Perspectives on activity theory

Activity theory is an interdisciplinary approach to human sciences that originates in the cultural-historical psychology initiated by Vygotsky, Leont'ev, and Luria. It takes the object-oriented, artifact-mediated collective activity system as its unit of analysis, thus bridging the gulf between the individual subject and the societal structure. This volume is the first comprehensive presentation of contemporary work in activity theory, with 26 original chapters by authors from 10 countries.

In Part I of the book, central theoretical issues are discussed from different points of view. Some topics addressed in this part are epistemology, methodology, and the relationship between biological and cultural factors. Part II is devoted to the acquisition and development of language – a theme that played a central role in the work of Vygotsky and Luria. This part includes a chapter that analyzes writing activity in Japanese classrooms and an original case study of literacy skills in a man with cerebral palsy.

Part III contains chapters on play, learning, and education, and Part IV addresses the meaning of new technology and the development of work activities. The final part covers issues of therapy and addiction.

Yrjö Engeström is Professor of Communication at the University of California at San Diego and Academy Professor at The Academy of Finland. He is the coeditor, with David Middleton, of *Cognition and Communication at Work.*

Reijo Miettinen is Associate Professor in the Department of Education, University of Helsinki.

Raija-Leena Punamäki is Senior Researcher in the Department of Psychology, University of Helsinki.

LEARNING IN DOING:
Social, Cognitive, and Computational Perspectives

Series Editor Emeritus
JOHN SEELY BROWN, Xerox Palo Alto Research Center

General Editors
ROY PEA, *Professor of Education and the Learning Sciences and Director, Stanford Center for Innovations in Learning, Stanford University*
CHRISTIAN HEATH, *The Management Centre, King's College, London*
LUCY A. SUCHMAN, *Centre for Science Studies and Department of Sociology, Lancaster University, UK*

Continued on page following the Index

Perspectives on activity theory

Edited by

YRJÖ ENGESTRÖM

REIJO MIETTINEN

RAIJA-LEENA PUNAMÄKI

CAMBRIDGE
UNIVERSITY PRESS

PUBLISHED BY THE PRESS SYNDICATE OF THE UNIVERSITY OF CAMBRIDGE
The Pitt Building, Trumpington Street, Cambridge, United Kingdom

CAMBRIDGE UNIVERSITY PRESS
The Edinburgh Building, Cambridge CB2 2RU, UK
40 West 20th Street, New York, NY 10011-4211, USA
10 Stamford Road, Oakleigh, Melbourne 3207, Australia
Ruiz de Alarcón 13, 28014 Madrid, Spain
Dock House, The Waterfront, Cape Town 8001, South Africa

http://www.cambridge.org

© Cambridge University Press 1999

First published 1999
Reprinted 2003, 2004

Printed in the United States of America

Typeface Ehrhardt 11/13 pt.   *System* AMS-T$_E$X

A catalog record for this book is available from the British Library

Library of Congress Cataloging in Publication data is available

ISBN 0 521 43127 1 hardback
ISBN 0 521 43730 X paperback

Contents

vii

Contributors

Kyoshi Amano, Chuo University

Stig Broström, Royal Danish School of Educational Studies, Copenhagen

Matthias Bujarski, Freie Universität Berlin

Jacques Carpay, Free University of Amsterdam

Michael Cole, University of California, San Diego

Francesco Paolo Colucci, Universita degli Studi di Milano

Vassily V. Davydov, The Russian Academy of Education

Yrjö Engeström, University of California, San Diego, and The Academy of Finland

Antti Eskola, University of Tampere

Bernd Fichtner, University of Siegen

Pentti Hakkarainen, Institute for Educational Research, University of Jyväskylä

Yrjö-Paavo Häyrynen, University of Joensuu

Mariane Hedegaard, Aarhus University

Martin Hildebrand-Nilshon, Freie Universität Berlin

Jan Kordt, Freie Universität Berlin

Anja Koski-Jännes, University of Helsinki

Kari Kuutti, University of Oulu

Mikael Leiman, University of Joensuu

Vladimir A. Lektorsky, Russian Academy of Science, Moscow

Joachim Lompscher, Potsdam University

Reijo Miettinen, University of Helsinki

Yuji Moro, University of Tsukuba

Raija-Leena Punamäki, University of Helsinki

Anthony Ryle, St. Thomas's Hospital, London

Oleg K. Tikhomirov, Moscow University

Ethel Tobach, American Museum of Natural History,
    New York

Charles W. Tolman, University of Victoria, British Columbia

Stephen Toulmin, University of Southern California

Bert Van Oers, Free University of Amsterdam

Series foreword

This series for Cambridge University Press is becoming widely known as an international forum for studies of situated learning and cognition.

Innovative contributions are being made in anthropology; in cognitive, developmental, and cultural psychology; in computer science; in education; and in social theory. These contributions are providing the basis for new ways of understanding the social, historical, and contextual nature of the learning, thinking, and practice emerging from human activity. The empirical settings of these research inquiries range from the classroom, to the workplace, to the high-technology office, to learning in the streets and in other communities of practice.

The situated nature of learning and remembering through activity is a central fact. It may appear obvious that human minds develop in social situations and extend their sphere of activity and communicative competencies. But cognitive theories of knowledge representation and learning alone have not provided sufficient insight into these relationships.

This series was born of the conviction that new and exciting interdisciplinary syntheses are under way, as scholars and practitioners from diverse fields seek to develop theories and empirical investigations adequate for characterizing the complex relations of social and mental life, and for understanding successful learning wherever it occurs. The series invites contributions that advance our understanding of these seminal issues.

Roy Pea
John Seely Brown
Jan Hawkins

Introduction

Yrjö Engeström and Reijo Miettinen

Activity theory: A well-kept secret

Activity theory is a commonly accepted name for a line of theorizing and research initiated by the founders of the cultural-historical
school of Russian psychology, L. S. Vygotsky, A. N. Leont'ev, and A. R.
Luria, in the 1920s and 1930s. The approach has been elaborated further
by a large number of contemporary scholars both in the former socialist countries and in the West. Although certain key works of Vygotsky
and Luria are widely accessible and have become classic references in
behavioral sciences (e.g., Vygotsky, 1978; Luria, 1976), the bulk of more
recent activity-theoretical publications remain scattered and often difficult to obtain.

In the United States, very few books have been published that address the central theoretical concept of activity. These include Leont'ev's
(1978) *Activity, Consciousness, and Personality* and two edited volumes of
translated texts, *The Concept of Activity in Soviet Psychology* (Wertsch,
1981) and *Activity: Theories, Methodology and Problems* (Lektorsky, 1990).
The first two have been out of print for quite a while. Moreover, all three
books represent exclusively Soviet views.

Activity-theoretical ideas are having increased impact in specific fields
of inquiry, such as learning and teaching (e.g., Moll, 1990) and human–
computer interaction (e.g., Nardi, 1996). Activity theory is discussed
in books attempting to formulate theories of practice (Chaiklin & Lave,
1993), distributed cognition (Salomon, 1993), and sociocultural psychology (Martin, Nelson, & Tobach, 1995). A new journal, *Mind, Culture
and Activity*, publishes a steady flow of articles inspired by activity theory. However, in all these contexts, activity theory still tends to appear as
an intriguing alternative approach only partially and briefly revealed to

1

the readers. To this day, its rich texture remains a well-kept secret to the Western scientific community.

Although we cannot claim to offer a complete overview, we at least want to pull aside the curtain of secrecy that has covered much of activity theory. This volume is the first attempt to present a somewhat balanced variety of the theoretical views and practical applications of activity theory currently developed by researchers in different parts of the world.

In 1986, the First International Congress for Research on Activity Theory was organized in Berlin. In 1987, an international scientific society for research based on activity theory (ISCRAT) was founded. In 1990, the Second International Congress for Research on Activity Theory was held in Lahti, Finland. The third congress was held in Moscow in 1995. The chapters in this volume originate mainly from selected contributions to the second congress. These chapters are authored by scholars from 10 countries.

In the post–World War II decades, activity theory was mostly developed within the psychology of play, learning, cognition, and child development. It was applied in research on language acquisition and experimental development of instruction, mainly in the context of schools and other educational institutions. Although these domains continue to be central, activity-theoretical research has become broader in the 1980s and 1990s. It now encompasses such topics as development of work activities, implementation of new cultural tools such as computer technologies, and issues of therapy.

It is important to point out the nondogmatic nature of the current phase of discussion and collaboration in activity theory. A prominent feature of the chapters in this book is their multifaceted search for connections and hybrids between activity theory and other related traditions. Examples include Stephen Toulmin discussing the relationship between Vygotsky and Wittgenstein (Chapter 3), Michael Cole discussing the relationship between activity theory and cultural psychology (Chapter 6), Ethel Tobach discussing the relationship between activity theory and the theory of integrative levels (Chapter 9), Francesco Paolo Colucci discussing the relationship between Leont'ev and Gramsci (Chapter 10), and Anthony Ryle discussing the relationship between psychoanalytic object relations theory and activity theory (Chapter 24) – to name just a few. Such parallels and hybrids make the implications and potentials of activity theory more accessible in multiple fields of research and practice without compromising the search for and elaboration of a common conceptual and methodological core.

Philosophical sources and discussion partners of activity theory

First and foremost among the philosophical roots of activity theory is the work of Karl Marx. It is not an exaggeration to say that Marx, in his *Theses on Feuerbach*, was the first philosopher to explicate pointedly the theoretical and methodological core of the concept of activity. The first and third theses condense the point of departure for activity theory.

The chief defect of hitherto existing materialism (that of Feuerbach included) is that the thing, reality, sensuousness, is conceived only in the form of the *object or of contemplation*, but not as *sensuous human activity, practice*, not subjectively. Hence, in contradistinction to materialism, the *active* side was developed abstractly by idealism – which, of course, does not know real, sensous activity as such. Feuerbach wants sensuous objects, really distinct from the thought objects, but he does not conceive of the human activity itself as *objective* activity. Hence, in *Das Wesen des Christenthums*, he regards the theoretical attitude as the only genuinely human attitude, while practice is conceived and fixed only in its dirty-judaical manifestation. Hence he does not grasp the significance of "revolutionary," of "practical-critical" activity.

(3) The materialist doctrine concerning the changing of circumstances and upbringing forgets that circumstances are changed by men and that it is essential to educate the educator himself. This doctrine must, therefore, divide society into two parts, one of which is superior to society.

The coincidence of the changing of circumstances and human activity or self-changing can be conceived and rationally understood only as *revolutionary practice*. (Marx & Engels, 1968, pp. 659–660)

Marx is doing several things in these short paragraphs. First, he shows that neither mechanical materialism nor idealism will do. Mechanical materialism eliminates human agency, and idealism puts it in the head or soul of the individual. What both are missing is the concept of activity that overcomes and transcends the dualism between the individual subject and objective societal circumstances. Second, Marx shows that the concept of activity opens up a new way to understand change. Change is not brought about from above, nor is it reducible to purely individual self-change of subjects. The key is "revolutionary practice," which is not to be understood in narrowly political terms but as joint "practical-critical activity," potentially embedded in any mundane everyday practice.

Marx's concept of labor, or production of use values, was the paradigmatic model of human object-oriented activity for Leont'ev when he formulated the concept of *activity*. Drawing directly on Marx and Engels, he emphasized the two mutually dependent aspects of mediation in labor activity.

The first is the use and making of tools. "Labour," Engels said, "begins with the making of tools."

The second feature of the labour process is that it is performed in conditions of joint, collective activity, so that man functions in this process not only in a certain relationship with nature but also to other people, members of a given society. Only through a relation with other people does man relate to nature itself, which means that labour appears from the very beginning as a process mediated by tools (in the broad sense) and at the same time mediated socially. (Leont'ev, 1981, p. 208)

In the early work of the cultural-historical school, led by Vygotsky, the unit of analysis was object-oriented action mediated by cultural tools and signs (see Vygotsky, 1978, p. 40). Mediation by other human beings and social relations was not theoretically integrated into the triangular model of action. Such an integration required a breakthrough to the concept of activity by distinguishing between collective activity and individual action. This step was achieved by Leont'ev by means of reconstructing the emergence of division of labor. This analytical feat, prompted by Leont'ev's careful reading of Marx, is summarized in the following famous passage.

A beater, for example, taking part in a primeval collective hunt, was stimulated by a need for food or, perhaps, a need for clothing, which the skin of the dead animal would meet for him. At what, however, was his activity directly aimed? It may have been directed, for example, at frightening a herd of animals and sending them toward other hunters, hiding in ambush. That, properly speaking, is what should be the result of the activity of this man. And the activity of this individual member of the hunt ends with that. The rest is completed by the other members. This result, i.e., the frightening of game, etc., understandably does not in itself, and may not, lead to satisfaction of the beater's need for food, or the skin of the animal. What the processes of his activity were directed to did not, consequently, coincide with what stimulated them, i.e., did not coincide with the motive of his activity; the two were divided from one another in this instance. Processes, the object and motive of which do not coincide with one another, we shall call "actions." We can say, for example, that *the beater's activity is the hunt, and the frightening of the game his action.* (Leont'ev, 1981, p. 210; italics added)

This distinction between activity and action became the basis of Leont'ev's three-level model of activity. The uppermost level of collective activity is driven by an object-related motive; the middle level of individual (or group) action is driven by a goal; and the bottom level of automatic operations is driven by the conditions and tools of action at hand.

It has become commonplace to omit Marx as an essential theoretical source from discussions of activity theory, in particular in assessments of Vygotsky's work. This omission occurs largely for political and ideological reasons. However, the appropriation and creative development of central theoretical ideas of activity theory presuppose a careful and critical study of Marx's work.

In the *Economic and Philosophical Manuscripts of 1844* Marx (1964) presented a materialist interpretation of the Hegelian conception of self-creation through labor as the essence of humanity. According to this interpretation, in the production of use values, humans change the outer nature and their own nature as well. Human nature is not found within the human individual but in the movement between the inside and outside, in the worlds of artifact use and artifact creation.

We see, that the history of industry and the established objective existence of industry are the open book of man's essential powers, the perceptibly existing human psychology. (. . .) We have before us the objectified essential powers of man in the form of sensuous, alien, useful objects, in the form of estrangement, displayed in ordinary material industry. (. . .) A psychology for which this, the part of history most contemporary and accessible to sense, remains a closed book, cannot become a genuine, comprehensive and real science. (Marx, 1964, p. 142)

Most of the works of Marx developed the idea of alienated labor, work under the specific circumstances of capitalism. The idea of total submission of concrete work to abstract work and production of surplus value, combined with a weak empirical analysis of the creation and uses of technologies, makes much of his analysis of the effects of labor on humans a somewhat abstract and exaggerated history of ever-increasing misery and exploitation. That is also why the creative and dynamic potential of concrete work process and technologies remains underdeveloped in his work. This dilemma is unfortunately repeated in much of the modern Marxist literature on work (e.g., Braverman, 1974).

However, Marx's analysis of capitalism includes invaluable analytical instruments, above all the concept of commodity as a contradictory unity of use value and exchange value. This dialectical concept is crucial for any serious analysis of the contradictory motives of human activities and human psyche in capitalist society. As Leont'ev (1981, p. 255) put it, "to ignore these peculiarities and remove them from the context of psychological research is to deprive psychology of historical concreteness, converting it into a science solely of the psyche of an abstract man, of 'man in general'."

Many of the ideas of pragmatism have common features with activity theory. The program of "transcending the dualisms" between thought and activity, theory and practice, facts and values has much in common with the theoretical aims of activity theory. John Dewey and George Herbert Mead developed conceptions of action, of practice, and at times even of collective activity. In his *Essays in Experimental Logic,* Dewey gives the following definition of practice.

It means that knowing is literally something which we do; that analysis is ultimately physical and active; that meanings in their logical quality are standpoints, attitudes and methods of behaving toward facts, and that active experimentation is essential to verifications. (Dewey, 1916, p. 331)

And Dewey goes on:

The object of knowledge is not something with which thinking sets out; but something with which it ends: something which the processes of inquiry and testing, that constitute thinking, themselves produce. Thus the object of knowledge is practical in the sense that it depends upon a specific kind of practice for its existence. (Dewey, 1916, p. 334)

These ideas are fully viable from the point of view of current epistemological debates in social sciences. They also have a family relationship to Leont'ev's ideas of object and motive construction as central mechanisms of transformation of activity.

Thus, the object of activity is twofold: first, in its independent existence as subordinating to itself and transforming the activity of the subject; second, as an image of the object, as a product of its property of psychological reflection that is realized as an activity of the subject and cannot exist otherwise. (Leont'ev, 1978, p. 52)

In *Human Nature and Conduct,* Dewey (1922) argues forcefully that goals are formulated and developed during the process of studying and orienting to the objective conditions of activity. Goals are therefore "milestones" in the course of activity, not its purpose or ultimate motive. Again, we see an affinity to Leont'ev's thinking.

Besides, isolation and perception of goals by no means occurs automatically, nor is it an instantaneous act but a relatively long process of approbation of the goals by action and by their objective filling, if this can be expressed in such a way. The individual, justly notes Hegel, "cannot determine the goal of his acting as long as he has not acted. . . ." (Leont'ev, 1978, p. 65)

In contrast to activity theory, the absence of cultural mediation is evident in much of Dewey's work. The study of Dewey's extensive production, however, reveals continually interesting theoretical openings and parallels with activity theory. Dewey's analyses of technology may be mentioned as a case in point (see Hickman, 1990).

G. H. Mead developed his theory of significant symbols within the context of division of labor in society (e.g., Bhattacharya, 1978). It is cooperative activity based on division of labor that makes the reciprocal role taking necessary. In *The Philosophy of Act,* Mead (1938) speaks of the nonindividual "social act," "whole act," or "whole social act," thus moving toward the concept of collective activity. According to Mead, an act of an individual is "abstracted" from the whole social act that is the prime object of study.

Building on Mead's theoretical legacy, Anselm Strauss and his colleagues have created a tradition of symbolic-interactionist studies of work that is in many ways parallel to efforts within activity theory (see Strauss, Fagerhaugh, Suczek, & Wiener, 1985; Strauss, 1993; Maines, 1991). Star (Star & Griesemer, 1989), Fujimura (1992), and Henderson (1991) have studied what happens in encounters between different *social worlds* – a unit of analysis roughly equivalent to the activity system.

They have developed the concepts of *boundary object, translation,* and *boundary crossing* to analyze the unfolding of object-oriented cooperative activity of several actors, focusing on tools and means of construction of boundary objects in concrete work processes. This work represents obvious challenges and opportunities for activity theory. It is no longer sufficient to focus on singular, relatively isolated activity systems. Activity theory needs to develop tools for analyzing and transforming networks of culturally heterogeneous activities through dialogue and debate.

The work of Ludwig Wittgenstein has been an important inspiration for many relevant studies on discourse and human practices. In his *Philosophical Investigations* (1958), Wittgenstein contended that the meanings of concepts and words can be understood only as part of a specific language game with its specific rules. Such a language game must be understood as part of a broader context. Wittgenstein calls this broader context "form of life." Both the significance of actions and the meaning of speech can be understood as a part of forms of lives. Wittgenstein uses the example of communication between a mason and his assistant in building a house (Wittgenstein, 1958, §24). The words used on communication are closely related to the objects (bricks) and their qualities (different shapes and sizes) significant to the common object of work: house construction.

Wittgenstein's idea of language game as an aspect of form of life has a strong affinity to activity-theoretical conceptions of communication as an integral aspect of object-oriented practical activity. Yet Wittgenstein's legacy is a healthy reminder of a potentially one-sided emphasis on the physical, tool-mediated aspect of human conduct in activity theory. In recent years, an increasing number of activity-theoretical studies have focused on issues of discourse and signification, often drawing on Wittgenstein and on the work of the Russian literary theorist and philosopher Mikhail Bakhtin (see Bakhtin, 1982). However, the integration of discourse into the theory of activity has only begun.

The current relevance of activity theory

In psychology, we have recently witnessed a wave of interest in contextual and cultural theories. In cognitive science, a similar phenomenon is associated with the concepts of *situated cognition* and *distributed cognition*. In education, situated learning in communities of practice has emerged as an attractive and controversial new approach. In sociology of science and technology, the concept of *practice* and the notion of *actor networks* have taken center stage.

Activity theory has much to contribute to the ongoing multidisciplinary wave of interest in cultural practices and practice-bound cognition. Activity theory should not be regarded as a narrowly psychological theory but rather as a broad approach that takes a new perspective on and develops novel conceptual tools for tackling many of the theoretical and methodological questions that cut across the social sciences today.

One of these pervasive and persistent issues is the relationship between the micro and macro levels of analysis. Various microsociologies have produced eye-opening works that uncover the local, idiosyncratic, and contingent nature of action, interaction, and knowledge. Empirical studies of concrete, situated practices can uncover the local pattern of activity and the cultural specificity of thought, speech, and discourse. Yet these microstudies tend to have little connection to macrotheories of social institutions and the structure of society. Various approaches to analysis of social networks may be seen as attempts to bridge the gap. However, a single network, though interconnected with a number of other networks, typically still in no way represents any general or lawful development in society.

According to activity theory, any local activity resorts to some historically formed mediating artifacts, cultural resources that are common to the society at large. Networks between activity systems provide for movement of artifacts. These resources can be combined, used, and transformed in novel ways in local joint activity. Local, concrete activities, therefore, are simultaneously unique and general, momentary and durable. In their unique ways, they solve problems by using general cultural means created by previous generations. Coming from a different tradition, Bruno Latour arrives at the same principle.

Everything in the definition of macro social order is due to the enrollment of nonhumans – that is, to technical mediation. Even the simple effect of duration, of long-lasting social force, cannot be obtained without the durability of nonhumans to which human local interactions have been shifted. (. . .) Society is the outcome of local construction, but we are not alone at the construction site, since there we also mobilize the many nonhumans through which the order of space and time has been reshuffled. To be human requires sharing with nonhumans. (Latour, 1994, p. 51)

Another important methodological discussion concerns the nature of causation and explanation in social sciences. Prigogine and Stengers (1985), among others, demonstrate how linear and monocausal concepts of causation taken from classical physics are unsatisfactory in explaining development determined by multiple systemically interacting elements typical to social and economic phenomena. The new sociology of science and technology tries to get rid of monocausal explanations by introducing the principle of *coevolution* of social, material, and technical factors (Bijker, Hughes, & Pinch, 1987). In a similar vein, Freeman (1994) proposes that an *interactive system model* is needed in studies of innovations, taking into account complex interactions between science, technology, and market, between designers and users of new technology. In developmental psychology, Valsiner (1988) proposes *co-construction* as the central explanatory principle.

To be able to analyze such complex interactions and relationships, a theoretical account of the constitutive elements of the system under investigation is needed. In other words, there is a demand for a new unit of analysis. Activity theory has a strong candidate for such a unit of analysis in the concept of *object-oriented, collective,* and *culturally mediated human activity,* or *activity system.* Minimum elements of this system include the object, subject, mediating artifacts (signs and tools), rules, community, and division of labor (Engeström, 1987; Cole & Engeström, 1993). The internal tensions and contradictions of such a system are the motive force of change and development. They are accentuated by continuous transitions and transformations between these components of an activity system, and between the embedded hierarchical levels of collective motive-driven activity, individual goal-driven action, and automatic operations driven by the tools and conditions of action (Leont'ev, 1978). This kind of explanation makes it possible to include both historical continuity and local, situated contingency in the analysis.

The rise of constructivism has led to justified skepticism regarding ideas of natural determinism and objective representation of facts "out there." However, much of constructivism is quite narrowly focused on the construction of texts. Van Maanen's recent essay on representation in ethnography provides an example.

My reading of the current turn toward text and language in ethnography is governed by a belief that holds rhetoric, broadly defined, to be the medium through which all truths or certainties are established (and shaken). Thus, for example, to look closely at well-received or persuasive ethnographic texts, to their compositional practices rather than through them, to the worlds they portray is to examine how a culture becomes a substantial reality for a given set of readers and perhaps beyond. (Van Maanen, 1995, p. 13)

Exclusive focus on text may lead to a belief that knowledge, artifacts, and institutions are modifiable at will by means of rhetoric used by an author. Activity theory sees construction more broadly. People construct their institutions and activities above all by means of material and discursive, object-oriented actions. On this view, the rhetorical construction of research texts is much less omnipotent than many versions of constructivism would have us believe. This suggests that the researcher's constructive endeavors may be fruitful when positioned less as stand-alone texts and more as voices and utterances in ongoing dialogues within and between collective activity systems under investigation.

Activity system as a unit of analysis calls for complementarity of the system view and the subject's view. The analyst constructs the activity system as if looking at it from above. At the same time, the analyst must select a subject, a member (or better yet, multiple different members) of the local activity, through whose eyes and interpretations the activity is constructed. This dialectic between the systemic and subjective-partisan views brings the researcher into a dialogical relationship with the local activity under investigation. The study of an activity system becomes a collective, multivoiced construction of its past, present, and future zones of proximal development (Engeström, 1987).

Activity theory recognizes two basic processes operating continuously at every level of human activities: internalization and externalization. Internalization is related to reproduction of culture; externalization as creation of new artifacts makes possible its transformation. These two processes are inseparably intertwined. Roy Bhaskar, elaborating on the notion of emancipatory social activity, comes to essentially the same conclusion.

It is no longer true to say that human agents create it [the society]. Rather we must say: they *reproduce* or *transform* it. That is to say, if society is already made, then any concrete human praxis, if you like, act of objectivation, can only modify it; and the totality of such acts sustain or change it. It is not the product of their activity (any more than their actions are completely determined by it). Society stands to individuals, then, as something that they never make, but that exists only by virtue of their activity (. . .) People do not create society, for it always preexists them. Rather it is an ensemble of structures, practices and conventions that individuals reproduce or transform. But which would not exist unless they did so. Society does not exist independently of conscious human activity (the error of reification). But it is not product of the latter (the error of voluntarism). (Bhaskar, 1989, p. xx)

The dialectical relationship between continuity and change, reproduction and transformation, is a challenge to concrete research in local activity systems. The underlying principles of historicity and material continuity do not imply a teleology or an evolutionist ideology of progress. They are simply methodological conditions for understanding and analyzing change and resistance to change, transformation and stagnation. In the past, activity theorists concentrated mainly on internalization of cultural means. Today externalization, the transformative construction of new instruments and forms of activity at collective and individual levels, has become an equally central theme of research.

In the current wave of contextual and culturally situated theories of mind and practice, two approaches are particularly close to activity theory. These are the sociocultural theory of mediated action (Wertsch, del Rio, & Alvarez, 1995b) and the theory of situated learning, or legitimate peripheral participation (Lave & Wenger, 1991). Both of these approaches have been inspired by Vygotsky's work. Both share with activity theory an emphasis on mediation of human action by cultural artifacts. Yet these approaches differ in important ways from activity theory.

The point of departure of the sociocultural theory of action is the Vygotskian idea of mediation of behavior by signs and other cultural artifacts, enhanced and enriched with Bakhtin's (1982) notions of social language, speech genre, and voice (Wertsch, 1991). Wertsch (1995) emphasizes that the proper unit of analysis is mediated action. The focus is on the individual performing actions in a sociocultural setting. Wertsch and his colleagues explicitly distance themselves from ideas of historicity, object orientedness, and the collective nature of human activity, emphasizing the sign-mediated and interactional aspects of action instead (Wertsch, del Rio, & Alvarez, 1995a).

The semiotic and interactional emphasis is obviously productive. But it seems problematic when considered as an attempt to understand context. Individuals act in collective practices, communities, and institutions. Such collective practices are not reducible to sums of individual action; they require theoretical conceptualization in their own right. When the individual action is the privileged unit of analysis, collective practice can only be added on as a more or less external envelope. Human conduct tends to appear as a string of goal-directed acts of rational actors. This leads to difficulties in analysis of the irrational aspects of actions and, more generally, of relationships between collective motives and individual goals.

As an attempt to go beyond this admittedly limited focus on the actor and mediational means alone, Wertsch (1995, pp. 71–72) turns to Burke's (1962) pentad of literary analysis (act, scene, agent, agency, and purpose). However, the embeddedness of action in collective practice receives mainly a metaphorical, not an analytical, acknowledgment from Burke's pentad. The key issue to be conceptually unfolded and analyzed is still hiding within the opaque notion of *scene*. Interestingly enough, in his earlier work, Wertsch saw Leont'ev's concept of activity as a way of tackling productively this very problem, pointing out that "the notion of an activity setting with its motive provides a means for relating social institutional and individual psychological phenomena" (Wertsch, 1985, p. 215).

Another important strand of cultural-contextual theorizing is the situated learning, or legitimate peripheral participation, approach of Lave and Wenger (1991). The central concept and unit of analysis here is the *community of practice* (see also Rogoff's [1994] related concept of *community of learners*). While acknowledging the importance of mediational means, this unit is decidedly broader than individual action. Moreover, practical, object-oriented work is investigated on a par with interaction and sign-mediated communication.

One could say that community of practice is *sociospatially* a wider and more encompassing unit of analysis than mediated action. The problem here is in the *temporal* dimension. The theory of legitimate peripheral participation depicts learning and development primarily as a one-way movement from the periphery, occupied by novices, to the center, inhabited by experienced masters of the given practice. What seems to be missing is movement outward and in unexpected directions: questioning of authority, criticism, innovation, initiation of change. Instability and inner contradictions of practice are all but missing – ironically, a feature of which Lave and Wenger (1991, pp. 47–48) themselves criticize Vygotskian notions of internalization.

The coexistence of and dialogue between such different but closely related approaches as activity theory and the other theories mentioned in this section is a sign of vital development in the field. Novel hybrid concepts and research paradigms are emerging. Activity theory has deep historical roots and an accumulated record of theory and research that is still only fragmentarily known in the West. Although activity theorists should self-consciously examine and exploit this history, they also need to face the exciting new challenges and opportunities for collaboration.

Structure and contents of the book

In Part I of this volume, central theoretical issues of activity theory are discussed from multiple points of view. In Chapter 1, Yrjö Engeström identifies six conceptual dilemmas facing activity theory and suggests ways to tackle those dilemmas based on the idea of mediation as the "germ cell" of the activity approach. In Chapter 2, Vassily Davydov, a leading contemporary Russian activity theorist, continues with the same theme, identifying central priciples of activity theory and challenging problems facing it.

In Chapter 3, Stephen Toulmin takes up the theory of knowledge inherent in activity theory. He compares the epistemological ideas of Vygotsky and Wittgenstein, finding rather surprising commonalities between them. In Chapter 4, Vladimir Lektorsky continues the epistemological theme, outlining a dialogical rationality as the basis of activity theory in the post–cold war era.

In Chapter 5, Charles Tolman takes up the notion of context and the specific form of contextualism represented by activity theory. In Chapter 6, Michael Cole introduces the dimension of culture into the discourse of activity theory. He weaves together methodological principles of the cultural-historical tradition and current methodological concerns of interventionist research involving participants in different social systems and activity settings trying to coordinate and communicate with each other. In Chapter 7, Antti Eskola continues the methodological theme, arguing for a reconceptualization of the meaning of *lawfulness* and *freedom* in research based on activity theory.

In Chapter 8, Yrjö-Paavo Häyrynen employs concepts from activity theory, life-span developmental psychology, and Bourdieu's sociology in an analysis of psychological change associated with the transformation of Europe after the fall of the socialist regimes. In Chapter 9, Ethel Tobach focuses on the relationship between biological and cultural factors in activity, discussing in particular the complementary conceptual frameworks of activity theory and Schneirla's theory of integrative levels of evolution. In Chapter 10, Francesco Paolo Colucci discusses Antonio Gramsci's ideas of common sense, relating them to Leont'ev's concepts of sense and meaning.

Part II is devoted to the acquisition and development of language, a theme that played a central role in the foundational work of Vygotsky and Luria in the formative period of cultural-historical activity theory. In Chapter 11, Yuji Moro elaborates the dialogic idea of language, analyzing writing activity in Japanese classrooms. In Chapter 12, Kiyoshi Amano presents an elaborate instructional approach to enhancing children's linguistic awareness with the help of mediating symbolic models. In Chapter 13, Matthias Bujarski, Martin Hildebrand-Nilshon, and Jan Kordt present a highly original case study of remediation of literacy skills in a nonspeaking young man with a severe cerebral palsy.

Part III consists of chapters on play, learning, and education. In Chapter 14, Pentti Hakkarainen presents a theoretical analysis of motivation in play activity, drawing on his research in preschool institutions. In Chapter 15, Stig Broström discusses the interplay of internalization and externalization in children's dramatic play activity.

In Chapter 16, Joachim Lompscher introduces the concept of *learning activity* and presents central findings from a decade of experimental research based on Davydov's theory of ascending from the abstract to the concrete in instruction and learning. In Chapter 17, Mariane Hedegaard presents an experimental study on history instruction, also based on Davydov's theory.

In Chapter 18, Jacques Carpay and Bert Van Oers critically assess Leont'ev's and Davydov's notions of learning and instruction, complementing them with ideas of discursive intersubjectivity and polyphony in learning activity. In Chapter 19, Bernd Fichtner adds another imaginative and metaphorical dimension to the concept of learning activity. In Chapter 20, Reijo Miettinen expands the analysis of learning activity to include social networks of learning that transcend the boundaries of school as an institutional activity system.

In Part IV, three chapters address the meaning of new technologies and the development of work activities. In Chapter 21, Oleg Tikhomirov discusses the implications of information technology for the development of activity theory, emphasizing particularly the integration of creativity into the conceptualization of activity. In Chapter 22, Kari Kuutti introduces the concept of *developmental work research* as an application of activity theory in information systems design. In Chapter 23, Yrjö Engeström presents a case study of knowledge creation in an industrial work team, using his theory of expansive learning as a conceptual framework.

Finally in Part V, three authors discuss activity theory and issues of therapy and addiction. In Chapter 24, Anthony Ryle considers the similarities and differences between activity theory and psychoanalytic object relations theory, suggesting his own cognitive analytic therapy as a hybrid that draws on both traditions. In Chapter 25, Mikael Leiman discusses internalization and externalization as interpsychological processes in therapy. And in Chapter 26, Anja Koski-Jännes examines activity theory as a framework for explaining addiction, particularly the role of mediating signs as instruments for achieving self-governance.

References

Bakhtin, M. M. (1982). *The dialogic imagination.* Austin: University of Texas Press.

Bhaskar, R. (1989). *Reclaiming reality. A critical introduction to contemporary philosophy.* London: Verso.

Bhattacharya, N. (1978). Psychology and rationality: The structure of Mead's problem. *The Philosophical Forum, 10*(1), 112–138.

Bijker, W. E., Hughes, T. P., & Pinch, T. (Eds.). (1987). *The social construction of technological systems: New directions in the sociology and history of technology.* Cambridge, MA: MIT Press.

Braverman, H. (1974). *Labor and monopoly capital.* New York: Monthly Review Press.

Burke, K. (1962). *A grammar of motives.* Berkeley: University of California Press.

Chaiklin, S., & Lave, J. (Eds.). (1993). *Understanding practice: Perspectives on activity and context.* Cambridge: Cambridge University Press.

Cole, M., & Engeström, Y. (1993). A cultural-historical approach to distributed cognition. In G. Salomon (Ed.), *Distributed cognitions: Psychological and educational considerations.* Cambridge: Cambridge University Press.

Dewey, J. (1916). *Essays on experimental logic.* New York: Dover.

Dewey, J. (1922). *Human nature and conduct: An introduction to social psychology.* London: George Allen & Unwin.

Engeström, Y. (1987). *Learning by expanding. An activity-theoretical approach to developmental research.* Helsinki: Orienta-Konsultit.

Freeman, C. (1994). The economics of technical change. *Cambridge Journal of Economics, 18*, 463–514.

Fujimura, J. (1992). Crafting science: Standardized packages, boundary objects, and "translations." In A. Pickering (Ed.), *Science as practice and culture.* Chicago: University of Chicago Press.

Henderson, K. (1991). Flexible sketches and inflexible data bases – visual communication, conscription devices, and boundary objects in design engineering. *Science, Technology and Human Values, 16*(4), 448–273.

Hickman, L. A. (1990). *John Dewey's pragmatic technology.* Bloomington: Indiana University Press.

Latour, B. (1994) *We have never been modern.* Hertfordshire: Harvester Wheatsheaf.

Lave, J., & Wenger, E. (1991). *Situated learning: Legitimate peripheral participation.* Cambridge: Cambridge University Press.

Lektorsky, V. A. (Ed.). (1990). *Activity: Theories, methodology and problems.* Orlando: Paul M. Deutsch Press.

Leont'ev, A. N. (1978). *Activity, consciousness, and personality.* Englewood Cliffs: Prentice-Hall.

Leont'ev (Leontyev), A. N. (1981). *Problems of the development of the mind.* Moscow: Progress.

Luria, A. R. (1976). *Cognitive development: Its cultural and social foundations.* Cambridge, MA: Harvard University Press.

Maines, D. (Ed.). (1991). *Social organization and social process: Essays in honor of Anselm Strauss.* Hawthorne: Aldine de Gruyter.

Marx, K. (1964). *Economic and philosophical manuscripts of 1844.* New York: International Publishers.

Marx, K., & Engels, F. (1968). *The German ideology.* Moscow: Progress.

Mead, G. H. (1938). *The philosophy of act.* Chicago: University of Chicago Press.

Moll, L. C. (Ed.). (1990). *Vygotsky and education: Instructional implications and applications of sociohistorical psychology.* Cambridge: Cambridge University Press.

Nardi, B. A. (Ed.). (1966). *Context and consciousness: Activity theory and human–computer interaction.* Cambridge, MA: MIT Press.

Prigogine, I., & Stengers, I. (1985). *Order out of chaos: Man's new dialogue with nature.* London: Fontana.

Salomon, G. (Ed.). (1993). *Distributed cognitions: Psychological and educational considerations.* Cambridge: Cambridge University Press.

Star, S. L., & Griesemer, J. R. (1989). Institutional ecology, "translations," and boundary objects: Amateurs and professionals in Berkeley's Museum of Vertebrate Zoology, 1907–39. *Social Studies of Science, 19,* 387–420.

Strauss A. L. (1993). *Continual permutations of action.* New York: Aldine de Gruyter.

Strauss, A. L., Fagerhaugh, S., Suczek, B., & Wiener, C. (1985). *Social organization of medical work.* Chicago: University of Chicago Press.

Valsiner, J. (1988). Ontogeny of co-construction of culture within socially organized environmental settings. In J. Valsiner (Ed.), *Child development within culturally structured environments.* Vol. 2: *Social co-construction and environmental guidance of development.* Norwood: Ablex.

Van Maanen, J. (1995). An end to innocence: the ethnography of ethnography. In J. Van Maanen (Ed.), *Representation in ethnography.* Thousand Oaks: Sage.

Vygotsky, L. S. (1978). *Mind in society: The development of higher psychological processes.* Cambridge, MA: Harvard University Press.

Wertsch, J. V. (Ed.). (1981). *The concept of activity in Soviet psychology.* Armonk: M. E. Sharpe.

Wertsch, J. V. (1991). *Voices of the mind: A sociocultural approach to mediated action.* Cambridge, MA: Harvard University Press.

Wertsch, J. V. (1995). The need for action in sociocultural research. In J. V. Wertsch, P. del Rio, & A. Alvarez (Eds.), *Sociocultural studies of mind.* Cambridge: Cambridge University Press.

Wertsch, J. V., del Rio, P., & Alvarez, A. (1995a). Sociocultural studies: History, action, and mediation. In J. V. Wertsch, P. del Rio, & A. Alvarez (Eds.), *Sociocultural studies of mind.* Cambridge: Cambridge University Press.

Wertsch, J. V., del Rio, P., & Alvarez, A. (Eds.). (1995b). *Sociocultural studies of mind.* Cambridge: Cambridge University Press.

Wittgenstein, L. (1958). *Philosophical investigations.* Oxford: Basil Blackwell.

Part I

Theoretical issues

1   Activity theory and individual and social transformation

Yrjö Engeström

Introduction

The internationalization of activity theory in the 1980s and 1990s has taken place in the midst of sweeping changes in the political and economic systems of our planet. During a few months, the Berlin Wall came down and Nelson Mandela was freed from prison. Those were only two among the visible symbols of the transformations that continue to amaze the most sophisticated observers.

Many of the current changes share two fundamental features. First, they are manifestations of activities from below, not just outcomes of traditional maneuvering among the elite of political decision makers. Second, they are unexpected or at least very sudden and rapidly escalating. These two features pose a serious challenge to behavioral and social sciences.

The behavioral and social sciences have cherished a division of labor that separates the study of socioeconomic structures from the study of individual behavior and human agency. In this traditional framework, the socioeconomic structures look stable, all-powerful, and self-sufficient. The individual may be seen as an acting subject who learns and develops, but somehow the actions of the individual do not seem to have any impact on the surrounding structures.

This traditional dualistic framework does not help us to understand today's deep social transformations. More than ever before, there is a need for an approach that can dialectically link the individual and the social structure. From its very beginnings, the cultural-historical theory of activity has been elaborated with this task in mind.

Activity theory: What kind of theory?

Activity theory has its threefold historical origins in classical German philosophy (from Kant to Hegel), in the writings of Marx and

19

Engels, and in the Soviet Russian cultural-historical psychology of Vygotsky, Leont'ev, and Luria. Today activity theory is transcending its own origins: It is becoming truly international and multidisciplinary. This process entails the discovery of new and old related approaches, discussion partners, and allies, from American pragmatism and Wittgenstein to ethnomethodology and theories of self-organizing systems.

This expansion is not unproblematic. Some may fear that activity theory will turn into an eclectic combination of ideas before it has a chance to redefine its own core. Although I realize that such a possibility exists, I anticipate that the current expansive reconstruction of activity theory will actually lead to a new type of theory. Essential to this emerging theory is multivoicedness coexisting with monism. This may sound like a contradiction, and that is exactly what it is.

In dialectical philosophy, monism is understood as a principle according to which it is possible to develop any whole theory and its multiple concepts consistently on the basis of one initial idea or *cell* (see Davydov, 1990). If such monism is combined with the standard realistic notion of *theory*, the whole endeavor will easily lead to single-minded elaboration of a closed, artificially static system of logically interlocking concepts (Jensen, 1989).

If anything, the current societal transformations should teach us that closed systems of thought do not work. But monism does not have to be interpreted that way. Human activity is endlessly multifaceted, mobile, and rich in variations of content and form. It is perfectly understandable and probably necessary that the theory of activity should reflect that richness and mobility. Such a multivoiced theory should not regard internal contradictions and debates as signs of weakness; rather, they are an essential feature of the theory. However, this requires at least a shared understanding of the character of the initial cell and a continuous collective attempt to elucidate that cell, as well as the multiple mediating steps from the cell to specific concepts.

Can activity theory develop as such a self-organizing system of interacting subjects? Obviously we are here dealing with a tension between two forces, or directions of development. One force pulls researchers toward individual applications and separate variations of certain general, often vague ideas. The other force pulls researchers toward learning from each other, questioning and contesting each other's ideas and applications, making explicit claims about the theoretical core of the activity approach. The key issue seems to be: Can we have sufficient shared understanding of the idea of activity to make it the cell of an evolving multivoiced activity theory?

In the following sections, I discuss six themes that may help us narrow down and define key dimensions of the very idea of activity. These themes emerged as I went through a number of recent publications containing critical debates on the concept of activity. The publications range from the materials of the First International Congress on Activity Theory (Hildebrand-Nilshon & Rückriem, 1988) and subsequent articles published in the *Multidisciplinary Newsletter for Activity Theory* and also as translations in the journal *Soviet Psychology* (now *Russian and East European Psychology*), to recent edited collections published in Denmark (Hedegaard, Hansen, & Thyssen, 1989), Germany (Holodynski & Jantzen, 1989), and Russia (Lektorsky, 1990), and to contributions that have appeared in an ongoing international electronic mail discussion on activity theory, coordinated by the Laboratory of Comparative Human Cognition in San Diego. I present each theme in the form of a dichotomy or two opposing standpoints. That is the form that often emerges in heated discussions.

After identifying the themes of debate, I try to delineate ways to overcome and transcend those dichotomies – possible elements toward a dynamically evolving cell concept of activity.

Dichotomies

1. Psychic process versus object-related activity

One of the basic issues concerning activity theory is the relationship between *activeness* (as opposed to *passivity*) as a general description of animal and human forms of life and the more specific idea of *activity* as an object-oriented and cultural formation that has its own structure. It has been argued that the English term *activity* is unable to carry the deeper philosophical meaning of the original German concept of *Tätigkeit* (Schurig, 1988).

With due respect to original philosophical terms, I cannot see how insistence on a term could prevent conceptual blurring. Actually there seems to exist a widespread awareness of the fundamental difference between *activeness* and *activity*. But there is a theoretically much more interesting disagreement that concerns the relationship between *object-related activity* and *psychic process*. This distinction stems from the theoretical tradition of S. L. Rubinstein and is championed today by A. V. Brushlinsky, among others.

Brushlinsky (1990; see also Brushlinsky, 1987) argues that the psyche acts objectively first and foremost as a process, always uninterrupted, live, extremely plastic and flexible, never fully predetermined. He goes on to claim that object-related activity of the subject is discontinuous, whereas the psychic process is not, which makes only the latter a *process* in the strict sense. The implication is that object-related actions and activities are secondary formations that emerge as products or results of the continuous psychic process.

The problem here is that the origin of activity seems to be reduced to an individual and internal psychic source. This would eliminate the fundamentally cultural and societal nature of activity so powerfully emphasized by the priciple of object-relatedness of activity. On the other hand, the question of continuity and discontinuity in human activity has to be taken seriously. This question pertains directly to the second dichotomy.

2. Goal-directed action versus object-related activity

In recent years, a large and varied psychological literature has emerged on the nature of goal-directed actions (see, e.g., von Cranach & Harré, 1982; Frese & Sabini, 1985; Ginsburg, Brenner, & von Cranach, 1985; Hacker, Volpert, & von Cranach, 1982). In cognitive science, situated action has become an important alternative to purely mentalistic and computational notions of information processing (e.g., Suchman, 1987). In sociology, the notion of action has been used in attempts to overcome the dualism of imposed structure and individual experience (e.g., Alexander, 1988; Fielding, 1988; Giddens, 1984).

In most of these theories, individual action is regarded as the unit of analysis and as the key to understanding human functioning. The orienting function of goals and plans, the sequential structure, and the levels of regulation of actions have received a lot of attention. But these theories seem to have difficulties in accounting for the socially distributed or collective aspects as well as the artifact-mediated or cultural aspects of purposeful human behavior. Also, the notion of time tends to be reduced to relatively discrete slices, often described in algorithmic terms with clear-cut beginnings and ends, dictated by given goals or tasks. The continuous, self-reproducing, systemic, and longitudinal-historical aspects of human functioning seem to escape most theories of action. As Oleg Tikhomirov (1988, p. 113) points out, focusing exclusively on the level of actions highlights goal attainment and problem solving but makes it very difficult to analyze the sociocultural and motivational basis of goal formation and problem finding.

In the First International Congress on Activity Theory, Hans Aebli, the well-known theorist of action, expressed the importance of a level beyond actions as a personal discovery. He stated:

Also the child is a newcomer in a complex system, in a system of her world: she is born in a family, she then enters a school, later a workplace. She tries to understand the system: "What makes it tick?" What moves the system? What are its mechanisms, its interconnections? (. . .) It is a question of solving this puzzle, of letting it gradually take shape, of understanding what are its structural features and the motives functioning within it. (Aebli, 1988, p. 151)

Leont'ev's (1978, 1981) famous three-level scheme of

> *activity*
> *action*
> *operation*

and, correspondingly,

> *motive*
> *goal*
> *instrumental conditions*

extended the sphere of analysis and directed our attention to the transformations going on between the levels. However, merely proclaiming that activity is a superior level of analysis does not help. And it is not at all clear that those who use the concept of activity are actually able to overcome the individualist and ahistorical biases inherent in theories of action. In the First Congress on Activity Theory, Mario von Cranach, another prominent action theorist, criticized the prevalent accounts of activity theory for these same weaknesses.

History is a concrete process, and it is not enough that one philosophizes a bit about the early humans, how they ran after antelopes, and then takes a huge step right to the distinction between capitalism and socialism. (. . .) Concrete analyses are difficult, however, because institutions and people in power often dislike concrete analyses of their activities and their history. (von Cranach, 1988, pp. 153–155)

3. Instrumental tool-mediated production versus expressive sign-mediated communication

Leont'ev's seminal works on activity theory in particular have repeatedly been criticized for an allegedly rigid and restrictive emphasis on tool-mediated production of objects as the prototypical form of activity. It is said that communication and mediation by signs are neglected or suppressed in this version of activity theory. There are at least two versions of essentially the same criticism. One version (e.g., Kozulin, 1984; Valsiner, 1988) portrays Leont'ev's work as a suppression of the original Vygotskian idea of semiotic mediation. Another version (e.g., Lomov, 1980) accuses activity theory of attempting to subsume everything under one concept and presents *communication* as the parallel or alternative fundamental idea of psychology.

These criticisms lead to a twofold opposition. First, mediation by signs is opposed to mediation by tools. Second, subject–subject relations are opposed to subject–object relations. At a more general level, we may identify a third opposition, namely, that between expressive or communicative action and instrumental or productive activity. This latter opposition figures prominently in the work of Habermas (1984), for example.

A careful reading of Leont'ev's work reveals that both mediation by signs and subject–subject relations do play an important role in his theory. Proponents of the cultural-historical school repeatedly point out that communication is an inherent aspect of all object-related activities. Leont'ev's (1981, pp. 219–220) account of the emergence of speech and language emphasizes the original unity of labor actions and social intercourse. And in his famous study of the emergence of consciousness in deaf and blind children, Meshcheryakov (1979) puts such a strong emphasis on this unity that he chooses to call his unit of analysis *shared object action.*

It is somewhat ironic that at the same time that the concept of object-related activity is criticized by some psychologists and philosophers for neglect of sign mediation, language, and communication, some prominent linguists are finding the same concept of activity increasingly attractive as a means of conceptualizing the interface between the sociocultural and linguistic realms. The following quotation from Elinor Ochs is a case in point.

First, language activities are at the same time linguistic and sociocultural phenomena. They are structured by linguistic and sociocultural principles. Second, the sociocultural contexts that language activities engender or reflect become part of the pragmatic or social meaning of particular linguistic structures carrying out these tasks. This idea is rooted in the work of Vygotsky (1962; 1978), Leontyev (1981), and Wittgenstein (1958). Drawing on Marx, Leontyev used the notion of "objectivization," that objects (and hence words) take their meanings from the variety of activities in which they participate. (Ochs, 1988, p. 17)

So there is a curious discrepancy between the ways Leont'ev is read by the critics and by those sympathetic to his ideas. Partly this discrepancy may be due to the fact that the systemic structure of activity was not very thoroughly analyzed and modeled by Leont'ev and his immediate collaborators. Leont'ev postulated the three levels of activity mentioned earlier. But what are the interacting fundamental components of an activity system? Often they are reduced to the subject, the object, and the mediating artifact (which may refer to either tools or signs). This triangle was, however, presented by Vygotsky (1978, p. 40) as a simplified model of mediated *action;* the conceptual distinction between activity and action was not yet worked out at the time Vygotsky presented his model. To my knowledge, Leont'ev did not elaborate on how the triangular model of action should be developed or extended in order to depict the structure of a collective activity system.

4. Relativism versus historicity

Activity theory evolved from the cultural-historical school of psychology. A key principle of this approach is historicity. The concrete implications of this principle have been surprisingly little discussed, a notable exception being Sylvia Scribner's (1985) impressive article on Vygotsky's uses of history. When Asmolov (1987) presented a list of the principles of activity approach, historicism was mentioned at the end in half a sentence: "the principle of historicism, which pervades all investigations using the activity approach" (p. 99). Such assertions cannot hide the fact that the principle of historicity, understood as concrete historical analysis of the activities under investigation, has mostly been neglected in empirical research based on or inspired by activity theory.

There is one obvious and another, less obvious, reason for this neglect. The obvious one stems from problems with rigid interpretations of the Marxist–Leninist view of history. Any conceptual framework that postulates a predetermined sequence of stages of sociohistorical development will easily entail suspicious notions of what is "primitive" and what is "advanced," what is backward and what is good. Such notions reduce the rich diversity of sociocultural forms of life to a one-dimensional scale. This problem was already evident in Luria's classic studies in Central Asia (Luria, 1976), carefully and sympathetically criticized by Cole and Griffin (1980; see also Cole, 1988).

It is surely appropriate to avoid imposing rigid, one-dimensional sequences on social reality. But especially among Anglo-Saxon researchers adhering to the ideas of Vygotsky, the standard alternative seems to be to avoid history altogether. Differences in cognition across cultures, social groups, and domains of practice are thus commonly explained without seriously analyzing the historical development that has led to those differences. The underlying relativistic notion is that we should not make value judgments concerning whose cognition is better or more advanced – that all kinds of thinking and practice are equally valuable. Although this liberal stance may be a comfortable basis for academic discourse, it ignores the reality that in all domains of societal practice value judgments and decisions have to be made every day. People have to decide where they want to go, which way is up. If behavioral and social sciences want to avoid that issue, they will be unable to work out useful yet theoretically ambitious intellectual tools for practitioners making those crucial decisions.

The less obvious reason for the neglect of history has to do with the point I mentioned earlier, namely, the underdevelopment of models of the structure of an activity system. Historical analyses must be focused on units of manageable size. If the unit is the individual or the individually constructed situation, history is reduced to ontogeny or biography. If the unit is the culture or the society, history becomes very general or endlessly complex. If a collective activity system is taken as the unit, history may become manageable, and yet it steps beyond the confines of individual biography.

5. Internalization versus creation and externalization

Both in the East and in the West, it has been almost a truism that internalization is the key psychological mechanism discovered by the cultural-historical school. When internalization is, in turn, reduced to children's learning of skills and knowledge in interaction with adults and more experienced peers, we get a version of Vygotskian research that looks very much like social learning theory flavored with fashionable terminology. Symptomatically, Vygotsky's writings that deal with creation and externalization, especially *The Psychology of Art* (1971), have received very little attention. And it seems to be all but forgotten that the early studies led by Vygotsky, Leont'ev, and Luria not only examined the role of *given* artifacts as mediators of cognition but were also interested in how children *created* artifacts of their own in order to facilitate their performance (see Luria, 1979).

In a Russian collection on the concept of activity edited by Lektorsky (1990), this emphasis was suddenly almost turned around. Nearly all authors emphasized that the most important aspect of human activity is its creativity and its ability to exceed or transcend given constraints and instructions. Perhaps this conclusion reflected the impact of perestroika in philosophy and psychology (for different views on this impact, see the round table discussion "Restructuring Psychology" in *Soviet Psychology,* *27*(6) [1989] and *28*(1) [1990]).

Be that as it may, concrete research and experimentation inspired by activity theory have been strongly dominated by the paradigm of internalization. There has been very little concrete research on creation of artifacts, production of novel social patterns, and expansive transformation of activity contexts. Vera John-Steiner's (1985) work on creativity and the *developmental work research* approach originated in Finland (e.g., Engeström, 1987, 1990) may be mentioned as openings in this direction.

6. *Principle of explanation versus object of study*

In the 1970s, the Soviet philosopher E. G. Yudin (1978) pointed out that the concept of activity may be understood either as a principle of explanation or as an object of study. Ever since that distinction was made, it has been used in various discussions for various purposes. Although Yudin's idea was probably not to create another dichotomy, in the ensuing discussions this distinction has often frozen into such a fixed opposition.

Reading through recent theoretical discussions and debates concerning the concept of activity forced me to observe that when activity is taken *only* as a principle of explanation, it seems that the outcome is often an endless conceptual exercise with meager empirical grounding. I suppose that V. A. Lektorsky had this in mind when he wrote:

If the discussion proceeds only at the level of formulating general positions and is not accompanied by attempts to apply them constructively or to realize them in a more or less elaborate conceptual system applied to explain a specific objective area, the discussion proves relatively ineffective since to any principle formulated in abstract terms it is always possible to oppose another.

(. . .) I believe that we can never have a truly fruitful activity approach if we simply superimpose the concept of activity on known facts (. . .). In this latter case, the concept and principle of activity essentially turn into empty terms and, no matter how we manipulate them, we shall not advance in a substantive analysis at all. Indeed, do we begin to understand such phenomena as association, dialogue, self-awareness, reflection, etc., better by simply calling them different "forms and types of activity" (. . .)?" (Lektorsky, 1990, p. xx)

Here we are dealing with the heavy ballast of the "grand theories" type of thinking and writing, often attributed to activity theory by its critics. However, a look at the works of Vygotsky, Leont'ev, and Luria reveals that these scholars were primarily and consistently interested in real human activities, concretely present in space and time. Even Il'enkov, perhaps the most important and theoretically the most demanding philosopher influential in the Soviet activity approach, grounded his conceptual work in a painstaking analysis of the methodological procedure that gave rise to a specific text, namely, the *Capital* of Karl Marx (Il'enkov, 1982). In other words, the core conceptual works of activity theory are very much grounded in concrete-historical materials and cases. Indeed, the ensuing openness and "incompleteness" of the conceptual systems may be aggravating for a researcher who would like to simply apply in practice a well-defined theoretical frame.

On the other hand, especially in the domains of learning and play, there is a fair amount of empirical, practice-oriented research that takes concrete activities as its objects of study. Quite commonly in such studies, the concept and structure of activity are treated as rather self-explanatory things. In such cases, the specific methods and findings may not enrich and push forward the elaboration of the conceptual and methodological basis.

Mediation as a key

The six dichotomies outlined earlier may be condensed into three crucial questions:

> First, how can we depict the cell of activity theory or, more specifically, what would be a viable way of modeling the structure and dynamic relations of an activity system?
>
> Second, how can we incorporate historicity and developmental judgment into activity-theoretical analyses, yet take fully into account the diversity and multiplicity inherent in human activities?
>
> And third, what kind of a methodology is appropriate for activity-theoretical research – one that could bridge the gaps between the basic and the applied, between conceptualization and intervention?

Before I present some personal views on these three questions, I want to emphasize what I see as the first prerequisite for any fruitful elaboration of these issues. This is the idea of *mediation*.

It is somewhat amazing that in the recent theoretical discussion concerning the concept of activity, very little attention is paid to the idea of mediation. Yet it is this idea that runs as the unifying and connecting lifeline throughout the works of Vygotsky, Leont'ev, Luria, and the other important representatives of the Soviet cultural-historical school, making attempts to prove "theoretical oppositions" between these scholars look more like trickery than serious and original analysis.

Mediation by tools and signs is not merely a psychological idea. It is an idea that breaks down the Cartesian walls that isolate the individual mind from the culture and the society.

This expansive potential is evident if we look at the notion of *control*. The traditional division between social sciences and psychology has created the still prevalent dichotomous notion according to which humans are controlled either from the outside by society or from the inside by themselves. In the former case, the possibility of human agency and transformation of social structures from below becomes an unexplained mystery. In the latter case, the origins of individual self-determination are attributed to the equally mysterious sources of biological urges or inherent free will. When Vygotsky formulated his idea of mediation, he was very conscious of the revolutionary implications concerning control. Calling the mediating artifact *auxiliary stimulus,* he wrote:

> Because this auxiliary stimulus possesses the specific function of reverse action, it transfers the psychological operation to higher and qualitatively new forms and permits the humans, by the aid of extrinsic stimuli, *to control their behavior from the outside.* (Vygotsky, 1978, p. 40; italics in the original)

The idea is that humans can control their own behavior – not "from the inside," on the basis of biological urges, but "from the outside," using and creating artifacts. This perspective is not only optimistic concerning human self-determination, it is an invitation to serious study of artifacts as integral and inseparable components of human functioning. As Marx Wartofsky (1979, p. 205) put it, "the *artifact* is to cultural evolution what the *gene* is to biological evolution." It is no accident that some of the most creative researchers in cognitive science – Donald Norman and Ed Hutchins, for example – are today focusing their research on the role of artifacts in cognition (see Norman, 1988; Hutchins, 1990). Activity theory has the conceptual and methodological potential to be a pathbreaker in studies that help humans gain control over their own artifacts and thus over their future.

Modeling the activity system

I am convinced that in order to transcend the oppositions between activity and process, activity and action, and activity and communication,

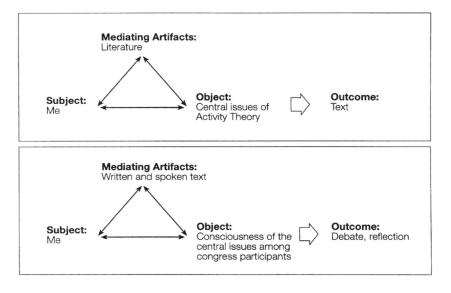

Figure 1.1. A triadic representation of actions.

and to take full advantage of the concept of activity in concrete research, we need to create and test models that explicate the components and internal relations of an activity system.

My actions of preparing and presenting the speech on which this chapter is based could be represented using the classical triadic model shown in Figure 1.1. The first triangle represents my actions of preparing and writing the speech with the help of available literature. The second triangle represents my subsequent actions of presenting the speech in the congress, using the written text and spoken words as my most important mediating artifacts.

The problem with this classical representation is that it does not fully explicate the societal and collaborative nature of my actions. In other words, it does not depict my actions as events in a collective activity system. The outcomes of my actions appear to be very limited and situation bound: a particular text, a momentary impact on the listeners. If this is all there is to gain, why did I bother to prepare this speech in the first place? Somehow, this level of representation hides or obscures the motive behind the actions.

To overcome these limitations, the model may be expanded as shown in Figure 1.2. Here I depict the structure of an emerging activity system

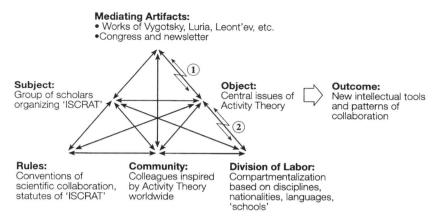

Figure 1.2. A complex model of an activity system.

that might be called *international activity-theoretical collaboration*. The subject has been changed. It is no longer "me" as an individual. Rather, I place myself into a diverse international group of scholars who created this organization. The central issues of activity theory remain the object – that is what connects my individual actions to the collective activity. However, the projected outcome is no longer momentary and situational; rather, it consists of societally important new, objectified meanings and relatively lasting new patterns of interaction. It is this projection from the object to the outcome that, no matter how vaguely envisioned, functions as the motive of this activity and gives broader meaning to my actions. In addition to the legacy of the cultural-historical school objectified in texts, the most important mediating artifacts in this activity system are the international meetings and publications.

The social basis of this activity is the rather loose worldwide community of scholars interested in activity theory. The rules are equally loose: largely tacit conventions of international scientific collaboration and the purposely very flexible statutes of the organizer of international congresses on activity theory, ISCRAT. Finally, the division of labor within this loose community seems to consist of multiple layers of fragmentation and compartmentalization.

In Figure 1.2, I have put lightning-shaped arrows between the object and the mediating artifacts, on the one hand (number 1), and between the object and the division of labor, on the other hand (number 2). These indicate contradictions between central components of the activity system.

In my analysis, the first contradiction exists currently between the very challenging issues activity theory is facing *and* the rather weak instruments of collaboration and discussion at our disposal. The second contradiction exists between those challenging issues *and* the fragmented division of labor that keeps pulling different disciplines, national groups, and schools of thought apart, preventing joint discussion.

This necessarily brief attempt to model the activity system of activity theorists will surely evoke objections and criticism, hopefully with further elaborations and alternatives as well. If so, the model is serving its purpose.

The models just presented indicate that it may be very fruitful to move from the analysis of individual actions to the analysis of their broader activity context and back again. Actions are not fully predictable, rational, and machine-like. The most well-planned and streamlined actions involve failures, disruptions, and unexpected innovations. These are very difficult to explain if one stays at the level of actions. The analysis of the activity system may illuminate the underlying contradictions that give rise to those failures and innovations as if "behind the backs" of the conscious actors.

The suggested model of activity system also highlights the subject–community relations – communicative relations – as an integral aspect of activity systems. There are other kinds of communicative relations, typically those in which representatives of different activity systems interact. Those relations need further elaborations of the model, perhaps entirely new models. But I am quite confident that serious research using and developing these integrated models will enable us to overcome the opposition between activity and communication.

Historicity and diversity

A key task in historical analysis is periodization. One must divide the stream of historical events into larger patterns that have meaningful characteristics of their own. What would be an appropriate period or pattern at the level of the historical evolution of an activity system such as the one in my example?

Zerubavel's (1979, 1981) analyses of time in organizations yield multiple layers of repetitive, cyclic time structures. However, cycles do not have to be repetitive; they can also lead to the emergence of new structures. G. P. Shchedrovitskii, one of the few Soviet activity theorists who has long been concerned with the development of collective activity systems, points out that "it is quite natural to endeavor to represent reproduction as *cycles* resulting in the formation of a new social structure on the basis of some preceding one" (Shchedrovitskii, 1988, p. 7; italics in the original). Such an irreversible time structure may be called an *expansive cycle* (Engeström, 1987).

Whether we are talking of repetitive or expansive cycles, it is important to note that activity time is qualitatively different from action time. Action time is basically linear and anticipates a finite termination. Activity time is recurrent and cyclic. Action time corresponds to "time's arrow" and activity time to "time's cycle," in the terminology of Stephen Jay Gould (1987).

For the historical understanding of activity systems, expansive cycles are of crucial importance. We know little of the dynamics and phases of such developmental cycles. It seems promising to analyze these cycles in terms of the stepwise formation and resolution of internal contradictions in activity systems. The trajectory of an activity system moving through such an expansive cycle seems to go through phases of "far from equilibrium" conditions (Prigogine & Stengers, 1984).

These observations have important consequences for some of the dichotomies discussed earlier. First of all, the opposition between continuous psychic process and discontinuous activity begins to look questionable. Perhaps this opposition is at least partially based on an insufficient differentiation between the time structures of action and activity.

Second, the opposition between internalization and creative externalization may be put in a new light. Obviously an expansive cycle is a developmental process that contains both internalization and externalization. The new activity structure does not emerge out of the blue. It requires reflective analysis of the existing activity structure – one must learn to know and understand what one wants to transcend. And it requires reflective appropriation of existing culturally advanced models and tools that offer ways out of the internal contradictions. However, these forms of internalization or appropriation are not enough for the emergence of a new structure. As the cycle advances, the actual design and implementation of a new model for the activity gain momentum: Externalization begins to dominate. This is schematically depicted in Figure 1.3.

In Figure 1.3, the expansive cycle of an activity system begins with an almost exclusive emphasis on internalization, on socializing and training the novices to become competent members of the activity as it is routinely carried out. Creative externalization occurs first in the form of discrete individual innovations. As the disruptions and contradictions of

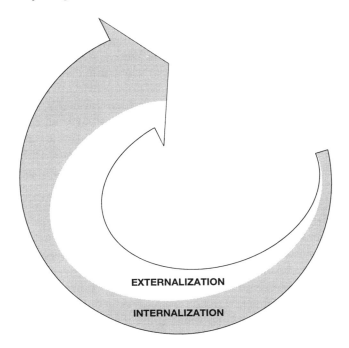

Figure 1.3. The expansive cycle.

the activity become more demanding, internalization increasingly takes the form of critical self-reflection – and externalization, a search for solutions, increases. Externalization reaches its peak when a new model for the activity is designed and implemented. As the new model stabilizes itself, internalization of its inherent ways and means again becomes the dominant form of learning and development.

At the level of collective activity systems, such an expansive cycle may be seen as the equivalent of the zone of proximal development, discussed by Vygotsky (1978) at the level of individual learning. From the viewpoint of historicity, the key feature of expansive cycles is that they are definitely not predetermined courses of one-dimensional development. What is more advanced, "which way is up," cannot be decided using externally given, fixed yardsticks. Those decisions are made locally, within the expansive cycles themselves, under conditions of uncertainty and intensive search. Yet they are not arbitrary decisions. The internal contradictions of the given activity system in a given phase of its evolution can be more or less adequately identified, and any model for the future that does not address and eliminate those contradictions will eventually turn out to be nonexpansive.

An activity system is by definition a multivoiced formation. An expansive cycle is a reorchestration of those voices, of the different viewpoints and approaches of the various participants. Historicity in this perspective means identifying the past cycles of the activity system. The reorchestration of the multiple voices is dramatically facilitated when the different voices are seen against their historical background as layers in a pool of complementary competencies within the activity system.

Back to transformations: The developmental method

It is often said that the formative or developmental experiment is the research method most adequate to and characteristic of activity theory. Sylvia Scribner (1985) has carefully demonstrated that Vygotsky's idea of the appropriate method is not reducible to any single technique. Scribner traces four moments or steps in the methodology sketched by Vygotsky: (1) observation of contemporary everyday behavior, or *rudimentary behavior,* (2) reconstruction of the historical phases of the cultural evolution of the behavior under investigation, (3) experimental production of change from rudimentary to higher forms of behavior, and (4) observation of actual development in naturally occurring behavior.

This is actually a cyclic methodology for understanding transformations at the individual level, emphasizing the internalization of culturally given higher psychological functions. Today it is increasingly evident that these are not the only kinds of transformations that must be understood and mastered. People face not only the challenge of acquiring established culture; they also face situations in which they must formulate desirable culture. In order to understand such transformations going on in human activity systems, we need a methodology for studying expansive cycles. Such a methodology does not easily fit into the boundaries of psychology or sociology or any other particular discipline.

I want to suggest that such a methodology is best developed when researchers enter actual activity systems undergoing such transformations. I am not suggesting a return to naive forms of action research, idealizing so-called spontaneous ideas and efforts coming from practitioners. To the contrary, the type of methodology I have in mind requires that general ideas of activity theory be put to the acid test of practical validity and relevance in interventions that aim at the construction of new models of activity jointly with the local participants. Such construction can be successful only when based on careful historical and empirical analyses of the activity in question.

This approach gives new contents to the notion of formative experiments. Instead of only forming experimentally skills and mental functions in the students, the researchers will be engaged in forming societally new artifacts and forms of practice jointly with their subjects. The validity and generalizability of the results will be decided by the viability, diffusion, and multiplication of those new models in similar activity systems.

Key findings and outcomes of such research are novel activity-specific, intermediate-level theoretical concepts and methods – intellectual tools for reflective mastery of practice. Such intermediate theoretical concepts provide a two-way bridge between general theory and specific practice. This way, the concept of activity as a principle of explanation may be continuously reexamined and reconstructed by making concrete activities the objects of study.

This approach implies a radical localism. The idea is that the fundamental societal relations and contradictions of the given socioeconomic formation – and thus the potential for qualitative change – are present in each and every local activity of that society. And conversely, the mightiest, most impersonal societal structures can be seen as consisting of local activities carried out by concrete human beings with the help of mediating artifacts, even if they may take place in high political offices and corporate boardrooms instead of factory floors and streetcorners. In this sense, it might be useful to try to look at the society more as a multilayered network of interconnected activity systems and less as a pyramid of rigid structures dependent on a single center of power.

References

Aebli, H. (1988). Panel discussion "Activity – Action – Operation." In M. Hildebrand-Nilshon & G. Rückriem (Eds.), *Activity theory in movement – discussions and controversies. Proceedings of the 1st International Congress on Activity Theory* (Vol. 4.1). West Berlin: System Druck.

Alexander, J. C. (1988). *Action and its environment: Toward a new synthesis.* New York: Columbia University Press.

Asmolov, A. G. (1987). Basic principles of a psychological analysis in the theory of activity. *Soviet Psychology, XXV* (2): 78–102.

Brushlinsky, A. V. (1987). Activity, action, and mind as process. *Soviet Psychology, XXV* (4): 59–81.

Brushlinsky, A. V. (1990). The activity of the subject and psychic activity. In V. A. Lektorsky (Ed.), *Activity: Theories, methodology and problems.* Orlando: Paul M. Deutsch Press.

Cole, M. (1988). Cross-cultural research in the socio-historical tradition. In M. Hilde-brand-Nilshon & G. Rückriem (Eds.), *Activity theory: A look into a multidisciplinary research area*. Proceedings of the 1st International Congress on Activity Theory (Vol. 1). West Berlin: System Druck.

Cole, M., & Griffin, P. (1980). Cultural amplifiers reconsidered. In D. R. Olson (Ed.), *The social foundations of language and thought*. New York: Norton.

von Cranach, M. (1988). Panel discussion "Activity – Action – Operation." In M. Hildebrand-Nilshon & G. Rückriem (Eds.), *Activity theory in movement – discussions and controversies*. Proceedings of the 1st International Congress on Activity Theory (Vol. 4.1). West Berlin: System Druck.

von Cranach, M., & Harré, R. (Eds.). (1982). *The analysis of action: Recent theoretical and empirical advances*. Cambridge: Cambridge University Press.

Davydov, V. V. (1990). Problems of activity as a mode of human existence and the principle of monism. In V. A. Lektorsky (Ed.), *Activity: Theories, methodology and problems*. Orlando: Paul M. Deutsch Press.

Engeström, Y. (1987). *Learning by expanding: An activity-theoretical approach to developmental research*. Helsinki: Orienta-Konsultit.

Engeström, Y. (1990). *Learning, working and imagining: Twelve studies in activity theory*. Helsiniki: Orienta-Konsultit.

Fielding, N. G. (Ed.). (1988). *Actions and structure: Research methods and social theory*. London: Sage.

Frese, M., & Sabini, J. (Eds.). (1985). *Goal-directed behavior: The concept of action in psychology*. Hillsdale: Lawrence Erlbaum.

Giddens, A. (1984). *The constitution of society: Outline of the theory of structuration*. Berkeley: University of California Press.

Ginsburg, G. P., Brenner, M., & von Cranach, M. (Eds.). (1985). *Discovery strategies in the psychology of action*. London: Academic Press.

Gould, S. J. (1987). *Time's arrow; time's cycle: Myth and metaphor in the discovery of geographical time*. Cambridge, MA: Harvard University Press.

Habermas, J. (1984). *Reason and the rationalization of society: Vol. 1. Theory of communicative action*. Boston: Beacon Press.

Hacker, W., Volpert, W., & von Cranach, M. (Eds.). (1982). *Cognitive and motivational aspects of action*. Amsterdam: North-Holland.

Hedegaard, M., Hansen, V. R., & Thyssen, S. (Eds.). (1989). *Et virksomt liv: Udforskning af virksomhedsteoriens praksis*. Aarhus: Aarhus Universitetsforlag.

Hildebrand-Nilshon, M., & Rückriem, G. (Eds.). (1988). *Proceedings of the 1st International Congress on Activity Theory* (Vols. 1–4). West Berlin: System Druck.

Holodynski, M., & Jantzen, W. (Eds.). (1989). *Persönlicher Sinn als gesellschaftliches Problem. Studien zur Tätigkeitstheorie 5*. Bielefeld: Universität Bielefeld.

Hutchins, E. (1990). The technology of team navigation. In J. Galegher, R. E. Kraut, & C. Egido (Eds.), *Intellectual teamwork: Social and technological foundations of cooperative work*. Hillsdale: Lawrence Erlbaum.

Il'enkov, E. V. (1982). *The dialectics of the abstract and the concrete in Marx's Capital*. Moscow: Progress.

Jensen, U. J. (1989). Den kulturhistoriske psykologi. Ideologisk metafysik eller objectiv teori? In M. Hedegaard, V. R. Hansen, & S. Thyssen (Eds.), *Et virksomt liv: Udforskning af virksomhedsteoriens praksis*. Aarhus: Aarhus Universitesforlag.

John-Steiner, V. (1985). *Notebooks of the mind: Explorations of thinking.* New York: Harper & Row.

Kozulin, A. (1984). *Psychology in utopia: Toward a social history of Soviet psychology.* Cambridge, MA: MIT Press.

Lektorsky, V. A. (1990). By way of conclusion. In V. A. Lektorsky (Ed.), *Activity: Theories, methodology and problems.* Orlando: Paul M. Deutsch Press.

Lektorsky, V. A. (Ed.) (1990). *Activity: Theories, methodology and problems.* Orlando: Paul M. Deutsch Press.

Leont'ev, A. N. (1978). *Activity, consciousness, and personality.* Englewood Cliffs: Prentice-Hall.

Leontyev, A. N. (1981). *Problems of the development of the mind.* Moscow: Progress.

Lomov, B. F. (1980). Die Kategorien Kommunikation und Tätigkeit in der Psychologie. *Sowjetwissenschaft / Gesellschaftswissenschaftliche Beiträge, 33,* 536–551.

Luria, A. R. (1976). *Cognitive development: Its cultural and social foundations.* Cambridge, MA: Harvard University Press.

Luria, A. R. (1979). *The making of mind: A personal account of Soviet psychology.* Cambridge, MA: Harvard University Press.

Norman, D. A. (1988). *The psychology of everyday things.* New York: Basic Books.

Ochs, E. (1988). *Culture and language development: Language acquisition and language socialization in a Samoan village.* Cambridge: Cambridge University Press.

Prigogine, I., & Stengers, I. (1984). *Order out of chaos: Man's new dialogue with nature.* London: Fontana.

Schurig, V. (1988). "Tätigkeit" or "activity"? The limits of translating key psychological concepts into other languages. *Multidisciplinary Newsletter for Activity Theory, 1,* 3–5.

Scribner, S. (1985). Vygotsky's uses of history. In J. V. Wertsch (Ed.), *Culture, communication, and cognition: Vygotskian perspectives.* New York: Cambridge University Press.

Shchedrovitskii, G. P. (1988). Basic principles of analyzing instruction and development from the perspective of the theory of activity. *Soviet Psychology, XXVI*(4): 5–41.

Suchman, L. A. (1987). *Plans and situated actions: The problem of human–machine communication.* Cambridge: Cambridge University Press.

Tikhomirov, O. K. (1988). *The psychology of thinking.* Moscow: Progress.

Valsiner, J. (1988). *Developmental psychology in the Soviet Union.* Bloomington: Indiana University Press.

Vygotsky, L. S. (1962). *Thought and language.* Cambridge, MA: MIT Press.

Vygotsky, L. S. (1971). *The psychology of art.* Cambridge, MA: MIT Press.

Vygotsky, L. S. (1978). *Mind in society: The development of higher psychological processes.* Cambridge, MA: Harvard University Press.

Wartofsky, M. (1979). *Models: Representation and scientific understanding.* Dordrecht: Reidel.

Wittgenstein, L. (1958). *Philosophical investigations.* Oxford: Basil Blackwell.

Yudin, E. G. (1978). *Sistemnyi podhod i printsip deyatel'nosti.* Moscow: IPL.

Zerubavel, E. (1979). *Patterns of time in hospital life.* Chicago: University of Chicago Press.

Zerubavel, E. (1981). *Hidden rhythms: Schedules and calendars in social life.* Chicago: University of Chicago Press.

2 The content and unsolved problems of activity theory

Vassily V. Davydov

Introduction

All the humanities have for their subjects different aspects of human activity. At present they have to face a great number of acute unsolved problems. But before stating those problems and looking for ways to solve them, it is important to explain the basic concept of activity as formulated by the followers of activity theory.

Activity is a specific form of the societal existence of humans consisting of purposeful changing of natural and social reality. In contrast to the laws of nature, societal laws manifest themselves only through human activity that constructs new forms and features of reality, thus turning the initial material into products. Any activity carried out by a subject includes goals, means, the process of molding the object, and the results. In fulfilling the activity, the subjects also change and develop themselves.

The goals of activity manifest themselves as images of the foreseen result of the creative effort. The transforming and purposeful character of activity allows the subject to step beyond the frames of a given situation and to see it in a wider historical and societal context. It makes it possible for the subject to find means that go beyond the given possibilities. Activity permanently and limitlessly overcomes all the "programs" on which it is based. That is why it cannot be limited to changing reality according to the stable cultural norms. Activity is, in principle, open and universal; it should be taken as the form of historical and cultural creativity. The formation of human activity is also the beginning of personality.

Notions of activity were elaborated by important idealist philosophers such as Kant, Fichte, and Hegel. The basis of a dialectical–materialist concept of activity was created by Marx, whose works drew on the achievements of classical German philosophy. The concept of activity formulated by Marx remains significant today. Here I review its content, taking into account that Marx's philosophical and sociological concepts

39

should be kept separate from his more specific economic and political views.

Basic contents of the concept of activity

In describing general characteristics of human labor, Marx depicts it, first, as human activity that changes nature. Human activity uses features of one natural object as tools for acting on other objects, thus turning the former into an organ of activity. Exerting influence on nature, human beings change their own nature at the same time (Marx & Engels, 1960, Vol. 23, p. 188). According to Marx, "labor is positive creative activity" (Marx & Engels, 1968, Vol. 46, Part II, p. 113) fulfilled within definite societal relations. In contrast to the one–sided production carried out by animals, the human being produces universally, reconstructs nature, and produces according to the measures of any kind and everywhere (Marx & Engels, 1974, Vol. 42, pp. 93–94).

In the framework of materialist dialectics, the notion of *activity* is an initial abstraction. Its concretization makes it possible to produce a general theory of development of social existence and its specific aspects. The initial form of activity is the production of material tools that help people produce objects satisfying their vital needs. Material production, or labor, has a universal character because it can produce any tools and objects. Such production is achieved in definite social relations. In the course of historical development of material production and social relations, spiritual production appeared and became relatively independent. But even in this sphere of labor, one can find the main properties of material production: its universal, transforming, and social character.

The process of material and spiritual activity is closely connected to people's ideal images that make it possible to foresee the product. Marx pointed out that "at the end of the process of labor one gets the result that existed in the notion, i.e., ideally" (Marx & Engels, 1960, Vol. 23, p. 189). Besides, if "production produces the object of consumption in its external form, . . . consumption considers the object in an ideal form, as an internal image, as a need, as an attraction and as a goal" (Marx & Engels, 1968, Vol. 46, Part I, p. 28).

Human notions considered as internal images, need and goal, different as they seem to be, can be united in the concept of an ideal. By means of this concept, one can understand the aspect of human activity that anticipates the production of an object.

Human activity is conscious. In order to reveal the sense of the notion *consciousness,* one should take into account the social character of human activity. Activity exists in both collective and individual forms when a person acts as a generic social being.

Individual and generic life of a human being are not different things, though the individual way of living may be either a more specific or a more universal manifestation of generic life. . . . (Marx & Engels, 1974, Vol. 42, p. 119)

Due to the possibility of its ideal existence, the universal character of collective tribal activity may be represented in an individual person. And the consciousness of persons is their ideal, subjective notion of their real social being, their tribal activity and social relations connected to this activity.

Thus one can regard activity as an initial category that determines the specific character of people's social being. The social laws can reveal themselves only in activity and through it.

At the end of the 19th century and early in the 20th, along with the dialectical materialist understanding of activity, other relevant ideas were developed pertaining particularly to the concept of action, the key component of activity. Within the philosophy of pragmatism, John Dewey created a theory of actions as instrumental contents of human notions (Dewey, 1910). Max Weber analyzed the different types of individual social actions, emphasizing their particular value orientations and purposes (Weber, 1978). An elaborate conception of action and human operational intelligence was worked out by Jean Piaget on the basis of logic, mathematics, and psychology (Piaget, 1952).

In my country after the Revolution, the problem of activity was studied by the various human sciences on the basis of dialectical materialist ideas. Such studies were conducted primarily in philosophy (by Kopnin, Il'enkov, Yudin, Ivanov, and others) and in psychology (by Basov, Rubinstein, Leont'ev, and others). At the end of the 1980s, we had a broad-based discussion on the status of the concept of activity, its multidisciplinary character, and its place among other central concepts of human sciences, such as *social relations* and *communication*. The explanatory potential of *activity* and *nonactivity* theories was also discussed (Lektorsky, 1990). Engeström continued this discussion in the opening address of the Second International Congress for Research on Activity Theory (Chapter 1, this volume).

Eight unsolved problems

I have very briefly formulated some of the main ideas of the interdisciplinary theory of activity. It is founded on a specific trend in modern philosophy, sociology, and psychology. Researchers now have at their disposal many facts that make it possible to render these ideas more concrete, to develop and expose their meaning. But at the same time, the analysis of such material shows that many important problems of activity theory are far from being solved. What problems are these? Let us discuss some of them.

1. Understanding transformation

The first complicated problem is connected with the necessity to determine a key notion of activity theory: *transformation.* Most frequently transformation is understood as changing the object. But careful examination shows that not every change is a transformation. Many changes of natural and social reality carried out by people affect the object externally without changing it internally. Such changes can hardly be called transformations. Transformation means changing an object internally, making evident its essence and altering it.

Unfortunately, modern logic does not offer a strict and clear understanding of essence. Far from it; for many decades, two approaches to this problem existed in opposition to each other. The first one has been stated by formal logic, the second by dialectical logic. According to the former, the essence of an object is something it has in common with other similar objects that makes them belong to the same class. In other words, any feature an object has in common with, or identical to, the characteristics of some other objects may be taken as essential.

That is why, when a person singles out more or less similar characteristics of objects, or identifies family and type relations, this involves movement in the sphere of essences, a step from one essence of a thing to its other essence. In this case, the object's transformation consists in the fact that a person changes its type to its family. For example, in a certain situation, the person considers boots and identifies their family characteristic as footwear. From the point of view of formal logic, the construction and use of various classification patterns by a person can be considered transformation of objects, or cognitive activity.

In dialectical logic, essence is a genetic initial or universal relation of a system of objects that gives birth to its specific and individual features. Essence is a law of development of the system itself. The most vivid example of a dialectical transformation is a purposeful growing up of an object as a complicated system. When we find and select wheat grains of full value, sow them, create conditions for their normal growth, and at last get a good crop, this process is an example of a real transformation of some part of nature by humans, or purposeful human activity.

Each of these two approaches to the essence of objects is expressed in a specific type of transformation. The first type is connected to the division of the variety of objects on the basis of their family and type relations, to the construction of adequate classifications, and to their use in order to achieve a practical orientation in reality. The second type of transformation is connected to the search for such an object in a certain domain of objects the development of which gives birth to all this variety. This transformation is connected to finding out and creating conditions necessary for the full realization of such development.

There are also two types of activity that correspond to the two types of transformation. One of them is aimed at changing the existing external order of objects. The other one is aimed at the realization of their inner potential, at understanding the conditions of origination of integral systems.

Activity theory has long been an object of serious criticism and has even been denied by several schools of philosophy and psychology. During the last few decades, this criticism has become more acute than ever. We see the reasons for this in certain deep social processes connected to the failure of a number of social experiments and to the ecological catastrophes we are witnessing. They are related to such changes and transformations of social and natural reality that have in fact occurred violently.

This criticism has some foundation, as the activity approach involves a certain technicist activism that has no humanistic origins. Instead of developing the essence of reality according to its own laws it disfigures it, mutilates it, and changes it without taking into account the historical interests of humans and realistic possibilities of the reality itself. Such activism does not coincide with the activity theory of Marx and Hegel, according to which people dealing with an object may only use the measure that belongs to that object. That is why humans, wrote Marx, build according to the laws of beauty as well (Marx & Engels, 1974, Vol. 42, p. 94).

It is certainly possible for people not to disfigure nature and society. But often there are no adequate conditions for the realization of this possibility. We need to analyze the historical reasons for the activism mentioned previously, and we need to explore the historical conditions for activity that transforms reality according to the laws of its own perfection. This is vitally important in order to show how narrow is the idea that humans must only understand, explain, and make themselves at home in the world, not change it (see Gaidenko, 1991, p. 8).

I have discussed the transformation problem. But it is this very problem that needs thorough study – first of all by logicians and sociologists who may be able to give other specialists a developed definition of essence and its different types and to reveal an inner connection between the transformation of an object's essence and the category of human activity.

2. Collective and individual activity

The second mostly unsolved problem of activity theory concerns the relation between collective and individual activity or between collective and individual subject. Numerous versions of activity theory admit the existence of an internalization process, that is, of the process of formation of individual activity on the basis of collective activity. While doing this, they notice that the structures of these two forms of activity are to a certain degree similar. But they pay very little attention to their difference. However, it is exactly the characteristics of this very difference that pose a particular problem for activity theory.

The interconnection of collective and individual activity is currently being investigated in various countries (e.g., Perret-Clermont, 1980; Rubtsov, 1987; Engeström, 1987). It is important that the analysis of the results of those studies be aimed at revealing the structure and functions of each form of activity. Some researchers still dismiss the internalization of collective activity. It is thus necessary to develop a more exact and comprehensive analysis of the stages of this process, emphasizing the importance of the conditions of its realization.

For a long time, social scientists refused to discuss the existence of the activity of *collective subjects*. Only recently has this term begun to be used. Lektorsky (1984) stresses that, in a certain sense, the collective subject exists outside particular individual subjects and reveals itself through external, objective-practical, collective activity rather than through individual consciousness.

I certainly agree with this. But then questions appear. If the collective subject is external to particular individuals, can it be imagined in the form of some totality or group of persons, and in what exact sense does it exist outside the particular individuals who form this group? Further, what must be the essential features of a group of persons who carry out the joint activity so that this group may be defined as a collective subject? What characteristics can help to distinguish collective and individual subjects? What are the particular characteristics of the individual subject, and in what ways does it differ from personality? What can be defined as the personal level of realizing individual activity?

These questions still have no concrete answers. That is why appropriate research is necessary. And while launching this work, it is important to take into account the theoretical conceptions that were formulated in the works of Durkheim, Blondel, Levy-Brühl, and their followers.

3. Structure and components of activity

The third problem concerns the difficulties of defining the general structure of activity. According to A. N. Leont'ev (1978), the structure of activity includes such components as needs, motives, goals, actions, and operations. If we examine this structure, we notice the absence of the means of solving a problem. It seems clear that this component should be added.

But the main question is how to relate this general activity structure to such traditional psychic processes as perception, imagination, memory, thinking, feelings, and will. Can these be considered as components of the general structure of activity, along with motives, problems, and actions? Or should they be considered as independent kinds of activity? If the latter thesis is accepted, we must admit the existence of sensoric, mnemonic, and thinking activity, and even of activity of feelings and activity of will.

It must be emphasized that at present in different sciences, and especially in psychology, these psychological processes are frequently regarded as particular kinds of activity. For example, human thinking is spoken of as thinking activity.

In my opinion, it is not correct to consider traditional cognitive processes as different forms of activity. They are no more than specific components of a general activity structure that promote the realization of its other components. For example, perception and thinking help a person to single out and concretize the conditions in which a sensory or cognitive problem can be solved and to choose the methods of its solution. But the problem itself is a component of some integral activity, for example, play, art, or learning.

4. Different kinds of activity

This question leads us to the fourth problem – that of classification of different kinds of activity. This problem is complicated by the various meanings attached to the term *activity* in different languages. The English equivalent of the Russian word *deyatel'nost* is *activity*. However, the common English use of the term *activity* is too inclusive and broad. Not all expressions of vital activeness can be defined as activity. True activity is always connected to the transformation of reality. This notion may be better expressed by the German terms *Tätigkeit* and *Handlung*.

Different disciplines have different bases for the classification of types of activity. Sociologists, for example, speak of labor, political, artistic, scientific, and other activity kinds. Educational scientists single out play, learning, and labor activity as the principal kinds. In psychology, activity can be identified with any psychic process (see the third problem). It is clear that, for example, labor or political activity includes the kinds of activity singled out by psychologists. What kind of classification is the principal one, and what is the general system of different types of activity?

I think that the main basis for classification must be the historical-sociological approach to activity, centered on labor in all the historical forms of its development. This approach will enable us to construct the whole variety of socially meaningful kinds of activity that appeared in history as forms of people's realization of social life (Levada, 1984). Historical sociology should reveal, study, and even make projections about the formation of all interconnected kinds and forms of human activity. It must study and explain the place and the role of every activity in people's social life. The character of historical reality consists in the fact that activity is the only possible method of its existence and development (Il'enkov, 1977a).

From this point of view, all sciences studying activity may be backed by the results of historical-sociological studies. But it is important that the materials from these sciences be used to render historico-sociological notions of activity more concrete. In this respect, investigations of learning activity are of considerable interest (e.g., Davydov, 1982; Engeström, 1987).

5. Understanding communication

One more problem concerns the interrelation between the notion of activity and the notion of interaction. Some philosophers and psychologists think that we must not exaggerate and absolutize the role of activity in people's social life; they believe that a considerable role in this sphere belongs to interaction and communication. These researchers suggest that we create a theory of human existence on the basis of those two notions of equal importance: activity and communication.

However, as pointed out earlier, activity is the only possible mode of people's historical and social existence and development. This is a crucial sociological conclusion (Voronovic & Pletnikov, 1975). The second conclusion, closely connected to the first one, is that collective and individual activity is realized in the form of material and spiritual social relationships. Communication is a processual expression of these relations. Communication can exist only in the process of different kinds of activity realization by people.

That is why the notions of activity and communication must not be opposed. At the same time, one cannot study communication and evaluate its role in people's lives without examining their activity. Communication only gives form to activity.

6. Connections to other theories

The sixth problem of activity theory concerns its connection to other approaches to the study of human conduct. Earlier in this chapter, I tried to show that the notion of activity is inseparable from those of ideal and consciousness.

In my opinion, first of all, one must take into account the theory of the ideal worked out by the Soviet philosopher Il'enkov (1977b). While doing this, activity theorists should also work on Freud's psychoanalytic theory of human consciousness. One needs to analyze the psychoanalytic conception from the point of view of activity theory. This should open up the possibility of enriching activity theory with various achievements of psychoanalysis (see Chapters 24 and 25 in this volume).

Genetic epistemology, created by Jean Piaget (1952) and his followers, is based on the notions of action and operation. Similarly, the theory of stepwise formation of mental actions, worked out by the outstanding Soviet psychologist Gal'perin (1976) and his followers, has as its foundation the notion of action. It is necessary to compare the theory of activity with the bases of the approaches of Piaget and Gal'perin, and to find their commonalities and differences.

7. The biological and the social

The seventh problem of activity theory has to do with understanding the relationship between the biological and the social in human existence. In recent years, expressions such as *biosocial human nature* and *biosocial human essence* have been frequently used. I will briefly present my own position.

According to a dialectical materialist approach, the human essence is societal, comprising the totality of the human being's social relations (Davydov, 1988, p. 3). However, Marx also wrote about the "natural bonds" that connect human beings. He pointed out that humans are natural beings endowed with vital corporeal forces (Marx & Engels, 1974, Vol. 42, p. 162). But neither for Marx nor for other adherents of his philosophy is the notion of *natural corporeal forces* of a human being equivalent to the notion of *biological forces* per se.

Natural human forces refer to the essential characteristics of human sensuous-objective activity directed to the transformation of nature, with humans themselves included as part of it. But this activity is essentially historical and societal. From this point of view, the biological is not directly present in sensuous-objective activity that constitutes the basis of human psychological development (Leont'ev, 1978).

The biological is inherent in the behavior of animals, realized as a unity of their needs and inborn ways of satisfying them. *Innateness* here means the predetermination of these ways by the peculiarities of morphophysiological organization of the animal as a representative of a certain species. The biological basis of animal behavior and the societal basis of human activity create two radically different types of existence.

Due to the societal essence of activity, the ways of satisfying human needs, even organic ones, are not predetermined by the organization of the human body. In the process of anthropogenesis, the human organism has evolved in a way that enables humans to create and engage in practically any form of activity. Such an organism comprises the universal character of humans as natural corporeal beings. The ways of satisfying human needs and conducting activity are connected to the use of means and tools, which Marx called the *nonorganic body* of the human being (Marx & Engels, 1974, Vol. 42, p. 92).

The organic body of a human being includes one's organic needs and the corporeal movements (actions) conducted to satisfy these needs. This organic body itself was formed during anthropogenesis and has a societal essence. Thus, Marx spoke about the social character of human hunger, which can be satisfied with the help of a knife and a fork and which differs greatly from the hunger of an animal (Marx & Engels, 1958, Vol. 12, p. 718). Even more social are the movements involved in the use of the knife and the fork.

Thus, the natural and the corporeal in a human being cannot be simply characterized as the *biological*. The natural and the corporeal may more adequately be labeled as the *organic*.

As pointed out earlier, the biological mode of existence, characteristic of animals, has a very important characteristic: a unity between organic needs and innate mechanisms of satisfying them. This unity constitutes the basis of instincts inherent in animal behavior. In the process of human anthropogenesis, a break occurred between organic needs and the means of satisfying them, that is, human beings lost their instincts. The organic needs that constitute human needs are still preserved, but the innate mechanisms of satisfying them have disappeared (Gal'perin, 1976). The organic needs of a human being become satisfied by the forms of activity acquired during one's lifetime. In this sense, the organics, corporeality, and "naturalism" of human beings remain, but the biological as the mode of animal existence has been lost.

In my view, the problems of biosocial human nature can be concretely resolved only in the course of interdisciplinary studies of the peculiarities of animal instincts and their disappearance during human anthropogenesis, as well as the origin of the relationship between the organic and nonorganic bodies of humans.

8. *Organizing interdisciplinarity*

The eighth problem concerns the methods of organizing the interdisciplinary study of human activity. Today separate disciplines generally study activity independently. Only in theoretical discussions may one see psychologists using conclusions made by a philosopher or a sociologist, or vice versa.

Very few experimental investigations are conducted in which representatives of different disciplines – logicians, sociologists, educators, psychologists, physiologists – participate. In our own experience, the organization of such studies requires considerable expenses and special conditions. But precisely this sort of research is of great importance today.

Four stages in the study of activity

In conclusion, I turn to the methodology of concrete research in human activity. Four stages of analysis may be identified in such studies.

In the course of life, the human being engages in various concrete types of activity that basically differ in their object contents. In other words, each specific activity has definite needs, motives, tasks, and goals as its contents. The objective of the first stage of the study of activity consists in identifying the object content of each type of activity. Only after this is done can one classify a particular psychological formation being observed as a concrete type of activity.

The second stage of studying activity consists of defining the object content and structure of its collective form, the interrelations of its constituents, the methods of their exchange, their various transformations, and the conditions and regularities of the emergence of individual activity. Although human activity in both collective and individual forms is conscious, the process of emergence of consciousness and its functions in activity are very difficult to analyze. There is a great need for a preliminary "morphological picture" of the two activity forms and their genetic interrelations.

The third stage of investigating activity concerns the study of the emergence of its ideal plane. In psychology this problem has been given very little attention, whereas in philosophy a number of serious works have dealt with it. In my opinion, the most promising approach to the problem of the ideal can be found in Il'enkov's (1977a, 1977b) writings. Il'enkov showed that the ideal is revealed in the human capacity to reproduce or re-create a material object resting on a word, a draft, or a model. The ideal exists in constant intertransitions of the activity elements according to the following scheme: object–action–word–action–object. The ideal is the existence of an object in the phase of its formation, in the subject's activity manifesting itself as a need and a goal.

At the third stage of investigating activity, one can study the genesis of its ideal components (needs, goals, and notions that precede achievement of its results), observing the special role of language, drafts, and various models in the process of their objectification and acquisition of corresponding social form. In the long run, at this stage, one can reveal conditions and regularities forming the human capacity to produce and re-create objects with joint activity. The ideal manifests itself in the realization of this particular capacity.

At the fourth stage of investigating activity, one may begin to study significant features of activity such as awareness. The ideal as the basis of consciousness is closely connected to the system of linguistic meanings. As to language, according to Marx, it exists practically for others, and for this reason, it also exists for my own self as real consciousness. Speech is a social event of verbal interaction. When producing an utterance, each person tries to take into consideration the listener's views, beliefs, likes, and dislikes.

In the consciousness of an individual there are ideally represented the needs, interests, and positions of other people involved in certain social relations and participating together with this individual in some kind of joint activity (in which individuals carry out various types of material and verbal communication). An individual's own activity is also ideally represented in his or her consciousness, so that it can be evaluated and planned in accordance with other people's positions.

These four stages of investigating activity are aimed at revealing its content and structure together with such fundamental characteristics as consciousness and the ideal. In the process of creating an interdisciplinary theory of activity, a number of problems emerge. I have identified only a few of them. Without persistent attempts to solve them, it may be impossible to work out theoretical approaches to practical improvement of human life.

References

Davydov, V. V. (1982). The psychological structure and contents of learning activity in school children. In R. Glaser & J. Lompscher (Eds.), *Cognitive and motivational aspects of instruction*. Berlin: Deutscher Verlag der Wissenschaften.

Davydov, V. V. (1988). About the concept of personality in modern psychology. *Psikhologicheskii Zhurnal, 9*(4), 22–32 (in Russian).

Dewey, J. (1910). *How we think*. Boston: D. C. Heath.

Engeström, Y. (1987). *Learning by expanding: An activity-theoretical approach to developmental research*. Helsinki: Orienta-Konsultit.

Gaidenko, P. P. (1991). The problem of rationality in the beginning of the 20th century. *Voprossy Filosofii, 6*, 3–14 (in Russian).

Gal'perin, P. Ia. (1976). *Introduction to psychology*. Moscow: Izd. MGU (in Russian).

Il'enkov, E. V. (1977a). *Dialectical logic: Essays in its history and theory*. Moscow: Progress.

Il'enkov, E. V. (1977b). The concept of the ideal. In *Philosophy in the USSR: Problems of dialectical materialism*. Moscow: Progress.

Lektorsky, V. A. (1984). *Subject, object, cognition*. Moscow: Progress.

Lektorsky, V. A. (Ed.). (1990). *Activity: Theories, methodology and problems*. Orlando: Paul M. Deutsch Press.

Leont'ev, A. N. (1978). *Activity, consciousness, and personality*. Englewood Cliffs: Prentice-Hall.

Levada, Yu. A. (1984). Play structures in the system of social actions. In *Sistemnye issledovaniya*. Moscow: Nauka (in Russian).

Marx, K., & Engels, F. (1958). *Collected works* (Vol. 12). Moscow: Gosudarstvennoje Izdatelstvo Politicheskoi Literatury (in Russian).

Marx, K., & Engels, F. (1960). *Collected works* (Vol. 23). Moscow: Gosudarstvennoje Izdatelstvo Politicheskoi Literatury (in Russian).

Marx, K., & Engels, F. (1968). *Collected works* (Vol. 46, Part I). Moscow: Gosudarstvennoje Izdatelstvo Politicheskoi Literatury (in Russian).

Marx, K., & Engels, F. (1969). *Collected works* (Vol. 46, Part II) Moscow: Gosudarstvennoje Izdatelstvo Politicheskoi Literatury (in Russian).

Marx, K., & Engels, F. (1974). *Collected works* (Vol. 42). Moscow: Gosudarstvennoje Izdatelstvo Politicheskoi Literatury (in Russian).

Perret-Clermont, A. N. (1980). *Social interaction and cognitive development in children.* London: Academic Press.

Piaget, J. (1952). *The origins of intelligence in children.* New York: International Universities Press.

Rubtsov, V. V. (1987). *Organization and development of children's joint actions in the teaching-learning process.* Moscow: Pedagogika (in Russian).

Voronovic, B. A., & Pletnikov, Y. K. (1975). *The category of activity in historical materialism.* Moscow: Znan'e (in Russian).

Weber, M. (1978). *Economy and society.* Berkeley: University of California Press.

3 Knowledge as shared procedures

Stephen Toulmin

Introduction

Most of the chapters in this volume are concerned with applying activity theory to different aspects of individual development and social transformation. From that point of view, the subject of this chapter (the relevance of L. S. Vygotsky's ideas to the philosophical theory of knowledge) may be peripheral. Still, something is gained if, for once, we stand back and view activity theory itself against its larger background in intellectual history. The questions to be raised here, then, have to do with the history of Western epistemology, and with the ways in which the work of Vygotsky and his successors helps throw light on current problems in this area.

To explain my personal interest in this subject: I have admired the work of Vygotsky and A. R. Luria for more than 20 years, having come to their writings through the American clinical neuroanatomist Norman Geschwind (1974). Geschwind's work on the aphasias and apraxias was closely related to the neurological work that Luria did during and after World War II. As Geschwind saw it, Luria's approach opened a new direction of attack on the cerebral localization of higher mental functions, and so on our whole understanding of sensory and cognitive systems (Luria, 1973). But that is not all: Going beyond neurology and psychology (he thought), Luria also suggested new ways of resolving other larger, more long-standing issues in the tradition of Western epistemology.

What is knowledge

How do human beings – how *can* they – come to know anything about the world?

What, if anything, do they (can they) know *for certain*, either one at a time, as individuals, or collectively, for example, as members of a profession?

53

Throughout the 20th century, there has been a deep crisis in this branch of philosophy. Edmund Husserl (1962) set out to locate this crisis early in the century. In the 1920s, John Dewey (1929) defined the intellectual confusion underlying the "quest for certainty" embodied in the agenda of 17th-century philosophy. In the 1930s and 1940s, this critique broadened into a more general philosophical skepticism through the later work of Ludwig Wittgenstein (1953). And, taken together, as Rorty (1989) has argued, the work of these writers, among others, finally destroyed the program for finding "unshakeable foundations" for human knowledge, which was dreamed up, from the 1630s on, by René Descartes (1968) and his successors. That program having run into the sand, the whole epistemological agenda now needs to be reformulated.

The present chapter has two aims. First, it attempts to indicate how the ideas of Vygotsky, Luria, and their associates help to point a way out of this epistemological crisis and define a more constructive way of moving ahead. Second, it considers on what conditions and in what ways a collaboration between philosophers concerned with the problems of knowledge, on the one hand, and human scientists engaged in studying "activity," on the other hand, may be profitable for both sides.

The roots of the 20th-century crisis

During the 350 years since René Descartes published his *Meditations* and *Discourse,* epistemology has gone through two distinct cycles of development. The first began with Descartes, was carried further by Leibniz and Locke, Berkeley and Hume, and culminated in Kant's (1976) *Critique of Pure Reason.* The second, briefer recapitulation began in the 1880s with the work of Ernst Mach, was carried further by Bertrand Russell and G. E. Moore, Moritz Schlick and Rudolf Carnap, and culminated in the later teachings of Ludwig Wittgenstein.

In both phases, the discussion began promisingly, was undertaken with vigor and self-confidence, but shipwrecked in the end for reasons that sprang from the excessively individualistic – if not narcissistic – nature of the philosophers' agenda. For Descartes and Locke as for Mach and Russell, the problem is how each human, as an individual, can arrive at any well-founded, even certain, knowledge about the world. From our standpoint, however, none of these writers gives a convincing account of the relationship between "knowledge" as the possession of individuals and "knowledge" as the collective property of communities of "knowers," for example, professional scientists. Descartes stated his initial question, "What if anything can I, René Descartes, know for certain?" in terms that invite the reader to slide into solipsism or, at least, into a belief that different individuals' personal experiences are hermetically sealed off from each other. Given this starting point, a miracle is required to guarantee that the "clear and distinct ideas" that gave Descartes a personal assurance of knowledge were available to other reflective and rational beings as well.

Nor, despite his best efforts, was the basic situation any better for John Locke (1959). He saw the "ideas of reflection" (*concepts*) available to any individual as produced by repeated experience of similar "ideas of sense" (*percepts*); but he had no way to demonstrate that different individuals placed in a sequence of similar situations would always, or necessarily, form identical concepts. In fact, we find out only as we go along how far concept acquisition has the same outcomes in different people; so, no certainty attaches to the resulting *collective* knowledge. (This difficulty arose once again, in the second phase, from Ernst Mach in the 1880s up to Bertrand Russell in 1912.)

At least Kant tried to make the crucial move when he denied that an intelligible account can be given of intellectual activities if we begin from so personal or individual an origin. Every cognitive judgment, even a direct report of perception, is in Kant's view "intersubjective." Still, his insistence that all cognitive achievements are, in principle at least, *shared* by all rational thinkers went hardly any further than this. He left it unclear just how, during their lifetimes, different individuals come to participate in this shared repertory of concepts and judgments. In this respect, the climax of the second phase (exemplified in the writings of Ludwig Wittgenstein and Ludvik Fleck) represents a true advance.

On the one hand, Wittgenstein's (1953) arguments not merely rejected but discredited the *ideas* and *impressions* that were the starting point of 17th-century epistemology, both rationalist and empiricist. If all our knowledge, concepts, and judgments are in principle intersubjective, there is a reason. All such units of understanding obtain their meaning by entering language not via the minds of single individuals but within "forms of life" (*Lebensformen*) that are essentially *collective*. As a result, the origin of any individual's questions and judgments is defined by the current state of the art in the relevant field of inquiry, what Fleck (1981) calls the *Wissensstand*. So, at the end of the second phase, we find ourselves facing an important scientific question: "How is it, then, that individuals can be successfully socialized, or enculturated, into the shared *Wissensstand* of any particular culture or profession?"

The *individualism* of 17th-century epistemology is, however, only part of the problem that led to the early-20th-century crisis. True, it is a significant part of the problem, appearing as a brand new issue in the time of Descartes, in the 1630s. But, looking back 40 years earlier, we find in Michel de Montaigne's *Essais* a treatment of knowledge and mental activity that is also individualistic but in no way tempts us toward solipsism (Montaigne, 1958). Far from seeing his own "mind" as a self-contained, hermetically sealed entity, Montaigne treats his activities, physical and mental equally, as being representative samples of the activities of all roughly similar human beings.

For Montaigne, that is, mental life was still *social* life. Montaigne's mental activities were an overt element in his public autobiography. He *described* them; he did not *explain* them. His "mind" was not yet trapped, as it was for Descartes, in the sensorium or "Inner Room" in which it was to remain up to the time of Jean Paul Sartre's play, *Huis Clos* (1962). Indeed, one of Montaigne's motives for writing the *Essais* was to present his own experience – whether from life or from reading – as contributing to the shared understanding of human experience as it presents itself to most (if not all) human beings in all its richness.

In the 1580s, Montaigne could still maintain this posture. By the 1620s or 1630s, the scale had tilted in the other direction. Why was this? Largely, it was because Descartes (1968) framed his theory of knowledge to match his particular view of theoretical physics (or *natural philosophy*, as it was then known) – a view of physics that was narrowly material, causal, and mechanical. Its counterpart was a view of human psychology (*mental philosophy*) that was immaterial, logical, and calculative. For any human person, to *be* is to *think* and to *think* is to *calculate*. During the 17th century, as a result, the *new mechanical philosophers* worked out an account of the physiological basis of mental life in general, and individual knowledge in particular, that banished the Mind inescapably into depths of Body.

That view, which insisted on the *interiority* of all mental events and activities, has remained influential among scientific writers up to the present. On this account, the data of sensory experience – ideas or vibrations, images or impulses – travel up the sensory nerves from the sense organs to the innermost brain. As Newton (1968) puts it: Is not the sensory (or sensorium) that place to which the sensible species (i.e., images) of things are carried through the nerves and brain, that there they may be perceived by their immediate presence to the (mental) substance?

Whatever is true of God, human beings are so unfavorably situated that, for them, only the "sensible images" of things are carried through the organs of sense into their little sensoriums, there seen and beheld by that which in them perceives and thinks.

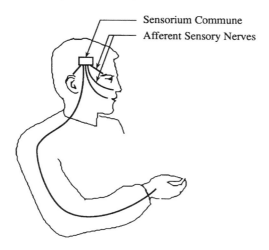

Figure 3.1. Traditional model of the internal sensorium as the locus of all perception.

Where exactly did the natural philosophers assume that the human sensorium was located? For lack of evidence, few of them hazarded more than a guess. Descartes leaned toward the pineal gland at the base of the brain – it had no other known function – but his successors placed it, vaguely, in or around the cerebral cortex. The crucial element of their theory was that the supposed *interiority* of mental life is an inescapable feature of the natural processes in our brain and central nervous system. If our mental lives are trapped within our brains, they are thus trapped there *from birth*. As Jean Paul Sartre's (1962) title suggests, our minds live the lives of prisoners who are born, live, and die in permanent deadlock.

The *inner–outer* problem, as it arises in cognitive psychology and epistemology, is thus a by-product of basic assumptions in 17th-century mechanical theory; and so it remains today, even though physics itself has long since abandoned so mechanical an account of the natural world. We find a particularly striking expression of this 17th-century model in one of the essays in T. H. Huxley's book *Science and Culture* (1881): this speaks of our sense organs not as *instruments* that help us to acquire knowledge of the world, but as *obstacles* that need to be penetrated or surmounted if we are to establish any connections between the *inner* mental life of the knower and the *outer* physical objects known about.

The underlying theoretical model can conveniently be represented in a diagram (Figure 3.1). Here the sensory nerves act as intermediate tubes, fibers, or other connections, standing between the interior Mind of the Knower and the physical state of the Known World.

The way ahead

At this point, we can see how the psychological, neurological, and cultural results of Vygotsky, Luria, and their colleagues throw light on the problems of 20th-century philosophers like John Dewey and Ludwig Wittgenstein. Four points are worth considering.

(1.) In the later Wittgenstein, the basic reason why the theory of knowledge cannot treat knowledge as primarily the possession of individuals is this: All *meanings* are created in the public domain in the context of *collective* situations and activities. True: Once this is done, individuals can internalize those meanings, for example, in the learning processes by which we master first everyday language and subsequently the conceptual content (Fleck's *Wissensstand*) of more sophisticated enterprises. But the effect of internalizing is quite unlike, and distinct from, the permanent interiority of mental life as Descartes, Newton, and their followers understood it. The *inner* character of internalized mental experiences is *acquired*, but the *interiority* of mental life that traditional philosophers take for granted is *lifelong* and so unchangeable.

Here Vygotsky has something very definite to teach us. As he argues in the essays reprinted as *Mind in Society* (Vygotsky, 1978), language is the instrument that we use, during enculturation and socialization, not merely to master practical procedures, but also to internalize the meanings and patterns of thought that are current in our culture or profession. In this way, we "make up" our own minds and, in time, acquire inner experiences modeled on the public activities of our culture and society.

2. The work of Vygotsky and Luria also makes it clear that the term *internalization* covers a variety of cases and procedures. On the one hand, we learn to do sums "in our heads" – doing "in the mind's eye" sums that might alternatively be performed with pencil and paper. Again, we "read to ourselves," following the example of Ambrose of Milan – a contemporary of Augustine's in the 4th century A.D., who is the first person clearly recorded as having this ability. In this way, we get information from the page more quickly than we can if reading aloud – the skill that led Ambrose's contemporaries to take him for a magician.

(In passing: Once reading to oneself became a generally available skill, scribes changed their ways of writing manuscripts and laying out pages. Earlier, they had run words, sentences, and paragraphs together without breaks or written across them at right angles to save parchment. This made it very difficult to scan a text quickly without articulating individual words. But now it was worthwhile to introduce clear breaks between the parts of a text so that a reader could follow it rapidly without having, in every case, to figure out where one word or sentence ended and the next began.)

In addition, we learn to "think to ourselves" as a way of concealing from other people plans that we do not wish to reveal. Finally, we learn to "judge ourselves" inwardly, so embittering "the sessions of sweet silent thought" by inward self-reproach. Far from being a single, clear-cut procedure, internalization therefore embodies a *family* of techniques that make mental life and activity more efficacious in a number of very different ways.

3. In neurophysiology, A. R. Luria has offered some revealing new ideas about how pure mental processes enter cognitive activity. Rather than accept the traditional image of the Mental Theater (or sensorium) as the interior locus of all mental activity, he argues that different layers of the cortex are mobilized and called into play in different activities. Whereas T. H. Huxley still thought of the inner self as penetrating and surmounting the sensory nerves that stand between the Knowing Mind and the Known World, Luria allows us to focus on the intellectual activities of entire human beings and so call into play appropriate parts of the higher nervous system.

(The same parts of the higher nervous system need not be called into play for any given purpose in all human knowers. As Luria shows, the grasp of linguistic procedures draws on different parts of the cortex among different peoples: In ideographic cultures like Chinese, the cerebral processes called into play in language use differ from those found in alphabetic cultures. After similar brain injuries, too, individuals can relearn intellectual or practical procedures by mobilizing alternative neural networks that stand in for those destroyed in the injury.)

4. The central respect in which Vygotsky's work converges on Wittgenstein's later arguments, however, is in their shared concern with *practice*. For both men, language has a definite meaning only when it is related to a given constellation of practical activities. Each lexical term is meaningful within a *Sprachspiel* (or "language game"); but a language game is meaningful only if construed in the context of a given *Lebensform* (or "form of life").

In one familiar American sense, for example, we understand the meaning of the word *strike* only if we are familiar with the game of baseball:

"Playing baseball" is the *form of life* that provides the background against which the word *strike* has this meaning. To put the point more generally, the shared intelligibility of any utterance requires it to have a standard place in a specific practical context: In the jargon of activity theory, this meaning is determined by its place in a given *typified action sequence.*

These four points imply several other conclusions. First, there is no single, universal solution to the inside–outside problem. We acquire (and handle) knowledge of people and things in everyday life in ways that are *in part* culturally universal and spontaneous, *in part* the result of the individual's internalizing of *his or her own* native culture. Paul Ekman's (1982) studies on the facial expression of emotions, for instance, carry further research started by Charles Darwin a century ago: Ekman shows that our ability to recognize, say, shame, joy, or curiosity in other people's faces is a spontaneous skill and does not need to be learned, yet it remains the case that the exact ways in which we put this innate capacity to work depend strongly on what culture we grow up in.

Hence, we face an important *scientific* question: namely, "Which aspects of our experience and abilities are universal and transcultural and which are products of enculturation?" Only when we have a full answer to that question can we go on to address the underlying question, at once scientific and philosophical: "How far are *Lebensformen* and *Sprachspielen* species specific and how far are they cultural variables?"

Meanwhile, the relevance of Vygotsky's (1978) ideas to, say, the philosophy of science or legal philosophy is clear enough. In any professional work, we master the relevant knowledge by making our own the *Wissensstand* of the discipline involved – the procedures that constitute the collective state of understanding in that field at present. This state of knowledge comprises the standard repertory of well-established procedures that are in good standing in the discipline *at a given time,* but the standards by which we judge the merits of the procedures are historical variables. This means that the *rationality* of a scientific or judicial procedure, say, is not a matter of clarity and distinctness or logical coherence *alone.* Rather, it depends on the way in which these procedures develop in the historical evolution of any given discipline.

So understood, shared procedures are neither the exclusive property of collective professions nor the exclusive property of individual agents. Rather, the rational history of a human discipline involves a continuing interchange between the innovations of creative individuals and their acceptance or rejection by the professional community. The procedures constitutive of different arts or sciences thus exist at the boundary of the individual and the collective: They have a life story independent of the individuals or groups that embody them at any time, in the same way as, say, operas or symphonies, which are performed several times in a single season by one orchestra and cast or another.

Conclusions

Where do we go from here? Taking this constellation of concepts (collective activities, shared procedures, "sums in the head," and so on) seriously, we have to go back before Descartes, and the whole model of the Mind as a Theater in the Head, and look at ideas that were familiar to the Middle Ages and the Renaissance, not to mention to Aristotle himself. For all these thinkers, *philosophy* was as much practical as theoretical: a field for practical wisdom (*prudence*) as much as for intellectual grasp. In ethics, they were concerned less with the abstract theories of moral philosophy than with the *concrete particulars* of specific moral issues, such as those in today's medical ethics. In logic, they were concerned less with the formalisms of the propositional calculus than with questions about the *substantive soundness* of the varied arguments to be found in different practical enterprises. In the human sciences, they were less concerned with the pursuit of universal generalizations than with the kinds of *local, particular* knowledge discussed today by Clifford Geertz (1983). And in fields of practical decision making, such as medicine, they saw that all our formal calculations need to be complemented by questions about the *timeliness* of our decisions.

The explanatory procedures of a physical scientist are one thing, the diagnostic procedures of a clinician another, the judicial procedures of a law court still another. We should not look for universal standards of, for example, "soundness" of arguments in all fields equally: In each case, the first step is to assemble detailed descriptive accounts of the procedures or typified action sequences involved in all these activities.

We need these descriptions, indeed, before theoretical issues can even be *raised*. To cite Aristotle's own example: We can ask *why* chicken is good to eat only if we are already certain *that* chicken is good to eat, just as today we can asky *why* aspirin relieves headaches only because we already know *that* aspirin relieves headaches. Until the basic empirical or experimental facts are established in the human sciences too, we are not in a position to develop theoretical explanations, and the pursuit of theoretical generalizations is premature.

With this last comment before us, we can raise two final queries.

1. In addressing the issues that arise in the study of human activity at the convergence point between Vygotsky and Wittgenstein, are we *ready*

to move on to theory? Or is the habit of calling this field of study *activity theory* another hangover from the age of Cartesianism? No doubt we can benefit by developing new patterns or paradigms to use in studying human activity, but we should consider models that defer the move to theory and focus on the richer preliminary task of describing these activities in full and relevant detail.

The step of "appealing to theory" is, in fact, only one specialized language game (rhetorical move, *topos*) within the broader activities on which we are hoping to throw light, and we need not be in too much of a hurry to make this move to theory. By now, it is notorious how far the human sciences were misdirected by trying to achieve, at a stroke, the universal, abstract theoretical structure found in Newtonian dynamics. Concentrating on the humbler task of giving accurate *descriptions* of human activities may put us in a better position to judge at what points, to what extent, and in what respects formal theories of activity can do us any good.

2. Historically speaking, the repeated attempts to elevate theory and explanation over practice and description have regularly tended to serve *antiegalitarian* interests. Plato's snide comments on the mean, mechanical nature (*banausia*) of practical craft activities provide one illustration; the current nickname for the Palo Alto Center for Advanced Study in the Behavioral Sciences – "the leisure of the theory class" – is a more recent one. Certainly, we all understand how theorizing spares us the labor of making detailed, concrete observations and so allows us to keep our hands clean. But such intellectualism cannot claim a monopoly on serious knowledge. Knowing how a chair is made (even how to make it yourself) may not be *less* subtle and rich than knowing how a differential equation is to be solved (or how to solve it yourself) but *more;* and, even in mathematics, handling formal algorithms is only one small part of a larger art (*techne*) that requires us to recognize when, in what ways, and for what purposes the algorithm can be applied to concrete practical situations.

For the future, then, the key notion in any new theory of knowledge needs to be *practice*. In place of the *foundationalist* theories that held center stage from Descartes to Russell, we shall do better to develop a new *praxiology* – the term is Kotarbinski's (1965) – that asks what procedures are efficacious in any given rational enterprise, on what conditions, and for what practical purposes. Such a theory of knowledge (incidentally) has an additional merit: Its practitioners are not ashamed of getting their hands dirty. Instead, they are ready to work with, and alongside, the professionals whose enterprises they study: practical or theoretical, scientific or diagnostic, legal or technical.

(Another passing comment: The "learning environments" created by Michael Cole and his colleagues at La Jolla [see Chapter 6, this volume] are effective instruments of research and teaching, but they carry a further risk of their own. In the contemporary world, a novel class distinction is developing between those who do and those who do not learn to use computers. We are thus at risk of creating a new mandarin class for whom all knowledge is mediated by way of computer screens. Michael Cole's "wizard" will no doubt work out ways of stimulating children to do many other creative things also, which bring them closer to the actual material of the world than a computer keyboard ever does, but the problem remains.)

A last postscript: I have followed up some convergences between Vygotsky's work and Wittgenstein's, and the question naturally arises, "Have we any reason to think that either man was personally acquainted with, or even aware of, the other?" The answer is, "No." Wittgenstein had long discussions about philosophy with Bakhtin's emigré brother (who lived in England), and he paid one quick visit to the USSR; this is as close as we can get to connecting the two men. Given Wittgenstein's deep *moral* commitment to "humanly useful" work, as reflected in the works of Leo Tolstoy, however, he was always on the lookout for people – and situations – in which those values were respected. (He did his best, e.g., to make sure that his disciples refrained from joining the "theory class," urging them to work for the benefit of their fellows as, say, physicians.) Still, if Ludwig Wittgenstein had by chance met Lev Vygotsky in person, I suspect that he would have found in him just the basic human insights and deep-seated seriousness he strove for in his own life.

References

Descartes, R. (1968). *Discourse on the method and the meditations.* Harmondsworth: Penguin Books.

Dewey, J. (1929). *The quest for certainty.* New York: Minton, Balch & Co.

Ekman, P. (Ed.). (1982). *Emotion in the human face.* Cambridge: Cambridge University Press.

Fleck, L. (1981). *Genesis and development of a scientific fact.* Chicago: University of Chicago Press.

Husserl, E. (1962). *Die Krisis der europäischen Wissenschaften und die transzendentale Phänomenologie.* Husserliana VI. The Hague: Martinus Nijhoff.

Huxley, T. H. (1881). *Science and culture, and other essays.* London: Macmillan.

Geertz, C. (1983). *Local knowledge.* New York: Basic Books.

Geschwind, N. (1974). *Selected papers on language and the brain.* Dordrecht: Reidel.

Kant, I. (1976). *Critique of pure reason.* London: Macmillan.

Kotarbinski, T. (1965). *Praxiology: An introduction to the sciences of efficient action.* Oxford: Pergamon Press.

Locke, J. (1959). *Essay concerning human understanding.* New York: Dover.

Luria, A. (1973). *The working brain. An introduction to neuropsychology.* Harmondsworth: Penguin Books.

Montaigne, M. de (1958). *Complete essays.* Stanford: Stanford University Press.

Newton, I., Sir (1968). *The mathematical principles of natural philosophy.* London: Dawson.

Rorty, R. (1989). *Philosophy and the mirror of nature.* Oxford: Basil Blackwell.

Sartre, J. P. (1962). *Huis clos.* New York: Appleton-Century-Crofts.

Wittgenstein, L. (1953). *Philosophical investigations.* London: Basil Blackwell.

Vygotsky, L. S. (1978). *Mind in society: The development of higher psychological processes.* Cambridge, MA: Harvard University Press.

4   Activity theory in a new era

Vladimir A. Lektorsky

Introduction

In Russia currently, activity theory is being criticized whole-
sale by some philosophers and psychologists because it is alleged to be
an expression of totalitarian ideology. Among these critics are people
who were themselves not long ago advocates of activity theory. They
are referring mainly to such versions of activity theory as those of A. N.
Leont'ev (1978) and P. J. Gal'perin (1992). These conceptions are interpreted by the critics as representing humans not as creative beings
but as simple executors of plans, orders, and standards imposed from
outside.

These critics think that activity theory, with its stress on actions, operations, and internalization of ready-made standards of behavior and
cognition, corresponds to what *command socialism* demanded of people,
namely, to be simple executors.

I think that this criticism is justified to a certain degree. It is possible to
show that some versions of activity theory (in particular the conception
of Leont'ev) are one-sided. It is true that the formulation and elaboration of some ideas of this theory in the 1930s and 1940s were influenced
by the ideological situation in the USSR. This, by the way, does not
mean that all ideas that are ideologically stimulated and influenced must
be false: Most fruitful hypotheses in the history of science were influenced by their nonscientific context.

At the same time, I only partly agree with these critics. First, not all
the ideas of Leont'ev and Gal'perin are outdated. Second, activity theory cannot be exclusively equated with the versions elaborated by these
scholars. Third, we should not repudiate activity theory as a whole but
develop it in new directions.

Rubinstein, Leont'ev, and Vygotsky

It is well known that the variant of activity theory proposed by Leont'ev was severely criticized by the famous psychologist and philosopher S. L. Rubinstein (1976). The latter stressed that human activity cannot be understood as simple internalization of ready-made standards. Rubinstein wrote about the creative character of human activity and the self-realization of human beings in this process.

I think that Rubinstein pointed out some real drawbacks of Leont'ev's conception. But the version of the theory of activity proposed by Rubinstein himself also has a great drawback. His version does not take into account the very specific and important role of artificial things, human-made objects, in the process of human activity. In other words, this version of activity theory underestimates the role of mediation in the process.

Leont'ev wrote about the significance of mediation in human activity. Nevertheless, in his theory the greatest attention was given to the relations between activity, actions, and operations; in other words, to the subjective but not the intersubjective side of activity. The intersubjective relations that arise in the context of artificial objects have not really been investigated in his works.

This problem has, however, played a very important role in the conception of Lev Vygotsky, Leont'ev's colleague and mentor. L. S. Vygotsky (1978) stressed the mediated character of all specifically human phenomena. He pointed out that human beings themselves create stimuli that determine their own reactions and are used as means for mastering their own behavior. Human beings themselves determine their behavior with the help of artificial stimulus means. Free human activity is not the same as the spontaneous behavior of an animal. The former presupposes behavior that is mastered and controlled.

This is possible only by means of artificial stimuli, signs, and artifacts. Human freedom can exist only in the world of artificial things, in the sphere of mediated, interindividual activity.

We would do well to return to the ideas of Vygotsky for understanding activity. I would like to stress that according to Vygotsky, human activity presupposes not only the process of internalization (about which Leont'ev wrote) but also the process of externalization. Humans not only internalize ready-made standards and rules of activity but externalize themselves as well, creating new standards and rules. Human beings determine themselves through objects that they create. They are essentially creative beings. Vygotsky wrote about signs and symbols as typical examples of human-made objects determining human activity. Nowadays we include among these objects many other artificial things, from ordinary objects of everyday life to instruments, tools, and laboratory devices. In other words, intersubjective relations arising in the mediation of human activity exist not only where we observe communication in an obvious form, but in other cases as well.

Dialectics of the subject and the object

I think that if we interpret the activity approach with the help of such a key, it will be possible to show that it has interesting philosophical consequences. In particular, this approach can eliminate the sharp dichotomy between the worlds of subjective and objective phenomena, which has been a distinctive feature of Western philosophy and psychology since Descartes (Lektorsky, 1984). The notion of activity provides a means to overcome this dichotomy. Supporters of this conception follow the tradition of German philosophy, especially the ideas of Kant, Fichte, Hegel, and the early Marx, giving it their own interpretation.

The so-called inner world (and all processes connected with it) arises as a result of the outer activity of a subject mediated by intersubjective relations. In order to create or to change "inner" or subjective phenomena, it is necessary to create some objective thing. A process of *objectification* is a necessary presupposition for the existence and development of the inner world. Thus, what is most important about the features of human beings is that these features are not naturally given, but instead mediated by artificial objects produced by human activity. These artificial objects are produced by one particular human being for another (one or ones). In other words, they are means of interindividual relations.

The processes of production, cognition, and interindividual communication therefore appear as closely interconnected and interpenetrating. The primary mode of existence of many familiar phenomena is that in which their subjective form is connected with the "space" of these interindividual, intersubjective relations. This applies to such phenomena as, for example, the ideal, meanings, and cognitive structures.

The dialogical nature of activity

I think that this interpretation of the activity approach is important and fruitful for philosophy and other human sciences (especially psychology) and cannot be abandoned because of the criticism of certain versions of the theory. At the same time, I believe that nowadays it is not sufficient to limit the activity approach to these ideas. It seems to me that it is necessary to study specific features of intersubjective relations connected with activity.

First of all, I am referring to the creative, nonpredictable character of human communication, which cannot be completely managed and controlled (e.g., Bibler, 1983–1984). The ideas of the famous Russian philosopher and literary theorist Mikhail Bakhtin concerning the nature of dialogue are very interesting in that respect (Bakhtin, 1982). Bakhtin has shown very clearly that it is impossible to equate subject–object and intersubjective relations. The latter include different kinds of subject–object relations but can't be reduced to them.

Activity in the process of a genuine dialogue is not a simple transformation of a co-interlocutor in accordance with the aims and plans of another; it includes the self-realization of the participants at the same time. Successful communicative activity presupposes taking into account the position and values of the other, an ability to look at oneself from this position and to perform an "inner dialogue." It is a complicated system of interactions between "my own image of myself," "the image of me by another," and "the other's image of him- or herself." It is an activity, it is a process of change, but it is not like the process of transforming physical things. The latter is included in intersubjective relations and can be understood only in this context.

Toward a new rationality

I think it is clear that these features of interhuman communication have not only not been investigated by those who elaborated activity theory up to now but have also been underestimated. For example, although Vygotsky wrote about the creativity of human beings, his scientific ideals were connected with mastering and controlling spontaneous natural and social processes. But this is not a feature that is unique to his scientific thinking. It is a distinction of a certain type of rationality that was dominant in European culture beginning in the 18th century.

According to this conception of rationality, all natural and social processes can in principle be put under complete human control, can be manipulated and used for human needs. This is the process of *rationalization* of nature and society. Humans appear as masters of natural and social processes who can give orders and commands suppressing these processes and transforming them.

But now we have reasons to speak of the appearance of another type of rationality. The main feature of this new type is its attitude of profound value: not to think of natural and social processes as things subjugated to human intervention, as things to be manipulated, controlled, and strictly predicted. Natural and social processes have their own activity; the ways of their transformations can be unique and unpredictable. Many of them are unsteady and cannot be described with the help of universal laws. So the notions of uniqueness and individuality, which were considered for a long time as specific to the description of human reality, should be considered as necessary concerns for reasoning in the natural sciences as well.

Many ideas concerning this type of rationality were formulated by the famous scientist and Nobel Prize winner Ilya Prigogine (e.g., Prigogine & Stengers, 1985), who refers to these ideas as a *philosophy of instability*. It is interesting to note that within the framework of this type of rationality, the sharp opposition between natural sciences and the study of the sphere of subjectivity disappears. Both natural and human sciences deal not only with universal laws, but also with the realms of unstable, unpredictable, creative, and unique processes.

Most interesting, however, is that now in many cases it is necessary to include human activity in considerations of objective natural processes. Subjects cannot be conceived as something outside the object of their action and cognition but must be thought of as partners in the objective process. This means that in many cases the relations between subjective and objective processes can be considered as a kind of communication.

I think that in the light of this new type of rationality, it is both possible and necessary to elaborate new versions of activity theory.

References

Bakhtin, M. M. (1982). *The dialogic imagination.* Austin: University of Texas Press.

Bibler, V. S. (1983–1984). Thinking as creation: Introduction to the logic of mental dialogue. *Soviet Psychology, XXII,* 33–54.

Gal'perin, P. J. (1992). The problem of activity in Soviet psychology. *Journal of Russian and East European Psychology, 30*(4), 37–59.

Lektorsky, V. A. (1984). *Subject, object, cognition.* Moscow: Progress.

Leont'ev, A. N. (1978). *Activity, consciousness, and personality.* Englewood Cliffs: Prentice-Hall.

Prigogine, I., & Stengers, I. (1985). *Order out of chaos: Man's new dialogue with nature.* London: Fontana Paperbacks.

Rubinstein, S. L. (1976). *Problemy obshchei psikhologii.* Moscow: Pedagogika.

Vygotsky, L. S. (1978). *Mind in society: The development of higher psychological processes.* Cambridge, MA: Harvard University Press.

5 Society versus context in individual development: Does theory make a difference?

Charles W. Tolman

Introduction

In studying development of the child psyche, we must . . . start by analysing the development of the child's activity, as this activity is built up in the concrete conditions of its life. (Leont'ev, 1981, p. 395)

What is meant by the term *concrete conditions of life*? Activity theory answers in terms of the societal nature of the individual human being. Anglo–American contextualists have recently emphasized the *embeddedness* of the individual in the *sociocultural milieu* or *ecology* (e.g., Lerner, 1979; Jaeger & Rosnow, 1988; Dixon, Lerner, & Hultsch, 1991). Is there a theoretical convergence here, or do significant theoretical and methodological differences remain? This is the question I wish to address here.

Activity theory on the societal nature of the individual

It is fundamental to activity theory that the relation of individuals to every aspect of the world around them is *essentially* societal. Conceptually, this idea can be traced to the fourth of Marx's *Thesen über Feuerbach* (1845/1968, pp. 339–341): *"In seiner Wirklichkeit ist [das menschliche Wesen] das Ensemble der gesellschaftlichen Verhältnisse."* I cite the original German statement here because the usual English translation (e.g., p. 14) can be confusing with respect to precisely the matter here at issue. The translation of *gesellschaftlich* as "social" does not fully capture the intended meaning. Animals often behave or are organized by their instinctive natures in such a way that can be called "social," and this is normally expressed in German by *sozial*. German usage distinguishes the way in which humans *organize themselves* socially by the adjective *gesellschaftlich*. The English translation as "social-historical" is an improvement over the mere "social," but "societal," derived from "society," just as *gesellschaftlich* is derived from *Gesellschaft* (as opposed to *Sozium*), is preferred.

70

This would count as mere pedantry were it not that it is exactly on the *societal* nature of the *human* individual, as distinct from the social, that activity theory insists. The theory is not referring merely to the social fact that individuals find themselves in relations with other people. In order to clarify this point, I describe, first, activity theory's conception of the societal nature of the functioning adult human being; second, the implications of this nature for the development of the individual personality; and, third, its methodological implications. By then contrasting these understandings with those of Anglo-American contextualism, I hope to make it clear that the activity approach represents an approach to both theory and practice that is fundamentally and significantly different from that of empiricist social science.

The societal nature of adult activity

Activity theory elaborates Marx's understanding of the human essence as the ensemble of societal relations, but it must not be assumed that this excludes the natural–historical (and therefore social) foundations for these relations. As Messmann and Rückriem (1978) so clearly put it:

Das Wesen des Menschen ist aus seiner Wirklichkeit als Ensemble der gesellschaftlichen Verhältnisse *allein nicht* zu erklären. Für eine zureichende Erklärung muss vielmehr diese Wirklichkeit als Realisierung einer Möglichkeit, eines Vermögens, betrachtet werden, das den Menschen "von der Natur aus" qualifiziert, Produzent dieser Verhältnisse zu sein. (p. 80)

A detailed account of the natural history of human societality was already assembled by Leont'ev (1959/1981; Leontjew, 1959/1975) and has since been elaborated and brought up-to-date by Schurig (1975a, 1975b, 1976) and Holzkamp (1973/1978, 1983). I shall not dwell on this here, but it must be recognized as assumed in the discussion that follows. Although the distinctness of human societal nature will be stressed, there is no entailment here of the mind–body dualism sometimes associated with the *Geisteswissenschaften*.

Human activity begins in the process that we know as *labor*. Marx gave labor its classic definition in *Capital:*

Labour is, in the first place, a process in which both man and Nature participate, and in which man of his own accord starts, regulates, and controls the material re-actions between himself and Nature. He opposes himself to Nature as one of her own forces, setting in motion arms and legs, head and hands, the natural forces of his body, in order to appropriate Nature's productions in a form adapted to his own wants. By thus acting on the external world and changing it, he at the same time changes his own nature. He develops his slumbering powers and compels them to act in obedience to his sway. We are not now dealing with those primitive instinctive forms of labour that remind us of the mere animal. An immeasurable interval of time separates the state of things in which a man brings his labour-power to market for sale as a commodity, from that state in which human labour was still in its first instinctive stage. We presuppose labour in a form that stamps it as exclusively human. (1867/1954, pp. 173–174)

Tool use and tool making are often considered the defining features of labor, but although these may indeed be necessary to the process, they are not sufficient. Even when Marx was writing, instances of animals' using and even preparing tools were known. As he went on to emphasize, the crucial features are individual consciousness and the collectivity of the activity. Indeed, as Leont'ev compellingly argues (1959/1981, pp. 207ff.), it is precisely in the collective nature of labor that consciousness emerges in its distinctively human form. The two working together are clearly portrayed in Leont'ev's example of the beater participating in a primitive hunt in which it is his function to drive the quarry toward his companions, who are lying in wait to make the kill. The collective nature of the activity is manifested in a division of labor. No single individual carries out the activity required to satisfy his or her needs. Rather, the activity is divided into separate actions, each of which is then assumed by a particular individual in coordination with the others.

In our own society, the enormous complexity of the division of labor is patently obvious. We are psychologists, carpenters, computer analysts, or whatever. Each of us carries out only a very few of the sum total of actions required to maintain our own and our society's existence. I mow my own lawn, but I did not invent landscaping and I did not make my own mower. I may go into the mountains to show that I can "live off the land," but I will wear clothing made by others and take with me implements invented and produced by others. Even if I go naked and implementless, I go with knowledge given me by others. Survival in the strictest sense is impossible for individual members of our species on their absolute own.

Our societal nature is perhaps most importantly indicated by the knowledge that is accumulated by society in the course of its history and that we receive from others. The information required by individuals for functioning in society and for the survival of society itself is not carried in our biotic genes but in our societal institutions, most notably those associated with the educational function, such as schools, libraries, and other cultural forms.

This implies the importance of consciousness. In the example of the beater in the primitive hunt, it is already obvious that a degree of consciousness is required that is lacking in other animals, no matter how complex their behavior patterns or social organizations. The beater who needs food for survival is engaged in actions that result in the opposite of what he is immediately seeking. Instead of closing the distance with the quarry, he is driving it away. This makes sense only if he knows that someone is waiting to achieve his goal (consciously shared with others) at the other end. The sense of his action lies not in the action itself but in his relation to other members of the group. As Leont'ev argues:

The separation of an action necessarily presupposes the possibility of the active subject's psychic reflection of the relation between the objective motive [getting food] and the object of the action [driving it away]. . . . [T]he beater's action is possible only on condition of his reflecting the link between the expected result of the action performed by him and the end result of the hunt as a whole. . . . (1959/1981, p. 212)

The emergence of action as a coordinated part of social activity performed by an individual must be accompanied by a shared meaning of the action that is reflected consciously by the actor. This is reflected in the fact (among others) that the roles of beater and bagger in the hunt are in principle interchangeable. The role of each participant must be decided beforehand. One participant may prove to be better in one role than another and the assignment of roles may come to appear fixed, but this does not affect the underlying interchangeability. Although the situation is immensely more complicated in our own society by the dependence of essential actions on training and education, the underlying principle remains the same.

Thus the necessary, conscious division of labor in human society is the most obvious indicator of the individual human's *societal* nature. The individual is truly human *only* in society. Indeed, a still stronger conclusion can be argued: that human individuality itself is achievable only in society. The *abstract* individual of bourgeois individualism is a figment of the ideological imagination.

Implications for the development of individual personality

The societal nature of the human psychological process of development is evident from a consideration of the kinds of experience that a human child requires. Leont'ev distinguished two kinds of experience in animals:

(a) that accumulated phylogenetically and reinforced by heredity; and (b) individual experience acquired during life. Two kinds of behaviour mechanism correspond to them. On the one hand there are hereditary mechanisms that are either already completely ready

for action at the moment of birth or that gradually mature during ontogenetic development; these mechanisms are formed in accordance with the general laws of biological
evolution; it is a slow process corresponding to slow changes in the environment. In animals these mechanisms are of *fundamental* adaptive importance (1959/1981, p. 420)

The second kind of experience is one that evolves gradually and
achieves a highly refined and effective state in "higher" animals. But
this ability must be correctly understood:

The basic function performed in animals by the mechanisms of the forming of individual experience consists, moreover, *in the adaptation of species behaviour to variable elements
of the environment.* Animals' ontogenetic development can hence be represented as the
accumulation of individual experience mediating the performance of their instinctive activity progressively better in complex, dynamic, external conditions. (1959/1981, p. 420)

Although most Anglo–American theories of human psychological development take this kind of learning to be *the* ontogenetic task of the
child, Leont'ev insists that this is not the case. Development cannot be
fully understood in terms of the acquisition of adaptive behaviors. The
task for the human child is different because the information required for
human existence is different: it is *societal* information. This kind of information *cannot* be "learned" in the way that animals learn to adapt to
the changing demands of their external worlds; it must be *appropriated*,
reflecting an evolutionary new process linked to the new societal nature
of the human species.

Leont'ev defines *appropriation* as "mastering . . . the experience accumulated by mankind in the course of social history" (1959/1981, p. 419).
It is not reducible to biological adaptation or to any form of adaptive behavior, but supersedes adaptation as a specifically human mode of dealing
with and living in the world. Unlike adaptation, appropriation "results in
the individual's reproduction of historically formed human capacities and
functions," and "the capacities and functions formed . . . in the course of
this are psychological new formations" (Leont'ev, 1959/1981, p. 296). It
is a developmental process in which the individual is drawn into societal
practice; at the same time, it is a societal process by which new "psychological formations" are developed.

Consider a child learning to drive nails with a hammer. Is it merely
learning responses? Is it merely learning to adapt to the demands of the
wood, the nails, or the hammer? The child *is* learning responses and *is*
learning to adapt to demands, but not *merely.* The hammer, like all objects
made by human beings, from the simplest implements to the computer,
embodies meaning, the accumulated historical experience of the society

into which the child is born, and it is this above all that the child is acquiring. It is the knowledge of making things and of the need to do so, of the utility of wood, of the functions of nails and hammers. The child is appropriating societal experience. And given that human society is characterized by a complex division of labor, the child is also acquiring the possibility of entering the productive life of society. At the same time, the child is being integrated into a process in which its own practice will create new ways of carpentering, thus altering the accumulated body of societal meanings that the succeeding generation will appropriate. None of this applies to the rat learning to press a lever in a Skinner box.

Consider one further aspect of learning to use a hammer. Can the child learn from the hammer itself, as animals learn directly from the demands of their environments? Is it the world of objects from which the child learns to speak a language, to read, and to develop other cognitive skills? Surely not! There is always another human being in the picture. It is a function of adults and older children to teach younger ones to do these things. This function becomes institutionalized in families, schools, and other cultural organizations precisely because the child cannot learn simply by interacting on its own with the world of objects.

It was this sort of thinking that was expressed in Vygotsky's term *zone of proximal development*. Too often, however, it has been interpreted simply as a way in which the teacher can aid the learning of a pupil. This completely misses its theoretical intent, which is to reveal the essentially societally mediated nature of human learning. Engeström comes closer to the mark when he describes this zone as the "distance between the everyday actions of individuals and the historically new form of the societal activity that can be collectively generated as a solution to the double bind potentially embedded in . . . everyday actions" (1987, p. 174).[1]

The conclusion, it appears to me, is inescapable: At its heart, human ontogeny is a uniquely human, societal process of appropriating historical experience in the form of actions and meanings.

Methodological implications

The implications of what was said earlier can be roughly divided into two groups: formal and practical. The formal aspect can be approached by way of an observation Leont'ev made in connection with teaching arithmetic to children:

If the persons training a child primarily set themselves the goal of imparting knowledge of some sort or other and pay little attention to how the child itself goes about it, by what operations it solves the school problems it has been set, and does not check whether a further transformation is taking place at the proper time in these operations, their development can be disturbed. (1959/1981, p. 432)

To discover "how the child itself goes about it" is to reveal the actual nature of the underlying process, which, for Leont'ev, was the aim of all social scientific investigation. The problem for us is to see what the method entails.

A first approximation to specifying the principles of an appropriate method was made by Vygotsky in 1930 (Vygotsky, 1978, chapter 5). It was expressed in three principles. The first was "analysing process, not objects." He wrote: "Any psychological process, whether the development of thought or voluntary behaviour, is a process undergoing changes right before our eyes" (p. 61). It was possible to "trace this development" by setting up situations that "provoke" it: "Our method may be called experimental-developmental in the sense that it artificially provokes or creates a process of psychological development" (p. 61). The aim was "a reconstruction of each stage in the development of the process" (p. 62). That this leads to experiments that look quite different from those that have become familiar in the Anglo-American tradition is evident from examples throughout the book. I shall return to this in a moment.

The second principle was "explanation versus description" (p. 62). It was explanation that Vygotsky was seeking, and here he turned to Kurt Lewin's distinction between *phenotype* and *genotype*, a recognition that underlying processes are not always evident from the surface appearance of actions. An example is the relation between overt speech and action in young children and adults, which appears to be the same in each case but is accounted for by quite distinct "causal dynamic bases."

The third principle was referred to as "the problem of 'fossilized behaviour'" (p. 63). Fully developed behavior patterns cannot be adequately understood from studying them in their developed forms. Vygotsky showed how this can be quite misleading. Only by looking at behavior "genetically," by observing its development, can one hope to reveal its underlying dynamics.

It remained, however, for Evald Il'enkov, a philosopher, to articulate the methodology in more generalized terms (e.g., Il'enkov, 1960/1982). He expressed the general unifying methodological principle as that of the "ascent from the abstract to the concrete," which requires a particular understanding of *abstract* and *concrete*. To say that all things are concrete does not mean merely that they are things as opposed to ideas, but also that they are integral wholes within a larger system that also forms an integral whole. Things represent a "unity in diversity." *Abstract*, by contrast, refers to the stripping of these relations, either objectively or in thought. The goal of scientific theory is the "reproduction of the concrete in thought" (Il'enkov, 1960/1982, p. 102).

The methodological "ascent from the abstract to the concrete" is a complex notion that we cannot hope to capture fully here. I am concerned only with revealing enough to highlight its contrast with standard Anglo-American empiricist methodology. Suppose we find, as in Leont'ev's example, that school children in some classes, though apparently competent in elementary arithmetic, are having difficulty mastering more advanced arithmetic skills. We note that this problem seems to be distributed not individually but by classes, and therefore we suspect that something the teachers are doing is responsible. Somehow we hit on the hypothesis that the teachers' attitudes are important. We divide the teachers into two groups, designated as "lenient" and "strict" (independent variable). The performance of the pupils (dependent variable) is then measured, and we discover a statistically significant correlation accounting for more than, say, 60% of the variance. We conclude that leniency accounts for the poorer skills.

Although this procedure describes a typical investigation in the Anglo-American tradition, from Il'enkov's, Vygotsky's, and Leont'ev's point of view, it is headed in the wrong direction. We started, as is necessarily the case, with an abstraction, a phenotype, of the children's performance on arithmetic problems. Instead of seeking the underlying genetic, dynamic process that caused this performance ("how the child itself goes about it"), we linked it statistically to another abstraction, teachers' leniency. We imagined ourselves to have made some kind of vital discovery by identifying the degree of correlation, whereas in fact we merely created a higher-order abstraction by showing how the relation between the two original abstractions can be generalized. We may repeat the investigation innumerable times, finding no exceptions, even approaching the ideal of universality. Yet we will not come a millimeter closer to understanding what is actually going on. This requires a genetic reconstruction of the concrete, causal dynamic process. The abstractions must be made concrete by finding their real connections within the concrete, integral whole of learning/teaching within the societal process.

How is this done? What rules of procedure will lead us to the truly concrete knowledge of a process? Certainly, one of the most seductive features of the empiricist methodology that purports to construct theoretical knowledge out of the correlations of arbitrarily selected variables is that it is readily reduced to rules of procedure, the basic mastery of which can be achieved by university undergraduates. By contrast, the

"Leont'evian" must take a more difficult route. The principles of the methodology (as distinct from methods and procedures) must be mastered. These cannot be translated into appropriate procedures without experience, intuition, and intelligence, coupled with a sound theoretical understanding of the phenomenon under study. In short, there are no rules. The very idea of a fixed set of abstract rules violates the concrete conception of the problem.[2]

The literature of activity theory is replete with examples of concrete research. They reveal three determinants: (1) an existing theoretical understanding of the general process; (2) a focus on the concrete nature of the immediate problem; and (3) an aim of revealing underlying causal dynamics. In a report of research on the development of the learning motive in children, Leont'ev (Leontjew, 1959/1975, pp. 344–355; an article omitted from the English edition) gave a very detailed account of how the play motive is transformed into the learning motive during the preschool and early school years. The work depended on (1) a general understanding of the societal structure of activity and its motivation, and of the senses and meanings that goals and motives have for individual children; (2) a clear specification of what was involved in children's learning in school; and (3) information gained from casual conversations with the children, as well as from observing their participation in organized games and their reactions to irregularities in school routine. In some instances, dependent and independent variables are identifiable *after the fact*, but it is clear that Leont'ev was not thinking in those terms. Large samples and measurement played a role in the studies, but there is no indication that statistical analyses were ever used or needed.

In contrasting the methodology and experimental procedures of activity theory with those of Anglo–American empiricist psychology, we continually encounter the problem of *variables*. If there is a single diagnostic feature of the two methodologies, it is the utter indifference of activity theory to variables, in contrast to empiricist methodology's insistence and dependence on them. It is useful to remind ourselves here that the critique of the analysis of variables has not gone unvoiced within American social science. A well-known instance is that of Herbert Blumer's presidential address before the American Sociological Society in 1956 (Blumer, 1969, pp. 127–139). Blumer identified three "shortcomings" of variable analysis: (1) "there seems to be little limit to what may be chosen or designated as a variable" (anything measurable will do); (2) many variables claim to be generic but are demonstrably not (measures of "integration" in fact measure different things in different cases but create the illusion that there is something generic called *integration*); and (3) some variables represent characteristics that are in fact generic, like "age," but then serve to overlook how age may be different in different societies and at different historical times. Blumer was obviously alarmed by the abstractness being imported into social science by the variable concept.

The "contextualist" approach to individual development

The *contextualist* approach to human development is a good foil for activity theory because (1) it is a fair representative of Anglo–American empiricist positions and (2) it claims more than most to accomplish the goals I have identified with activity theory. It self-consciously seeks to overcome the limitations of both mechanism (e.g., behaviorism) and organicism (e.g., Piaget) and avows a *dialectical* view of psychological process that integrates the individual into the social milieu (e.g., Lerner, 1979, p. 272). It is a position, therefore, that can lead one to believe that activity theory is not really different from what has been proposed in American psychology.

The key to any distinction lies in how the individual–society relationship and the role of that relationship in the development of the individual personality are understood.

Individual and society in contextualism

Richard Lerner (1979) leads into his discussion of social relations by outlining the contextualist view of individual–environment relationships generally. Here he speaks of "direct exchanges," "reciprocal outcomes," "reciprocities," "interdependent relations," and "congruity" (p. 275). He states that there is a "continuous interdependency of organism and environmental processes" (p. 276). There is a "dialectical intermeshing" of the two that is conditioned by the organism's biological maturation and experience, with each being interdependent with the other (pp. 275–276). Lerner stresses the reciprocity of this process:

As each person's maturation–experience interactions intermesh to provide a distinct individual, this individual concomitantly interacts differently with his or her environment as a consequence of this individuality. In turn, these new interactions are a component of the individual's further experience, and thus serve to further promote his or her individuality. (p. 278)

It appears that the "organism–organism" or social relationship is merely a variant of the organism–environment relationship. Lerner's language here, however, becomes a bit stronger. The relationship is not just reciprocal but "circular" (p. 279). But social relationships appear to be not the only "circular" ones:

> Although organism interactions with animate and non-conspecific organisms certainly exist, and at least for the latter type of interactions circular functions are also certainly involved, the conspecific organism–organism interaction – the social relation – has been used to exemplify the nature of circular functions. (p. 280)

This exemplification, Lerner asserts, is based on the fact that "development by its very nature is basically a social relation phenomenon" (p. 280). He goes on to say that, despite their being a mere form of nonsocial reciprocities, social relations are "particular" because they "invariably involve processes of reciprocal stimulation and hence interdependent influencing" and because "they involve relations with stimuli on the basis of stimulus association value or meaning, rather than merely on the basis of stimuli's immediate physiological import" (p. 280).

Lerner proceeds to a discussion of the "sociocultural-historical" context in which the dependence of the social relation on the "sociocultural milieu of the relation" (p. 281) is stressed:

> Parents in one setting may be more or less permissive than parents in another. Furthermore, the sociocultural milieu also influences the physical setting of any social interaction, and it may be expected that in physical environmental situations varying in such socioculturally related variables as noise level, pollution level, housing conditions, crowding, and recreational facilities, the quality and timing of person–person exchanges will show variation and provide differential feedback to all involved individuals. (p. 281)

As might be expected, history is treated the same way: It is simply a contextual milieu that changes with time. Lerner's example is the influence of the advent of television.

Two interrelated conclusions appear to be warranted. First, this understanding of the individual–society relationship is not the same as that found in activity theory. Rather than being characterized by the internal and necessary relationship between the two, contextualism confines itself to external and contingent relations that are not essentially, or even qualitatively, different from any other kind of relations.[3]

Second, despite the claims of Lerner and other contextualists, their position does not differ essentially from that of mechanistic behaviorists. Except for its "dialectical" posturing, Lerner's account is much like that of Skinner (1953, esp. chapter 19). Even the account of *meaning* in terms of association is the same. In both contextualist and behaviorist positions, the individual is treated as preexisting, coming to society to be further shaped by external influences encountered there. The essentially societal individual of activity theory is absent.

The contextualist account of individual development

Given the mechanistic understanding of social relations, it comes as no surprise that development is similarly understood:

From this [contextualist] perspective, developmental changes occur as a consequence of reciprocal (bidirectional) relations between the active organism and the active context. Just as the context changes the individual, the individual changes the context. (Lerner, Hultsch, & Dixon, 1983, p. 103)

It is diagnostic here that contextualists recognize only two types of process in development: biological maturation and experience, with the latter understood exclusively in terms of response acquisition. A key to the distinctive nature of Leont'ev's theory, one that followed from his understanding of the internal and essential connection between individual and society, was the recognition of a third process, namely, appropriation. This or anything comparable is lacking in the contextualist account.

Indeed, to the extent that the contrast of appropriation and adaptation as central moments of ontogenetic development is diagnostic, it is informative to note that much of Lerner's recent empirical research on child development has been guided by what he calls the *goodness-of-fit* model.

The studies we have conducted in our laboratory have focused on how the demands regarding characteristics of behavioral or physical individuality (e.g., temperament or physical attractiveness, respectively) held by a child's or an adolescent's parents, teachers, or peers are associated with different levels of adaptation, or adjustment, among children with various repertoires of temperamental individuality or characteristics of physical attractiveness. . . . [T]his notion is termed the *goodness-of-fit* model. (Lerner & Tubman, 1991, p. 198)

In short, goodness-of-fit, as the name applies, is little more than an elaborated version of complexified adaptation. An examination of the original reports again reveals nothing resembling the process of appropriation.

Contextualism and variable analysis

Contextualists claim that their position represents the "emergence" of a "major organizational philosophy" (Lerner et al., 1983, p. 101). It is hailed as a "new model," a "new view of reality," with "different assumptions about human nature" (Lerner, 1979, p. 274). Clearly, this is vastly overstated, and it is significant that of the two "paradigms" against which contextualists contrast their own position, it is not the organismic one of Piaget's to which they remain tied but the still more empiricistic, mechanistic one.[4] Piaget was at least attempting to discover the nature of the developmental *process,* not only the effects of external influence. He also did not speak in terms of variables.

Contextualism remains captive to the variable conception and analysis of its subject matter. Consider, for instance, the claim that

the phenomena that characterize developmental change arise from a dynamic interaction between nature variables, such as maturation, and nurture variables, such as experience. The contribution of each source of development is influenced by the quality and timing of the other. . . . (Lerner, 1979, p. 274)

Given that the "source of development" is a set of variables that is distinguished only by the fact that it is more complex than that ordinarily recognized by psychologists, the methodological implications contextualists draw from their philosophy pertain to the elaboration of standard variable analysis:

[I]n order to study the complex interrelations among organism and context life-span developmentalists [contextualists] promote the use of particular research designs and methodologies [sic] (e.g., sequential designs, multivariate statistics, cohort analysis). (Lerner et al., 1983, p. 105)

Lerner uses a diagram to illustrate the contextualist model (1979, p. 277). It consists of an outer ring labeled "history" and one inside that is labeled "sociocultural milieu," inside of which are the "extraorganism environmental influences," within which are located smaller circles, one labeled "target organism" and three labeled simply "organism." Double-headed arrows denoting interactions connect all components of the diagram. Professor Lerner displayed this diagram as part of a lecture at the University of Victoria a couple of years ago. After pointing out all the possible interactions, he sought to relieve those dismayed by the diagram's apparent complexity by granting that all of these relationships cannot be studied at once; the approved strategy was to pick one or two at a time, holding the others constant.[5]

But for the individual, the "historical-sociocultural milieu," that is, "society," is not a set of variables that can be subtracted from the focus of concern by being held constant. The individual *is* society manifested in a single organism. And its nature is not that of variables but of process!

Conclusions

If *context* is a collection of variables that influence the already existing individual, then it cannot be identical to society. Also, therefore, activity theory and contextualism are not saying the same thing with different words. They are fundamentally different theories because they are based on fundamentally different philosophies: Activity theory is a consequence of classical German philosophy; contextualism is one of the many natural offspring of British empiricism. As a result, their methodologies are distinct, yielding different methods and procedures. They also yield different kinds of knowledge: one of underlying processual dynamics, the other of external correlations among variables.

Danziger (1991) has demonstrated that the Anglo–American preoccupation with measurement and prediction based on the statistical analysis of variables arose in response to the needs of educational administrators to order pupils within the statistical aggregate (p. 79 and chapter 7). He writes:

> By contrast, the main consumers of educational psychological research in Germany appear at first to have been classroom teachers. . . . Unlike administrators, classroom teachers were directly concerned with psychological processes in the minds of individual children and therefore had an interest in psychological research conducted on that basis. (1991, p. 131)

Indeed, as Leont'ev, an inheritor of the German tradition, reminded us, if we are truly concerned with imparting knowledge but "pay little attention to how the child itself goes about it," that child's "development can be disturbed" (Leont'ev, 1959/1981, p. 432). In the real promotion of children's development – as opposed to merely sorting them out – *theory does make a difference*, and when it comes to the choice between activity theory and contextualism (or any other popular Anglo–American form of empiricism), these differences will repay careful attention.

Notes

1. In a book remarkable for its clarity and concreteness, Jean Lave and Etienne Wenger (1991) have elaborated a theory of appropriation (though they do not call it that) in a manner that is in keeping with the societal and historical spirit of Leont'ev's activity theory (and that in significant ways may surpass it). They speak of "situated learning" as the "legitimate peripheral participation" of individuals, both children and adults, in "communities of practice." I cannot describe these ideas here; readers sympathetic to the distinction I am trying to make in this chapter between societal and nonsocietal conceptions of psychological functioning are urged to consult this book for a lucid, positive example of the former.

   Other examples of what I call the *societal conception of context* are found in the works of some of the recent social constructionists, notably John Shotter (1993), and of ethnolinguists such as Duranti and Goodwin (1992; especially the excellent introductory chapter by the editors). It is interesting to note the influence of Vygotsky in all these recent societal or cultural treatments of context.
2. Aside from the work of Il'enkov that I have cited, an excellent, brief discussion in concrete psychological terms – though in the somewhat modified terminology of substantial versus empirical generalization – can be found in a paper by Davydov (1984).

A very useful summary of Il'enkov's thinking on the subject is contained in a recent book by Bakhurst (1991, chapter 5). Both of these sources are highly recommended.

3. The undifferentiated emphasis on relations to context has been extended by some contextualists to the object of knowledge, and from there to *truth*, yielding – understandably – a straightforward epistemological relativism (Rosnow & Georgoudi, 1986, chapter 1). This is usually accompanied by a hostility to the kind of realism that forms a necessary part of activity theory.

4. Lerner and his associates appear more recently to have adopted a softer stand on their differences with mechanism. They now see contextualism as one of a "pluralism" of positions that can be ranged on various dimensions between mechanism and organicism, but always falling closer to the former than to the latter (Dixon et al., 1991, esp. Fig. 2, p. 291).

5. There is ample evidence in the literature that Lerner and his associates are not alone in understanding context as an independent variable. A chapter on "assessing the family context" by Carlson (1990) is particularly instructive. Despite a nominal commitment to what some regard as the relatively more liberated positions of ecological psychology and systems theory, the author presses on to identify the "two basic decisions" involved in assessing the context as "choosing which aspects of the family [variables – CT] to measure and selecting a satisfactory method of measurement" (p. 551). The earlier and more classical ecological/systems statement on context by Bronfenbrenner (1977), despite its distinctly positive contribution, had also failed to free itself from the conception of reality as a collection of variables.

A recent book, *Context and Development*, edited by Cohen and Siegel (1991), is especially interesting in connection with the problem of variables. The book consists of 13 chapters contributed by 17 authors. Although it contains the chapter by Lerner and Tubman referred to earlier, it is evident that many of the remaining 15 authors are striving – with varying degrees of success – to free themselves from the constraints of conventional methods. Although this indicates a recognition that conventional methods are obstructing a more adequate understanding of context, there is little evidence of recognition that the problem may lie in the entailed conception of the subject matter in terms of variables.

One must be encouraged, however, by the editors' concluding observations that "contexts are more than just environments" (p. 308); that "contexts can neither be defined nor understood independent of the people who create them and inhabit them" (p. 309); that "contexts are essentially social" (p. 309); and that "context is not additive" (p. 310). In their introduction, however, the editors share with readers their enthusiasm that "many social scientists are turning toward explanations that embrace the examination of contextual variables" (p. 4). To be fair, it must be acknowledged that the editors go on, in the same paragraph, to suggest that there may be something more than this in context. Without an explicit treatment of the problem, however, it remains only a promise; but it *is* promising.

References

Bakhurst, D. (1991). *Consciousness and revolution in Soviet philosophy: From the Bolsheviks to Evald Ilyenkov.* Cambridge: Cambridge University Press.

Blumer, H. (1969). *Symbolic interactionism: Perspective and method.* Englewood Cliffs: Prentice-Hall.

Bronfenbrenner, U. (1977). Toward an experimental ecology of human development. *American Psychologist, 32*, 513–531.

Carlson, C. I. (1990). Assessing the family context. In C. R. Reynolds & R. W. Kamphaus (Eds.), *Handbook of psychological and educational assessment of children: Personality, behavior, and context* (pp. 546–575). New York: Guilford Press.

Cohen, R., & Siegel, A. W. (Eds.). (1991). *Context and development*. Hillsdale: Lawrence Erlbaum.

Danziger, K. (1990). *Constructing the subject: Historical origins of psychological research*. Cambridge: Cambridge University Press.

Davydov, V. V. (1984). Substantial generalization and the dialectical-materialist theory of thinking. In M. Hedegaard, P. Hakkarainen, & Y. Engeström (Eds.), *Learning and teaching on a scientific basis* (pp. 11–32). Aarhus: Aarhus Universitet, Psykologisk Institut.

Dixon, R. A., Lerner, R. M., & Hultsch, D. F. (1991). The concept of development in the study of individual and social change. In P. van Geert & L. P. Mos (Eds.), *Annals of theoretical psychology* (Vol. 7, pp. 279–323). New York: Plenum Press.

Duranti, A., & Goodwin, C. (1992). *Rethinking context: Language as interactive phenomenon*. New York: Cambridge University Press.

Engeström, Y. (1987). *Learning by expanding: An activity-theoretical approach to developmental research*. Helsinki: Orienta-Konsultit.

Holzkamp, K. (1983). *Grundlegung der Psychologie*. Frankfurt am Main: Campus Verlag.

Holzkamp, K. (1978). *Sinnliche Erkenntnis: Historischer Ursprung und gesellschaftliche Funktion der Wahrnehmung* (4. Auflage). Königstein: Athenäum Verlag. (Original work published 1973)

Il'enkov, E. V. (1982). *The dialectics of the abstract and the concrete in Marx' Capital*. Moscow: Progress. (Original work published 1960)

Jaeger, M. E., & Rosnow, R. L. (1988). Contextualism and its implications for psychological inquiry. *British Journal of Psychology, 79*, 63–75.

Lave, J., & Wenger, E. (1991). *Situated learning: Legitimate peripheral participation*. New York: Cambridge University Press.

Leontjew, A. N. (1975). *Probleme der Entwicklung des Psychischen* (5. Auflage, Elske Däbritz, Trans.). Berlin: Volk und Wissen. (Original work published in Russian, 1959)

Leont'ev (Leontyev), A. N. (1981). *Problems of the development of the mind* (Anonymous Trans.). Moscow: Progress. (Original work published in Russian, 1959)

Lerner, R. M. (1979). A dynamic interactional concept of individual and social relationship development. In R. L. Burgess & T. L. Huston (Eds.), *Social exchange in developing relationships* (pp. 271–305). New York: Academic Press.

Lerner, R. M., Hultsch, D. F., & Dixon, R. A. (1983). Contextualism and the character of developmental psychology in the 1970s. *Annals of the New York Academy of Sciences, 412*, 101–128.

Lerner, R. M., & Tubman, J. G. (1991). Developmental contextualism and the study of early adolescent development. In R. Cohen & A. W. Siegel (Eds.), *Context and development* (pp. 183–210). Hillsdale: Lawrence Erlbaum.

Marx, K. (1954). *Capital* (Vol. 1, S. Moore & E. Aveling, Trans.). Moscow: Progress. (Original work published 1867)

Marx, K. (1968). Thesen über Feuerbach. In S. Landshut (Ed.), *Karl Marx: die Frühschriften*. Stuttgart: Alfred Kröner Verlag. (Original work written 1845)

Messmann, A., & Rückriem, G. (1978). Zum Verständnis der menschlichen Natur in der Auffassung des Psychischen bei A. N. Leontjew. In G. Rückriem (Ed.), *Historischer Materialismus und menschliche Natur* (pp. 80–133). Cologne: Pahl-Rugenstein.

Rosnow, R. L., & Georgoudi, M. (Eds.). (1986). *Contextualism and understanding in behavioral science.* New York: Praeger.

Schurig, V. (1975a). *Naturgeschichte des Psychischen 1: Psychogenese und elementare Formen der Tierkommunikation.* Frankfurt am Main: Campus Verlag.

Schurig, V. (1975b). *Naturgeschichte des Psychischen 2: Lernen und Abstraktionsleistungen bei Tieren.* Frankfurt am Main: Campus Verlag.

Schurig, V. (1976). *Die Entstehung des Bewusstseins.* Frankfurt am Main: Campus Verlag.

Shotter, J. (1993). *Conversational realities: The construction of life through language.* London: Sage.

Skinner, B. F. (1953). *Science and human behaviour.* New York: Free Press / Macmillan.

Vygotsky, L. S. (1978). *Mind and society: The development of higher psychological processes.* (M. Cole, V. John-Steiner, S. Scribner, & E. Souberman, Eds.). Cambridge, MA: Harvard University Press.

6 Cultural psychology: Some general principles and a concrete example

Michael Cole

Introduction

In an earlier paper, I discussed the uses of cross-cultural research by the originators of the Soviet cultural-historical school. My focus was on the ways in which their ideas intersect with certain streams of American cross-cultural research (Cole, 1988).[1] In that paper I argued that continued progress in developing the ideas of the cultural-historical school would be well served by combining their emphasis on the mediated structure of higher psychological functions and historically evolving modes of activity with the American approach emphasizing the importance of cultural context and empirical methods that begins with an analysis of concrete activity systems.

In this chapter, I begin where my previous discussion left off by presenting various contributions to the elaboration of a cultural theory of human nature that have come to prominence in the past decade under the rubric of *cultural psychology*.[2] After suggesting some ways in which these efforts complement the basic program of cultural-historical psychologists and their successors who work within the framework of activity theory, I present an example of research designed to apply the overall framework to a concrete problem of development in modern industrial societies.

Recent proposals for cultural psychology

Approximately a decade ago, Douglas Price-Williams (1979, 1980), a well-known cross-cultural developmental psychologist, published two papers suggesting that psychologists recognize the existence of *cultural psychology*, which he defined as "that branch of inquiry that delves into the contextual behavior of psychological processes" (1979, p. 14). In addition to urging that the category of culture be made the centerpiece of such a discipline, Price-Williams pointed to the great relevance of closely related thinking in the semiotic and pragmatic schools of linguistics and cultural studies.

A few years later, J. R. Kantor (1982) defined cultural psychology as the study of human beings' responses to "institutional stimuli." By *institutional stimuli*, Kantor meant stimuli that have acquired meaning as a consequence of their inclusion in prior meaningful human activity. He gave as an example the contrasting responses of a Hindu and a Christian to the sight of a cow. Both individuals share "non-cultural" perceptual responses to the biological properties of cows but have different cultural responses corresponding to the inclusion of cows in two different cultural meaning systems.

More recently, Richard Shweder, in a book entitled *Cultural Psychology: The Chicago Symposia on Human Development* (1990), wrote that the basic idea of cultural psychology is that "no socio-cultural environment exists or has identity independent of the way human beings seize meaning and resources from it, while every human being has her or his subjectivity and mental life altered through the processes of seizing meanings and resources from some socio-cultural environment and using them" (p. 2). Shweder's suggestions for appropriate models of theory and data collection include the study of expertise and event schemata in cognitive-developmental psychology, cognitive and symbolic anthropology, intentional worlds philosophy, discourse process studies in various disciplines, and many more.

Lutz Eckensberger is a student of Ernst Boesch, whose career combines the German historical tradition (see Whitman, 1984) with a form of action theory *and Piagetian* constructivism. In elaborating on Boesch's version of action theory, which takes seriously the cultural-historical constitution of mind, Eckensberger (1990) draws on Barker's (1968) ecological psychology, certain strains in German and American critical psychology, and anthropologically oriented developmental psychologists in the United States. Eckensberger, Krewer, and Kasper (1984) (see also Krewer, 1990) identify another central feature of cultural psychology: It implies a developmental approach to the study of human nature as a general methodological requirement.

This sampling of modern views about the nature of cultural psychology is not intended to be exhaustive. But it *is* taken to be representative of a rather broad consensus that seems to be building about the key features of a cultural psychology among American and European social scientists. These otherwise disparate authors seem to converge on the importance of word meaning, the centrality of context as the locus of mental life, and the necessity of methodological approaches that are broadly comparative and developmental.

Similarities to cultural-historical formulations

In the earliest Soviet publication on this topic to appear in English, entitled "The problem of the cultural development of the child," Alexander Luria (1928) began with the well-known premise that "Man differs from animals in that he can make and use tools." Following Marx and Engels (as well as Aristotle, Benjamin Franklin, and Henri Bergson, to name a few!), he said that tool use simultaneously transforms the conditions of human existence and the structure of human psychological processes. The distinctive structural change in human thought that arises in connection with tool use is that direct, "natural" processes are complemented by indirect (mediated) ones.

Vygotsky (1934/1987) also emphasized the qualitative change in human activity engendered by tool mediation. He called the resulting, specifically human, form of thought the *cultural method* of cognition, which he characterized as follows:

All processes forming part of that method form a complicated functional and structural unity. This unity is effected, first, by the task which must be solved by the given method, and secondly, by the means by which the method can be followed. . . . It is precisely the structure which combines all separate processes, which are component parts of the cultural habit of behavior, which transforms this habit into a psychological function, and which fulfills its task with respect to behavior as a whole. (Vygotsky, 1929, pp. 420–421)

Vygotsky believed that although humans are born into an environment transformed by the tool-mediated cultural transformations of prior generations, it is especially with the acquisition of language as a special form of mediated activity that cultural-historical genesis and phylogenesis become intertwined, thereby creating uniquely human psychological functions.

As is well known, although a number of these theses were widely accepted in the USSR, the formulations of the early cultural-historical psychologists were criticized on various grounds, one being the inappropriateness of distinguishing between natural and cultural processes in ontogenetic development, another being a putative underdeveloped treatment of the relation between mind and activity (Leont'ev & Luria, 1956; Brushlinsky, 1990). I have no intention of entering directly into disputes between Soviet adherents of rival activity-theory approaches developed after the official dismemberment of the cultural-historical school in the 1930s. Rather, drawing on a combination of Anglo–American and Soviet sources, I want to sketch out ways in which these two traditions, each placing culture at the center of a theory of human nature, may fruitfully be combined in the service of a practically useful theory of human behavior.

I focus on two core concepts that unite Soviet and non–Soviet formulations of culture and mind: artifact-mediated activity and a conception of culture as the unique *medium* of human existence, a medium that acts as both a constraint on and a resource for human action. These two concepts, which are intimately related, provide a way to think seriously about two other core concepts: word meaning and context.

Tools as artifacts

One of the central tenets of the cultural-historical school is that the process of the historical development of human behavior and the process of biological evolution do not coincide; one is not a continuation of the other. Rather, each of these processes is governed by its own laws. The key to this difference is to be found in the concept of an *artifact*, a material object that has been modified by human beings as a means of regulating their interactions with the world and each other. Artifacts carry within them successful adaptations of an earlier time (in the life of the individual who made them or in earlier generations) and, in this sense, combine the ideal and the material, such that in coming to adopt the artifacts provided by their culture, human beings simultaneously adopt the symbolic resources they embody. (This conception of artifacts is quite widespread. It is found, for example, in the writings of the American anthropologist Leslie White [1959], and the Soviet philosopher Evald Il'enkov [1977, p. 94], who asserts that "the world of things created by man for man, and, therefore, things whose forms are reified forms of human activity . . . is the condition for the existence of consciousness.")

In linking artifact-mediation and context, I find Marx Wartofsky's (1979) discussion of the nature of tools particularly useful.[3] In terms strongly reminiscent of those of the cultural-historical theorists (derived most likely from a common source in Marx and Engels, as he does not seem to have been aware of Soviet psychological or American anthropological research at the time), Wartofsky also asserts that what is distinctively human about the way *Homo sapiens* produces and reproduces the conditions of species existence is the creation of artifacts, including the words of one's language.

What makes Wartofsky's discussion of artifacts particularly useful for my present purposes is that he proposes a three-level hierarchy of artifacts that helps me to bridge tool-*mediated activity*, the key concept of the cultural-historical school, and *context*, a key concept in Western discussions of cultural psychology. The first level, *primary artifacts,* includes those directly used in production (as examples, Wartofsky mentions axes, clubs, needles, and bowls; my examples include computers, telecommunications networks, and mythical cultural personages). The second level, *secondary artifacts,* consists of representations both of primary artifacts and of modes of action using them. Secondary artifacts play a central role in preserving and transmitting modes of action. The third level is a class of artifacts

which can come to constitute a relatively autonomous "world," in which the rules, conventions and outcomes no longer appear directly practical, or which, indeed, seem to constitute an arena of non-practical, or "free" play or game activity. (p. 208)

Wartofsky calls these imagined worlds *tertiary artifacts.* He remarks that such "possible worlds" provide candidates for conceivable change in existing practices. Such imaginative artifacts, he suggests, can come to color the way we see the actual world, acting as tools for changing current praxis. In modern psychological jargon, modes of behavior acquired when interacting with tertiary artifacts can transfer beyond the immediate contexts of their use. Wartofsky applies this hierarchical conception of artifacts to works of art and the process of perception; I want to generalize his conception for use in designing activities for children that will promote their social and cognitive development. To make that link, I now turn to a second key concept: culture as a medium.

The garden as a metaphor for culture as a medium

The notion of culture as a special medium of human life is certainly familiar to cultural-historical and activity theorists. However, here I draw on its interpretation within the history of Anglo-Saxon thought, whose metaphors appear especially useful in dealing with critical methodological problems facing the field.

Raymond Williams, who has traced the English concept of culture back to its connection with Latin roots, notes that the core features that coalesce to produce modern conceptions of culture refer to the process of helping things to grow. "Culture," Williams wrote, "in all of its early uses was a noun of process: the tending of, something, basically crops or animals" (Williams, 1973, p. 87).

Sometime around the 16th century, the term *culture* began to refer to the tending of human children in addition to crops and animals. In the 18th century, culture when applied to human affairs began to differentiate quantitatively: Some people came to be considered more "cultured" or "cultivated" than others. It was not until the 19th century that the idea of culture as a social group's medium of adaptation to (and transformation of) its ecological circumstances forced attention to the variety of cultural forms and brought into question the linear scaling of cultures into more and less developed kinds. At present, these two latter conceptions live side by side in science and society.

From the beginning, the core idea of culture as a process of helping things to grow was combined with a general theory on how to promote growth: Create an artificial environment where young organisms could be provided optimal conditions for growth. Such tending required tools, of course, and it is somehow provocative to learn that one of the early means of culture was "plowshare."

Although it would be foolish to overinterpret the metaphorical parallels between the theory and practice of growing future generations of crops and of children, the exercise, I argue, has particular heuristic value for thinking about the processes of development and for designing new activity systems to promote development. Broadly speaking, like gardeners, activity theorists must attend simultaneously to two classes of concerns: what transpires inside the activity system ("garden") they study (or design and study) and what transpires around it. These issues often seem to be addressable independently of each other, but in reality they are as interdependent as tasks and context, thought of as the text and context of development. Inside the garden, for every kind of plant, there is the quality of the soil to consider, the best way to till the soil, the right kinds of nutrients to use, and the right amount of moisture, as well as the best time to plant and nurture the seeds and the need to protect the growing plants against predators, disease, and so on. Each of these tasks has its own material needs, associated tools, and knowledge. The theory and practice of development at this level focuses on finding exactly the right combination of factors to promote life within the garden walls.

Gardens do not, obviously, exist independently of the larger ecological system within which they are embedded. Although it is possible to raise any plant anywhere in the world, given the opportunity first to arrange the appropriate set of conditions, it is not always possible to create the right conditions, even for a short while. And if what one is interested in is not a short-run demonstration of the possibility of creating a development-promoting system, but rather the creation of conditions that sustain the needed properties of the artificial environment without much additional labor, then the system in which the garden is embedded is as important as the properties of the garden itself. In the extended example to be presented, I treat the garden-as-culture metaphor as a way of specifying a particular kind of cultural context, constituted jointly by tool-mediated practices that "wall the garden off" from its environment, thereby establishing it as a particular kind of cultural context. In doing so, I pay attention to the organization of activity both within the context ("garden/activity system") and between such contexts (between the "garden" and *its* environment).

Applying the garden metaphor: From tertiary artifact to the 5th Dimension

I now want to shift gears and describe a program of research that takes seriously the garden metaphor as the basis of a methodology for implementing a cultural theory of mind. In particular, this program assigns the researcher the role not only of an analyst but also of an active agent in attempting to "create gardens" and "grow plants."

The first of these attempts was directed at the problem of children who had failed to learn how to read following several years of elementary school instruction. Named *Field College,* it was an afterschool activity system that, in turn, was divided into two distinct kinds of activity. The first involved the children in a unique form of group reading inspired by the early work of A. R. Luria (1932). Since this work has already been described in some detail in recent publications, I will not dwell on it here (see Cole, 1990; Griffin, King, Cole, & Diaz, 1989, for accounts of this work). Instead, I describe recent work with the second activity system that we initiated in 1981 as it has evolved in the course of our subsequent research. We call this activity system the *5th Dimension.*

The purposes of the 5th Dimension include, but extend well beyond, the teaching of reading. In terms of the garden metaphor, the 5th Dimension is a specially designed cultural medium for promoting the all-around intellectual and social development of 6- to 12-year-old children while introducing them to computers and computer networking. In Wartofsky's terms, the 5th Dimension is a tertiary artifact – a bounded alternative world with its own social norms, tasks, and conventions. This artifact is a tool designed to address certain long-standing problems in American education, in particular the distressingly low academic achievement of many American youngsters, the widely perceived need for them to gain a qualitatively richer experience with new information technologies, and the failure of apparently successful educational innovations to survive beyond the period of innovation and external funding.

In order to transform this tertiary artifact into a material system of activity, we needed, of course, to provide participants with primary and secondary artifacts as crucial mediational means. We also needed to identify likely social institutions that would serve as environments for our proposed innovation. Once the system was in place, we needed both to promote its growth and to analyze the dynamics of growth over time. Then, after a suitable period, we withdrew to a prearranged position as participants in, but no longer principal instigators of, the innovation to determine if it would continue to grow quantitatively and qualitatively – for example, whether it would continue to develop. At present, we are in the fourth year of work directed specifically at institutionalization of the 5th Dimension and analysis of the dynamics of its growth, considering both the level of interpersonal interactions within it and the institutional arrangements that support it.

An overview of the 5th Dimension's activity system

Figure 6.1 provides an overview of the activity system that constitutes the 5th Dimension, with a close-up of one of its institutional loci, the Boys and Girls Club of Solana Beach, California, a suburb of San Diego. From the children's point of view, the heart of the 5th Dimension is shown at the top of the figure in the form of a cardboard maze approximately 1 square meter in area divided into 20 or so "rooms," each of which gives access to two activities. About three-quarters of the time, these activities are instantiated as computer programs that include computer games and educational software, some of which also have gamelike qualities; the remainder are noncomputer activities that include board games, arts and crafts, and physical exercise. According to the rules of the 5th Dimension (enshrined in a Constitution, which each child receives upon entering the activity system), children progress through the maze. In order to carry out a task, children must first consult a task card that defines progress on that task. More about task cards in a minute.

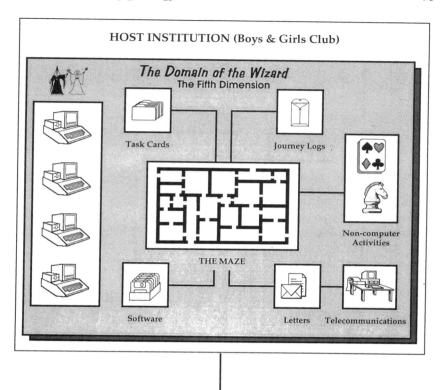

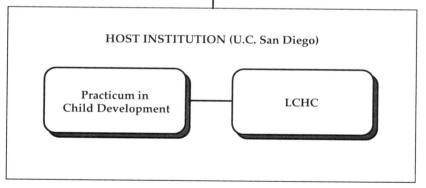

Figure 6.1. A schematic representation of a 5th Dimension site in its institutional setting. At the center of the figure is the maze controlling which games the children will play. Various supporting artifacts that further structure children's interactions within the 5th Dimension are arrayed around the maze. Along the walls of the room a variety of computers are arrayed.

This Map belongs to: _____

The Solana Beach Boy's and Girl's Club Fifth Dimension

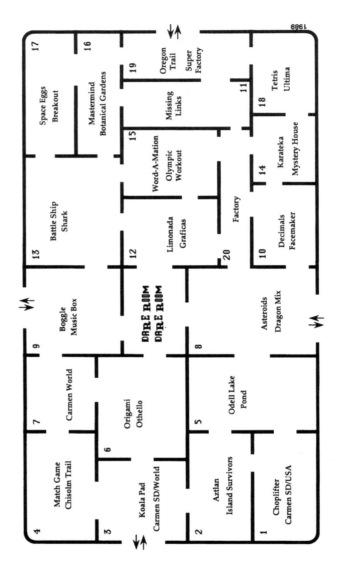

Figure 6.2. The contents of a 5th Dimension maze. The specific activities shift according to the availability of software. A wide variety of content is represented by the games and other activities within the maze.

In addition to the local goal of completing a task, the rules of the 5th Dimension provide for a variety of goals designed to appeal to a variety of children. For example, all children are given a plain-looking token figurine upon entering the 5th Dimension. By traversing a path that takes them in one door and out of another, they may "transform their cruddy creature" and obtain a more desirable figurine. Or they may choose to complete all of the rooms in the maze, thereby attaining expert status and access to new activities. In Leont'ev's terms, the 5th Dimension provides a variety of possible effective motives in addition to motives (such as the need to master new information technologies) that are merely understandable to the children.

Figure 6.2 provides a slightly more detailed schematic drawing of the 5th Dimension maze with a list of the software in use during the 1989–1990 academic year. Notice that by being provided with two activities in each room, as well as multiple paths through the maze, children are confronted with choices at every step of the way, allowing them to satisfy their own goals within the constraints provided by the microworld as a whole.

Figure 6.3 illustrates the way children's interactions within a task are structured using task cards. In this case, the task is an embodiment of a Piagetian formal operations problem. In reading the task card, note that the beginning level provides the child with a relatively accessible goal that remains entirely within the predesigned task structure. But for both the "good" and "excellent" levels, the child must not only complete actions specified by the software but also write about the strategies used and the knowledge gained to the "boss" of the 5th Dimension, the Wizard.

Before discussing the multiple significance of that archetypal artifact, the Wizard, it is useful to glance at Figure 6.4, which displays an important microstructural constraint on movement through the 5th Dimension. At the top of the figure we see the possible trajectories of activity should a child choose always to complete a task at the beginner level. Note that, by and large, beginner-level achievement quickly leads to a dead end, where the child oscillates between two rooms. At the bottom of the figure are the consequences of achievement at each level. Here the important point to note is that higher levels of achievement increase children's freedom of choice in moving within this quasi-make-believe world. They can use this freedom either to return to a favorite game or to pursue one of the other goals in the 5th Dimension.

Returning to Figure 6.1, it is time to examine that shadowy figure in the upper-left-hand corner, the Wizard. It is difficult for me to classify

FACTORY

Welcome to Willy Wonka's Wacky factory! As the new supervisor in charge of new product development, it is your job to create new things!!!! You have various machines you can use to do this! These machines can punch holes in your product, rotate your product to a variety of angles, and even stripe your product with various sizes of stripes. The purpose of your factory is to design some cool new products. In fact, your job as supervisor depends on it. You had better get STARTED!!!!!!!!

BEGINNER: Begin by testing the machines. To do this, type #1. At the bottom of the screen you have the choice to punch, rotate or stripe. Select punch. Then choose circle, then one. You will see the board enter the machine and the result will be a square with a circle punched in the middle. Test all the machines. Then make a product that is a square, with a cross made of two medium stripes, with a round hole right in the middle.

GOOD: Do the Beginner Level. Then go on and do some CHALLENGES! Do EASY level challenges with "Make a Product" until you get three right on your first try!! Write to the **Wizard** and describe what your challenge products looked like and tell the **Wiz** how many machines it took you to create the product. (HINT: Better keep track by writing some things down!!)

EXPERT: Pick "Make a Product" to try to figure out how to make the products that the computer challenges you to do!! Figure out how to make three different products at the ADVANCED LEVEL! Write to the **Wizard** and describe for **ME** what each product looked like and the machines you used to make them!! Or write to a child at another 5th Dimension with a Factory Challenge! Describe for them one of your products and challenge them to make an Expert level product of their own and write to YOU about it!

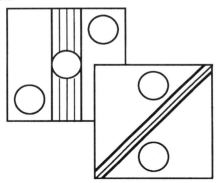

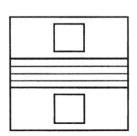

Figure 6.3. A sample task card for the game "Factory" (Sunburst Corporation). Movement from beginner to expert level involves increasingly complex actions afforded by the software and increasingly complex forms of communication about the actions with the software.

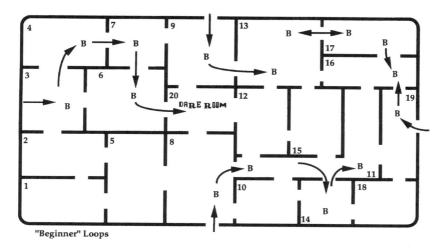

"Beginner" Loops

Consequences for All Levels

Figure 6.4. The arrangement of consequences for different levels of accomplishment with games in each room of the maze. In the upper half of the figure are the consequences of staying at the beginning level after entering the maze – a variety of dead ends. In the lower half of the figure are the consequences associated with each level of accomplishment; the higher the level of accomplishment, the more freedom there is to choose which rooms to travel to next.

the Wizard according to Wartofsky's hierarchy of artifacts because this figure seems to display properties of all three levels. In the life-world of the 5th Dimension, the Wizard is known as the ultimate authority. The Constitution of the 5th Dimension was created by the Wizard. This Constitution can be amended, but only through discussion with the Wizard. However, the Wizard is contactable only through the computer-mediated telecommunications system displayed in Figure 6.1 in the form of either electronic mail or a live chat. So, there is something tertiary about the Wizard. On the other hand, the Wizard does write to the children, and the resulting letters are important primary artifacts regulating their actions. The Wizard encourages the children when they have difficulty and chides them when they behave antisocially or perform a task in a fashion below their abilities. The Wizard is especially helpful in making and maintaining contacts with children in other geographical areas, whose local schedules often make continuity of interaction a problem.

The Wizard is also an essential tool in reordering power relations between adults and children in the 5th Dimension. This rearrangement comes about in part because when conflicts arise in the 5th Dimension, adults need not confront children directly since it is the Wizard, not the human participants, who has the power to adjudicate disputes. In such cases, adults as well as children must write to the Wizard, who decides how matters should proceed. It is also important that by subordinating themselves to the Wizard, the adults can collude with the children in the pretense of the Wizard's existence and thereby play *with* the children. Finally, since computer technology is not especially reliable and programs or computers often fail to work, adults can offload responsibility onto the Wizard at strategic moments, a possibility that has endeared the Wizard to all adults who have worked in the 5th Dimension.

Another purpose of the Wizard is to act as a tool for organizing mediated interaction that provides children with both the means and the motive to decrease their intense "figurative" involvement in the game-like tasks of the 5th Dimension and to formulate the knowledge they have gained in written language. As Vygotsky pointed out long ago, "The analysis of reality on the basis of a concept emerges much earlier than analysis of the concept itself" (1934/1987, p. 161). In the 5th Dimension we routinely observe children engaged in successful goal-directed activity who experience great difficulty in communicating the strategies and concepts that underpin their actions. Because progress within the 5th Dimension requires children to report their achievements to the Wizard, the children are constantly confronted with the need to explicate what they are doing and to communicate it to others. We believe this requirement to communicate is one of the major educational tools of the 5th Dimension. Whether motivated by Vygotsky and Luria's work on the cognitive significance of written language or by Piaget's concept of reflective abstraction, this kind of mediated activity is expected to promote intellectual development.

Now I want to examine another part of the activity system indicated in Figure 6.1 by the box labeled "UCSD – practicum in child development." The involvement of the university is important to the overall system in several ways. Each academic quarter, a course is offered at the University of California, San Diego (UCSD), that teaches principles of development through a course requiring students both to become familiar with theories of development and to combine their theoretical work with hands-on practice. The theory is derived from cultural psychology, and the practice consists of participating in 5th Dimension activities in the role of the Wizard's assistants. As the Wizard's assistants, undergraduates assist children in achieving their goals. As university students, the undergraduates themselves learn how to work through telecommunications systems, how to interact with children to promote their development (including how to adopt the persona of the Wizard offline), and how to document their interactions in written field notes. Subsequently, these field notes become one important source of data on the workings of the activity system.

The undergraduates' participation in local 5th Dimension activities makes available yet another source of goals to children. Not only do the children admire the undergraduates and seek their approval, the undergraduates want very much to be liked and admired by the children. As a consequence, in addition to play and education, the 5th Dimension includes a strong element of affiliation. Since a dozen or more children participate in the 5th Dimension during each session, it should be obvious that peer interaction is also a prominent source of motives for action. As a consequence of the coordination of all of these factors through the mediational artifacts in the environment, the 5th Dimension brings together all four leading activities of childhood – affiliation, play, education, and peer interaction – within a single activity system. The result is a unique medium for social and cognitive development, a special kind of garden for growing young citizens of the 21st century.

To complete my description of the elements of this system, I briefly note that UCSD provides both the human and material resources to interconnect local sites in geographically disparate areas. As shown in

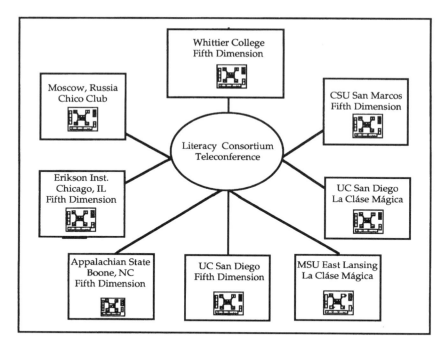

Figure 6.5. A full map of the coordinated network of activity systems, mediated by a teleconference of all the participants in what has come to be called the *Distributed Literacy Consortium.*

Figure 6.5, there are sites in distant locales, including Chicago and New Orleans in the United States and Moscow in Russia. Each of these sites has a local Wizard, and collectively the sites have a meta–Wizard who fosters intersite interaction between the children.

Some preliminary results

Before ending this description of our model activity system, I want to summarize a few results of the work so far.

First, there seems little doubt that, on a small scale, the 5th Dimension has achieved the social goal of providing children with additional time on academic tasks. We know from tracking children's progress that over the course of the year they achieve higher and higher levels within the tasks that the 5th Dimension provides and become familiar with a wide variety of computer-based activities, including telecommunications. In addition, although there is no longer any research money for the development of the 5th Dimension, it has continued to propagate itself. Instead of one Boys and Girls Club 5th Dimension, the regional Boys and Girls Clubs have adopted this activity. They provide not only space but also salaries for an on-site supervisor, computer, and telephone lines for telecommunications activity. In addition, one local school has made the 5th Dimension the organizing principle for its instructional program in computers, and others are asking to do so. Perhaps most interesting, other universities are asking if they can join in this kind of activity. They (correctly) see it as a benefit to their students, as well as to their communities.

Quite naturally we worry about the problem of scale. At present, this new cultural artifact is continuing to replicate itself with only modest input of energy from the university. But we are acutely aware that we can do little more than provide a model of possibilities for others to emulate or modify. We are encouraged by Wartofsky's observation that artifacts are to cultural evolution as genes are to biological evolution. Since cultural evolution proceeds by the Lamarckian principle that successful modifications are passed down to directly succeeding generations, if Lamarck is right, then a "culturogene" such as the 5th Dimension may be expected to continue gathering energy so long as it serves useful functions for the communities in which it has appeared. We are witnessing such growth at present, but how far it will go is necessarily uncertain.

As researchers, we are presently preoccupied with a number of pressing methodological problems. First, we are seeking to understand more fully the interaction between the 5th Dimension as medium/garden and the various institutional environments in which it is placed. This level of analysis has yielded several interesting results. For example, we know from analyzing 5th Dimension interactions in a variety of community institutions (libraries, schools, and churches, in addition to youth clubs) that the specific characteristics of interaction *within* a 5th Dimension depend on the nature of its institutional context. At the micro level, each 5th Dimension is unique. We are also studying the factors that determine whether or not institutions assimilate their 5th Dimensions and begin to nurture their growth; not all institutions are equally fertile environments for the 5th Dimension, and in some cases 5th Dimensions have been abandoned for lack of institutional support. Nor can a single university be expected to provide unlimited institutional support for such efforts if they diffuse widely. What appears to be needed is replication not only of local 5th Dimension sites but also of entire 5th Dimension activity systems, as pictured in Figure 6.1.

Nor can we ignore the micro-level interactions that determine the quality of experience for children who participate in our garden / micro worlds. In several analyses to date, we have worked out ways to trace relationships between the growth of local 5th Dimension cultures and the sociocognitive development of individual children who participate in them. We are quite encouraged by what we have observed so far, but detailed analyses challenge us to deal seriously with field notes as a source of data about psychological processes; it remains to be seen how far we can push the use of such data, which ideally would be complemented by data on children's school achievement and social behavior in other settings. We are also seeking to understand and document the conditions under which intersite coordination between children serves as a source of motives for communication and the cognitive analysis that it entails, since this is a major source of the intellectual benefits from participating in this specialized activity system.

Summing up

I hope that this discussion, brief as it has been, has successfully illustrated my contention that the initial ideas of the cultural-historical school of psychology are indeed usefully complemented by Anglo-American notions associated with the notion of cultural psychology. In our research, we have adhered to the necessity of considering simultaneously the goals and settings of activity and the mediational means placed at participants' disposal. Our approach is developmental, not only because we are working with children *within* an activity, but also because of the history of that activity itself. Consistent with a contextual approach, we have focused on both within-context and between-context interactions as constitutive of the activity itself.

It should be obvious that we need to continue to develop our theoretical approach even as we develop the methodology that links theory to practice. This effort is very much a collective enterprise to which I invite the readers' participation. For anyone who would like to enter into this activity with us, the needed course of action is clear. Simply write an electronic message to lchc@ucsd and ask to get in touch with the Wizard. I am confident that the Wizard will be happy to assist you.

Notes

1. In that paper I used the term *sociohistorical* to refer to the work of Leont'ev, Luria, Vygotsky, and their students as it was appropriated by American scholars. In part this

decision was based on my belief that since cultural phenomena are necessarily historical, the social nature of cultural-historical phenomena needed to be emphasized. It
might also be noted that Leont'ev (1981) used this term in his well-known monograph
on development. Subsequently, after many discussions of the issues involved, I came
to the conclusion that such a change in terminology does a disservice to the historical record and fails to add conceptual clarity, since cultural-historical phenomena are
also necessarily social. Consequently, I use the term *cultural-historical* throughout this
chapter.

2. For a discussion of the history of the notion of cultural psychology, see the special issue of *The Quarterly Newsletter of the Laboratory of Comparative Human Cognition* of
   January, 1990.
3. My thanks to Yrjö Engeström for bringing Wartofsky's discussion to my attention in
   his provocative article titled "When Is a Tool?" (Engeström, 1990).

References

Barker, R. G. (1968). *Ecological psychology: Concepts and methods for studying the environment of human behavior.* Stanford: Stanford University Press.

Brushlinsky, A. V. (1990). The activity of the subject and psychic activity. In V. A. Lektorsky (Ed.), *Activity: Theories, methodology, and problems.* Orlando: Paul M.
Deutsch Press.

Cole, M. (1988). Cross-cultural research in the sociohistorical tradition. *Human Development, 31,* 137–151.

Cole, M. (1990). Cultural psychology: A once and future discipline? In J. J. Berman (Ed.),
Nebraska symposium on motivation: Cross-cultural perspectives. Lincoln: University of Nebraska Press.

Eckensberger, L. (1990). From cross-cultural psychology to cultural psychology. *The
Quarterly Newsletter of the Laboratory of Comparative Human Cognition, 12,* 37–
52.

Eckensberger, L., Krewer, B., & Kasper, E. (1984). Simulation of cultural change by
cross-cultural research: Some metamethodological considerations. In K. A.
McCluskey & H. W. Reese (Eds.), *Life-span developmental psychology: Historical and generational effects.* Orlando: Academic Press.

Engeström, Y. (1990). *Learning, working and imagining: Twelve studies in activity theory.*
Helsinki: Orienta-Konsultit.

Griffin, P., King, C., Cole, M., & Diaz, E. (1989). *A socio-historical approach to remediation.* Moscow: Progress (in Russian).

Kantor, J. R. (1982). *Cultural psychology.* Chicago: Principia Press.

Krewer, B. (1990). Psyche and culture: Can a culture-free psychology take into account
the essential features of the species, *homo sapiens? The Quarterly Newsletter of
the Laboratory of Comparative Human Cognition, 12,* 24–36.

Il'enkov, E. V. (1977). The problem of the ideal. In *Philosophy in the USSR: Problems of
dialectical materialism.* Moscow: Progress.

Leont'ev, A. N. (1981). *Problems of the development of the mind.* Moscow: Progress.

Leont'ev, A. N., & Luria, A. R. (1956). Vygotsky's outlook on psychology. In L. S. Vygotsky, *Selected psychological works.* Moscow: Academy of Pedagogical Sciences
Press (in Russian).

Luria, A. R. (1928). The problem of the cultural development of the child. *Journal of Genetic Psychology, 35*, 493–506.

Luria, A. R. (1932). *The nature of human conflicts.* New York: Liveright.

Price-Williams, D. (1979). Modes of thought in cross-cultural psychology: A historical review. In A. J. Marsella, R. G. Tharp, & T. J. Ciborowski (Eds.) *Perspectives in cross-cultural psychology.* New York: Academic Press.

Price-Williams, D. (1980). Toward the idea of cultural psychology: A superordinate theme for study. *Journal of Cross-Cultural Psychology, 11*, 75–88.

Stigler, J. W., Shweder, R. A., & Herdt, G. (Eds.). (1990). *Cultural psychology: The Chicago symposia on human development.* Cambridge: Cambridge University Press.

Vygotsky, L. S. (1929). The problem of the cultural development of the child, II. *Journal of Genetic Psychology, 36*, 414–434.

Vygotsky, L. S. (1987). *Thinking and speech.* New York: Plenum. (Original work published 1934)

Wartofsky, M. (1979). *Models: Representation and scientific understanding.* Dordrecht: Reidel.

White, L. A. (1959). The concept of culture. *American Anthropologist, 61*, 227–251.

Whitman, J. (1984). From philology to anthropology in mid-nineteenth century Germany. In G. W. Stocking (Ed.), *Functional historicism historicized: History of anthropology* (Vol. II). Madison: University of Wisconsin Press.

Williams, R. (1973). *Keywords.* New York: Oxford University Press.

7 Laws, logics, and human activity

Antti Eskola

Introduction

There are two underlying ideas in the empirical studies of most psychologists and social scientists that deserve critical attention. The first idea is that the phenomenon that is being explained is determined by certain factors, not directly but through the mediation of certain mechanisms. This means we must first decide which are the dependent variables that represent the phenomenon we want to explain and which are the independent variables from which we will try to find our explanation. We then go on to examine whether there are any correlations between those two categories of variables. If such correlations exist, then it is assumed that they reflect some sort of universal laws, psychological, social, or biological (Figure 7.1). These laws exert their influence through mediating mechanisms, which are represented by intervening variables.

Among the earliest techniques that were developed for the analysis of complicated relationships between variables were factor analysis, regression analysis, and Lazarsfeld's (1955) method of elaboration. Today it is possible, by means of covariance structure analysis, to combine into one analysis the different steps for which the psychologist of the 1950s needed factor and regression analyses (Schoenberg, 1989) or, by means of log-linear models, to correct the technical deficiencies of the elaboration procedure of the 1960s (Hagernaas, 1990, p. 23). In methodological terms, however, these new and elegant techniques introduced nothing new compared to the idea described in Figure 7.1.

A second characteristic of empirical research in these fields is that the search for explanatory factors is restricted to two sources. Either those factors lie inside the person, in his or her dispositions or traits such as needs, abilities, attitudes, and so on, or they are hidden somewhere in the environment or situation. The final explanation may contain factors

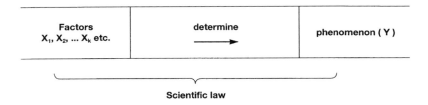

Figure 7.1. The mechanistic-deterministic research paradigm.

Figure 7.2. Two sources of explanation in traditional social psychology.

from both domains and in this sense may be based on the interaction of person and environment (Figure 7.2).

Over the years, psychology has no doubt made some progress in its search for explanations. However, it still remains trapped in the cul-de-sac represented by the dichotomy described in Figure 7.2. All that has happened is that the emphasis has shifted from the left to the right, that is, there has been "sequential progression from the dispositional strategy to the interactional strategy to the situational strategy" (Snyder & Ickes, 1985).

Transcending the trait–situation dichotomy

So what is wrong with the idea presented in Figure 7.2? According to it, there are two sources of explanatory factors. I will take a simple example from the field of historical psychology. Renvall (1949) studied the Finnish man of the 16th century using criminal court records. He found a phenomenon that seems to call for an explanation. In the 16th century, people seemed to be so interested in court sessions that they were "something of a popular entertainment," as Renvall says. Large numbers of people would always turn up on court session days, and their involvement in the court proceedings was so intense that serious disturbances sometimes occurred. How do we explain this phenomenon? Which of the two sources of explanation should we turn to?

Renvall himself turns to the person. According to him, people in those days were "affective" and unable to control their emotions. That is why they liked to attend court meetings and to take an active part in them. But the environment may also have played some part. That is, on court sessions days there was always beer for sale. This might have attracted people as well; and when people got drunk, they also got involved and interfered in the court proceedings. Perhaps both of these factors are relevant. Perhaps the active involvement of the audience is explained by the effect of inebriation on the person who was not very good at controlling his or her emotions in the first place. The final explanation would thus lie in the interaction of person and environment.

I do not believe that this explanation is totally irrelevant. But the most important thing of all is nevertheless still to be mentioned: the activity of "administration of justice," which transcends the person–environment dichotomy. That is, from Renvall's data we also learn that the presence and active participation of an audience was actually required at court sessions. It was one constitutive element of that activity. In many cases, decisions had to be made on the basis of oral tradition. Therefore, an audience had to be present whom the judge could consult. Renvall has evidence of cases where the judge was forced to call off the court session because not enough people had arrived. Not only that, those who failed to appear were fined.

My example dates back to the 16th century. But the truth that psychology needs not only the person and the environment but also the concept of activity still applies today. I refuse to believe that many of those who attended the 2nd International Congress for Research on Activity Theory in Lahti did so because they are certain types of persons, or because Lahti is such an attractive environment, or because the situation at home was so intolerable that they had to get away for a while. They went to Lahti in order to participate in an activity called an *international congress on activity theory*. This is the first thing we have to realize; only then can we see whether there is any room left for additional explanations referring to person and environment. This is why we have to add a third source of explanation – activity – and write beside it: START HERE! (Figure 7.3)

I am sure that the concept of *activity* could add an important new step to those analyses that now stop short at the concept of *situation*. Let us consider the following question by Ross and Nisbett (1991, pp. 2-4): "While walking briskly to a meeting some distance across a college campus, John comes across a man slumped in a doorway, asking him for help. Will John offer it, or will he continue on his way?"

We can agree with Ross and Nisbett that "nothing one is likely to know or learn about John would be of much use in helping predict John's

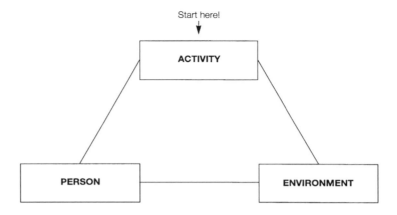

Figure 7.3. Activity as a starting point for interpretation.

behavior in the situation we've described." However, "details concerning the specifics of the situation would be invaluable." In the "situation," Ross and Nisbett include the appearance of the person in the doorway: "Was he clearly ill, or might he have been drunk or, even worse, a nodding dope addict?"

It is at this point that the concept of activity helps to clarify the analysis. The appearance of the person is an important clue because it is on that basis that John tries to decide whether the act of giving money would mean "helping the poor" or "financing drug abuse." These are very different types of activity in our society. The former is something that religious organizations and charities do; the latter is often an illegal business. Therefore it is important carefully to divide the situation into two parts. Some aspects of it (such as the appearance of the person who is asking for help) provide clues to what a certain behavior means as an activity; other aspects (such as whether it is raining or the sun is shining, or at which end of the street the episode is happening) are "only" part of the environment. Sometimes these will also have a part to play in the explanation; if, for instance, it is pouring, it is probably less likely that John will even stop to consider giving help than if it is a sunny day. In an exact analysis, all the elements of Figure 7.3 must be included.

Replacing the mechanistic-deterministic paradigm

Having now discovered activity as a third source of explanation, and as a primary source of explanation in relation to the other two, we

In activity the actor	takes into account, according to this or that logic, that	if X, then Y
		law, rule

Figure 7.4. Realistic paradigm for the study of human action.

also have to replace the mechanistic-deterministic paradigm represented in Figure 7.1 with a more realistic paradigm. I do not want to deny the meaning of laws and rules in our lives. But our activity is not determined by them. Instead, we take them into account on the basis of some form of logic (Figure 7.4).

Following this line of reasoning, our first concern is not to find out what is the "dependent variable," what are the "independent variables," and what are the "mediating mechanisms." Rather, this line of reasoning draws our attention to (1) the structure and development of activity and to its meaning to different actors; (2) the laws and rules that actors take into account in this activity; and (3) the logics on the basis of which they do so. We do not reject the concept of law that was so central in Figure 7.1; instead, we integrate it into the broader and more realistic concept of human activity.

As Leont'ev (1978, p. 50) pointed out, activity is "a system that has structure, its own internal transitions and transformations, its own development." All of these can be investigated without reference to individual actors. The same applies to logics that are possible in connection with a certain activity, as well as to laws and rules that are relevant in the context of a given logic. In a "pure" or "radical" form, the theory of activity seems to get rid of the person as well as the environment. In a less radical form, the theory describes the structures, laws, rules, and logics as they are represented in the actor's consciousness or as they appear in his or her subconscious sets (Uznadze, 1966).

One of the purposes of Figure 7.4 is to link the idea of lawfulness with the idea of freedom. That is why it refers to the actor who, in accordance with a given logic, takes into account a law of the type "if X, then Y." Let us assume that I am that actor and that the law is this: If I buy my food from the supermarket, I will also have to eat and my body absorb all the additives contained in these prepared foods, which in the long run may be a serious health hazard.

There are at least two logics on the basis of which I can take this law into account. First, I may reason that life is dangerous in any case; I might just as well eat what I please and ignore the health consequences. Second, I may reason that the most important thing in life is health, so I will move out to the country and grow my own food using biodynamic methods. In both cases, the law has an impact on me. In the former case, there is an accumulation of additives in my body; in the latter case, there is a change in my whole way of life. I cannot escape the law and step outside it, but I do have the freedom to choose what effects I allow those laws to have on me.

The conclusion is precisely the same even if Y, which follows from my act X, is the reaction of some other person or society, such as in the case of social interaction or social norms. Just as fish live and swim in water, we live our lives swimming in water that consists of laws and rules of the type "if X, then Y." However, the course of our lives is not determined by the laws any more than the course of swimming fish is determined by water. From this it follows that the analysis must start not with water but with swimming, as we are instructed to do in Figures 7.3 and 7.4.

Breaking loose from the power–knowledge coalition

At first glance, it seems quite obvious that if we want to understand the meanings attached by actors to their activities, the laws and rules they take into account, and the logics forming the basis on which they do this, it is useful to listen to their accounts, which is what so-called ethogenic techniques do (see Harré, 1979, pp. 124–128). By bending or breaking rules, which has been the trademark of ethnomethodological research techniques, we can grasp the logic of the practical consciousness that the actor cannot express discursively (e.g., Garfinkel, 1967, pp. 35–75). The study of activity turns as if by itself to techniques that Parker (1989) calls the methods of *new* social psychology in contrast to the laboratory experiment of *old* social psychology.

But is there anything radically new about new psychology as elaborated by Harré (1979) and others? Parker (1989) refers to Foucault's idea according to which power uses two types of knowledge for purposes of discipline: first, lawfulnesses that help to regulate behavior and, second, the confessions of the disciplined. If the laboratory experiment helps power by obtaining the first type of knowledge, new psychology helps it by obtaining confessions, also known as *accounts*.

I believe there are some research techniques that the study of activity could employ in its efforts to transcend these problems and to avoid being caught in the traps of power. I have in mind the technique known as *nonactive role playing.* In this technique, a group of people who have agreed to cooperate with the researcher are given a short script describing a certain episode. They are asked to imagine themselves in this situation and to imagine how it continues or, in another version, what must have preceded it; and then they are asked to write a short story. These stories form the material from which the researcher then attempts to extract the structures and meanings of the activities occurring in them, and to identify the laws and logics followed by the actors described in the stories. Experimenting is an integral part of this method in that the researcher makes minor modifications to the script and observes the effects of these changes on the stories (see Eskola, Kihlström, Kivinen, Weckroth, & Yli-joki, 1988, pp. 239–311).

However, the texts that are produced by this method should not be treated and analyzed as representations of a fixed reality. They are fictitious texts in the same sense as literary works, although they are not arbitrary or meaningless. The texts have been created under the guidance of the researcher's experimental thinking by human beings who have the skill to act and rich experience with various sorts of activity. This is why they not only replicate existing reality and its power relations but also produce new solutions, new logics, and new ways of acting. Useful methodological models for activity research operating with this type of material are provided by the approaches of textual deconstruction and social psychological discourse analysis (e.g., Parker, 1989; Potter & Wetherell, 1987). The logic of these methods is to open up escape routes and to uncover opportunities for resistance rather than to build traps and prisons for the purpose of controlling people.

Note

This chapter was written as part of a research project financed by the Academy of Finland. My research assistant in this project was David Kivinen.

References

Eskola, A., Kihlström, A., Kivinen, D., Weckroth, K., & Ylijoki, O.-H. (1988). *Blind alleys in social psychology: A search for ways out.* Amsterdam: North-Holland.

Garfinkel, H. (1967). *Studies in ethnomethodology.* Englewood Cliffs: Prentice-Hall.

Hagernaas, J. A. (1990). *Categorical longitudinal data.* Newbury Park: Sage.

Harré, R. (1979). *Social being.* Oxford: Basil Blackwell.

Lazarsfeld, P. F. (1955). Interpretation of statistical relations as a research operation. In P. F. Lazarsfeld & M. Rosenberg (Eds.), *The language of social research.* Glencoe: Free Press.

Leont'ev, A. N. (1978). *Activity, consciousness, and personality.* Englewood Cliffs: Prentice-Hall.

Parker, I. (1989). *The crisis in modern social psychology and how to end it.* London: Routledge.

Potter, J., & Wetherell, M. (1987). *Discourse and social psychology.* London: Sage.

Renvall, P. (1949). *Suomalainen 1500-luvun ihminen oikeuskatsomustensa valossa (The Finnish 16th century man in the light of his conceptions of justice).* Turku: Turun yliopisto.

Ross, L., & Nisbett, R. E. (1991). *The person and the situation.* New York: McGraw-Hill.

Schoenberg, R. (1989). Covariance structure models. In R. W. Scott & J. Blake (Eds.), *Annual review of sociology* (Vol. 15). Palo Alto: Annual Reviews.

Snyder, M., & Ickes, W. (1985). Personality and social behavior. In G. Lindzey & E. Aronson (Eds.), *The handbook of social psychology* (3rd ed., Vol. 2). New York: Random House.

Uznadze, D. N. (1966). *The psychology of set.* New York: Consultants Bureau.

8   Collapse, creation, and continuity in Europe: How do people change?

Yrjö-Paavo Häyrynen

Introduction

Recent changes in Europe have been swift and have altered the entire political landscape. As a result, the structures that were established after the Second World War have faded away. The last chain of conversions started with the rebellions in Poland, continued with perestroika in the Soviet Union, and culminated in 1989/1991 in the collapse of the socialist regimes of Eastern Europe. Fixed coalitions known as the Soviet Union, the German Democratic Republic, the Warsaw Pact, and Yugoslavia suddenly collapsed. As a consequence, the tension between the opposing military superpowers was alleviated and deep conflicts within the postsocialist sphere emerged.

But has this development actually been rapid? One may even say that what happened happened too late: What nurtured the tensions within the earlier socialist nations is that many preserved too long their centralist coalitions and provided no space for change. Present-day Europe is full of indications of a new relationship between the individual and society. One of the areas where these indications are manifested is the process of economic and political integration in Western Europe – a type of development seemingly opposite to the disintegration of socialism. How are these changes reflected in day-to-day activities? How swiftly can people change?

Mainstream psychology does not usually concern itself with these kinds of temporal problems. It has been extremely static in its premises and methods. To paraphrase Pierre Bourdieu, academic research has chiefly been concerned with the world of "preconstructed facts" mirroring the conventions of everyday life rather than the hidden, temporal, gender- and class-based flow of social behavior (Bourdieu, 1992). Couze Venn (1984, p. 130) suspects that the dominant social forms, such as a middle-class type of ability or male linguistic practice, are translated in

psychology into "facts" through quantification. Even activity theory suf-
fers from its persistent focus on the formal, "industrial" structure of
goal-directed activity, which is considered unchanging and timeless (see
Leont'ev, 1977, p. 198). Radzikhovskii (1991) criticizes this objectivist orientation in Soviet psychology for its neglect of human experience. But
what part does experience play in the study of social transformations?

What is suggested here is not the rejection of the study of experience
but a decomposition of experience by means of historical and sociological analysis. In her recent critique of cognitive psychology, Jacqueline
Goodnow (1990) outlines a similar aim. She assumes that cognitive psychology relies, at bottom, on a "free-market" model of society. In this
model, individuals are seen as free and isolated consumers of knowledge,
which is equally available to all. As a result, cognitive psychologists tend
to explain differences in intellectual competence as "innate" or "learned"
differences of individuals, with no regard to the social factors that regulate the acquisition of knowledge in a competitive society (Goodnow,
1990). Moreover, psychologists who try to expose the underlying "rules"
of cognition bypass the silent but obdurate argumentation of people that
remains undetectable in psychological experiments (Billig, 1991, p. 38).
To understand change, one must first study the nature of notions that
block this kind of subtle understanding in present research.

Psychology as a memory park

The German educationalist Johann Friedrich Herbart drafted in
1816 a program for psychology that illustrated a robust physicalist ambition. "The lawfulness of the human mind will completely resemble
that of the starry sky" (Herbart, cited in Ebbinghaus, 1920, p. 13). This
search for the firmament of innate laws remains to this day the ambition
of mainstream psychology. A landscape of knowledge, with its adherence to static rules, was described in Paul Valéry's poem *The Cemetery
at the Sea* in 1920. Composed of motionless gravestones, the cemetery
is a glorious but dead temple to time. Above is the midday sun, the
"perfect brain thinking only of itself." This "right-minded noon" is the
protector of the status quo, an analog of the academic system of refer-
ees whose task is to reveal heretical deviations rather than to appreciate any fresh movement. However, a fresh Mediterranean wind expels
the worshipers of the idols at the end of this ballad. If psychology is
compared to that kind of memorial park, then the gale's coming is still
delayed.

Valéry's poem describes a battle between the self and the frozen representation of knowledge. Some years earlier, Henri Bergson had revived the Greek philosophers' distinction between *kairos,* dynamic and irreversible social time, and *kronos,* the homogeneous and celestial time of the natural sciences (Bergson, 1985).

Bourdieu draws attention to the fact that for the Sophists *kairos* also denoted the "vital point": both the right moment and the right words for the moment. This was to be a well-timed blow that introduced a turning point in the debate: "As rhetoricians they were predisposed to make a philosophy of the practice of language as strategy" (Bourdieu, 1990, pp. 287–288). In this way, the Sophists also generated their being as polemicists or "intellectuals," those who deliver punches in the spiritual sphere. In general, humans create themselves in collective practices such as work, art, politics, and the various forms of dialogue. But conflicts are created in the course of the same self-development; as Henri Wallon writes, evolution tends to proceed through "leaps, breaks, and even catastrophes" (Wallon, 1951). Development can result in unanticipated consequences that drastically limit the realm of goal-directed activity (Elias, 1977, p. 47). But is it possible, then, to connect in one and the same study breaks and continuity, goal-directed activity and unanticipated effects? This is a nuclear question if we wish to study activity in the context of present change.

Dialectic of durations

Is not history, the dialectic of duration, the explication of the social in all its reality? asks the social historian Fernand Braudel (1958). He claims that the time perspective of human research is either too broad, so that concrete change remains unrecognized, or focused on timeless events. Braudel invites social researchers to consider processes of long duration that may indeed take centuries. This duration symbolizes the deep layer of habits, which are not altered instantly (see also Peeters, 1991):

Humans are prisoners of long-lasting centuries, of climates, of vegetations, of populations, of animals, of cultures; of a slowly constructed balance from which they cannot escape without the risks involved in wagering all. (Braudel, 1958, p. 731)

People do change, Braudel would answer, but they do so only slowly. However, Braudel also identifies shorter, conjunctural durations that last for a maximum of 50 years. Conjunctural changes may be recurrent; it is therefore essential to recognize in present history as well the changes that are irreversible and those that are not yet finished. The key concept in this thinking is the *dialectic of duration,* which means that during a single period different progressions of time emerge, supporting and/or contradicting each other. Conjuncture has connections with long-term changes but also with the life course of the individual and even with the isolated event.

Harry F. M. Peeters applies Braudel's theory in a promising classification of time levels in psychological research. Peeters studied the genesis of childhood in early Dutch and French capitalism. He believes that sound psychological research should always consist of three forms of history: general history, an individual's personal history, and the history of mental functions that are to be studied (Peeters, 1984, 1990, 1991; Peeters, Gielis, & Caspers, 1988). Although both Braudel and Peeters stress the slow unfolding of all social processes, I suggest that the potentials that are shaped by long-term processes, such as the acquisition of new abilities, manifest themselves abruptly when the right moment comes.

How are the different currents of psychology related to this idea of dialectical change? This question will be clarified if we discuss the nature of the representations of change in psychology. For this purpose, I make use of the ideas of Karl Riegel.

The enactive mind

In his final essay, *Psychology Mon Amour,* Riegel (1979) declares that the primary task of psychological research should be to estimate to what extent social change, especially transformations initiated by psychological knowledge itself, affects the future activities of people. Using Bruner's classification of thinking codes into the symbolic, iconic, and enactive, Riegel claims that the orientation of Western psychology is chiefly "symbolic-verbal" – that is, conceptual and abstract – or "iconic," related to sensory data, rather than enactive (i.e., pertaining to action that creates new conditions for life within society). Selectivity also exists: Some theories depict only human beings as active, whereas others include the environment. Riegel (1979) summarizes this contrast between passive and active representations in the scheme depicted in Figure 8.1.

Naturally, the model provokes a number of questions. For example, why is Vygotsky placed in the same segment as Skinner? Or could Riegel have also used Rousseau or Freud as paradigms of personal evolution (Segment C)? Segment D appeals naturally to dialectic psychologists, though one could ask whether there are no newer representatives of this

	INDIVIDUAL	
	PASSIVE	ACTIVE
PASSIVE	A. LOCKE HUME (HERBART) inter-action 'clockwork'	C. LEIBNIZ PIAGET CHOMSKY (FREUD) self-action & development 'inner force'
ENVIRONMENT		
ACTIVE	B. SKINNER VYGOTSKY acquirement & internalization 'outer force'	D. MARX RUBINSTEIN (WALLON BOURDIEU) enactment & agency 'dialectic'

Figure 8.1. Representations of change in psychology based on Klaus Riegel, *Psychology Mon Amour* (1979).

paradigm (active individual and active environment) than Karl Marx and S. L. Rubinstein, especially if one considers the changes that have taken place in everyday life and politics since the time of these two eminent thinkers. I propose that Bourdieu, Foucault, and Bakhtin, reinterpreting Marx in the domain of cultural power, all fulfill the criteria for enactive representation that Riegel sets.

Riegel explains Vygotsky's location in Figure 8.1 on the basis of the early works in which Vygotsky stressed the role of internalization as opposed to exteriorization. A still better parallel for Vygotsky might have been Émile Durkheim, who derived all individual psychological facts from the existing social laws. It was exactly on the basis of this "Durkheimian bias" that S. L. Rubinstein, in his monumental *Principles of General Psychology* (1948/1977), criticized Vygotsky's sociogenetic theory. Another point is that Vygotsky did not pay much attention to the conflicts that emerge *between* learners and instructors in formal education. As Goodnow (1990) remarks, Vygotsky's concept of internalization illustrates a motivated learner instructed by a benign adult, an ideal that rarely occurs even in the closest family circle. Can one say that Vygotsky failed to problematize the ambiguous contents of Soviet social reality? On the other hand, one might also ask whether he considered such contents, even in the 1930s, as phenomena of a transitory period. However this may be, the cultural-historical school of thought ignored for a long time the study of the manifestation of power in human processes such as learning and social development.

Riegel (1979) defends Rubinstein's position in Figure 8.1 on the basis of Rubinstein's notion of the *dual interaction* of activity. The leading doctrine in the works of Rubinstein is that every human act changes not only the world but the actor as well. This thought is formulated beautifully but in a somewhat difficult way in his essay on *creative self-activity*, in which Rubinstein suggests that education should be based on creative activity in which learners construe their objects and personal ideas (Rubinstein, 1919/1989). Rubinstein seems to reformulate what the philosophers of the Enlightenment understood by the notion of *imaginative power*, or *Einbildungskraft*, a cognitive process that fabricates new knowledge, the previously unknown, instead of processing only given sensory data (Engel, 1981). This is the "revolutionizing" activity that permits self-creation to exceed the frontiers of social actuality. However, Rubinstein did not draw attention, not even during the "thaw period" of the 1950s, to the way in which self-creation may conflict with the repressive order in a society (cf. Joravsky, 1989, pp. 457–460). Thus, he bypassed the question of power in his published writings.

Dialogical consciousness and the monologue of power

In Soviet psychological thinking, it was only the semiotician Mikhail Bakhtin who appears to have analyzed the distorting influence of ideological relationships on thinking. As Radzikhovskii writes, Bakhtin presents *dialogue* as the "social DNA" of human community (1991, p. 90; see also Radzikhovskii, 1988). Through dialogue, power relations penetrate the inner speech of individuals, subsequently modifying their consciousness and external communication. For Bakhtin, individual consciousness is composed of "copied dialogues" in which the individual's "Self" interacts with interlocutors who represent different outside forces. But it is important to see that the speech situation in a society is basically controlled by its implicit order, the seemingly insignificant demands for politeness and suitable behavior (Bourdieu, 1990, p. 88; see also Wertsch, 1991). Revolutionary crises may break this order and facilitate spontaneous verbal explosions, as Bourdieu points out. Bakhtin's characterization of these "breaks" highlights vividly the pressures that the everyday order imposes on dominated people in particular. Earlier, I called attention to the fact that contradictions among the "inner voices" of creative individuals also serve to explain defenses of scientific thinking, which may incarnate such stylized traits of academic communication as abstractness, monotony, or rigid adherence to accepted canons (Häyrynen, 1981).

Bourdieu (1990, pp. 32–33) attaches special importance to Bakhtin's critique of Saussurean theory, in which language is seen as a self-sufficient system of formal rules. Bourdieu's argument is that people use language in their practical world. Contrary to Leont'ev's supposition (1977, p. 201), people's comprehension of reality seems not to be restricted to the "ready-made" meanings they assimilate from without. Like Bakhtin, Bourdieu assumes that people can break, in carnivals and revolutionary situations, the external meanings or stereotypes to which their thinking is anchored. The specific form of understanding in human beings, Bourdieu stresses, is not a universal structuring of meanings but practical sense, including the ability of actors to develop new strategies of action and new meanings in the context of their experienced world. A central regulator of this process is the *habitus*, the system of durable dispositions through which people organize their practices and representations.

For Bourdieu, "habitus has an infinite capacity for generating products – thoughts, perceptions, expressions and actions – whose limits are set by the historically and socially situated conditions for its production" (1990, p. 55; see also Sabour, 1988, pp. 21–25). It should be observed that this notion of habitus has certain parallels with Rubinstein's scheme of *dual interaction* and, as Sabour notes, even with the circle of interiorization/exteriorization that Vygotsky elaborated in his works. Mutual relationships connect habitus to a certain social context. The incessant generation of new strategies of action renders this social world continuously mobile: Its "rules" last only as long as they have credibility, as long as the "elite" of a certain social field can legitimate themselves as the representatives of moral and cognitive superiority. The collapse of this kind of legitimacy is called a *symbolic revolution*. As an example, Bourdieu mentions the French university crisis of 1968, when the "symbolic capital" of the professors suddenly collapsed and the "hidden regulation" became visible to all. Students recognized, for the first time, the possibility of autonomous action. Political revolutions in Europe in the 1980s followed a similar pattern.

Creation in an academic generation: A case of "medium duration"

In the remainder of this chapter, two cases of conjunctural change are discussed that pertain both to generative aspects of human habitus and to a dialectic of various durations. The first case concerns the problem of the structure of changing potentials of creativity that emerged in a longitudinal study of Finnish students. The second case involves global changes in Europe today in light of Bourdieu's and Foucault's notions of power and resistance.

My own research program, concerned with Finnish students and academics, covers two decades and thus represents a typical duration of "conjunctural psychology" (Peeters, 1984). It comprises a longitudinal study of applicants to the University of Helsinki in 1965, with follow-up until 1983. In addition, we collected data on new applicants in 1980, which gave us a chance to compare cohort differences in the values guiding occupational choice. The study has been reported in several published articles (e.g., Häyrynen, 1987, 1989). Here I review some of the aspects of creativity as reflected in individual trajectories and as related to conjunctural change in the values of choice.

The expressions of creativity on which we gathered information represent a heterogeneous set of aspects. As our study target is a cohort of intellectuals, these include value orientations and self-evaluations, assessed literary and aesthetic production in 1983, Ph.D. dissertations, and the degree of autonomy in work, which were all linked with feelings of creativeness in our subjects. This heterogeneity characterizes the nature of creativity. Creativity may be seen as symbolic capital for middle-class people. Alternatively, it can be studied as an aspect of the self-images of the individuals who were investigated.

At the university, students who came from upper-middle-class homes activated the cultural capital their families had gathered; by this means, they also reproduced the class position of their family in their learning processes. Their cultural background was already visible in their self-image at the time they entered the university. In this case, the "creative" self-concept correlated with social origin and guided the individual's further selection of respected or autonomous jobs. But we could also identify the effect of career on the development of creative orientation. For those who were placed in positions in which work was self-directed, a strengthening of the orientation to independence and creativity occurred by 1983. This relationship between work and personal development has been investigated by Kohn and Schooler (1983) in longitudinal studies that include several cultural comparisons.

Despite the diversity of the various individual trajectories, we observed an overall rise between 1965 and 1983 in the creativity-oriented values of our cohort sample. Comparison of the two academic cohorts of students similarly indicated that the 1980 applicants displayed a higher level of creativity and achievement-oriented values than the applicants in 1965. This appears to be a general cultural trajectory of values change in Western Europe, with a rise in independence-oriented values along the lines demonstrated by Inglehart (1990) in his cross-national comparisons. I suppose that this is a typical case of "conjunctural transformation" of career values as it was linked to maturation of the welfare society during the 1970s.

The most interesting observation, however, concerned matters that could not be predicted by statistical analysis. These findings showed that women were generally less predictable than men in their occupational behavior, including the degree of productivity they displayed. This meant that a creative woman student often did not demonstrate this orientation in her later career, and that, while still students, some women writers or scholars did not reveal their subsequent interests. This unpredictability of women's life course has become well known from several follow-up studies. It may not be a sign of "indeterminate decisions" but signifies, rather, a higher developmental variation among women.

One conclusion is that women more often display abilities that are not directly linked with the prevailing forms of meritocratic career succession or prestige hierarchy. Instead, these abilities manifest themselves in informal life activities such as hobbies, social interaction, and so on. Thus, women form a potential reserve for future reforms in job structures. The transformation from an industrial to a postindustrial or postmodern pattern seems to increase the value of improvisation and social sensitivity, qualities that are more usual among women than among men.

The scales we used for evaluating creativity have shortcomings, however. For example, some students did not recognize themselves as creative when asked about this in the verbal rating scales. Even so, later in their life course they showed high inventiveness. Hence, creative practices may exist that are articulated neither in the public criteria for creativity nor in people's self-knowledge. In Finland, the academic tradition emphasizes symbolic-verbal rather than iconic or enactive mastery. Students who do not express themselves in a verbal-conceptual code may not, therefore, consider academic or literary careers even if they possess the necessary talent. To rate oneself as creative on a verbal rating scale involves internalization of the accepted norms of creativity (L. Häyrynen, 1992). However, creativity that will affect future development may be hidden in inarticulate forms that do not manifest themselves in the individual's verbalized self-conception.

Convulsion in Eastern Europe: Conjuncture or completed change?

It is a long leap from creativity to revolutions, especially if the academic norms of creativeness are considered. However, current developments in Eastern Europe offer a picturesque example of symbolic revolution as a component of changes in power relationships. In general, dominant ideological systems deteriorated first, leading to a gradual exhaustion of the political capital of the ruling elite. Political circumstances changed so fast that almost every central institution in the socialist system lost its symbolic power in a short period. But what were the psychological conditions of this macrostructural change?

In his study of the social conditions of Stalinism, Böröcz (1992) uses the notion of *dual dependence* to describe the operation of power relationships. He draws attention to the fact that although, politically and militarily, the Soviet Union controlled the Eastern European socialist semiperiphery, the semiperiphery did not stay totally independent of the world economic system. Eastern Europe was influenced by the technological, scientific, and political development of the Western "core." In the 1980s, the political center – Moscow – gradually lost its grip on the Eastern socialist periphery as the latter's dependence on the Western world system grew. This formed the context for the political collapse that followed in 1989–1991.

A new feature is the commercial impact of the Western mainstream on all sectors of life in the postsocialist sphere. This does not imply an unambiguous psychological adjustment of postsocialist society to a market economy. In place of Russian, Eastern European intellectuals now have to accept another mainstream language, English. Most are motivated to do this, but the new situation again reproduces the linguistic difference between periphery and center in a new form. The feelings of provinciality may be even stronger now for Eastern Europeans when they come face to face with fluent, materially well-equipped representatives of the new mainstream. Hence, acquisition of the new qualities of habitus – which may be more commercial, more individualistic, and less demanding of loyalty to one's group – may not be completely unproblematic for intellectuals in postsocialist countries.

The early phases of these revolutionary processes have perhaps been most carefully coded by the Polish sociologists and social psychologists who edited *Sisyphus,* the journal of the Polish Academy of Sciences, between 1980 and 1984. To some extent, the papers in this journal provide a psychological manual on spontaneous revolutions. Here Wladyslav Adamski (1982) attaches importance to the role played by the growing expectations of young, educated Poles frustrated by an economy that could not offer jobs matching their increased demands. The rebels of the 1980s had a different social character from those of the 1950s or 1960s. A number of incidents prior to the protest wave of 1980, also known as Poland's *hot August,* had diminished the credibility of the ruling class. During the previous winter floods, the government had proved incapable of organizing emergency relief, with a consequent decrease in its political capital. Pope John Paul II's visit had confirmed in people the belief that they were capable of organizing mass meetings without official management. The centralized political system demonstrated its fundamental weaknesses in that it had no channels for feedback from the population. The system had used monologue and lost its ability to engage in dialogue.

The keenest political pressures against the socialist regimes came usually from the highly educated. But did a change really occur in internal power relations as well? Here we come to the problem of the nature of power and how it operates. Foucault (1980) claims that since power in modern societies lies in the social microstructure, a real transformation can be achieved only by revealing and changing these structures. For Foucault, occupation of the state bureaucracy or a parliament building is a change that easily preserves the old forms of dominance. As he says, power lies beneath and apart from the state, in the capillaries located throughout the lower level of everyday life. But at the same time, power generates resistance. This is why coercion does not eliminate the mass inventiveness or silent argumentation of the people (Billig, 1991), though it forces this argumentation to take capillary forms similar to those that power assumes.

The aftermath of suppression and the problems of perestroika

Foucault's analysis of political power emphasizes the difference between ancient despotic and modern bourgeois society. In the ancient French monarchy, the king was its efficient and visible agent (Waltzer, 1989). When the king, Louis XVI, was killed, power was dispersed to a multitude of newly emerging agencies, such as social service centers, hospitals, planning offices, banks, the army, prisons, schools, factory organizations, and so on, which control the functioning of society but whose power is largely concealed.

This formulation facilitates attempts to analyze the cultures of power in the former Soviet Union. To understand what happens now, one should know the exact context of power in the past. We face a problem here: Was not Stalin the despot who used violence efficiently and who was visible to all, like Louis XVI of France? What capillary resistance – if any – did this evoke, and how did it influence the habitus of the Soviet people? It would be too simple to attribute violence to Stalin's personality: The existence of a gulag type of institution cannot be personal or historical caprice (Hacking, 1989, p. 37). Waltzer (1989, p. 63) draws attention to the fact that the Communist regime exercised power and control from the very heart of the social system and not from what Foucault calls the *capillaries,* that is, from the center, not the extremities. The crucial question is, then, why the brutal and visible exercise of power was able to win even though the subtle system had proven itself to be more suitable for modern society. Was the new socialist country not sufficiently modern to utilize the subtle modes of control?

The model of dual dependence posited by Böröcz (1992) may provide one answer to this question. If political and military expansion exists without a respective extension of the open forms of exchange (open trading and exchange of information, democratic elections), a movement toward totalitarianism will probably ensue. However, the picture of absolute control under Stalinism does not remain totally flawless. Soviet society was a huge conglomerate of divergent institutions in the 1920s. Although the regime could effectively suppress individuals and even nationalities, it was less efficient in controlling semiautonomous institutions such as the army and the *oblasts,* the various compartments of administration. This middle belt of the Soviet regime, known as the *nomenklatura,* had the most durable grasp on power. It was independent of the immediate control of central rule and could reproduce its position even in the later postsocialist order. In fact, there was a capillary form of power that still seems to exist.

The failure of *perestroika* can be related to this continuum of bureaucratic power that is the heir of Peter the Great's administrative order. It seems that the plan–command system provoked cynicism, indifference, aggression, and privatism, which the short period of *perestroika* was not able to eliminate. So, the curious alternation of advance and regression, which made the movement of *perestroika* so puzzling for Zinchenko (1989), was perhaps linked with the dynamics of intuitive and widely scattered capillary resistance, and was therefore very difficult to cope with politically.

The final part of this discussion is dedicated to the question of creative resistance and continuity of an intellectual tradition under these circumstances of oppression. When considering the strong intellectual tradition that existed in Russia in the 19th century, it seems improbable that the generative capacity of the intellectual habitus could have been fully blocked even during the last 70 years. In fact, brutal and visible political control can efficiently suffocate the expression of opinions, but it is usually unable to penetrate intimate modes of thinking (although identification with power is also a known defense mechanism). The situation was quite different in the Brezhnevian period, in which control was less manifest and perhaps more manipulative. In Brezhnevian society, individuals spoke in the public sphere very differently from the way they thought – a situation reminiscent of the milieu of *Wittgenstein's Vienna* at the beginning of this century; only that which was not said had significance (Janik & Toulmin, 1973). But the rapid return of intellectuals to the stage of Russian political life indicates that a critical tradition has survived in some form: in family circles, in distant libraries, in small, informal groups. In addition, no homogeneity of the Russian personality is now detectable, as might have been expected after such a long rule by a regime demanding conformity.

But the hindering of initiative in this social structure cannot be denied either. Yurevich (1989) describes the "dual dependence" of the discipline of psychology in the USSR: its seemingly rationalistic role and hidden social ties. Psychology was widely dependent on the modes of dominance and power in the socialist state, which nevertheless were ignored in psychological research and writing. Instead, a scientistic and highly abstract conception of psychology was introduced, claims Yurevich. One consequence was the isolation of psychological phenomena from the nuclear domains of social reality such as politics or the economy. This may also explain why the psychological roots of the personality cult still lack a systematic analysis in Russia. A parallel critique has been expressed by Radzikhovskii (1991), who maintains that Soviet psychology needed no external control from the 1950s on because it had become a self-censuring system.

Though one can agree with Radzikhovskii in that there is more space for pluralism in the West, one should not ignore the fact that many seminal lines of psychological thinking in the West have been condemned to a peripheral academic role (e.g., the ideas of Georg Herbert Mead, Henri Wallon, Georges Politzer, Theodor Adorno, Maurice Halbwachs, and even Freud, whose works have much less influence than standard applications of the experimental or differential psychological method). Freedom to express unpopular scientific ideas surely exists, but it is often applied at the extremes of the academic establishment where the midday sun of the mainstream does not shine brightly.

Despite this, the creative attitude rooted in the long-term processes of society is very enduring. As Bauer (1952) noted in *The New Man in Soviet Psychology*, a common mistake in the West was the belief that everything published in Soviet psychology bore an ideological stamp. In fact, one cannot but appreciate the pluralism in psychological thinking that evolved even during Stalinism. For example, while Rubinstein published his *Principles of General Psychology* in 1948, Pjotr Anokhin, in the same year, was developing his ideas on the image-based regulation of nervous activity. Under a Pavlovian disguise, versatile scientific traditions were developed (Kozulin, 1984).

"Long duration" and the temporal prospects of individuals

It seems that humans alter their manifest economic, political, and intellectual opinions swiftly when a revolution occurs and the overt forms of political power are replaced by new ones. This was clearly displayed in the attitudinal changes that Priit Järve (1989) reported in Estonia during the first years of *glasnost*. But the direction of political development has diverged strongly in the different postsocialist communities. In countries where the influence of the central power was embedded deeply in different networks of society, transformation is concomitantly rougher. One might ask, for instance, if Ceaucescu's sensational execution in 1990 actually safeguarded the capillary systems of power. It seems to have eliminated few of the political antagonisms displayed in developments in Romania.

If a total change occurs in the structure of power and no moral system emerges in which people can place their trust, a cultural vacuum develops that cannot resist the subsequent expansion of commercialism or anti-intellectualism. The situation may be different, for example, in Estonia, where there has been a revival of the intellectual values that were typical some 50 years ago (moderate religiosity, a form of petit bourgeois entrepreneurship, strong patriotism).

Though changes have been rapid, developments also expose continuities. Peeters seems to view the recent changes in Eastern Europe as a shift in the balance of power rather than a result of a deep dialectical process. Even the most unexpected changes may display a revival of old patterns of behavior and, thus, the aspects of "long duration" (Peeters, 1990). As such, a revival of old values may even act as a restraint on modern Western consciousness.

However this may be, deeply inculcated strategies of habitus – such as patterns of opposition, fears, and habits of economic behavior – may survive for decades despite overt political change. This also explains why the different postsocialist countries have such divergent models of change. Each period seems to involve a certain bottom layer of historical and social facts, which often remains neglected in contemporary research. If, therefore, one wishes to reveal the potentials for development in Russia, Poland, Germany, or Europe in general, these bottom layers should also be taken into account.

How much, then, can the future activities of people be influenced? Psychologists do not usually give advice on how revolutions should be conducted. Their role is predominantly that of specialists rather than of intellectuals or donators of blows. However, Foucault stresses that in addition to political forms of power there exists the power of truth. He describes the earlier model of the "universal" intellectual. This was the man of justice, the man of law, who opposed power and despotism (Foucault, 1981). The 1960s were perhaps the last historical manifestation of this prominent type of intellectual; in Eastern Europe it still plays an important role.

Since the 1960s, there has been an accelerated movement toward "specific" intellectuals, toward the savant/expert who exercises the power of truth only in a limited field. The chance that experts, such as psychologists, will have an effect on development depends on their capacity to deal with specific problems of health, the environment, or social policy. The vital point here would be to separate the different forms of power from each other. Foucault emphasizes that truth is of the world; it has been produced under multiple constraints. For him, the problem is not so much a question of emancipating truth from every power system but rather of detaching the power of truth from all other forms of hegemony: social, economic, and cultural (Foucault, 1981). In psychology, this kind of extraction of truth should include the reevaluation of static, person-centered methodologies and the introduction of cultural and dialogical approaches.

As some systems collapse, a fundamental process of integration also occurs in Europe. Integration is not limited to the economic coordination of nations but also contains the idea of open cultural and social exchange. The direction of development depends on the openness of the system of interaction through which ideas are circulated. Maurice Halbwachs (1938/1972), who stressed the collective aspect of creation in his psychological studies, vividly describes the conditions under which dialectical thinking originated in classical antiquity. It was in this historical milieu that the method gained its shape, not directly from Plato or Socrates but from their contact with the Sophists. "Dialectics was constructed in a very open and mobile society in which it reached not only individuals but also schools, where it confronted the ordeals and doctrines elaborated in different areas of Greece, Asia or Italy" (Halbwachs, 1938/1975, p. 145). A superior form of logic was constructed, a collective creation that carried the spirit of the ensemble of its developers. Could the model for cooperation in a future Europe resemble this?

References

Adamski, W. (1982). Structural and generational aspects of a social conflict. *Sisyphus Sociological Studies, III*, 49–57.

Bauer, R. W. (1952). *The new man in Soviet psychology*. London: Oxford University Press.

Bergson, H. (1985). *Denken und schöpferisches Werden*. ("Le Pensée et le Mouvant," 1946). Frankfurt am Main: Syndikat.

Billig, M. (1991). *Ideology and opinions: Studies in rhetorical psychology*. London: Sage.

Böröcz, J. (1992). Dual dependency and property vacuum. Social change on the state socialist semiperiphery. *Theory and Society, 21*, 77–104.

Bourdieu, P. (1990). *The logic of practice*. Cambridge: Polity Press.

Bourdieu, P. (1992). Thinking about limits. *Theory, Culture & Society, 9*, 37–49.

Braudel, F. (1959). Histoire et sciences sociales. La longue durée. *Annales économes, sociétés, civilisations, 13*, 725–753.

Ebbinghaus, H. (1920). *Abriss der Psychologie*. Berlin and Leipzig: Walter de Gruyter.

Elias, N. (1977). Adorno-Rede: Respekt und Kritik. In N. Elias & W. Lepenies (Eds.), *Zwei Reden anlässlich der Verleihung des Theodor W. Adorno-Preises 1977* (pp. 37–68). Frankfurt am Main: Suhrkamp.

Engel, J. (1981). *The creative imagination. Enlightenment to romanticism*. Cambridge, MA, and London: Harvard University Press.

Foucault, M. (1980). *Power/knowledge. Selected interviews and other writings 1972–1977* (C. Gordon, Ed.). New York: Pantheon Books.

Foucault, M. (1981). Truth and power. In C. C. Lemert (Ed.), *French sociology* (pp. 293–307). New York: Columbia University Press.

Goodnow, J. (1990). Using sociology to extend psychological accounts of cognitive development. *Human Development, 33*, 81–107.

Hacking, I. (1989). The archeology of Foucault. In D. C. Hoyn (Ed.), *Foucault: A critical reader* (pp. 51–68). Oxford: Basil Blackwell.

Halbwachs, M. (1972). La psychologie collective du raisonnement. In M. Halbwachs, *Classes sociales et morphologie* (pp. 164–173). Paris: Les Editions Minuit. (Originally published in 1938)

Häyrynen, L. (1992). How architects look on their history. In P. Korvenmaa (Ed.), *History of Finnish architects on their first centenary* (pp. 233–253). Helsinki: Rakennuskirja Oy.

Häyrynen, Y.-P. (1981). Tutkiva ajattelu ja korkeakoulujen sisäinen käytäntö (Explorative thinking and the implicit practice of universities). *Tiede ja Edistys, 1,* 55–59.

Häyrynen, Y.-P. (1987). The life contents and social types of Finnish intellectuals. In R. Eyerman, L. G. Svensson, & T. Söderqvist (Eds.), *Intellectuals, universities and the state in western modern societies* (pp. 211–234). Berkeley: University of California Press.

Häyrynen, Y.-P. (1989). Life trajectory, impact of university and intellectual position: 1965–1982. In M. A. Luszcz & T. Nettelbeck (Eds.), *Psychological development: Perspectives across the life-span* (pp. 345–355). Amsterdam: North-Holland.

Inglehart, R. (1990). *Culture shift.* Princeton: Princeton University Press.

Janik, A., & Toulmin, S. (1973). *Wittgenstein's Vienna.* New York: Simon & Schuster.

Järve, P. (1989). Attitude change in Estonia during *perestroika.* Poster presentation at the ISBD International Congress on Research into Development, Jyväskylä.

Joravsky, D. (1989). *Russian psychology: A critical history.* Oxford: Basil Blackwell.

Kohn, M. L., & Schooler, C. (Eds.). (1983). *Work and personality: An inquiry into the impact of social stratification.* Norwood: Ablex.   •

Kozulin, A. (1984). *Psychology in Utopia: Toward a social history of Soviet psychology.* Cambridge, MA: MIT Press.

Leont'ev, A. N. (1977). Activity and consciousness. In *Philosophy in the USSR: Problems of dialectical materialism* (pp. 180–202). Moscow: Progress.

Peeters, H. F. M. (1984). Theoretical orientations in a historical psychology. In K. J. Gergen & M. M. Gergen (Eds.), *Historical social psychology* (pp. 61–82). Hillsdale: Lawrence Erlbaum.

Peeters, H. F. M. (1990). *The life-span as a sequence of diachronic interactions.* Paper presented at the 2nd International Congress for Research in Activity Theory, Lahti, May 1990.

Peeters, H. F. M. (1991). Sosiaalisen konstruktivismin mahdollisuudet ja rajat (Possibilities and limits of social constructivism). *University of Joensuu Psychological Reports No. 12.*

Peeters, H. F. M., Gielis, M., & Caspers, C. (1988). *Historical behavioural sciences: A guide to the literature.* Tilburg, the Netherlands: Tilburg University Press.

Radzikhovskii, L. A. (1988). The dialogic quality of consciousness in the works of M. M. Bakhtin. *Soviet Psychology, 26*(1), 3–28.

Radzikhovskii, L. A. (1991). The historical meaning of the crisis in psychology. *Soviet Psychology, 24*(4), 71–96.

Riegel, K. (1979). *Psychology mon amour: A countertext.* Boston: Houghton Mifflin.

Rubinstein, S. L. (1977). *Grundlagen der Allgemeinen Psychologie.* Berlin: Volk und Wissen. (Original work published in Russian in 1948)

Rubinstein, S. L. (1989). The principle of creative self-activity (philosophical foundations of modern pedagogy). *Soviet Psychology, 27*(3), 6–21. (Original work published in 1919)

Sabour, M. (1988). Homo Arabicus academicus. *University of Joensuu Publications in Social Sciences,* No. 11.

Venn, C. (1984). The subject of psychology. In J. Henriques, W. Jollway, C. Urwin, C. Venn, & W. Walkerdine (Eds.), *Changing the subject* (pp. 119–152). London: Methuen.

Wallon, H. (1951). Psychologie et materialisme dialéctique. *Societa, 2.* Reprinted as Psychology and dialectical materialism. *International Journal of Mental Health* (1971), *4,* 75–79.

Waltzer, M. (1989). The politics of Michel Foucault. In D. C. Hoyn (Ed.), *Foucault: A critical reader* (pp. 51–68). Oxford: Basil Blackwell.

Wertsch, J. V. (1991). *Voices of the mind: A sociocultural approach to mediated action.* London: Harvester Wheatsheaf.

Yurevich, A. V. (1989). Influence of social factors on psychology and problems of perestroika. *Soviet Journal of Psychology, 10*(2), 3–13.

Zinchenko, V. P. (1989). Psychology – perestroika. *Soviet Psychology, 27*(5), 5–28.

9 Activity theory and the concept of integrative levels

Ethel Tobach

Introduction

The work and theory of Vygotsky (1978, 1987), Luria (1966, 1987), and Leont'ev (1978) reflect their commitment to dialectical and historical materialism. This commitment led to their interest in the phylogeny as well as the ontogeny of the activity of organisms. The personal and societal histories of these three leaders in human science did not make it possible for them to be aware of complex developments in the study of the evolution of behavior.

Vygotsky was clearly knowledgeable about the most well-known research in primate behavior, but the significant theoretical controversies about such work were to occur after his lifetime. Luria and Leont'ev were equally well read in the European and North American literature. However, they also were part of the Soviet scientific community and reflected the dominant thinking in the biological and physiological disciplines. Soviet scientists by and large accepted the traditional division between "animals" and humans; although humans had some "lower animal instincts, drives and emotions," they were reflective primarily of societal processes (Graham, 1987). The history of this view in relation to Marx, Engels, and Lenin requires its own treatment, but it is fair to say that it was the view held by those three dialectical materialists, as well as by Vygotsky, Luria, and Leont'ev (the "Troika" of activity theory).

This belief by the Troika does not detract from their significant development of human activity theory based on historical and dialectical materialism. It is possible, however, that some consideration of more recent thinking is warranted. One example of contemporary thought is the concept of *integrative levels*, an application of dialectical and historical materialism to the evolution and development of behavior.

The vitality of dialectical and historical materialism is at issue today in two of its most creative and useful expressions: activity theory and

133

the concept of integrative levels (Tobach, 1987). These two expressions are interconnected and interdependent. They provide the theory for developing a concomitant practice in the scientific community, in research and training, and in society in general for the struggle against antihuman ideologies and policies. In other words, they provide the guidelines for studying and informing individual humans and society.

The concept of integrative levels has a long history. I am constrained to cite its more modern beginnings: first, the work of Joseph Needham, a biochemist, who formulated the basic premises of the concept in the 1920s; second, the article by Alex Novikoff, also a biochemist, in 1945 in *Science* that was the first clear statement of the concept; and finally, the writings of T. C. Schneirla (1971), a comparative psychologist who specialized in the study of the behavior of ants. Comparative psychology is a subdiscipline of psychology studying the development and evolution of behavior in all living species, including plants, animals other than humans, and humans. The scientific backgrounds of these three psychologists are relevant in light of the interests of the Troika in phylogenetic aspects of activity.

The concept of integrative levels

The concept of integrative levels, as used in this chapter, should not be confused with the terms *levels of organization, hierarchy,* or *stages.* Organizational levels frequently emphasize structure; hierarchy connotes a predetermined relationship of greater or lesser status, as in the societal institutions of religion, the military, or the government; and stages seem more useful in defining developmental processes within categories and are definable in terms of integrative levels.

All matter, beginning with the inanimate, proceeding through intermediate forms that are both inanimate and animate, such as viruses, to the animate forms may be seen as a series of succeeding levels, each level being an integration of structure and function. Each level requires its own methods and instrumentalities and poses its own questions for analysis and study.

I offer the following working definition of *level* to show the concept's dialectical, materialistic, historical nature; its fusion of structure and function; and its basis in process and change.

A level is a temporal–spatial relationship of structures whose functions are sufficiently synthesized to be categorized as an entity. This structural–functional relationship, though temporally integrated or synthesized, is sufficiently antithetical, synchronous, or dissonant at the same time for the changing internal contradictions to produce a new level. This new level subsumes the preceding level. Thus levels are related to each other dialectically. Levels are serial, sequential, and successive. The succession explicates the temporal, processural contradictions within the structural–functional integration of each level, temporally and processually.

The conceptualization of matter as a series of integrated levels is one formulation by humans attempting to use their knowledge of the world. They develop categories through their activity with the inanimate and animate levels. They formulate categories to deal with the multiple quantities and qualities of their activity in that world. One such category is the category *organism*. The organism may be defined as the integrated structural–functional, spatial–temporal relationship of several levels beginning with the molecular biochemical level (e.g., genes and proteins in subcellular processes). As the internal contradictions of these molecules counter outer biochemical contradictions of other subcellular processes, they produce new structural–functional processes that become the succeeding level, a cell; the cells become integrated into tissues (new level), into organs, into physiological systems (such as the nervous system or the reproductive system). These levels are subsumed in the structural–functional, spatial–temporal integration category of organism. Each level requires its own methods of study. One would not study hormonal titers of the organism with a paper-and-pencil questionnaire addressed to some physiological or biochemical function; one would not do a blood test or karotype to study the organism's solution of a visual-spatial discrimination problem.

The causal relationship between and among levels is derived first from the contradictions within each level and then from the contradictions between the inner contradictions of any one level and its contraditions with preceding and succeeding levels. The causal relationship between and among levels is dialectical and multidirectional.

For example, an individual provokes an angry comment by a supervisor (the process may be entered for analysis at any stage of its development). This activity by the two individuals may be viewed in terms of at least two categories, each with its own series of integrative levels: the organism (the worker as one; the supervisor as the other) and social behavior (the relationships between the worker and the supervisor). Each individual organism is the integration of intraorganismic levels described earlier, with the succeeding psychological level for the category of human organism. The contradictions among these intraorganismic levels become sharpened in contradiction with the external social category, changing the relationship among the levels in terms of which is the major or minor contradictory.

In the organism category, the changes on the psychological level (most immediately, the contradictory of the social level) act on the physiological level (endocrine and neural systems), changing the biochemical level (adrenal hormones and neurotransmitters), effecting a change back to the subsuming physiological level (neuromusculature), resulting in change in the facial muscles, presenting an adequate change (social stimulus) to the supervisor. This changes the integration of the social behavior category, leading to a further development of the angry interchange. In the category of social behavior, the intraorganismic changes are integrated in the component individuals in the category relevant to the worker–supervisor relationship. The intraorganismic psychological level subsuming all the intraorganismic levels then brings about changes in the biochemical level, as well as the physiological level. Again, the physiological level functions upward to the psychological level, which functions downward to the physiological level, and so forth.

To understand fully the processes occurring on all levels, knowledge of the history of the individuals involved is also necessary (societal category). Causal explanations are not only dialectically "upward" and "downward" among levels but also interdependent with other categories in relation to the category being investigated.

The concept and method of levels of integration may be applied to any category. The definition of the levels, that is, how a fundamental, earlier level leads to succeeding levels and how these are integrated, makes it possible to define a category. Levels should be unique to a category and offer explanations of causality only within the category.

Categories, however, may act as external contradictions to each other, sharpening the internal contradictions of the relationship among levels within the categories. This is one process in which discontinuities are introduced. The following is an example of such relationships among categories and their levels.

There are three significant categories among other categories in the category "evolution of behavior." They are interdependent and interconnected in such a way that at every level within them, they bring about new levels within the other categories. Each category represents a behavioral continuum in evolution that becomes discontinuous as the other categories sharpen the inner contradictions within each category.

These three continuities, or categories, are (1) activity, (2) social behavior/organization, and (3) control of environmental change (environment comprising abiotic or nonliving and biotic or living processes). The interconnectedness and interdependencies of these three categories are evident in the evolution of intraorganismic morphological/physiological levels, particularly in the evolution of neural systems.

Two categories: Social organization/behavior and environmental control

The continuities and discontinuities in two of these categories, the social behavior/organization category and the environmental control category, will be discussed briefly and then related to the category of activity.

By definition, a living organism is one that reproduces itself. It is therefore not surprising that every species, beginning with blue-green algae, once thought to reproduce only by fission, or splitting in two, must at some time in its life cycle mix the gametes of one organism with the gametes of another to reproduce. Thus, there is no species that is not social at some time in its history: That is, it engages in an activity involving another organism, but the quality of its social activity is reproductive. The forms and activities involved in reproduction at succeeding species levels become increasingly subsumed within other types of interindividual activity (e.g., feeding, anti-predation). As the contradiction between reproductive and nonreproductive social behavior sharpens, the continuity of the category social behavior/organization becomes discontinuous on different phyletic levels and social behavior differentiates from reproductive behavior. These changing relationships within the levels of the category of social behavior/organization have been ignored or misinterpreted by ethologists and sociobiologists, who reduce social behavior to genetic perpetuation and make reproductive behavior dominant on all phyletic levels, including humans (Dawkins, 1976).

The category of behavioral environmental control applies to all forms of life and is evident in the earliest forms as the taxic behavior of acellular organisms. That is, organisms that are not attached to the substrate change location as a function of physical and chemical changes in the environment; they move toward or away from the gradient of change. An amoeba forms a pseudopod or "false foot," and moves to a particular chemical change in the environment whether the source of the chemical is another living organism, an amoeba of the same group, or not, or whether the chemical change is from an abiotic source, such as one produced by heat or light, from which it will withdraw or approach. The quantity and nature of the physical/chemical changes at the membrane surface constitute the external contradiction that sharpens the contradiction of the protoplasmic state on the other side (inner) of the membrane. This produces a change in the internal structure/function to produce a pseudopod. The integrative level is molecular/biochemical. The change in the organism's relationship to the environment, and the level of its environmental control, are limited.

As the individual members of a species act on and in their environment, the consequences of such actions become integrated intraorganismically, bringing about changes in structure/function on all levels from molecular to morphological/physiological systems. In the course of these evolutionary changes, the category of environmental control proceeds through succeeding levels of integration. Following the limited control of its environment by acellular individuals and other early organisms, at succeeding phyletic levels the organism's relation with the environment becomes more directed and selective as a function of past experience (adequate change with more than a trace [transient] effect on the organism). At succeeding phyletic levels, not only does the act change the organism's environment, but the activity itself becomes associated with the consequences (contingency), thus producing a new level in the category of environmental control: Goal-directed behavior and planning activity in regard to environmental control are now possible.

At this level, that is, goal-directed activity, the organism controls its environment not only by leaving it or staying in it (a taxis) but also by changing the environment actively, not merely by the concomitant effects of metabolism or taxis. This new level of planned problem-solving control of the environment produces new external contradictions. The activity controlling the environment changes the organism's relationship with conspecifics (major contradictions, e.g., spatial distribution between nests and communal foraging), as well as other biotic aspects of the environment (minor contradiction, e.g., plant material for nesting). Thus, as the category of environmental control evolves in succeeding, subsuming levels, the category of social organization/behavior changes also: The two categories sharpen each other's contradictions, facilitating the production of new levels in each. For example, cooperation in hunting is accompanied by increasingly interdependent social organization/behavior in wolves (Kleiman & Eisenberg, 1973).

One of the significant discontinuities of social behavior/organization as a function of the discontinuity in the category of environmental control is the increasing dependence of the individual on the group for survival.

In the human species, a new level of interdependence between the individual and the group was produced. Environmental changes produced objects to ensure survival of the object (e.g., sponge made to obtain water by an orangutan). This new level of environmental change is labor, or work, and by the production of this level in the category of environmental change, the contradictions within the category of social organization/behavior were sharpened, bringing about a new level, that is, society. These new levels, labor and society, are concomitant with the new level of "human" in the category of primates. Societies have their own laws of development, different from those of the social process on other phyletic levels. This new level, uniquely different in its quality, is demonstrated by the following.

It is a truism that species cannot survive unless individuals survive to reproduce viable offspring that can reproduce. However, the leap from the preeminence of reproduction on previous levels to the preeminence of labor on the human level as a necessity for perpetuating the human species represents a significant discontinuity.

The social processes pertinent to life processes (biological processes) mandatory for human survival are qualitatively different from those of other species, as they exist on the societal level. That is, societal practices for the care of offspring, while subsuming incubation and feeding (nursing), are significantly different from those of other species. Discontinuity in the social behavior/organization category at the human level is also evidenced by the qualities of the materials, methods, and spatial/temporal characteristics of the exchanges between and among individuals. This discontinuity is defined by the accumulation, storage, and retrievability of artifacts of past experiences and knowledge in symbolic form that make it possible for different generations and different populations to continue in societal relationships that are not spatially or temporally restricted in the present and future.

The third category: Activity

For Marx (Livergood, 1967) and Engels, the centrality of activity made the philosophical categories of dialectical and historical materialism definable. Activity (change) as a category is an expression of the fundamental quality of all matter. The succeeding levels of integration in the category of change of inanimate matter are relevant insofar as the process of change is continuous into animate matter. The activities (changes) or subatomic particles in inanimate matter are subsumed in the integration of succeeding complex matter, as in amino acids, a level in the category of animate matter. The contradictions of change produce new structural/functional integrations, or new levels. In this process of change and level production, mesolevels are produced. Two examples of such mesolevels are the virus, a level between the inanimate and animate levels in the category of matter, and euglena between the levels of plants and animals in the category of animate matter. The leap of discontinuity is seen at every level, including the genetic level. For example, gene function in eukaryotes (animal) is very different from that in prokaryotes (plant).

Within the category of change-activity in animals, the continuity that exists throughout all species, from the earliest acellular ones to the human species, is the energy transformations of living matter. These transformations are brought about through the opposition of the inner contradictions of the organism's environment. Such change, that is, metabolic change, is termed *passive* and is not considered activity by Leont'ev (1978).

It should be noted, however, that this passive activity is the fundamental level of all living organisms. As such, its penetration into all succeeding levels of integration is significant. For example, in dealing with hunger, drive, and motivation, the use of the concept of integrative levels describes this fundamental activity as the primary contradictory in succeeding levels. The metabolic change in the cells that store fat, functioning on the biochemical level, produces substances that are integrated in the tissues, organs, and physiological structure/functions to change the integrative function of the neural system. The psychological level of integration subsuming these changes makes goal-directed foraging and feeding possible. The primary contradictory on the biochemical level becomes a minor contradictory on the psychological level when the organism feeds past satiation in a socially facilitative situation, a well-known human behavior.

The amoeba may produce a pseudopod that will pull it away from or propel it to a new environment in which the by-products of its metabolism will be sufficiently diluted so as not to challenge its survival. In a meeting room, everyone is changing the environment by virtue of metabolic by-products. But the human response to these environmental changes (e.g., an increase in ambient temperature) is not to produce pseudopods, or even to withdraw from the room, if the societal level is dominant. Rather, the level of integration in the category of activity in this instance, for humans, involves developing appropriate ventilation systems to deal with environmental change.

The changing quality of activity from passive to active is reflected in the production of new levels. The activity category may be phyletic or ontogenetic (Tobach, 1981). The phyletic category has been discussed here in an effort to clarify the relationship among different integrative levels of activity in the organism and in the individual when applying activity theory to human psychology. The goal-directed activity of the human, the societally conscious, historical materialist activity of the human, subsumes the preceding levels of activity, both intraorganismically and phyletically. The contradictory relationships are integrated at each level in the production of new levels, changing the primacy of the contradictions. At the human level, societal consciousness becomes the dominant (major) contradiction. In a new species, the relatively passive, taxic nature of the earlier level of activity was integrated into a new level of activity, a discontinuity in which activity became directional in its interconnectedness and interdependence with the internal and external contradictions through neural systems. These new structural/functional levels in neural-type functions were seen in early multicellular organisms like hydra and social insects. These performed modified directional activities in feeding and reproduction based on associated past experience. These new levels of speciation, expressed in the activity of the organism in its social behavior/organization, in its control of the environment resulting from the discontinuity of contingency activity described earlier, were qualitatively different. Differences in activity meant planning and definition of goals and brought about new levels in the category of activity, as seen in later vertebrate phyletic levels.

The interdependent external contradictions among the three categories brought about discontinuities within all three categories: activity, social organization/behavior, and environmental control. At the same time, the contradictions among the three categories brought about intraorganismic changes on all phyletic levels. These are seen in the new discontinuities in the physiological/morphological structure/function not only of the nervous system, but also of the skeletal, muscular, respiratory, and hormonal systems, in fact at every intraorganismic level. These changes are seen in other categories, such as communication, leading to the level of language, and in the category of problem solving, leading to creative, cognitive, integrative levels. These, in turn, lead to new processes of control of the environment through social activity, consciousness, and labor.

These new levels, discontinuous and unique, are the delineated historical materialist processes of the dialectical materialist category of activity. Each of these new levels – communication (i.e., language), social behavior/organization (i.e., society), and environmental control (i.e., consciousness and labor) – evolve and may be defined as new categories, each of which must be defined in terms of its own levels of integration. The levels within the categories of language, society, consciousness, labor, and human activity need to be defined (Tobach, 1987, 1990b).

The evolutionary history of the category of activity shows its continuity and discontinuity in all living organisms, including humans. Unfortunately, the relation between the evolutionary or biological history of human activity and the societal or epistemological history of human activity is often described as dichotomous. This dichotomy is posed generally as follows: Human activity (consciousness, language, and labor) is genetically determined (evolutionary, biological) or human activity (consciousness, language, and labor) is a process of socialization.

The former ideology espouses genetic or hereditarian explanations of all behavior. Its proponents seem to have difficulty dealing with observable processes that are simultaneous and changing. They

1. cannot understand the true relationship between physiological activities expressed in metabolism, brain function, and simultaneous mental/cognitive/socialized conscious activity in which abstract ideas, symbols, and so on are used.
2. attempt to reduce all behavior to the biochemical level: They say that, as living organisms, humans, like all other organisms, are simply the vehicles through which genes operate to reproduce themselves and produce successive generations of genes. In other words, social behavior is ultimately and primarily reproductive behavior.
3. confuse the results of evolution, that is, the presence of species, with the causes – a rather old and simple error in logic.

The emphasis on reproduction (perpetuation of the gene) as the primary process in behavioral evolution has had a cooling effect on investigation of the processes whereby the unique characteristics of the human species may have evolved, such as labor, language, and consciousness. It has also resulted in a distortion of the relationship between life processes (biology) and social processes (social science). Humans may have physiological and biochemical processes in common with other species, but these factors have different significance in the context of the complex societal processes of political economy and culture, that is, the societal infrastructure and superstructure that are characteristic only of the human level.

Activity theory and the concept of integrative levels are views that are contrary to genetic determinism. The roots of activity theory and the concept of integrative levels are in dialectical and historical materialism, whereas the roots of genetic determinism are in reductionism, logical positivism, idealism, and scientific materialism.

Who are the proponents of the genetic determinist-hereditarian views? The Nobel Prize winner Konrad Lorenz best represented the ethological views that the explanation of human behaviors such as aggression, sex differences in parenting, and group formation could be extrapolated from what ethologists called the "instinctive, inherited, innate, inborn" behavior patterns described in animals (Lorenz, 1970, 1971; see also Lehrman, 1953). Today ethology is an accepted, accredited, and honored ideology in biology, psychology, psychiatry, anthropology, sociology, and so on in all academic and scientific communities in the world. There are those who profess a neoethology that involves developmental explanations of behavior. But these explanations are based on the concept that genes determine developmental patterns (Hinde, 1988).

Another expression of genetic determinism is *sociobiology*. J. P. Scott originally defined sociobiology as "the interdisciplinary science which lies between the fields of biology (particularly ecology and physiology) and psychology and sociology" (Scott, 1950, p. 1004). The term *sociobiology* has undergone significant reformulation, however. The first phase of this process was W. D. Hamilton's (1964) interpretation of evolutionary theory, which led to axiomatic formulations of the relationship between biology and social behavior. E. O. Wilson (1975) provided a new contextual meaning of sociobiology derived from Hamilton's work by analyzing human nature and society from a scientific materialistic approach.

C. J. Lumsden and E. O. Wilson (1981) then defined sociobiology as the "systematic study of the biological basis of all forms of social behavior, including sexual behavior and parent–offspring interaction, in all kinds of organisms." They elaborated this meaning further by postulating gene–culture coevolution, which provides an "internally consistent network of causal explanation between biology and the social sciences" (p. 243). Central to this proposal is the *culturegene,* defined by them as "the basic unit of culture. A relatively homogeneous set of artifacts, behaviors and mentifacts (mental constructs . . .)" (p. 268). These "are processed through a sequence of epigenetic rules" (p. 7) that are "ultimately genetic in basis" and channel "the development of an anatomical, physiological, cognitive, or behavioral trait in a particular direction" (p. 370). Gene–culture coevolution is governed by natural selection and genetic fitness, so that "human cultural transmission is ultimately gene–cultural transmission" (p. 24). Although Lumsden and Wilson propose that gene–culture co-evolution permits flexibility, individuality, and mechanisms for culture change, they state that "the genes hold culture on a leash" (p. 375).

In the sociobiological ideology, language, cognition, consciousness, and labor are mechanisms evolved to perpetuate the human species. Variations among individuals and populations are all to be attributed to and explained by natural selection and genetic fitness.

How do these ideologies relate to an alternative view that can be based on the interdependent and interconnected processes and concepts of activity and integrative levels?

In the United States today and in many other industrialized nations, the struggle against racism and sexism requires an alternative scientific explanation for individual differences and societal variation. The public is easily convinced that "success" (in other words, achievement of the ownership of goods and services) is based on such irrelevancies as skin pigmentation, ethnic identity, or possession of feminine or masculine reproductive systems. These ideologies are expressed in consciousness and societal activity, as well as in language.

Sexist and racist theory and practice are societally engendered. The scientific community is continuously engaged and supported in research to justify racism and sexism.

One of the most lucrative enterprises for scientific research is the plethora of twin studies designed to prove that genes can overcome any experiences the individual may have during the course of development. These studies, when scrutinized, are poor in their experimental design and procedures, incorrect in the statistical treatment of their faulty data, and specious in the inferences they draw (Bouchard, 1984; Plomin, 1990; see also Tobach, 1990c).

In addition to these studies, there are investigations showing the inferiority of poor African-American and Hispanic-American children compared to children of European background, particularly if Teutonic or Anglo-Saxon.

The third area of research designed to bolster genetic determinism is research concerning differences in the neurophysiology of women and men, in their psychophysical perceptions, and so on in which women come off a poor second in the allegedly important aspects of human activity.

Should one argue against understanding the relationships among different levels of integration, including genetic, physiological, and psychological/societal? Not at all.

There are many ways to understand genetic function. However, to extrapolate from the biochemical level of the gene to the societal level of political values (as some of the twin studies do) is patently questionable as good science.

The concepts of integrative levels and activity are most helpful in presenting an alternative approach. For example, to understand the pathways through which the genes are expressed in structure, through the function (activity) of the developing organism that lead to the uniqueness of each individual, is important. The geneticists have made it clear: Each organism is genetically unique. Having large numbers of genes in common does not predict the variation possible among species; then why should this sharing of genes between individuals be any more significant? There are behavioral continuities between the apes and the human; they also have many genes in common. However, the differences in behavior among the different categories of apes themselves, and the differences between them and humans, demonstrate the significance of the discontinuities in a small number of genetic structures and the qualitatively great discontinuities in behavior.

The powerful toolkit of dialectical and historical materialism, particularly as expressed in activity theory and the concept of integrative levels, can be effectively used in the arena of societal policy. The natural world is not chaotic; it has profound laws that can be studied, defined, and understood. The animate world is self-organizing. But this is because of the inner and outer contradictions that make for change; the self-organizing process also has laws that can be studied and understood.

These tools can help the scientific community contribute to social consciousness and activity in order to do away with the exploitation of peoples based on ethnicity and gender and to help humanity learn to control the environment for its welfare and that of the entire planet.

References

Bouchard, T. (1984). Twins reared together and apart: What they tell us about human diversity. In S. W. Fox (Ed.), *Individuality and determinism: Chemical and biological bases.* New York: Plenum.

Dawkins, R. (1976). *The selfish gene.* Oxford: Oxford University Press.

Graham, L. R. (1987). *Science, philosophy and human behavior in the Soviet Union.* New York: Columbia University Press.

Hamilton, W. D. (1964). The genetical evolution of social behavior. I and II. *Journal of Theoretical Biology, 7,* 1–51.

Hinde, R. A. (1988). *Individuals, relationships and culture: Links between ethology and the social sciences.* Cambridge: Cambridge University Press.

Kleiman, D. G., & Eisenberg, J. F. (1973). Comparisons of canid and felid social systems from an evolutionary perspective. *Animal Behavior, 21,* 637–659.

Lehrman, D. S. (1953). A critique of Lorenz's "objectivistic" theory of animal behavior. *Quarterly Review of Biology, 28,* 337–363.

Leont'ev, A. N. (1978). *Activity, consciousness and personality.* Englewood Cliffs: Prentice-Hall.

Livergood, N. D. (1967). *Activity in Marx' philosophy.* The Hague: Martinus Nijhoff.

Lorenz, K. (1970). *Studies in animal and human behaviour* (Vol. 1). Cambridge, MA: Harvard University Press.

Lorenz, K. (1971). *Studies in animal and human behaviour* (Vol. 2). Cambridge, MA: Harvard University Press.

Lumsden, C. J., & Wilson, E. O. (1981). *Genes, mind and culture: The coevolutionary process.* Cambridge, MA: Harvard University Press.

Luria, A. R. (1966). *Higher cortical functions in man.* New York: Basic Books.

Luria, A. R. (1987). Afterword to the Russian edition. In R. W. Rieber & A. S. Carton (Eds.), *The collected works of L. S. Vygotsky: Vol. I. Problems in general psychology.* New York: Plenum.

Novikoff, A. B. (1945). The concept of integrative levels and biology. *Science, 101,* 209–215.

Plomin, R. (1990). The role of inheritance in behavior. *Science, 248,* 183–188.

Schneirla, T. C. (1971). Selected writings of T. C. Schneirla (L. R. Aronson, E. Tobach, D. S. Lehrman, & J. S. Rosenblatt, Eds.). San Francisco: Freeman.

Scott, J. P. (1950). Foreword. Methodology and techniques for the study of animal societies. *Annals of the New York Academy of Sciences, 51*(10003), 1–5.

Tobach, E. (1981). Evolutionary aspects of the activity of the organism and its development. In R. M. Lerner & N. A. Busch-Rossnagle (Eds.), *Individuals as producers of their development: A lifespan perspective.* New York: Academic Press.

Tobach, E. (1987). Integrative levels in the comparative psychology of cognition, language and consciousness. In G. Greenberg & E. Tobach (Eds.), *Cognition, language and consciousness.* Hillsdale: Lawrence Erlbaum.

Tobach, E. (1990a). Biologie und Sozialwissenschaften. In H. J. Sandkühler & A. Regenbogen (Eds.), *Europäische Enzyklopädie zu Philosophie und Wissenschaften.* Hamburg: Felix Meiner Verlag.

Tobach, E. (1990b). The amoeba and Einstein. In G. Greenberg & E. Tobach (Eds.), *Evolution of knowledge.* Hillsdale: Lawrence Erlbaum.

Tobach, E. (1990c). If it were easy it would have been done: Genetic processes make a hard row to hoe. Commentary on article by P. Roubertoux and C. Capron. *Cahiers de Psychologie Cognitive, 10,* 681–685.

Wilson, E. O. (1975). *Sociobiology: The new synthesis.* Cambridge, MA: Harvard University Press.

Vygotsky, L. S. (1978). *Mind and society: The psychology of higher mental functions* (M. Cole, V. John-Steiner, S. Scribner, & E. Souberman, Eds.). Cambridge, MA: Harvard University Press.

Vygotsky, L. S. (1987). Thinking and speech. In R. W. Rieber & A. S. Carton (Eds.), *The collected works of L. S. Vygotsky: Vol. I. Problems in general psychology.* New York: Plenum.

10 The relevance to psychology of Antonio Gramsci's ideas on activity and common sense

Francesco Paolo Colucci

> *Le bon sens est la chose du monde la mieux partagée.*
> Descartes

Introduction

Common sense is a key concept in the study of man. Its relevance has been further underlined by recent social transformations and political events. Take, for example, the role it played in the collapse of the Communist regimes in Eastern Europe and the breakup of the partitocracy in Italy. In general, common sense orientates and at the same time is the product of activity, a process that includes communication, cooperation, conflict, and negotiation.

Although Gramsci's ideas on common sense are in the tradition of Enlightenment thought, some aspects are remarkably modern and useful in current psychological research. They link up with the problem of social representations, which is now crucial in social cognitive psychology. Furthermore, these ideas are founded on the Marxist concepts of *praxis* and *historicity,* which are in important respects in line with the cultural-historical school founded by the Russian psychologist Vygotsky and, hence, with the concept of *activity* as developed by this psychological school.

I have chosen to concentrate here on Gramsci's ideas in order to help psychologists, well versed in their own fields of research, in making their own observations on the problems put forward. The underlying assumption is that these ideas can serve as a basis for a comparison of different psychological theories, above all between cognitive social psychology and activity theory, and thus contribute to the advance of psychology.

147

The relevance of the problem of common sense in Gramsci

The importance of common sense has been a typical feature of modern culture from its very beginnings. It is linked to the significance attributed to subjectivity or, in other words, the freedom and potentiality of the human subject. In the 18th century, common sense became the main object of study by the Scottish school (Thomas Reid), which formulated this concept in its dispute with Hume and in defense of tradition. On the other hand, it was developed in more problematic and modern terms during the Enlightenment. The questions posed by common sense, its diverse and also conflicting facets, and its "polysemy" are already apparent in the ambiguous, perhaps deliberately ironic, idea expressed by Descartes in the epigraph to this chapter. Moreover, as will be seen, these aspects characterize the way the subject is considered by both Gramsci and the recent literature. It is worthwhile to recall that an important, though short, explanation of the term *sens commun* is found in both Diderot and d'Alembert's *Encyclopédie* and Voltaire's *Dictionnaire Philosophique*. To begin with its definition, common sense was viewed by Enlightenment thinkers as standing in a complex and problematic relation with scientific thought; this is why, in some cases, it was contrasted with the abstruseness of philosophers.

The problem of common sense is not only of central importance in Gramsci's thought, it is also strictly connected with its other essential elements, above all the concepts of praxis and history, and dovetails perfectly with the typically Gramscian use of subjectivity. Particularly with regard to this last aspect, it is significant that in tackling the problem of common sense in his *Prison Notebooks* (*Quaderni del carcere* – hereafter Q.), Gramsci (1975) goes back to "the thought of the 17th and 18th centuries . . . which in reaction to the principle of authority represented by the Bible and Aristotle could not but extol common sense" (Q. 10, p. 1334). At the same time, being a Marxist and living in the 20th century, Gramsci was obviously opposed to the metaphysical concepts of nature and reason and to the consequent "generalizations" that underpinned the Enlightenment.

It is impossible to examine here the importance and the role of the problem of common sense in Marx's writings, where it is often referred to by other terms (*Weltanschauung, ideology*). There is little doubt, however, that the problems of common sense and all its implications have been largely neglected by Marxist culture. This is highly significant since the nonconsideration of common sense and the associated concept of subjectivity or an incorrect consideration (by, for example, idealizing "the people's way of thinking") go hand in hand with the notion of the ineluctable laws of society and historical development and also with the universalized concept of the proletariat. A further result is that this attitude toward subjectivity and, hence, common sense ends up justifying various political practices.

However, the concepts and the political practices that prevailed particularly in the so-called Communist world, with the consequences that have recently become obvious to all, were opposed by Gramsci, who analyzed common sense and underlined its importance. Naturally, this does not in any way mean that Gramsci's thought solves all the problems of Marxism or is free of internal contradictions; nor does it imply that if it had been dominant at the political level, the outcome would have been necessarily positive.

Essential points concerning the problem of common sense in Gramsci

An analysis of the essential points in the Gramscian approach to the problem of common sense, or *spontaneous philosophy*, must take into account the fragmentary and creative nature of the *Quaderni del carcere* and their lack of a systematic structure. The same theme is mentioned and developed in several places in different contexts and with various shades of meaning. It is generally thought, however, that the correct starting point is Gramsci's assertion that his thought derives from the Enlightenment:

It is therefore necessary to demonstrate as a preliminary step that "all men are philosophers" ["*tous sont philosophes*," *Encyclopédie*, heading *Sens Commun*] by defining the limits and characteristics of this "spontaneous philosophy" typical of "everybody"; namely, the philosophy which is contained: 1) in language itself, which is an ensemble of certain notions and concepts and not simply, and only, of words; 2) in common sense and good sense; 3) in popular religion and, thus, also in the entire system of beliefs, superstitions, opinions and ways of seeing and of operating which come out in what is generally called "folklore." Having demonstrated that all men are unconsciously philosophers, though in their own way, since even behind the slightest manifestation of intellectual activity – "language" – lies a particular worldview, we proceed to the second step, that of criticism and awareness. . . . (Q. 11, p. 1375)

Keeping in mind the fundamental role that Gramsci attributes to language when putting forward the problem of common sense, I now attempt to clarify the relation between the latter and good sense. The "sound nucleus" of common sense, good sense "deserves to be developed and made unitary and consistent" (Q. 11, p. 1380). It reveals itself in the "expressions of common language" and consists, moreover, in understanding philosophy above all as an "invitation to reflect, to understand that what happens is basically rational and, as such, must be faced by focusing one's rational powers and not letting oneself be carried away by violent impulses" (ibid.). More important, common sense, inasmuch as it is good sense, is able to "identify in a series of judgments . . . the exact simple cause and is not led astray by metaphysical abstruseness and falsely profound pseudo-scientific elaboration, etc." (Q. 10, p. 1334). Whereas good sense reacts against such cultural degeneration, common sense, in contrast, "purveys Philistinism, mummifies a justified reaction into a permanent state of mind" (Q. 8, pp. 958–959, and Q. 11, pp. 1399, 1483).

To these principal basic elements Gramsci adds more complex distinctions and characteristics that further define common sense in general. Here we start with the distinction between common sense and *folklore*, defined earlier as one of the three components of spontaneous philosophy. Although he frequently uses the terms *common sense* and *folklore* as synonyms, there is an important distinction:

Common sense [which, together with good sense, is "the most widespread conception of life and man" among the different social strata] is not something rigid and immobile, but is continually transformed, enriched with scientific notions and philosophical opinions that have entered the public domain. Common sense is the folklore of philosophy and is always halfway between true folklore (that is, as it is commonly understood) and philosophy, science and the economics of scientists. Common sense creates future folklore, namely a relatively rigid phase of popular knowledge of a certain time and place. (Q. 24, p. 2271, and Q. 1, p. 76; Q. 5, paragraph 156; Q. 9, paragraph 15; Q. 27, paragraphs 1 and 2)

Common sense, in the true meaning of the term, therefore represents, in contrast to folklore, the moment of becoming and of transformation. It must be pointed out, however, that being polysemic good sense, folklore and common sense are present in people's minds in mixed forms, in which one aspect rather than another may predominate. Consequently, common sense may, for instance, appear alien to philosophical abstruseness and hairsplitting, but at the same time may be fatalistic and teleological and conceive the connection between causes and effects in a mechanical way.

In all its aspects (i.e., folklore, but also the changes in common sense and the creation of a "new common sense"), the concept of common sense establishes a nonmechanical relation to what Gramsci means by historicity and "real life conditions." The latter refer to the entire set of characteristics (economic, social, institutional, legal, etc.) of a specific historical period in a specific place. This relation is so important that common sense is sometimes defined by Gramsci as "historical consciousness" (Q. 16, pp. 1874–1875). Since "real life conditions" may be different for the various social groups that make up a particular society, there will be different "historical group consciousnesses." Thus, it is in this context that the connection between social groups and common sense, repeatedly mentioned by Gramsci, assumes importance. Furthermore, this connection poses the "question of conformism": "Due to our own worldview, we always belong to a given group, in precise terms, to the one whose members all share a specific way of thinking and acting. We are conformists of some conformism or other; we are always mass-men or collective-men" (Q. 11, p. 1376).

Gramsci's reference to historicity is, then, intended to oppose a universalistic way of understanding the world as "eternal and unchangeable." This implies rejection of the idea of "generalization as the assumption of homogeneity," which can be traced back to the Enlightenment conception of "nature," and instead the adoption of the idea of "abstraction" as reference point. "Abstraction will always be abstraction of a determinate historical category, viewed precisely as a category and not as a many-sided individuality" (Q. 10, p. 1276). It follows that common sense, and also philosophy, can be understood only through a historical, hence genetic, analysis that shows its origin and formation in the past and the way it is rooted in the real conditions of life. A historical analysis of this type is particularly necessary in order to understand folklore and its importance: "[F]olklore must not be conceived as something bizarre or strange, or as a picturesque element, but as something that is very serious and to be taken seriously" (Q. 5, sect. 156; Q. 9, sect. 15; q. 27, sects. 1 and 2). Common sense as folklore is also a serious matter because it is part of the problem of the complex, and sometimes contradictory, relation between worldviews and rules of conduct (Q. 11, pp. 1378–1380).

Apart from the basic and general characteristic of historicity, common sense/folklore, as it usually appears in social reality, reveals other particular aspects, among which Gramsci insists most on "inconsistency," "contradictoriness," "acriticalness," and "unawareness." Above all, it presents different elements from many sources contemporaneously: for example, elements deriving from ancient religions, popular superstitions, and various past philosophies, but also from recent scientific ideas. The result is that all these elements appear in a jumble of various strata. In short, the predominant characteristics of common sense as folklore are polysemy and polymorphism.[1] The implication is that common sense as folklore may even contain truths. But, with regard to new truths, "common sense is purely misoneist and conservative and if we succeed in penetrating it with a new truth, this is proof that such a truth is powerfully clear and expansive" (Q. 11, p. 1400). Finally, common sense as folklore is characterized by the prevalence of "realistic and materialistic elements," understood as "the immediate product of coarse sensation" (Q. 11, p. 1397).

The next step is to analyze the essential elements in the formation of common sense. As we have already seen, the most important formative factor in common sense is philosophical-scientific thought, which stands in a complex relation with common sense (Q. 10, p. 1280; Q. 11, pp. 1396–1397, 1400). Also highly relevant is the role Gramsci assigns to language: There is a continuity in the passage, which implies a change in meaning, from philosophical and scientific to common language (Q. 8, pp. 958–959). For this reason, language is also an important indicator of common sense and must become an object of analysis: "If it is true that every language contains the elements of a worldview and a culture, it will also be true that from the language of each individual can be judged the greater or lesser complexity of his worldview" (Q. 11, p. 1377).

All Gramscian analysis of common sense, however, is significant inasmuch as its end is the formation of a "conscious," "critical," and "consistent" common sense, consonant with the revolutionary transformation of society. As Gramsci points out, Marx himself insists on this necessity (Q. 11, p. 1400). It involves both the masses and individuals, implying cooperation and conflict between men. Gramsci poses the rhetorical question:

. . . [I]s it preferable to "participate" in a worldview "imposed" by one of the many social groups in which each person is automatically involved from the very moment he enters the conscious world . . . or is it preferable to formulate one's own worldview consciously and critically and thus, in connection with this intense working of one's own mind, to choose one's own sphere of activity, actively participate in producing world history, be one's own guide and not accept in a passive and servile way the hallmark of one's own personality from the outside? (Q. 11, pp. 1375–1376)

As this quotation makes clear, the essential aspect of the "new common sense" consists in its being "critical." Furthermore, "conformism," which for Gramsci must also characterize it, can become meaningful only if we bear in mind that it is set in a dialectical relation with this critical aspect. It is therefore a new and "different" conformism.

The need to form a "new common sense" interacts in a complex way with the "reform" and transformation of society but, at the same time, it helps to prepare and foster the process by acting as a decisive factor for change (in the Western societies to which Gramsci refers).

In general, the coming into being and the transformation of common sense or, more precisely, the formation of the new common sense brings us once more to the centrality of the concept of *historicity*. Gramsci maintains that historicity is the criterion of validity for ideas, worldviews, and philosophies. Some of the causes singled out by Gramsci to explain the diffusion of new worldviews could be defined as psychological: As well as the "authority of the exhibitor" or the "authoritative element" (what is nowadays called *authority of the source*), there is the "rational form" in which the new concept is exhibited. But he reaffirms that the presupposition of the diffusion of new concepts is of the "political and social expectation type." This means, above all, that "adherence by the masses to an ideology, or their non-adherence, is the way in which real criticism of the rationality and historicity of ways of thinking occurs" and that "the mental constructs which correspond to the needs of a complex and organic historical period always end up by asserting themselves and prevailing even if through many intermediate phases" (Q. 11, p. 1393).

This Gramscian notion cannot be understood unless we recall what Gramsci means here by "historicity" and "needs of a historical period." Passing from the general criteria for the formation and diffusion of common sense to the conditions under which the new common sense is formed as a necessary aim, historicity is defined as being in relation to both the needs and practical existence of the masses. The formation of the new common sense is thus founded on the dialectical relation between theory and praxis (Q. 15, p. 1780). In political (social) praxis, it assumes the form of a dialectical relation between the intellectual elites and the masses in accordance with the forms of hegemony that are possible in civil society and with the philosophy of praxis as a synthesis of philosophy and politics.

It is the foundational nature of these concepts and of the central concept of praxis that allows us to understand correctly the great importance Gramsci attaches to pedagogy and educational activity in order also, and above all, to form a new common sense. What's more, if considered separately from the central foundational concepts in his thought, Gramsci's pedagogy and ideas on the formation of humanity run the risk of being viewed as a generic pedagogical willingness. For the previously mentioned reasons, educational activity, understood as formation of the new common sense in the masses by elites, cannot be considered simply as an activity that starts from the historical analysis of common sense in the masses and then acts on them from above (through elites). This is because such educational activity must, in turn, depend for its efficacy on its linkage with the practical life of the masses: In this the elites depend on the masses.

If this dialectical relation between elites and the masses is not constituted, or is not "organic," the formation or educational activity will not achieve its aims, just as, for example, the popular universities did not achieve their objectives. They were criticized by Gramsci as being places where the exchange between intellectuals and the people had assumed the form of the relationship between British merchants (the intellectuals) and natives (the people) based on the exchange of junk for gold nuggets. Only in these terms is it possible to distinguish the formation of the new common sense in the masses, undertaken by the philosophy of praxis, from the pedagogical action carried out by other cultural formations and elites. Take, as an example, the pedagogical action of the Church and, in particular, the Catholic Church. The latter is characterized by its intention to spread a "religion for the people" and keep it distinct from a "religion for intellectuals."

There are some aspects in Gramsci's thought on common sense that can be considered as outdated and in need of critical revision. Take, for example, Gramsci's ideas on the function of the Party in the formation of the new common sense and in the organization of the relation between elites and the masses (the general idea of the "modern prince-Party"). It is undeniable that this relation is more complex inasfar as this is true of society as a whole. At the same time, it must be remembered that the problem of elites posed by Gramsci, though in different terms and with different connotations, is a topical one in contemporary psychology, where it is called *minority influence* or *influence des minorités actives*.

Common sense and social representations

Apart from this respect, there are others that appear in current psychological debates, as will be evident to psychologists themselves from what has already been said. Thus, when we read Gramsci's scattered observations on common sense, several similarities and points of agreement with the theory of social representations immediately become apparent. Developed in recent years by Moscovici, this theory is today one of the principal research approaches in European social psychology. Furthermore, the concept of *social representation* is in fact strictly related to the concept of common sense (Moscovici, 1984; Jodelet, 1984). Here I indicate some common points in order to stimulate more detailed analysis.

Just as Moscovici was to do many years later when working out his psychology, Gramsci emphasizes the polysemy and polymorphism of common sense: its being made up of numerous interwoven layers. It is clear that Gramsci had realized the importance of the relation between common sense and conduct, even though the terms he used were different from those of current psychology. Also, the "realistic and materialistic elements" that according to Gramsci (Q. 11, p. 1397) predominate in common sense can be linked to the "anchoring" and "objectifying" processes developed by Moscovici (1981, pp. 192–203). A further common point is the problem of social groups ("historical group consciousness"), considered by Gramsci when dealing with common sense and of fundamental importance for the theory of social representations and all modern psychology. In other words, in Gramsci's writings we find social groups viewed as a kind of subjectivity distinct from the collective subject of the Marxist tradition (the masses, the proletariat, etc.), even if he appears to consider the specific differentiations within groups as a consequence of the contradictoriness of existing social relations, which is reflected in current common sense and must be overcome (Q. 11, p. 1376; Q. 16, p. 1875).

Nevertheless, even more than from the points of agreement, the relevance of Gramsci's thought emerges from those aspects that differentiate it from Moscovici's psychology. As Moscovici does at a later date, Gramsci poses the problem of the passage of ideas from scientific thought to common sense, and it is already here that the differences come to light. Summarizing, in Moscovici science and social representations are presented as radically and profoundly different from each other, to the point of constituting distinct "universes": "Consensual universes" constitute the domain of social representations, and "reified universes" constitute the domain of science (Moscovici, 1981). This difference is for Moscovici so great that we can speak of a dualistic concept.

In Gramsci, on the contrary, the relationship between common sense and philosophical-scientific thought is far more structured and complex or, to use an old term, *dialectical*. It starts from the basic capacity of reasoning common to everyone ("all men are philosophers") and from good sense as the sound nucleus of common sense, aspects that seem to place Gramsci closer to Heider (1958) than to Moscovici. Furthermore, there is Gramsci's hypothesis of the possibility of certain ideas passing from common sense to philosophical-scientific thought: for example, the idea – a very old one for common sense – of the natural equality of all men, adopted by philosophical thought in the 18th century.

It is this dialectical relation between common sense and philosophical-scientific thought that underlies the fundamental difference between Gramsci and Moscovici. In the latter, it is not quite clear how there can be a reunification of the reified and consensual universes, of science and social representations. Moscovici assigns to social representations the task of reunification within the "opus nostrum," within a genuinely human reality, but how they are to perform this task is not evident. The reason is that human activity is given a limited and merely implicit role in his psychology. In Gramsci, by contrast, there is no dualistic splitting because common sense and philosophical scientific thought are both embedded in historical reality; they are part of it inasfar as they depend on the real conditions and, above all, on the practical life of the masses. However, the reference to historical reality certainly does not imply realism or objectivism or that the concept of dependence on the practical life of the masses is a generic one. Both the latter concept and the reference to historical reality are a consequence of the foundational role that Gramsci gives to praxis.

Gramsci, Vygotsky, and activity theory

The topicality of the Gramscian concept of *praxis* and of its relevance to psychology is a subject that requires its own particular analysis. Such an analysis, based on the relation between praxis and *activity* (as this last concept was put forward by Vygotsky and developed by Leont'ev), would enable us to underline both the similarities and differences between Gramsci's thought and that of the cultural-historical school. A comparison of the two, useful to activity theory and also to psychology in general, offers many hints. Consider, for example, the fact that Gramsci (1891–1937) and Vygotsky (1896–1934) were contemporaries. Although far apart and under different conditions, they lived through the same great political events and in cultural climates that displayed important common aspects.

As far as their cultural formation is concerned, the two men have in common the necessarily fragmentary nature of their work, which, nonetheless and thanks to their creativity, has in both cases stimulated further developments, as the topicality of their ideas demonstrates. One of the most immediately evident common aspects in their work is the importance they attribute to the problem of education in the context of a shared Marxist frame of reference and in connection with precise elements of their theory that are rooted directly in the concept of activity or of praxis. Even the importance Gramsci attaches to folklore is far from alien to Vygotsky, as shown by the research conducted on his initiative in Uzbekistan, which looks at the subject from a more strictly psychological standpoint (Luria, 1976).

However, the central concepts both in Gramsci's thought and in the psychology of Vygotsky and Leont'ev are historicity and activity. As to the first, the following explication of the essential meaning of the historical approach in the cultural–historical school also applies to Gramsci.

The historical approach does not simply mean that historical situations become the object of analysis or that certain phenomena are treated in their historical context and so "relativized." Even more than this, the method of scientific knowledge itself is in a certain sense a historical method. Explaining an object scientifically means understanding it through its genesis. (Holzkamp & Schurig, 1980, p. xxv)

Nevertheless, the genetic aspect attributed to the historical approach constitutes the major difference between Gramsci and the cultural-historical school. It is well known that in the latter, historicity, insofar as it is genetic analysis, also refers to natural history. The consideration of phylogenesis, of natural and biological development, which is given great weight in the cultural-historical school, remains in the background in Gramscian thought. In this respect, Gramsci is more directly influenced by Benedetto Croce and his closed mind toward the natural sciences and, more generally, by the limits of a certain approach to culture in the Italy of that period.

In particular, however, it is through a consideration of the concept of activity that we are able to focus on the shared roots and common elements. Attention will now be drawn to some aspects of the Gramscian concept of praxis so that students of activity theory, and those who are well acquainted with the works of Vygotsky and Leont'ev, can develop further the comparison made here. The importance and the various aspects of the relation between praxis and common sense have been underlined several times. Without this relation, common sense would not have the specificity it takes on in Gramsci's thought. It can thus be maintained that in Gramsci's theory and praxis, intellectuals and masses and, on a plane closer to the problems of psychology, common sense and praxis or human activity as a whole are set in the same dialectical relation of two-way influence. If, as we have seen, common sense helps to explain the rules of conduct, it can then be maintained that, in turn, all the activities carried out in society (an important one, but not the only one, is work) exert an influence on common sense. This contributes either to changing it or, on the contrary, to its sedimentation in folklore, according to the type of activity and the real historical context in which it is exercised.

At the same time, the point of departure and the essential premise for all these dialectical relations are the given material and objective conditions. It is precisely the latter that make these dialectical relations, and more particularly that between common sense and the activities of subjects, appear completely consonant with that "almost circular movement formed by the passages: subject – activity – object" (Leont'ev, 1978) that is at the basis of Leont'ev's psychology. The activity theory of Gramsci and that of Leont'ev have several aspects in common. Consider the "object-related character," which in Leont'ev combines the mental activities with the productive ones, and the corresponding Gramscian notion of praxis as a validity criterion for each individual's philosophy. Then there is the importance Gramsci attaches to language, which in Vygotsky but also in Leont'ev plays a central role and is closely related to their activity theories, as Engeström (Chapter 1, this volume) points out.

The most important aspect that links Gramsci's theory with that of the cultural-historical school is also the one that distinguishes them most in the context of Marxist thought; it is also the most problematic. What I am referring to is the particular value that both theories attribute to the individual subject in relation to the collective and social subject, to the "working class, the subject of historical praxis." This takes us back to the problem of the difficult relation, and at times opposition, between society and individual. This is a constant problem for all of psychology, but one that is particularly dramatic in Marxist psychologies. One reason is that a certain version of Marxism came up with a deleterious solution: The process of historical development and the laws of society were viewed in a deterministic and mechanistic way. This was done in the name of the superior interests of the proletariat, the masses, and the collectivity, whereas in reality, any form and expression of collective or individual subjectivity was suppressed and the value of the activities, consciousness, and needs of classes and social groups, as well as of individuals, was denied.

This is precisely the solution of mechanistic determinism against which Gramsci fought a constant battle and that the cultural-historical school opposes with its central concept of activity. But in the context of Marxist psychology, the fight against mechanistic determinism neither solves nor tackles adequately the problem of the relation between individual subjectivity and collective or supraindividual subjectivity, between the activity of the concrete individual and the social praxis. If anything, this is because the concept of activity in question here is plainly supraindividual in nature as a result of its Hegelian and then Marxist theoretical origins.

Gramsci and the cultural-historical school posed and addressed the previously mentioned problem in similar ways, though without solving it. Put in other terms, briefly the problem consists in recognizing the entire value of the individual subject and, thus, of the way he or she acts in the world, his or her consciousness and needs, without negating what is positive and essential in the Marxian conception of activity.

The value attributed by Gramsci to subjectivity and, in context, to the individual subject may be considered as one of the most characteristic aspects of his theory. As a consequence, when he refers to the concept of *hegemony* (one of the components in his thought that most explicitly differentiates it from that of Lenin and even more so from the particular version of Leninism prevalent in Soviet Marxism), it has the meaning of "cultural guidance" alongside that of "political guidance" (Bobbio, 1990). Also, it supposes the utilization of the subjectivity of both the masses, the "wide strata of society" and "social groups," and single individuals, involving their common sense and action in the institutions of the "civil society." Indeed, often and in various contexts, Gramsci confirms that no individual (not only intellectuals, who have greater responsibilities, but anyone since "every man, even if in his own way, is a philosopher or intellectual") can be or should feel divested of responsibility by delegating his duties and actions to a collective subject.

Thus, in his frequent references to the field of education, Gramsci sees action aimed at hegemonizing areas in favor of the subaltern classes and against the dominant culture as the concern not only of teachers as a social group or class but also of each individual teacher, who cannot get out of it by transferring his or her duties and tasks to the group. The culture, common sense, and activity of, on one side, the masses and social groups and, on the other, single individuals do not exclude each other or stand in simple opposition. However, this cannot be considered a solution to the previously mentioned problem. Gramsci reaffirms the priority role of the masses, "identifies the active historical subject in the collective will" (Bobbio, 1990), and points to a number of unresolved questions and inner contradictions.

In the cultural-historical school, for which the unifying concept of activity comprises both social action and individual conduct, the problem of the relation between individual subject and collective subject obviously assumes, compared to Gramsci, more distinctly psychological connotations. The utilization of the individual subject is based essentially on the *personality principle* and on the principles of *internalization* and *appropriation*. The first principle establishes that external causes always act through the mediation of a single personality, understood as "all the internal conditions linked together in a whole," and that, in the end, the intervention and commitment of single individuals is required.

The development of single individuals – in as much as it is the appropriation of social experience – does not simply unfold from within: rather, it is a task assigned to each person by society, which he or she takes upon him- or herself more and more consciously as the years go by. (Holzkamp & Schurig, 1980, p. xxiv)

A more important role is played by the principles of *internalization* and *appropriation,* which in Vygotsky's original formulation directly involve the active intervention of the subject in the developmental process (Vygotsky, 1978). Moreover, it is on this theoretical foundation that Vygotsky, like Gramsci, attributes importance to the role and responsibility of the adult in the educational process. The work of Luria also goes in the direction of the utilization of individual responsibility, a particularly significant example being his "romantic science," in the sense of clinical analysis that is not merely descriptive but relates the concrete case to cultural-historical theory (Luria, 1972, 1978).

Some aspects of this theory, however, such as the concept of appropriation or the personality principle, remain at a generic level despite their importance. Above all, a still open question in Leont'ev's work is a kind of "opposition between sociality, in the preeminent figure of work, and nature, in the individualistic determination of the conditions of necessity; the concept according to which the participation of the single individual in collective activity has to be brought about by external coercion" (Conti & Romano, 1979, p. 145). It should be noted that the Berlin school of critical psychology has made an important contribution in this area (Holzkamp-Osterkamp, 1976; Tolman & Maiers, 1991).

Nevertheless, this question is now being posed in increasingly complex terms. In their analysis of activity, both Gramsci and Leont'ev refer above all to the big factory,[2] which is going through what is probably an irreversible crisis. Moreover, the means of production and communication and the organization of work have changed radically. From a more general perspective, as Rückriem (1991, p. 3) observes, "not only the principle of activity is charged with the destruction of outer nature in the name of ruling over nature, but there is also the destruction of inner nature, the suppression of senses, of the body and sexuality." Given all this, the assumption can be made that common sense is becoming more and more important. This increasing importance of common sense follows from its capacity to cope with change, not only by assimilating it through the function of "familiarization" (Moscovici) but also by helping to bring it about.

In conclusion, I believe that it is necessary as well as opportune to undertake a comparison of different theories. Gramsci, like Marx but contrary to many Marxists enclosed in their monolithic theories, assimilated several theoretical and cultural currents. These include the Enlightenment, Italian philosophy (Benedetto Croce, Giovanni Gentile), and the Italian cultural tradition, but also Catholic culture in its many pervasive aspects. The receptiveness of Gramsci's thought to various influences allows us to use him as a catalyst for a direct comparison between the cultural-historical school and developments within a wider range of contemporary psychological research, in particular, Moscovici's theory of social representations. Originally, the cultural-historical school displayed a similarly open attitude toward establishing significant links with, above all, Gestalt psychology and Kurt Lewin (see Stadler, 1988).

Finally, it is important to point out that if the proposed comparison were based on each theory's shedding its own particular identity, it would inevitably fail or could even give rise to misunderstanding. That is to say, it is necessary to reaffirm that although the cultural-historical school and Gramsci's thought are open to the most varied influences, at the same time they are both entirely and structurally Marxist. Hence, the fundamental concepts of these theories, starting with activity, derive directly from Marxist thought and so stand in the Hegelian tradition.

Notes

This study was financed by research grants from the Italian Ministry for Universities and Scientific Research to Paola Belpassi and Francesco Paolo Colucci, at the time both of the Institute of Philosophy at Urbino University.
1. In a recent essay on Gramsci, which was well received in the United States and also elsewhere, M. Walzer (1988) puts forward an only partial, and hence substantially incorrect, interpretation of the Gramscian concept of common sense. Without taking into account its polysemy, he emphasizes merely the negative aspects, that is, common sense as Gramsci's version of false consciousness, as a folklore philosophy, and so on. This author thus falls into what, in my opinion, is a serious misunderstanding of the intellectuals–masses relation and of the Gramscian vision of politics.

2. Rückriem (1991) maintains that it is possible and useful to take the Gramscian category of activity, and therefore the formative function attributed by Gramsci to the organization of work in the modern big factory, as the starting point for an explanation of subjectivity.

References

Bobbio, N. (1990). *Saggi su Gramsci.* Milan: Feltrinelli editore.

Conti, C., & Romano, D. F. (1979). *Il dramma uniforme. Per una teoria della vita quotidiana.* Bologna: Il Mulino.

Gramsci, A. (1975). *Quaderni del carcere.* Critical edition by V. Gerratana. Turin: Einaudi editore.

Heider, F. (1958). *The psychology of interpersonal relations.* New York: Wiley.

Holzkamp, K., & Schurig, V. (1980). *Zur Einführung in A. N. Leontjew's Probleme der Entwicklung des Psychischen.* Königstein: Athenäum.

Holzkamp-Osterkamp, U. (1976). *Grundlagen der psychologischen Motivationsforschung.* Frankfurt: Campus.

Jodelet, D. (1984). Représentations sociales. In S. Moscovici (Ed.), *Psychologie Sociale.* Paris: PUF.

Leont'ev, A. N. (1978). *Activity, consciousness, and personality.* Englewood Cliffs: Prentice-Hall.

Luria, A. R. (1972). *The man with a shattered world: The history of a brain wound.* New York: Basic Books.

Luria, A. R. (1976). *Cognitive development: Its cultural and social foundations.* Cambridge, MA: Harvard University Press.

Luria, A. R. (1978). *The making of mind: A personal account of Soviet psychology.* Cambridge, MA: Harvard University Press.

Moscovici, S. (1981). On social representations. In J. P. Forgas (Ed.), *Social cognition.* London: Academic Press.

Moscovici, S. (1984). The phenomenon of social representations. In R. M. Farr & S. Moscovici (Eds.), *Social representations.* Cambridge: Cambridge University Press.

Rückriem, G. (1991). *Common sense and the concepts of "sense" and "meaning."* Paper presented at the International Symposium "Praxis, Common Sense and Hegemony," Bologna, December 4–5.

Stadler, M. (1988). Theory of activity and Lewin's field theory. In M. Hildebrand-Nilshon & G. Rückriem (Eds.), *Proceedings of the 1st International Congress on Activity Theory* (Vol. 4.1). Berlin: System Druck.

Tolman, C. W., & Maiers, W. (Eds.). (1991). *Critical psychology: Contributions to an historical science of the subject.* Cambridge: Cambridge University Press.

Vygotsky, L. S. (1978). *Mind in society.* Cambridge, MA: Harvard University Press.

Walzer, M. (1988). *The company of critics.* New York: Basic Books.

Part II

Language and its acquisition

11 The expanded dialogic sphere: Writing activity and authoring of self in Japanese classrooms

Yuji Moro

Introduction

Writing is a multifunctional activity. Writing enables us to send messages to or receive information from people displaced in time and space. With the aid of written symbols, we can regulate our own actions and behaviors in the future. Among the various functions of writing, however, I would like to focus on the function of constructing a dialogic sphere. The following composition, which illustrates this function, was written by a second-grade girl in a Japanese elementary school.

Example 1
TADPOLE IS A BABY FROG
Today, we decided that we were going to keep tadpoles in our classroom. I know that a tadpole is a baby frog but I don't know it really. Tomoki said we would see hind legs first but Naomi insisted that forelegs and hind legs grow out at the same time.
    Mr. Kuwabara [the teacher of the class] didn't know what to answer. I'm really looking forward to seeing how the tadpoles would grow.

This composition, taken for a classroom journal, is a typical example of writing in the Japanese classroom. Its most characteristic feature is that it is writer-based (Britton, 1977; Kitagawa & Kitagawa, 1987). It is not an autonomous text, as characterized by Olson (1977), but one dependent on the classroom community in which children and teachers share experience and senses.

The composition cannot be seen merely as a report of classroom discussion. It cannot be read as a mere memorandum for future activity, either. It serves to construct a special sphere where the writer appreciates the reality of tadpoles. In the second sentence, the writer presents two propositions that contradict each other. She says she knows that tadpoles are baby frogs, and she also says that she does not know it. The first proposition may be a quotation of adults' speech or knowledge acquired from books. The second one is her evaluation of the first proposition.

165

It seems that the writer succeeded in constructing a special sphere where she interfaces two kinds of utterances (Bakhtin, 1986). And by interfacing them, she generated a will to anticipate and appreciate the growth of the tadpoles in the future. She also succeeded in individualizing her form of speech in the sphere.

The purpose of this chapter is to shed light on this function of writing activity: constructing a dialogically expanded sphere and interfacing utterances in the sphere.

Vygotsky's proposal

In the last chapter of *Thinking and Speech*, Vygotsky proposes a view on child development: "[T]he central tendency of the child's development is not a gradual socialization introduced from outside, but a gradual individualization that emerges on the foundation of the child's internal socialization" (Vygotsky, 1987, p. 259).

Vygotsky's view on child development, though it changed his perspective on egocentric speech, seems not to have been fully developed by Vygotsky himself. His proposal has great significance and important implications for the activity-based theory and practice of language development and education.

Vygotsky proposed two theses. The first thesis is that child development originates in social processes. The second thesis is that with the aid of social processes, children transform and differentiate the processes themselves and construct their own selves. The first thesis has now become very popular. A number of researchers have endeavored to explicate the idea that various functions of mind are of social origin and to show how these functions are formed in social processes. The second thesis, however, has not yet been appreciated sufficiently. My task here is to explicate the process of individualization through social interactions, or the process of social formation of the self.

As Vygotsky's theory of tools and mediation posits, individualization is achieved through mediation and tool usage. The most powerful mediational means are manifested in the process of making one's own "ways with words" (Heath, 1983) or making one's "voice" (Wertsch, 1985).

But it must be pointed out that Vygotsky's characterization of speech and discourse is insufficient as a tool for examining the process of individualization. He characterized the main unit of speech in terms of words and identified the main function of speech with directives or commands.

In his later years he adopted the unit of analysis based on the discourse studies of that time, for example, those of Yakubinsky (1923). But most frequently in his psychological writings, Vygotsky used the word as a unit for the analysis of speech. This concept of unit seems to have enabled him to succeed in revealing the semiotic nature of speech and the child's word-concept development. But at the same time, this unit became a limitation in his studies.

Vygotsky's notion of speech function, focused on directives or commands and inspired by the French psychologist Pierre Janet (Wertsch, 1985), also limited his analysis of speech. Individualization is a process of acquiring self-control. As they develop, children make use of adult directives and commands as tools to control themselves. But the directive function itself does not reveal the content of the situation in which it is used. When directing or commanding, speakers and hearers are assuming particular roles, recognizing the situation as some kind of social institution, and adopting certain forms of speech closely tied to the institution. The word as the unit of analysis and the directive function of speech cannot serve as sufficient tools for investigating such concrete speech situations.

Bakhtin's theory of utterance

Mikhail Bakhtin's theory of utterance (Bakhtin, 1981, 1986; Bakhtin/Voloshinov, 1973) provides a powerful basis for looking into the process of dialogic sphere construction and individualization. Bakhtin's discussion appears intricate because of his irritating and disorganized style, but the core of his theory seems to me very simple and therefore powerful.

Bakhtin starts his discussion with the situation of dialogue. The notion of *utterance* is "a real unit of speech communion" (Bakhtin, 1986, p. 67). Utterance is not an abstract unit such as the word and the sentence, but a real one, reflecting a real speech situation and real speech activity in it.

Bakhtin criticized the traditional linguistic notion of language, especially the Saussurean notion, which is based on a fictional speech situation. The fictional situation is presented in "diagrams of the active speech processes of the speaker and the corresponding passive processes of the listener's perception and understanding of the speech" (Bakhtin, 1986, p. 68). The diagram represents an autonomous view of language in which language is a self-sufficient system dissociated from societal and historical processes.

In contrast to this view, Bakhtin constructed his notion of utterance in a concrete dialogic situation where equally active and responsive persons, the addressor and the addressee, meet and each becomes the other for each of them. The situation can never be reduced to one person's intention. This is a condition for realizing a situation in which there exist active, speaking subjects.

The persons in the situation of utterance are concrete. Thus, utterance is "oriented toward an addressee, toward who that addressee might be: a fellow-member or not of the same social group, of higher or lower standing, someone connected with the speaker by close social ties or not" (Bakhtin/Voloshinov, 1973, p. 85). Utterances are "determined equally by whose word (utterance) it is and for whom it is meant" (ibid., p. 86). In other words, utterances have the "quality of being directed to someone" or "addressivity" (Bakhtin, 1986, p. 95).

Utterances serve as a verbal medium with which addressor and addressee can participate in the speech communication and can produce evaluative responses to the other's utterances. Utterances can be seen as a positive extension of de Saussure's *parole*, which is considered an unsocial or individualistic verbal performance. For Bakhtin, "the structure of the utterance is a purely sociological (social) structure" (Bakhtin/Voloshinov, 1973, p. 98).

Utterances have common features, regardless of their variation in length, content, and compositional structure. The common features may be divided into two kinds: structural and phenomenal. The common structural features of utterances are "boundaries" (Bakhtin, 1986, p. 71) and "finalization" (ibid., p. 76), which are reciprocally dependent on each other.

Utterances have clear-cut boundaries. The boundaries are determined by a change of speaking subjects. Every utterance has an absolute beginning and end, regardless of its length. Whether it is a single word or a long scientific treatise, an utterance is a response to another utterance and is an object to which other addressors make responses. At the beginning and end is a change of subject. Ordinary dialogues are the most typical examples revealing the change of speaking subjects. In the case of ordinary dialogues, the real speaker corresponds to the speaking subject. However, in the case of a culturally complex domain such as artistic work and writing activity, the real speaking person does not have to correspond to the speaking subjects. In those cases, "the change of speaking subjects has been internalized" (Bakhtin, 1986, p. 92). The feature of finalization enables changes of speaking subjects. The change of speaking subjects takes place when an addressor has said everything he or she wished to say.

The phenomenal features represent how utterances appear to both the addressor and addressee in the situation of utterance. The phenomenal features also serve as a factor determining the composition and style of utterances. The first phenomenal feature is that utterances have "evaluative accents" (Bakhtin, 1986; Bakhtin/Voloshinov, 1973). When producing utterances, active interlocutors are not only responding to each other's utterances but also evaluating and judging them and developing a valuative attitude toward them. Speakers are judging whether the utterances are true or false, good or bad, and beautiful or not.

The second phenomenal feature is that an utterance emerges as a "voice" with the speaker's expression and intonation (Bakhtin, 1986). Speakers are not abstract beings. They are concrete persons with specific purposes and particular statements to present, and they are located in specific social and historical positions. Utterances not only have specific logical and referential contents, they also have specific speakers' intonation and expression.

Dialogizing utterances

An utterance is not a mere reflection of the structure of the situation in which the addressor and addressee dialogize. It is determined by the broader social milieu. The milieu provides a "zone" (Bakhtin, 1981, p. 302) in which a variety of utterances interact and penetrate each other. Bakhtin discusses how meaning is constructed in an utterance; how one's utterance meets another's; how one's utterance is refracted by another's; and how the meaning of one's utterance is renewed. Thus the theory of utterance is a theory of meaning in movement. In the verbal medium, in each utterance, however trivial it may be, this living dialectical synthesis is constantly taking place again and again between the psyche and ideology, between the inner and the outer. In each speech act, subjective experience perishes in the objective fact of the enunciated word-utterance, and the enunciated word is subjectified in the act of responsive understanding in order to generate, sooner or later, a counter statement (Bakhtin/Voloshinov, 1973, pp. 40–41).

Heteroglossia (Bakhtin, 1981, p. 263) is the most striking characteristic of utterances that supports the meaning in movement. Utterances are "heteroglot in that they are a function of forces practically impossible to recoup, and therefore impossible to resolve" (Holquist, 1981, p. 428). Borrowing Bakhtin's term, utterance is an *arena*. Each word (utterance) is a little arena for the clashing and crisscrossing of differently oriented social accents. A word in the mouth of a particular individual is a product of the living interaction of social forces (Bakhtin/Voloshinov, 1973, p. 41).

The broader sociohistorical milieu of utterances is also heteroglot. Language is stratified into sublanguages, or "social languages" (Bakhtin, 1981, p. 356), such as "social dialects, characteristic group behaviors, professional jargons, generic languages, languages of generations and age groups, tendentious languages, languages of authorities, of various circles and of passing fashions, language that serves the specific sociopolitical purposes of the day" (Bakhtin, 1981, p. 263). Stratification is the basic depiction of language, contrastive to a unitary language, an abstract entity often presupposed in linguistics.

Behind the notion of heteroglossia is Bakhtin's view that any language is in the process of centralization and decentralization. On the one hand, as national languages and scientific languages, language has a tendency to unify itself and centralize into a unitary whole. At the same time, there is a tendency to decentralize and stratify into sublanguages. These two incompatible forces produce the movement of the meaning in utterances.

This movement occurs on two planes: the plane of the contents of an utterance and the plane of inner speech. Every utterance has a semantically and referentially specific content. In referring to some object, we establish a certain relationship with the object. The relationship cannot be neutral. In making an utterance, we find the object "entangled, shot through with shared thoughts, points of view, alien words that have already been spoken about it" (Bakhtin, 1981, p. 276).

The second plane of the dialogizing movement exists as an internal compositional construction of utterances. Each utterance has its own boundary. But boundaries of utterances do not always correspond to the changes of actual speaking subjects. In some cases, when a single speaker is "doing" the utterance, there are multiple speech subjects in the utterance. In other words, utterances of others are assimilated within the boundary of the utterance. In terms of voice, utterances are multivoiced.

Bakhtin's view on inner speech, "internalized changed speech subjects" (1986, p. 92), represents a sharp contrast to Vygotsky's and Luria's characterization of it. In the Vygotsky–Luria line of thinking, features of inner speech are abbreviation, predictability, and dominance of "sense" over "meaning." Although the last feature, dominance of sense, is shared by Bakhtin and Vygotsky–Luria, the other two are treated differently in the two lines of thinking. Vygotsky and Luria emphasize the difference between outer and inner speech. Bakhtin stressed the movement of meaning in multivoiced utterance rather than the location of speech. As Radzikhovskii (1986–1987) points out, utterances form a "dialogically expanded" sphere in which the movement of meaning is maximized.

Interfacing utterances: Tendency of language development

According to Bakhtin's theory of utterance, it may be proposed that speech is an activity to create interfaces between diverse utterances, between different voices, and between various social languages. A general tendency of language development may be characterized as the process of assimilating others' language, interfacing it with one's own, and strengthening one's utterance boundary in the dialogic sphere.

We can distinguish different phases that appear as the interfacing of utterances develops. In some cases, speakers use different social languages without thinking and without conflicts. These languages are "inviolable and predetermined" (Bakhtin, 1981, p. 296). Contrary to this is the phase of "critical interanimation of languages" (ibid.). In the interanimation phase, the languages are found to be in mutual conflict and it becomes necessary to choose one's orientation from among them.

There are various resources with which speech subjects assimilate others' language, create an utterance interface, and then construct individualized speech events. Such resources include forms for assimilating others' language (e.g., various forms of quotation and reported speech); degrees of dialogizing quality (e.g., degree of internal persuasiveness or, in contrast, degree of authoritativeness); speech genres that provide the speaking subject with the compositional structure of communicative situations particular to the speech genre; and generic forms of utterances particular to the genre. These resources are interrelated.

Let us now examine several genres of utterance because they seem to have great potential as powerful analytic tools for writing activity in the classroom. Speech genres are "relatively stable types" (Bakhtin, 1986, p. 60), and they are extremely varied. In ordinary situations, we frequently use "primary speech genres" (ibid.) without being aware of it. With the aid of primary genres, the utterances are equipped with intonation and expression of speaking subjects. The secondary genres arise in more complex and comparatively highly organized situations of communication. One resource provided in the secondary speech genre is the "posited author" (Bakhtin, 1981, p. 312). The speaker sets up as a posited author, and assimilates and interfaces others' language in the secondary genre.

Writing in the classroom is a kind of secondary speech genre, which develops highly organized and complex speech communication. Now let us return to the composition (Example 1) presented earlier. The child sets herself up as an author who adopts the genre of the classroom journal. With the aid of this genre, she is able to construct a dialogic sphere in which she interfaces two mutually incompatible utterances.

Seikatsu Tsuzurikata

Seikatsu Tsuzurikata, or "life experience writing" (Kitagawa & Kitagawa, 1987), is a traditional grass-roots movement in writing education in Japan. It has been practiced for over 60 years in various parts of Japan. Let us examine the movement briefly to understand the background of this writing activity in Japan and to illustrate the function and development of interfacing utterances in the expanded dialogic sphere.

Over a period of more than 60 years, Seikatsu Tsuzurikata has been changing in its emphasis on objects and methodology. Theorists and researchers have given it a wide variety of evaluations and characterizations due to the multifaceted nature of this movement. Its aspects range from the development of a classroom community, to education for achieving a total person rather than proficiency in just language arts, to resistance to the repression imposed by the military government during World War II. In this section, I would like to comment on two characteristics of Seikatsu Tsuzurikata: the emphasis on contextualized writing activity and the orientation to a connection between the writer and the reality of the writer's ordinary world.

The prevailing view is that writing leads to decontextualization. According to this view, writing is a tool to send messages in a detached mode, that is, no matter who the writer or the reader is, writing serves as a tool. In other words, writing is regarded as producing autonomous symbols. According to Kitagawa and Kitagawa (1987), writing is regarded as a reader-biased process. But in the Seikatsu classroom, children's writing is seen as a contextualized process, located in a specific time and place and oriented to particular readers.

The following examples are a composition written by a first grader and a note by her teacher commenting on it (translated by Kitagawa & Kitagawa, 1987).

Example 2
EARTHWORM
I saw an earthworm the earthworm Suzuki grabbed the earthworm.

Example 3
TEACHER'S COMMENT
I understood this composition because I happened to be there and to see her face at the time of the event. But even if I did not, still I would want to read into it and to appreciate the mind of the child who wants to express herself through the writing.

As seen in this comment, the teachers in the Seikatsu movement regard a child's composition as a clue to understanding and appreciating the mind of the child. The written symbols are, first of all, considered as a bridge connecting the child, the teacher, and the other children in the class. Through the bridge, the child and the teacher can talk to each other. Metaphorically speaking, the written symbols are regarded as scribblings made by preliterate children.

Let us turn to the second characteristic. Children's ordinary life is a topic selected most frequently for their writing. Fantasy stories, poems, and scientific reports are also written, but ordinary life events are preferred topics for compositions. This reflects the popular view among the Japanese that writing is a tool for self-reflection and appreciation of the real world in which the writer is located.

Izumi's confession: Authoring of self in the dialogic sphere

Let us examine a series of compositions written by a boy named Izumi in Niwa's Seikatsu classroom (Niwa, 1982). Niwa is a teacher in an elementary school located in Ena, a rural area of central Japan. Ena is known as a unique area that has developed education based on the belief that the legitimate purpose of education is to teach children how to live as people and what it means to be a member of a community. Ena is an area where teachers develop and create classrooms focused at the local level rather than being oriented to national standards.

Niwa's object in education is to show the children the reality of the world around them. Using writing, she tries to construct an audience community in her classroom. To the audience, the children write what they want when they want to do so. The audience community serves as a resource of others' languages, social languages, and various generic forms of speech with which children strengthen their utterance boundaries and interface their utterances with various evaluative utterances of others. In Niwa's classroom, each child writes a journal and, with the writer's permission, some of the compositions are read to his or her classmates for discussion.

The main theme of the following series of compositions is how Izumi came to realize the existence of his disabled aunt, who lived with him. These compositions depict the process by which Izumi came to face the reality of her existence, his attitude to it, and its effect on his family. Before he decided to write about it in an involved manner, he hesitated throughout his fifth-grade period. At this time, he wrote the following composition.

Example 4
GRANDFATHER (fifth grade, July)
My grandfather is seventy years old now. He is laid up with paralysis. When I was in the third grade he was not so bad, but since then he has become more and more physically disabled, so he can't walk without a stick and when speaking he can't speak well because of saliva.

My grandmother takes care of him. I think it is hard for her because she also has to cultivate a rice field alone. My mother goes out for work and isn't at home every day, so grandmother seems to be working the hardest in my family.

And in my family there is a person who is my father's sister [neuter gender] and the person is handicapped a little so it is hard for grandmother, I feel. I wish my grandfather was well. I think it is hard for anyone whose family members are not healthy. I hope that I can be of help in working hard for grandmother. But now I can only help her by bringing meals to grandfather's bed.

The narrative of the classroom journal is the dominant speech genre of this composition. The speech genre leads to a composition design consisting of a description of some events or the situation and a statement of a moral or solution located at the end. The speech genre dominates throughout the writing. The speech genre makes this composition monologous rather than dialogizing. It is clearly expressed in the third paragraph, where the writer treats his aunt as someone dissociated from his family's situation. He refers to his aunt by using the neuter gender in an objective and abstract way. In terms of the speaking subject, Izumi was able to assimilate into himself a posited author who adoped a narrative genre but failed to introduce himself as the main character to dialogize with the actual writer.

The following composition was written four months after Izumi wrote Example 4.

Example 5
MY BURDEN (fifth grade, December)
When I read and discussed Oono's composition, I was surprised that he had a courage to write the composition.

I have something that I want to write but I cannot make up my mind to do so. My grandfather is laid up with paralysis. It cannot be helped since most of old persons seem to get paralysis. I think it inevitable but it is hard for me that the person who is father's sister [the neuter gender] at my home is disabled. That is known only to my neighbors. But mother said that it is not inherent nor hereditary and we had no need get anxious.

I think Oono's situation is not as difficult as my family's.

I do want to write, but I do not want to. I think when something is really difficult, one cannot write.

As the composition shows, by discussing several compositions of his classmates, Izumi began to change his way of speaking in writing. He wrote about his conflicting and ambivalent evaluation of his family's problem. In other words, Izumi began to assimilate himself to the "confession" type of speech genre, which was borrowed from other children in the classroom community. But he did not succeed in interfacing the two speech genres: the classroom journal and the confession–type speech. He still used a detached, abstract way of referring to his aunt.

Example 6
GRADUALLY I BEGAN TO FEEL LIKE WRITING WHAT I DON'T WANT TO WRITE (fifth grade, February, excerpts)
When we read Miyuki's composition and Kumi's on her younger brother in the third term, I have more and more things that I want to write. . . .

When Mijuki read out her composition, she added tearfully, "I thought you would understand, and so I wanted all of you to know. First I thought I wanted only the teacher to read it, but as I trusted the teacher, I trusted you [the class], too." . . .

At that moment, I felt that I could write, too. I felt that I could write about Hatchan honestly. Since then I have been thinking hard how I would write it. . . .

In the composition (Example 6), though Izumi did not yet write about his aunt, we notice his changed way of writing. The resources provided by other children enhanced the change. He came to use the classroom journal genre to speak to his classmates and the teacher straightforwardly. In this speech genre, Izumi was able to create a main character who talked about the process he could use to write about "Hatchan."

Example 7
ME WHO CAME TO THINK ABOUT HATCHAN EARNESTLY
(sixth grade, May, excerpts)
When I was a third grader, Madoka came to my house to play with me. He looked at Hatchan when she looked into the room in which we were playing, and he said "Who is that?" I answered, hoping that she would go out, "Well, she is Hatchan. When she was small she was taken ill, and became like that," and Madoka said "Pity." But I felt ashamed, I wished Hatchan was not at my home. . . .

This composition (Example 7), written 10 months after Example 4, is 17 pages long. Izumi constructed a dialogic sphere in which he set himself up as a posited author describing his difficult problem to his classmates and to the teacher. In this composition he is taking a double role. The first role is that of the posited author who assimilates various utterances into the sphere. The other role is that of the main character. By taking this double role – in other words, by acting as a split speaking subject – Izumi depicted Hatchan vividly. In Example 7, he frequently quotes others' utterances and describes the scenes and events in which he acted on and interacted with other people around him.

The development of Izumi's interface of utterances seems to consist of three phases, as illustrated in Figure 11.1.

Introduction of the posited author into language arts classes

Let us examine the practice we used in collaboration with Mr. Wakabayashi, a teacher of Nagata Elementary School in Yokohama City (Wakabayashi, Moro, & Satou, 1992). The objective of the practice was to provide children with others' language, enabling them to interface their own ways of writing with those of others.

As Bakhtin (1981) states, an utterance is produced by a specific speaking subject who has a unique point of view. Each speaking subject takes a specific standpoint, and he or she has a perspective related to that standpoint. To interface utterances is to present one's own perspective in contrast to those of others, and in a successful case it results in an awareness of the specificity of one's own standpoint and perspective. The point of view is constructed according to the structure of the activity that the speaking subject is engaged in.

So far, we have set up two types of writing classwork, both of which provide children with language and points of view of others that are not usually introduced in a language art class. The first type is a film maker's

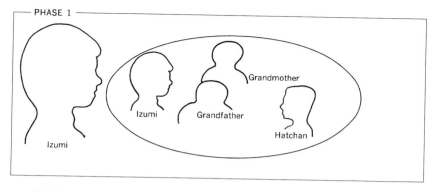

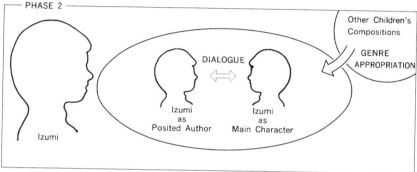

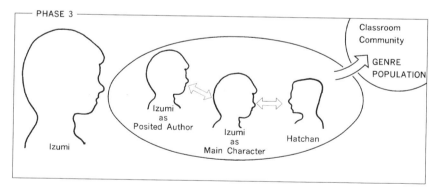

Figure 11.1. Three phases of interfacing utterances in Izumi's composition.

language; the second one is a cultural anthropologist's viewpoint. Here I focus on the first one.

The practice was motivated by the unsatisfactory outcome of the language art lesson preceding the practice. In the lesson, in order to explain the basic mechanisms of point of view, a picture of a soccer game was presented to the children for a discussion on how they should write if they take the viewpoint of each of the three players in the picture. Then the children were asked to compose a story by rewriting the famous fairy tale of Momotaro. Afterward we asked them to make a memorandum and draw pictures to decide which event in the Momotaro story should be highlighted to impress readers. After instruction, the children wrote longer compositions than usual but they still failed to incorporate the viewpoint in their writing. They could not use the viewpoint activity to construct the story world because the lesson failed to render the activity inevitable and necessary for them. It seemed that the children misunderstood the object of the Momotaro lesson as making an outrageous story that no one could ever create.

The film-maker practice consisted of several units of activity. First, children were asked how they would write if they had to make a story based on a four-frame cartoon, *The First Shopping*, presented in Figure 11.2. They discussed the theme of the cartoon among themselves.

Thus the children engaged themselves in studying a director's activity. We explained the role and behaviors of a director who made a film, illustrating them with scenes from motion pictures and TV programs. In particular, we told the children that, using continuity sketches, a director determines a camera angle and the type of shot (long shot, middle shot, or close-up) to be used for each scene. The children watched a video film on samurais. Afterward, they were given the following questions for discussion:

1. Where was the camera?
2. What was shot by the camera?
3. How did the director instruct the actors?

Then they each drew continuity sketches to divide the whole story into scenes and to determine subthemes for each scene, setting themselves up as directors who intended to make a film from the cartoon story. Finally, each of them wrote a new story based on his or her continuity sketches.

Some of the children seemed to succeed in gaining a new way of writing. Here I examine two compositions written by a girl in Mr. Wakabayashi's class before and after studying the director's activity. The following is a composition written before the study.

Example 8
THE FIRST SHOPPING
One day, Kurichan was asked to go shopping by his father. Because it was the first time for him to go shopping by himself, he was excited and went out rigorously.

Figure 11.2. The first shopping experience.

But his father was anxious about him. So, being careful not to be seen, he followed Kurichan.

Having seen Kurichan coming out from a cigar store and feeling relieved, father hurried back home.

Figure 11.3. Continuity sketches.

Kurichan came back just as father returned and sat down with an innocent look. Kurichan felt very happy that he was able to go shopping by himself. Father and mother felt relieved. Kurichan thought it was good. Praised by father and mother, Kurichan felt very good.

As shown in this composition, the children adopted two strategies when they wrote without the director's viewpoint. The first strategy was to translate pictures into paragraphs; the second, third, and fourth paragraphs correspond to the first, second, and fourth frames of the cartoon, respectively. The children seemed to regard writing as a way of translating the picture into sentences. The second strategy was based on a speech genre akin to the story grammar. The children added the setting or motive frame and also added evaluation or a moral to the last part of the story.

The same girl, after learning how to take a director's viewpoint, wrote the following composition with the aid of the continuity sketches shown in Figure 11.3.

Example 9
THE FIRST SHOPPING (excerpt)
"I have no pack of cigarettes" said Kuri's father. Kurichan, throwing away the book that he had been reading, rushed to father and said "I'll go to buy them." He took the money and went out rigorously, saying "I'll be back soon."

Kuri's father and mother were getting anxious and uneasy about him. They were silent for a while. Suddenly father said "I'll follow him" and hurried out. Kuri's father followed Kuri slowly, so as not to be noticed.

On entering the cigar store, Kurichan said to the old woman in the store, "Give me two packs of Sevenstar, please." She received money and patted him on the head, praising and saying "Good boy, you are able to come shopping by yourself."

At that moment Kuri's mother was ironing. She was very anxious about him. She was absent-minded and burned shirts and pants with the hot iron.

Behind a telegraph pole at the corner, Kuri's father was nervous, jiggling his knees so fast that we could not see it. His face looked like a chimp's face. He crinkled his face like an aggressive chimp that was fighting with another chimp. He waited for Kuri for ten minutes. But Kuri did not come out of the store. When he decided to rush into the store, Kurichan came out, smiling, with packs of cigarettes in his hand. Father, looking at Kuri, wrinkled his face more, with joy, and he was relieved. . . .

The girl succeeded in assimilating into herself a posited author who dialogized with the characters in the story. The posited author was created through her process of appreciating the director's activity. Compositions written after studying the director's activity had two characteristics: utilization of quotations and detailed description of the scenes in the story. As in the previous example, almost all of the children quoted the characters' speech. Children were able to add various details: the characters' appearance and behaviors, their action and body movement, and their locative relationship. These were details seen by a posited author who was sent by the actual writer.

In this chapter, I have proposed an approach to writing activity based on the idea that this activity involves creating interfaces of utterances utilizing various genres and social languages. Through the creation of interfaces, children achieve individualization of speech.

References

Bakhtin, M. M. (1981). *The dialogic imagination.* Austin: University of Texas Press.

Bakhtin, M. M. (1986). *Speech genres and other essays.* Austin: University of Texas Press.

Bakhtin, M. M. / Voloshinov, V. N. (1973). *Marxism and the philosophy of language.* Cambridge, MA: Harvard University Press.

Britton, J. (1977). Language and the nature of learning: An individual perspective. In *The seventy-sixth yearbook of the National Society for the Study of Education.* Chicago: University of Chicago Press.

Heath, S. B. (1983). *Ways with words.* Cambridge, MA: Harvard University Press.

Holquist, M. (1981). The politics of representation. In S. Greenblatt (Ed.), *Allegory in representation: Selected papers from the English Institute* (pp. 163–185). Baltimore: Johns Hopkins University Press.

Kitagawa, M. M., & Kitagawa, C. (1987). *Making connection with writing: An expressive writing model in Japanese school.* Portsmouth: Heinemann.

Niwa, N. (1982). *Asu ni mukatte (Toward tomorrow).* Tokyo: Soodo Bunka.

Olson, D. R. (1977). From utterance to text: The bias of language in speech and writing. *Harvard Educational Review, 47,* 257–281.

Radzikhovskii, L. A. (1986–1987). The dialogic quality of consciousness in the works of M. M. Bakhtin. *Soviet Psychology, 25,* 3–28.

Vygotsky, L. S. (1987). *The collected works of L. S. Vygotsky: Vol. 1. Problems of general psychology.* New York: Plenum.

Wakabayashi, K., Moro, Y., & Satou, Y. (1992). Writing from a virtual point of view: A dialogic approach for writing activities in classroom. *The National Language Research Institute Occasional Papers, 13,* 123–164.

Wertsch, J. V. (1985). *Vygotsky and the social formation of mind.* Cambridge, MA: Harvard University Press.

Yakubinsky, L. P. (1923). On verbal dialogue. *Despositio, 4,* 231–336. Department of Romance Language, University of Michigan.

12 Improvement of schoolchildren's reading and writing ability through the formation of linguistic awareness

Kyoshi Amano

Introduction

Reading and writing are complex, conscious speech activities that require awareness of various aspects of linguistic reality: the phonological structure of words, the meaning of words, and the syntactic–semantic structure of sentences. L. S. Vygotsky characterized the peculiarity of reading and writing in the sentence "written speech is the algebra of speech." According to him, writing "is a more difficult and a more complex form of intentional and conscious speech activity" (1987, pp. 204–205). He also pointed out that the real cause of difficulties for children in learning written speech is that "when instruction in written speech begins, the basic mental functions that underlie it are not fully developed; indeed their development has not yet begun" (ibid., p. 205).

Vygotsky's view of written speech is of particular importance when we construct literacy programs for teaching children with learning difficulties or learning disabilities. It suggests that if we can foster and develop a certain degree of linguistic awareness by some appropriate method before children begin to learn to read and write, we can decrease their difficulties and promote their success.

The idea of teaching phonological analysis of words to children at the beginning of literacy training originated historically with the phonological method for reading established by the Russian educator K. D. Ushinsky (1974) in the 19th century. For a long time, psychologists did not pay attention to his idea. It was A. R. Luria who first demonstrated the role of phonological analysis in writing in a psychological study. In 1948 he found that patients with lesions of the inferior part of the premotor zone had severe difficulty with phonological analysis of successions of words and could not spell words correctly. Based on this fact, he argued that phonological analysis of words is one of the necessary operations of writing activity (Luria, 1950).

Following Luria in 1956, D. B. El'konin (1956) proved in his experiment, using the stage-by-stage formation method of P. Ya. Gal'perin (1956, 1959), that phonological analysis forms the most important basis for acquisition of reading by children. He proposed a new teaching program for reading (El'konin, 1956, 1962, 1976). In the 1960s, I began to study phonological analysis and reading acquisition by preschool children in Japan (Amano, 1967). Only after 1970 did problems of phonological analysis and the acquisition of literacy by children become the object of systematic research by psychologists in the West, especially in English-speaking countries. Since then these issues have been investigated systematically by different methods, including confirmation test methods (e.g., Liberman, Shankweiter, Fisher, & Carter, 1974), cross-sectional correlational methods (Calfee, Lindamood, & Lindamood, 1973; Wallach & Wallach, 1979; Tunmer & Nesdale, 1985), and longitudinal methods (Share, Jorm, Maclean, & Mattews, 1984; Perfetti, 1985).

The important role of phonological analysis in learning literacy has also been confirmed by several teaching or training experiments using children learning different kinds of writing systems, for example Russian (El'konin & Zhurova, 1963; Zhurova, 1974), Japanese (Amano, 1977, 1978, 1986), English (Fox & Routh, 1984; Treiman & Baron, 1983; Gleitman & Rozin, 1973, 1977a, 1977b), and Swedish (Lundberg, Frost, & Peterson, 1988; Torne'us, 1984). These training studies showed that preparatory formation of awareness of the phonological structure of words in children promoted their learning in reading and writing words. On the basis of these findings, it is natural to think that the same relationship holds between the formation of linguistic awareness of the syntactico-semantic struture of sentences and learning to read and write sentences.

Over the past 10 years, I have been involved in a project to construct a teaching program for schoolchildren with learning difficulties and learning disabilities. The program consists of (1) an orthography program using syllabic letters, (2) a syntax program, and (3) a lexico-semantic cognitive program. The orthography program was designed to teach children the rules of reading and writing in Japanese syllabic letters (Hiragana) through the development of awareness of the syllabic structure of words. It was based on the idea of D. B. El'konin's phonemic analysis method and the stage-by-stage formation method (Gal'perin, 1956, 1959). The syntax program, designed for forming and developing linguistic awareness of the syntactico-semantic structure of sentences in children and for teaching them to read and write sentences in Hiragana correctly, was based on the theory of case grammar (Fillmore, 1976) and the genetic modeling

The 2nd International Congress of Research for Activity Theory is held in Lahti in Finland.

第二回活動理論会議が　　　フィンランドのラハチで　　　開かれている。

| The 2nd International Congress of Research for Activity Theory | of Finland | in Lahti | is held |

第二回活動理論会議, 開　　: Chinese characters

が, の, で, かれている　: syllabic letters, Hiragana

フィンランド, ラハチ　　: syllabic letters, Katakana

Figure 12.1. An example of a sentence written in the Japanese symbolic system.

method (Davydov, 1990). Finally, the lexico-semantic cognitive program focused on helping children develop classification skills, including single and double classification, in order to master the concept of class inclusion and at the same time learn many kinds of lower- and higher-level concepts (e.g., animals and birds, men and women, tools, traffic facilities).

The purpose of this chapter is to outline the experimental training studies of this teaching program. I examine the role of phonological analysis of words and clarify the role of syntactico-semantic analysis of sentences in the acquisition of reading and writing skills by schoolchildren.

The Japanese writing system

The Japanese symbol system consists of Chinese characters, Kanji, and two types of syllabic letters, Hiragana and Katakana. Usually Japanese adults use these three kinds of letters in a certain combination. An example is shown in Figure 12.1.

Usually we express the names of persons, objects, concepts, and the stems of verbs and adjectives using Chinese characters. Other parts of sentences representing the case relations of words, conjugations of verbs, adjectives, and so on are expressed by syllabic letters, Hiragana. But when we write the names of places, persons in foreign countries, and words of foreign origin, we usually use the second type of syllabic letter, Katakana.

As with other writing systems, many years are required to learn the Japanese writing system so that the children may master it in reading and writing. In particular, learning over 2,000 Chinese characters, which is the minimum essential to modern Japanese, requires much time and practice. But the Japanese have a so-called writing system for children, that is, a syllabic writing system, Hiragana. Books for preschool children are always printed in Hiragana, which has 71 symbols. Preschool children who have mastered it can easily learn to read picture books and write letters.

Learning of syllabic letters by children

In the preschool period, Hiragana is always used at home, in kindergarten, and in nursery school to represent the names of children, other persons, and objects. Children can often find sign boards and name-plates written in Hiragana in the streets. In any railway stations in Japan the names are always written also in Hiragana.

This cultural circumstance, of course, stimulates preschool children to learn to read and write Hiragana letters. Usually Japanese children begin to learn to read Hiragana in the early preschool period or, to be more exact, at about 4 years of age. Almost all of them can master the fundamental skills of reading in Hiragana before entering school without any systematic instruction in reading in kindergarten (Muraishi & Amano, 1972). Why can Japanese preschool children begin to learn to read syllabic letters when they are about 4 years old, and why can they acquire the most basic skills of reading in Hiragana before school without any systematic instruction? These were the first questions I had to answer when I began my research on child literacy in the National Language Research Institute 28 years ago.

A series of experimental studies (Amano, 1967, 1970, 1977) on the relationship between the development of syllabic analysis and the acquisition of reading in syllabic letters produced the following answers to these questions:

1. Syllabic analysis or, more exactly, the act of analyzing the succession of syllabic components of words, is the most important and necessary prerequisite condition for acquisition of reading and writing in Hiragana. Without syllabic analysis, children can never learn to use Hiragana letters.
2. Syllabic analysis and syllabic awareness begin to develop at the age of 4.

3. Development of rhythmic motor coordinate actions and the concept of order through different kinds of play between ages 3 and 4 at home and in kindergarten serves as the basis of development of syllabic analysis.

4. There is a strong reciprocal relationship between development of the act of analyzing the succession of syllabic components of words and reading and writing acquisition by children in Hiragana, particularly in the fundamental syllables (letters) that have a one-to-one correspondence between syllable and symbol. Analysis of the syllabic components of words is one of the necessary prerequisite conditions for acquisition of reading and writing by children in Hiragana. Conversely, reading and writing by children facilitates internalization of the act of syllabic analysis.

But these findings do not mean that Japanese children never have difficulty acquiring literacy in Hiragana. Our further studies (Amano, 1978, 1986) showed that preschool children and lower-grade schoolchildren, particularly those with learning difficulties and learning disabilities, encounter great difficulties in learning to read and write words with special syllables of Hiragana. In Japanese, besides the 71 fundamental syllables there are 4 kinds of special syllables – long, contracted, contracted long, and assimilated – which do not maintain a one-to-one correspondence between syllable and symbol. They are presented in a combination of fundamental syllabic letters. For example, long syllables are represented by two symbols and contracted long ones by three.

Our studies also showed that when children do not have linguistic awareness of the features of syllables, that is, length, contraction, and assimilation of syllables, they often make typical mistakes in spelling these syllables. For example, children with no awareness of long and short syllables often use the same spelling for the words *obasan* (an aunt) and *oba:san* (a grandmother), *ojisan* (an uncle) and *oji:san* (a grandfather), by omitting the vowel that should be added in the case of the long syllable. This fact suggested that it was necessary for children to acquire linguistic awareness of special syllables so that they can correctly write words, including those with special syllables. This holds true particularly for children with learning difficulties or learning disabilities.

But how can we form such linguistic awareness in children? We constructed a model corresponding to the syllabic structure of a word to serve this purpose. If we represent four kinds of syllables, short fundamental syllables including a nasal consonant, long ones, contracted ones,

Figure 12.2. Examples of the models of the syllabic structure of words.

and contracted long ones, with a square, a rectangle, a circle, and an oval, respectively, and a pause (or stop) mora in an assimilated syllable with a triangle, we can symbolize words with all kinds of syllabic structures in Japanese by combining these figures. For example, the syllabic structures of the words *sakura* (cherry), *bo:shi* (a hat), *syo:bo:sya* (a fire truck), and *kyu:ko:ressya* (an express) can be represented as shown in Figure 12.2.

Mainly on the basis of this idea, we constructed an experimental reading and writing teaching program for preschool children (Amano, 1977b) and for lower-grade schoolchildren with learning difficulties (Amano, 1982). This program consisted of seven parts comprising 26 steps. In the first part, children learn to analyze the succession of syllabic components of words consisting of only fundamental syllables, and to read and write these words correctly. In the second part, they learn to construct models of words with assimilated syllables and to read and write them correctly. Then they do the same with words containing a long syllable, a contracted one, and a long-contracted one, respectively, in the third to fifth parts of the program. And in the last part of the program, they learn to make syllabic models of words and to read and write them with complex words including two or three kinds of special syllables in one word.

Using the stage-by-stage formation method (Gal'perin, 1956, 1959), we organized children's learning of model construction of words with a special syllable in the following five stages.

1. First, children are taught the linguistic features of each special syllable necessary to identify it in a word.

2. Second, they learn to construct models of syllabic structures of words using different forms of wooden blocks (or small plastic plates), with the help of a visual schema of models of words drawn under pictures.

3. At the third stage, the visual schema of the model is simplified into series of dots expressing only the number of syllables in the words and requiring the children to construct models by analyzing the syllabic structure of words orally.

4. At the fourth stage, the visual schema of the models is omitted completely and children are required to construct models by analyzing the syllabic structure of words only.

5. Finally, the children are required to construct models of words without any help immediately on recognizing words presented orally.

After learning model construction with words, children learn the correspondence between syllables and symbols or the orthographic rules of these syllables. For example, in the program on the orthographic rules of a long syllable, training proceeds in the following steps.

1. First, children learn the features of symbols and sounds and the differences between them.

2. Second, they learn the vowels and identify long vowels contained in a long syllable of the word.

3. Third, they learn to classify words according to the long vowel in the long syllable of the word.

4. Then they learn the orthographic rules of long syllables.

5. Finally, they repeat the practice of reading and writing words containing long syllables.

We repeated such teaching experiments first with preschool children and then with children with learning difficulties. Figure 12.3 shows the results of the experimental training of long syllables with preschool children. In this study (Amano, 1977b), based on data from preliminary tests, seven pairs of 4- and 5-year-old children, each equal in terms of level of acquisition of Hiragana letters, level of acquisition of awareness, and word construction of long syllables, were selected and randomly divided into training and control groups. Children in the training group were trained in model construction and then in spelling long syllables individually. Their performance (mean percentage correct) in the model construction and word construction tasks during the study period was

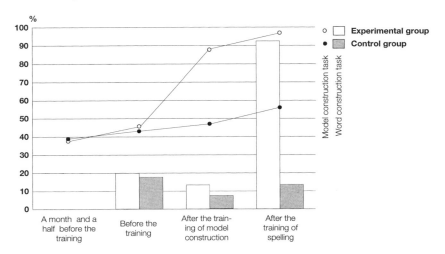

Figure 12.3. The effect of training in model construction and word construction on learning of long syllables by preschool children.

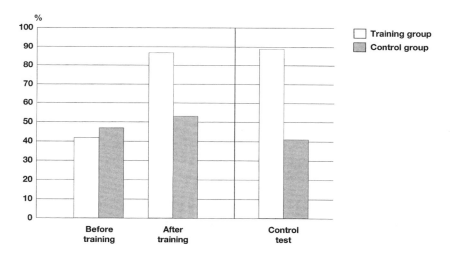

Figure 12.4. The effect of training in model construction of syllabic structure of words on school children.

compared with that of children in the control group, who did not undergo any training.

Figure 12.4 shows the results of the experimental training in special syllables in schoolchildren with learning difficulties. In this study (Amano,

1982), six second-grade children underwent individual training under the previously mentioned seven-part program. The figure compares the progress (mean percentage correct) of the training group on model construction of words containing different kinds of special syllables with that of the control group. In Figure 12.4 the results (mean percent correct) of a control test administered to both groups after the training, using 20 tasks of model construction of words with various kinds of special syllables, is also shown.

These studies revealed that even preschool children and children with learning difficulties could acquire linguistic awareness of the syllabic structure of words with special syllables through model construction of words. After becoming aware of special syllables, they could learn to read and to write words containing different kinds of special syllables.

Phonological analysis in the acquisition of reading and writing

We may now define the role of phonological analysis in the acquisition of reading and writing by children as follows.

1. Phonological analysis, as D. B. El'konin (1956) pointed out, consists of two kinds of analysis: analysis of the succession of phonological components of words and analysis of the phonological structure of words.
2. The role of phonological analysis of words in developing children's literacy in phonological symbol systems is due to the fact that reading and writing in phonological symbol systems always contain the transformation of codes, from graphic to phonological and from phonetic or phonological to graphic.
3. Phonological analysis in the process of writing prepares students for the transformation from phonological code into symbols. The links of phonological analysis in the transformation of word codes from perceptive-acoustic code to phonological symbol code in writing are schematically illustrated in Figure 12.5.
4. Phonological analysis of words in learning to read prepares students for the transformation of codes from graphic to phonological through the development of linguistic awareness of the phonological succession and structure of words.

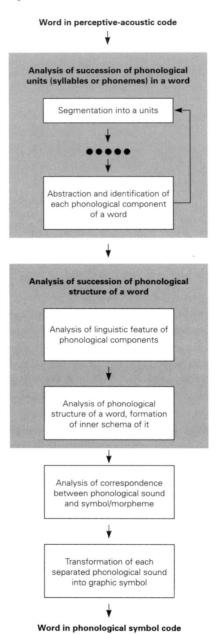

Figure 12.5. Schema of processes of transformation of a word from an acoustic or phonological code into a graphic one in writing a word.

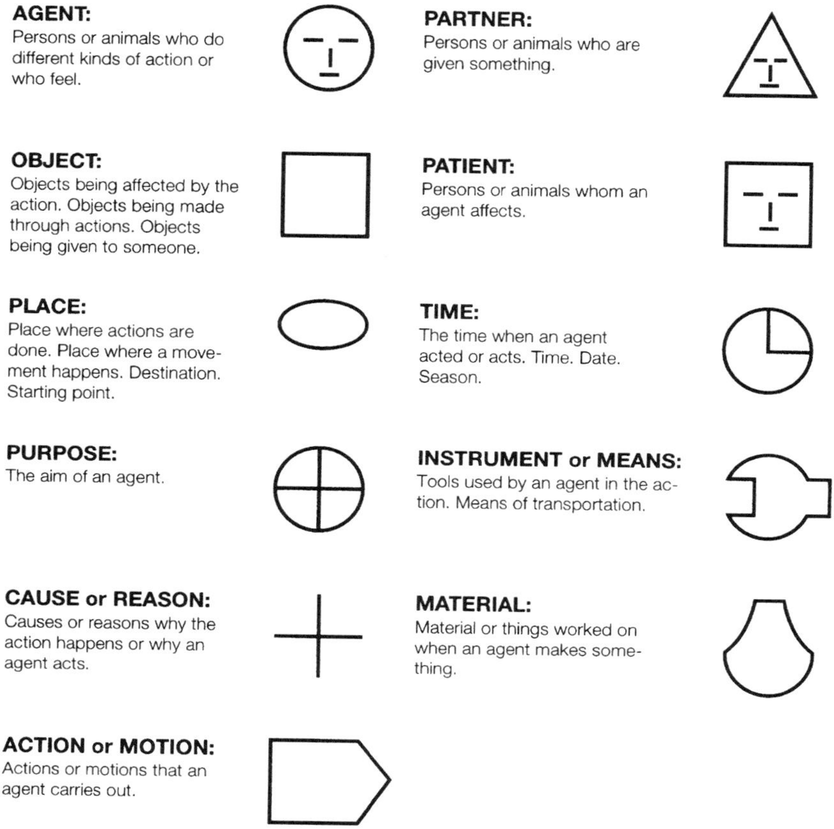

AGENT:
Persons or animals who do different kinds of action or who feel.

PARTNER:
Persons or animals who are given something.

OBJECT:
Objects being affected by the action. Objects being made through actions. Objects being given to someone.

PATIENT:
Persons or animals whom an agent affects.

PLACE:
Place where actions are done. Place where a movement happens. Destination. Starting point.

TIME:
The time when an agent acted or acts. Time. Date. Season.

PURPOSE:
The aim of an agent.

INSTRUMENT or MEANS:
Tools used by an agent in the action. Means of transportation.

CAUSE or REASON:
Causes or reasons why the action happens or why an agent acts.

MATERIAL:
Material or things worked on when an agent makes something.

ACTION or MOTION:
Actions or motions that an agent carries out.

Figure 12.6. The illustrative figures of symbols.

Linguistic awareness of the syntactico-semantic structure of sentences and acquisition of reading and writing in children

In our experimental teaching, we give children a sentence model construction task under what we call the *syntax program*. The main aim of this program is to develop in children linguistic awareness of the syntactico-semantic structure of sentences. In this program we use 10 or 11 kinds of symbols that represent the syntactico-semantic categories of sentences: agent, object, partner, patient, instrument, material, purpose, cause and reason, time, place, and action. They are shown in Figure 12.6.

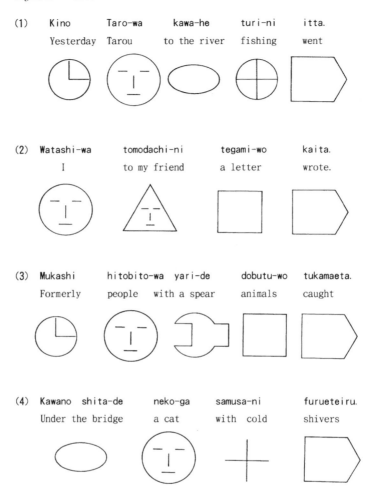

Figure 12.7. Examples of models of the syntactico-semantic structure of sentences.

With the aid of these symbols, one can easily construct a model of the syntactico-semantic structure of a sentence, as long as one has more or less obvious linguistic awareness of the syntactico-semantic components of sentences. The following examples, shown in Figure 12.7, serve as an explanation.

As the reader can see in these examples, in Japanese the case relations of words, that is, the syntactico-semantic meaning of words, is expressed not by prepositions or word order as in English, but by postpositions, for example, *ga, wa, de, ni, wo, kara*, and so on. There are some 15 postpositions in Japanese. But like prepositions in English, Japanese postpositions are always multivocal and represent different kinds of syntactico-semantic categories. For example, the postposition *de* sometimes represents "place" but at other times "cause and reason" or "instrument" or "material," depending on the context of a word in the sentence. Moreover one syntactico-semantic category can often be expressed by different kinds of postpositions. For example, the "place" can be expressed by *de, ni, he, kara*, and so on.

Usually children with learning difficulties or learning disabilities have serious difficulty not only in writing but also in oral speech. They can hardly compose and write any sentence, or at best can write a simply constructed sentence. Related to the previously mentioned characteristics of Japanese syntax, they often show errors or ellipses of postpositions in written sentences and in oral speech. This defect in their syntactic ability may result, on the one hand, from poor development of sentence construction but also, on the other hand, from nonawareness of syntactico-semantic categories and components of sentences. Of course, in Japan children learn grammar in elementary school, but usually the lessons in grammar begin with teaching the concepts of the *subject* and *predicate* of sentences in the third grade. These concepts of formal grammar never help children with learning difficulties acquire the necessary linguistic awareness in sentence composition. For these reasons, we intended to develop this new type of syntax program in order to promote the development of linguistic awareness in children with learning difficulties or learning disabilities in reading and writing.

But how can we teach children to construct a syntactico-semantic model of sentences? Over the past 10 years, we repeated many teaching experiments with different categories of children: normal elementary schoolchildren, preschool children, children with learning difficulties, and children with mental retardation. The methods of teaching were slightly different, depending on the degree of their development. When we teach Japanese adults or students to construct models, it may be sufficient to give them a brief explanation of each category with the aid of the illustrative figure. But when teaching lower-grade schoolchildren, much less children with learning difficulties, it is clearly insufficient to give them only explanations of the meaning of each symbol. It is necessary to teach some objective acts or operations, by which they can identify correctly each of the syntactico-semantic components or categories in the sentences. The following two acts or operations serve this purpose.

1. The act of analyzing and identifying the syntactico-semantic category of a certain component of a sentence by composing an interrogative sentence with the interrogative word corresponding to the category of the component in question. For example, when a child is required to identify the category of *kawa-he* ("to the river") in the following sentence,

> Kino Taro-wa kawa-he turi-ni itta.
> (Yesterday Taro went to the river fishing.)

he or she can identify it by constructing the interrogative sentence with the interrogative word, which corresponds to the category of *kawa-he*, by asking "Kino Taro-wa doko-he ittanodesuka?" ("Yesterday where did Taro go fishing?"). In order to help children learn this act, a supplementary illustrative figure representing the correspondence between the symbol mark of category and interrogative words is shown to children in the training programs.

2. The act of analyzing and identifying the syntactico-semantic category of a certain component of a sentence by composing a sentence expressing an unfolded syntactico-semantic meaning of the category of the component in question. For example, when a child is required to identify the category of "to the river" in the previously mentioned sentence, he or she can do so by constructing the sentence "Kino Taro-ha kawato iu basyo-he turi-ni itta" ("Yesterday Taro went fishing to the place of a river"). In order to help children learn this act, we prepare a supplementary illustrative figure representing the meaning of each symbol mark of category words in teaching.

In addition to these acts, a concrete pretending act, in which a child makes small toy dolls play the role of agent, partner, or patient in the same miniature situation as in a given sentence, is used to help children learn the function of each syntactico-semantic category.

In training normal lower-grade schoolchildren, the content of a sentence is presented in printed text. For children with learning difficulties or learning disabilities, the content is presented in a picture with the schema of a model of the sentence.

In the sentence model construction task, a child is asked to make a model of a sentence with small symbol plates on which a symbol figure is drawn. At the first stage, he or she is asked to make a sentence, saying aloud each word, taking the corresponding symbol plates one by one from the right side of a schema of the sentence with the help of a schema of the sentence. Then different tasks are given stage by stage.

The first training experiment (Amano, 1982) was conducted with normal second-grade schoolchildren (four children each in the experimental and control groups) applying a six-step program. The steps of the training are illustrated in the flow chart shown in Figure 12.8.

In this program, training began with teaching the function of each syntactico-semantic category through the concrete pretending act of using toys in miniature garden situations. The program then moved to the model construction of sentences through learning the previously mentioned two kinds of operation. This method proved to be very effective in developing the sentence model constructive skill in children.

Figure 12.9 shows the effect of the training, comparing the mean percentages correct on model construction tasks before and after training.

Subsequently, we moved to a training program with lower-grade schoolchildren with learning difficulties. The program was administered to first-grade children who apparently could not learn to read and write due to a learning disability or slight mental retardation. For the time being, the program consists of two parts.

In the first part of the program, children composed declarative and interrogative sentences with different constructions in oral speech, such as constructing the model of a sentence on the basis of a schema of the model. The aim of training in this stage is to improve their sentence construction in oral speech and, at the same time, to develop syntactico-semantic categories and functions of each figurative symbol with the aid of the explanatory figure. Then they learn to compose declarative and interrogative sentences with the interrogative words *who, what,* and *where* in oral speech. In this step, pictures expressing the content of sentences are used as training materials. Each picture is drawn on a sheet; below it is a schema of the model of the sentence corresponding to it. The schema is usually covered by a small sheet of opaque paper, but it can be uncovered if needed.

The training in sentence composition is conducted in the following order.

1. Training in sentence composition without a schema of the model and model construction. First, the child is asked to compose a sentence, viewing a picture presented with the schema covered. If the child succeeds, the trainer gives praise and asks the child to construct a model of the sentence.
2. Sentence composition based on schema and model construction. If the child fails to compose the required sentence or makes mistakes in the use of postposition, the trainer points out the errors,

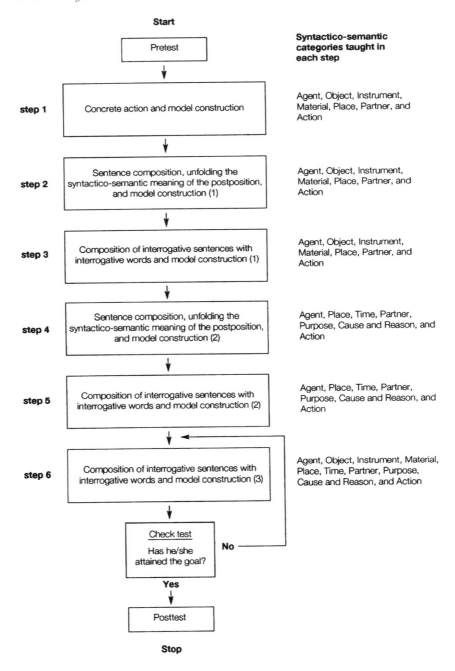

Figure 12.8. Flowchart of the experimental training program.

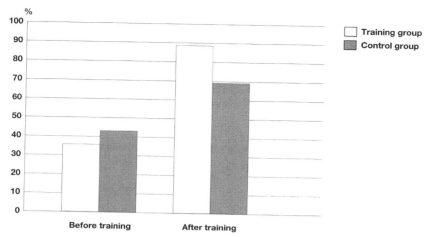

Figure 12.9. The effect of the training: comparison of mean percentages of correct model construction tests before and after training.

uncovers the schema, and asks the child to compose the sentence correctly, putting the corresponding symbol plates on the schema and constructing a model of it.

3. Composition of an interrogative sentence with interrogative sentences. After the child has constructed the model of a sentence, he or she is required to compose an interrogative sentence, asking for one component (agent, object, or place of the sentence) and constructing a model of the sentence with the aid of the supplementary figures for interrogative sentences. The trainer first demonstrates constructing the interrogative sentences once with each type of interrogative sentence.

4. Test of model construction. After exercises with 14 sentences, the trainer asks the child to make a model of each sentence correctly again in order to evelute his or her learning. In steps 2–4, similar training is done with 10 different sentences with different syntactico-semantic components. But in each step, the child learns to compose different kinds of interrogative sentences.

In the second part of the program, written sentences are introduced and children learn to read and write sentences based on the model of sentences constructed by themselves. In step 5, written text and a miniature garden, small dolls (a mother, a boy, a girl, a cup, poles, a sheet of paper, a block of clay, etc.) are prepared. After the sentence is read aloud, the child is asked to make himself or herself or a toy doll perform the action described in the text and to construct a model of the sentence. By confirming the correspondence between syntactico-semantic categories and components of the concrete action performed, the child learns the function of each category.

In steps 6–9, the child learns to read and write in the following order, using the materials in steps 1–4, respectively.

1. Reading sentences. A written sentence on a small sheet of paper is put on the schema of the sentence under the picture. The child is required to read correctly. When he or she makes errors, the trainer points them out and asks the child to read the sentence again correctly.

2. Sentence composition based on model construction. When the child reads the sentence correctly, he or she is required to construct a model of it, putting symbols on the sheet of paper one by one, sequentially reading aloud the corresponding component of the sentence.

3. Sentence composition based on model construction. The written sentence is covered, and the schema of the sentence is uncovered. The child is asked to compose a sentence aloud while constructing a model of the sentence.

4. Writing sentences. After constructing a model of the sentence, the child is asked to write the sentence with a pencil in his or her notebook while looking at the syntactico-semantic model of the sentence that the child constructed.

We conducted experimental training of five first-grade boys with learning difficulties in reading and writing (four of the boys demonstrated what appeared to be learning disabilities; the fifth boy apparently had slight mental retardation) for 1.5 years using this syntax program in addition to the previously mentioned orthography program in syllabic letters and the lexico-semantic-cognitive program. The training was conducted individually with each boy two times a week in the speech clinic centers in Kawasaki City.

As a result of the training, all children successfully acquired the basic ability to construct the syntactico-semantic models of sentences, to read, and to write sentences with different kinds of constructions on the basis of the model construction of sentences. Table 12.1 shows the comparison of the results of tests on syllabic analysis of words (syllabic model construction), sentence model construction, oral sentence construction, class inclusion, and revised Japanese Wechsler Intelligence Scale for Children

Table 12.1. *Comparison of test results of children with learning disabilities before and after the training*

Subjects	Before training					After training				
	T.M.	N.T.	M.Y.	I.T.	N.D.	T.M.	N.T.	M.Y.	I.T.	N.D.
Age[a]										
(years : months)	7 : 5	7 : 0	7 : 0	6 : 10	7 : 4	8 : 9	8 : 5	8 : 6	8 : 4	9 : 8
WISC-R[b] VIQ	84	107	85	68	69	101	103	107	113	79
PIQ	113	95	113	90	59	111	93	84	95	61
IQ	97	102	99	76	61	106	98	96	105	68
Syllabic models										
construction	4	3	5	16	11	20	19	20	20	20
(20 words), %	20.0	15.0	25.0	80.0	55.0	100.0	95.0	100.0	100.0	100.0
Sentence model										
construction task	4	7	12	23	15	28	28	27	27	28
(29 items), %	13.8	24.1	41.4	79.3	51.8	96.6	96.6	93.1	93.1	96.6
Oral sentence										
construction task	5	8	12	10	4	19	19	20	19	13
(22 items), %	22.7	36.4	54.5	45.5	18.2	86.4	86.4	90.9	86.4	50.9
Class inclusion										
task[c]	0	0	1	0	0	6	6	6	6	6
(6 items), %	0.0	0.0	16.7	0	0	100.0	100.0	100.0	100.0	100.0

[a] Age of the child when tested.
[b] The test was administered in 1983 and 1985. However, the scores of VIQ, PIQ, and IQ are modified on the basis of the score table of the WISC-R test revised in 1989 in Japan.
[c] The task consisted of three items with concrete objects and three verbal items.

(WISC-R) tests before and after training. After the training, we also gave the children a sentence composition task using a certain model sentence and the task of writing an essay on a certain theme ("On a person whom I like best"). These results showed clearly that the children had acquired a linguistic awareness of syllabic word construction and sentence construction, as well as the basic skills required to write a sentence and an essay correctly through the training by our complex language teaching programs.

The very important and interesting result obtained by this experimental training is that the verbal IQs (VIQs) on WISC-R tests improved significantly for three boys (T.M., M.Y., and I.T.) of the five who underwent our complex training program. In contrast, one boy (N.T.), whose performance IQ (PIQ) on WISC-R tests had been lower than his VIQ before the training, did not improve in VIQ, although his awareness of the syllabic structure of words, the syntactico-semantic structure of sentences, and his sentence composition abilities were significantly improved by the training. The fifth boy (N.D.), who had considerably lower scores in both VIQ and PIQ before the training, seemingly due to slight mental retardation, also showed improvement in VIQ, but the gain was smaller.

These results indicate that the training of children with learning disabilities by our complex teaching programs not only improved their reading and writing abilities but also contributed much to the development of general verbal abilities, especially in children whose VIQs were depressed. Our complex language teaching programs were more effective for children with verbal learning disabilities.

Conclusion

I have outlined a long series of studies that started nearly 30 years ago, stimulated by the ideas of Vygotsky and El'konin on reading acquisition by children. To conclude, I point out some of the problems concerning the relationship between the development of linguistic awareness and learning to read and write.

As I mentioned earlier, we observed a strong reciprocal relationship between the development of the act of analyzing the succession of syllabic components of words and reading and writing acquisition by children in Hiragana, particularly in the fundamental syllables (letters), which have a one-to-one correspondence between syllable and symbol. But a different pattern was observed in reading and writing words containing special syllables, especially those with long or long contracted ones. When we were able to form and develop linguistic awareness of special syllables in children before they learned to read and write words with them, we observed the appearance of a reciprocal relation between development of linguistic awareness of special syllables and reading and writing activity of children. However, when we did not teach them the linguistic features of special syllables, we did not observe this relation. That is, some children began to read and write words using their own strategy, with no linguistic awareness of special syllables. As a result, their awareness developed very slowly, and they repeated errors in reading and spelling words for a long time. A similar relationship was observed between the development of linguistic awareness of syntactico-semantic structures of sentences and learning to read and write sentences.

In our training studies, we observed that children's construction of models of the syntactico-semantic structures of sentences played a role in facilitating learning to read and to write sentences in the following two ways: (1) the syntactico-semantic model of sentences constructed by children served as a schema of sentences when they constructed sentences orally and then in written speech; (2) the linguistic awareness of each syntactico-semantic category developed through model-constructing actions made children more conscious of the relations between the case of words and the form of words in sentences and facilitated their learning to read and write. In these cases children's reading and writing activity also facilitated their development of linguistic awareness. But when we did not organize their formation of linguistic awareness, their reading and writing activity did not always facilitate the development of linguistic awareness of syntactico-semantic structures of sentences because, as mentioned earlier, they could hardly learn such linguistic knowledge spontaneously.

On the basis of our research, we may conclude that the optimal way of organizing the teaching of reading and writing in a phonological symbol system is to organize the learning so that development of linguistic awareness is interrelated with reading and writing activities in a reciprocal way. In other words, instruction that leads to linguistic awareness at the beginning of teaching literacy is one of the most effective ways to enlarge the zone of proximal development for children engaged in learning to read and write.

References

Amano, K. (1967). An experimental study on the ability of preschool children to analyze phonological structure of words. *Study of Language, 3*, 51–87 (National Language Research Institute).

Amano, K. (1970). Formation of the act of analyzing phonemic structure of word and its relation to learning Japanese syllabic characters (kana-moji). *Japanese Journal of Educational Psychology, 18*(2), 76–89.

Amano, K. (1977). On the formation of the act of analyzing syllabic structure of words and the learning of Japanese syllabic characters in moderately mentally retarded children. *Japanese Journal of Educational Psychology, 25*(2), 73–84.

Amano, K. (1978). *Formation of the act of analyzing syllabic structure of words and the learning of Japanese syllabic characters: Formation of awareness on long syllable and teaching reading and spelling in preschool children.* Paper presented at the 20th Annual Conference of the Association of Japanese Educational Psychology, Yokohama, September 2–4.

Amano, K. (1982). Improvement of language abilities of school children through the formation of awareness to linguistic reality. *Bulletin of the National Institute for Educational Research, 102*, 1–112.

Amano, K. (1986). *Processes of acquisition of Japanese syllabic characters.* Tokyo: Akiyama-syoten.

Calfee, R. C., Lindamood, P. A., & Lindamood, C. (1973). Acoustic-phonetic skills and reading: Kindergarten through twelfth grades. *Journal of Educational Psychology, 64,* 293–298.

Davydov, V. V. (1990). *Types of generalization in instruction: Logical and psychological problems in the structuring of school curricula.* Reston: National Council of Teachers of Mathematics.

El'konin, D. B. (1956). Nekotorye voprosy psikhologii usvoeniya gramoty. *Voprosy Psikhologii, 5,* 38–53.

El'konin, D. B. (1976). *Kak uchit' detei chitach'.* Moscow: Znanie.

El'konin, D. B., & Zhurova, L. E. (1963). K voprosy o formirovaniya fonematicheskogo vospitaniya u detei doshkol'nogo vozrasta. In *Sehsorhoe vospitanie doshkol'nikov.* Moscow: Izd-vo APN RSFSR.

Fillmore, C. J. (1976). The case of case. In E. Bach & R. T. Harms (Eds.), *Universals in linguistic theory.* New York: Holt.

Fox, B., & Routh, D. K. (1984). Phonemic analysis and synthesis as word attack skills. *Journal of Educational Psychology, 76,* 1059–1064.

Gal'perin, P. Ya. (1956). O formirobanii chuvstvennykh obrazov i panyatii. In *Materialy soveschaniya po psikhologii.* Moscow: Izd-vo APN RSFSR.

Gal'perin, P. Ya. (1959). Razvitie issledovanii po formirovaniyu umstvennykh deistvii. In *Psikhologichekaya Nauka v SSSR.* Tom 1. Moscow: Izd-vo APN RSFSR.

Gleitman, L. R., & Rozin, P. (1973). Teaching reading by syllabary. *Reading Research Quarterly, 8,* 447–483.

Gleitman, L. R., & Rozin, P. (1977a). The structure and acquisition of reading 1: Relations between orthographies and the structure of language. In A. S. Reber and D. L. Scarborough (Eds.), *Toward a psychology of reading: The proceeding of CUNY conferences.* Hillsdale: Lawrence Erlbaum.

Gleitman, L. R., & Rozin, P. (1977b). The structure and acquisition of reading 2: The reading process and acquisition of the alphabetic principle. In A. S. Reber and D. L. Scarborough (Eds.), *Toward a psychology of reading: The proceeding of CUNY conferences.* Hillsdale: Lawrence Erlbaum.

Liberman, I. Y., Shankweiter, D., Fisher, F. W., & Carter, B. (1974). Explicit phoneme and syllable segmentation in the young child. *Journal of Experimental Child Psychology, 18,* 201–212.

Lundberg, I., Frost, J., & Petersen, O. P. (1988). Effect of an extensive program for stimulating phonological awareness in preschool children. *Reading Research Quarterly, 23,* 263–284.

Luria, A. R. (1950). *Ocherki psikhofiziologii pis'ma.* Moscow: Izd-vo APN RSFSR.

Muraishi, S., & Amano, K. (1972). Reading and writing ability in preschool children. *National Language Research Institute, Report No. 45.* Tokyo: Tokyo Syoseki.

Perfetti, C. A. (1985). *Reading ability.* Oxford: Oxford University Press.

Share, D., Jorm, A., Maclean, R., & Mattews, R. (1984). Sources of individual differences in reading acquisition. *Journal of Educational Psychology, 76,* 1209–1224.

Torne'us, M. (1984). Phonological awareness and reading: A chicken and egg problem? *Journal of Educational Psychology, 76,* 1246–1258.

Treiman, R., & Baron, J. (1983). Phoneme analysis training helps children benefit from spelling-sound rules. *Memory & Cognition, 11,* 382–389.

Tunmer, W., & Nesdale, A. R. (1985). Phoneme segmentation skill and beginning reading. *Journal of Educational Psychology, 77,* 417–427.

Ushinsky, K. D. (1974). *Izbrannye pedagogicheskie sochneniya.* Tom 1–2. Moscow: Peda-gogika.

Vygotsky, L. S. (1987). Thinking and speech. In *The collected works of L. S. Vygotsky: Vol. 1: Problems of general psychology* (R. W. Rieber & A. S. Carton, Eds.). New York: Plenum.

Wallach, M. A., & Wallach, L. (1979). Helping disadvantaged children to learn to read by teaching phonemic identification skills. In L. Resnick & P. A. Weaver (Eds.), *Theory and practice of early reading* (Vol. 3). Hillsdale: Lawrence Erlbaum.

Zhurova, L. E. (1974). *Obuchenie gramote v detskom sadu.* Moscow: Pedagogika.

13 Psychomotor and socioemotional processes in literacy acquisition: Results of an ongoing case study involving a nonvocal cerebral palsic young man

Matthias Bujarski, Martin Hildebrand-Nilshon, and Jan Kordt

Introduction

The case study presented here is one of the first six to be involved in an Augmentative and Alternative Communication (AAC) research project led by Professor Siegfried Schubenz. Its aim is to examine new communication forms and approaches with physically severely disabled students.

The intervention strategy that we use is derived from *psychological-educational therapy* (*Pädagogisch-Psychologische Therapie;* see Schubenz, 1993; Pilz, 1982; Schlösser, 1980). Grounded in activity theory, this therapy integrates psychotherapeutic and educational aspects into a model of ambulant psychosocial intervention.

The AAC medium most widely used in our work is Blissymbolics (Bliss, 1965). This is a picto- and ideographic symbol communication system consisting of 26 basic "symbol elements" (McDonald, 1980, p. 21). These elements are combined according to standardized rules to form terms and can be grammatically arranged into sentences.

In order that the symbols be understood by persons not fluent in Bliss, the meaning of each symbol is also written in traditional orthography (TO) above the symbol. Currently there are about 3,000 standardized Blissymbols worldwide.

In order to communicate with the help of such a nonverbal symbolic communication system (Musselwhite & St. Louis, 1982), or aided system (Lloyd, 1985; Lloyd, Quist, & Windsor, 1990), not only the meaning of the symbols but also ways to produce them have to be learned. If writing or drawing are out of the question, some form of indicating or coding strategy becomes necessary as a substitute, using the remaining range of voluntary movements.

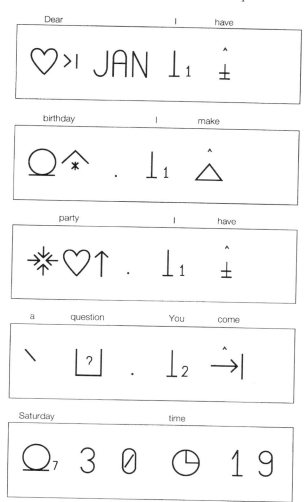

Figure 13.1. An invitation written in Blissymbols.

Transcription and translation:

Dear Jan,
It's my birthday soon. I'll have a party. I have a question.
Would you come on Saturday the 30th at 19 hours?

Note that the Bliss text follows the German grammar correctly, with one exception: Michael writes "Du kommen," whereas the correct form would be "Kommen Du."

In our work, questions arising from the construction and use of adequate coding strategies are of great importance, not only for the use of alternative communication systems, but also for the acquisition of literacy.

Case study of Michael B.

Michael was 18 years old when he became involved in our research work. His voluntary movements are restricted almost entirely to his upper torso, neck, and face due to a quadriplegic cerebral palsy caused by an oxygen deficiency during birth. He can turn his head to either side quite freely and can also move his upper torso, neck, and head forward with some difficulty. Michael is labeled anarthric, that is, his speech is not intelligible, except for a few words, and these are understood only by people who know him well. On the other hand, he understands spoken language perfectly well, having mastered language comprehension in his childhood apparently without delay.

Although it is not the topic of this chapter, it must be noted that this skill alone is far from normal for people with physical disabilities of this kind and magnitude in Germany. From the outset, Michael was fortunate to have very dedicated parents who were convinced that their son would develop in a normal way. They participated in organizing a parent–infant play group at a private therapeutic center. Later, Michael attended kindergarten and preschool at the same center in an integrated group of handicapped and nonhandicapped children of the same age. Michael and his parents have fond memories of the time he spent at the center.

Despite strong efforts by the staff of the center and his parents, the board of education for his district did not allow Michael to continue his schooling with this group of children at a normal primary school. Currently, the situation in the Berlin school system has been liberalized so that integration is possible under certain circumstances, but at that time – in the mid-1970s – the concept of segregating children with special needs was still being actively pursued. From the age of 7 until the age of 20 (1989), Michael thus attended a special school for the learning-disabled and mentally handicapped that also schooled a number of multiply handicapped students.

During his 13 years of education, Michael acquired and maintained a tenacious dyslexia, which prevented him from learning to read texts written in TO and impaired his writing skills. Since many different methods of instruction in reading and writing skills showed little success, skepticism concerning his learning abilities grew over the years.

Michael was exposed to Blissymbolics for the first time in 1984. As a result of his success in learning Blissymbols, the efforts to teach him reading and writing in TO were minimized from then on. However, Michael always refused to give up on literacy acquisition.

Bliss soon became a powerful means of communication for him, used for "speaking" as well as for writing activities. Reading letters and other literature available in Bliss was now also possible, although to a much lesser degree. This is largely due to the fact that not many people are writing in Bliss.

The seriousness of Blissymbolics was considerably enhanced by the introduction of a microcomputer. When we first met Michael at school, he was a competent user of the Talking-Blissapple program (Kelso & Vanderheiden, 1985) on the Apple II computer. He used a small, specially adapted numerical keyboard, striking the keys with this head. In order for him to be able to do this, a headpointer was attached to his forehead and his arms were tied to his body to give him enough stability.

Patterns of head movements for Blissymbols

Due to the limitations of the Talking-Blissapple software and the large number of symbols he wanted to use, Michael had to learn a three-digit numerical code for each symbol in order to produce it on the computer screen. To facilitate the learning of these codes and to be able to use the Blissymbols when communicating without the computer – that is, to gain more independence from others – a counting strategy was introduced by which the digits were converted into head movements. Thus, an important sensorimotor dimension was added to support the symbolic representation. Now each Blissymbol had its own movement pattern, enabling Michael to "speak" in numerical terms.

This numerical strategy proved to be efficient and adaptable to conversation situations when technical assistance is either not available or undesired. The strategy is as follows: After catching the attention of the person he wants to talk to, Michael indicates that the person should take his Blissbook out of the pack attached to the back of his wheelchair. This book contains a list of Blissymbols and some words written in TO. On each page, the symbols and words are arranged in rows and columns. Michael indicates the term he wishes to convey by moving his head to the left. His vis-à-vis has to count Michael's head movements. The first number of movements indicates the page, followed by those indicating the row and, finally, those for the column in which the word or symbol

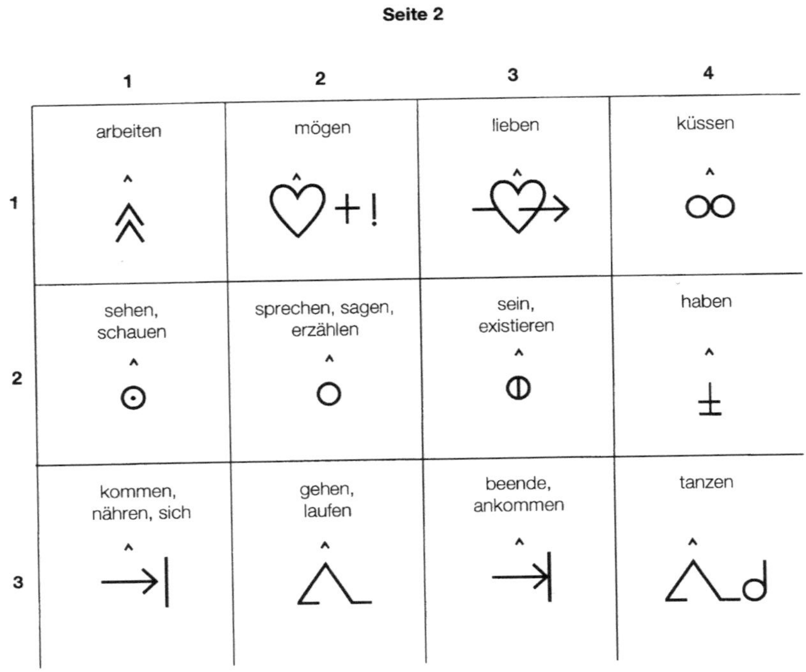

Seite 2

	1	2	3	4
1	arbeiten	mögen	lieben	küssen
2	sehen, schauen	sprechen, sagen, erzählen	sein, existieren	haben
3	kommen, nähren, sich	gehen, laufen	beende, ankommen	tanzen

The procedure to select "sehen" (see):

First step:	Selection of page:	2 head movements =	Page No. 2;
Second step:	Selection of row:	2 head movements =	Row No. 2;
Third step:	Selection of column:	1 head movement =	Column No. 1;

code 221 = sehen.

Figure 13.2. Part of page 2 of Michael's Blissbook.

is located. For example, "I like to go (to a) coffee house" would be expressed as 111,I – 212,like – 232,go – 453,coffee house.

Of course, there are serious limitations to this way of communicating. First and foremost, it is comparatively slow. Second, up to now, the vocabulary used has remained limited to some 650 terms. Third, Michael is not encouraged to use more complex sentences since the capacity of the so-called nonhandicapped to keep track of the head movements and content at the same time is limited.

However, by using the numerical strategy as he does, Michael was able to develop his own way of talking for the first time. He could show his capacity for learning hundreds of symbols and their numerical representation at the same time. The use of the numerical code deemphasizes the importance of the graphic aspects of the symbols. New terms added to his book are now written in TO, and some of the old Blissymbols have also been replaced by TO words.

A two-way approach to literacy: The integration of micro and macro processes within activity theory

Part one: Providing movement patterns for the alphabet

The continuing improvement of communication with Blissymbolics, that is, the growth of active, self-initiated use of the symbols, as well as the successful addition of written words to the Blissbook, encouraged Michael and us to make a fresh effort with regard to literacy.

Over the years, Michael's teachers used various educational methods – synthetical, analytical, syllable and morpheme oriented – in attempting to teach him reading and writing, without lasting success. He had learned however, to identify all the letters and could produce them on a typewriter using a headpointer. Thus he was able to process the letters phonetically and optically and even produce them with his headpointer. These movements, however, never became established as a finite set of motorically controlled patterns comparable to those Michael had developed for the Blissymbols. Optical fixation of the keyboard was necessary, which, of course, also meant that the movements could not be used without the apparatus. Using the headpointer was very impractical, tiring, and demotivating, further supporting the hypothesis that the movement patterns we were looking for had to be created differently.

Michael had learned the traditional Morse code, with some promising results. However, the differentiation between long and short signals using head movements had proved to be too uncertain, so this method had to be abandoned. But the concept of voluntary head movements remained and was applied successfully for the first time in learning Blissymbolics.

Thus a first hypothetical explanation for why Michael had not been able to progress in reading and writing was found. His difficulties could be attributed to the fact that he had always lacked a facility to actively produce letters by distinct, voluntary movements either by speaking (larynx, tongue, and lip movements) or by writing (finger or hand movements).

This leads to the first hypothesis concerning the importance of the sensorimotor (or micro) level for the acquisition of literacy: If the articulatory, gesticulatory, and graphomotor functions are severely handicapped, they have to be compensated for by learning some other voluntary movement patterns as representations for letters and other symbols. Furthermore, the use of these patterns is one of the prerequisites for the process of analyzing and synthesizing the letter strings of words in reading and writing.

In the normal course of development, articulatory movement patterns are unconscious. They are normally developed in the early stages of language acquisition. While learning to read and write, which usually takes place in school, supported by different educational strategies (e.g., conscious, goal-directed spelling of single letters), the child attains access to hitherto unconscious articulatory structures, thus enabling orthographic and morphological analysis. Each letter is learned as a set of voluntary movements on an articulatory and a graphomotor level. With use, not only do the movement patterns necessary for the production of the articulatory and graphic structures become automatized, so does the ability to move from one level to the other.

Our explanation for the lack of progress in literacy acquisition in this case study is twofold. The second hypothesis regarding this apparent lack of progress in reading and writing competence deals with the macro level of personality development. Both hypotheses and their interrelation are derived from activity theory. We discuss personality development and integration of the micro and macro levels into activity theory in Part Two. Before that, we continue to consider the practical implications of the first part of our approach.

Since the numerical code for the processing of Blissymbols had been so successful, we decided to create an equivalent code system of head movements for the letters of the alphabet. We hoped to find out whether learning to produce the letters actively through individual patterns of head movements would help Michael to complete his literacy acquisition on the sensorimotor level, that is, to connect the ongoing visual and acoustic processes, on the one hand, with a substitute for the missing articulatory and graphomotor processes, on the other, thus enabling him finally to close the gap in the field of phonological and orthographic analysis.

Keyboard simulation SIMULA_1 and SIMULA_2

To test our hypothesis concerning the sensorimotor aspects of literacy acquisition in practice, distinct and acceptable movement patterns

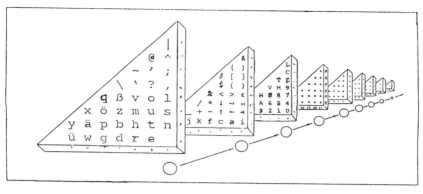

Graphical model of the nine consecutive triangles
containing up to 140 characters

Figure 13.3. The keyboard simulation program SIMULA_1 and SIMULA_2.

for every letter of the alphabet had to be created. This was done by developing a software program allowing the simulation of the entire keyboard of any standard MS-DOS microcomputer with either a one- or two-switch input device. We named it SIMULA_1 and SIMULA_2.

The program consists of nine consecutive triangular tables, which contain all the letters of the alphabet as well as all the other keys of the extended PC keyboard (140 total). The nine tables – seen as a whole – form a tetrahedron. The first triangle is largest, with each successive triangle smaller than the preceding one. This allows the number of steps needed to select a character to be minimized; the character in the most unfavorable position can be reached with just 12 strokes. Each key on the keyboard is represented exactly once in the simulation program, and the search for each key begins at the same starting point. Another advantage of the triangular arrangement is that the space on the screen needed for the tetrahedron is very small, thus minimizing interference with other complementing software (e.g., word processing programs).

The procedure used to choose a key requires three steps. First, the triangle is chosen, then the row of characters, and finally the character within the chosen row. Regardless of whether SIMULA_1 or SIMULA_2 is used, any character in any of the nine triangles has its own individual pattern. However, whereas in SIMULA_2 each character is actively retrieved by the user at his or her own pace, SIMULA_1 is based on a scanning procedure. With a certain period of time, which can be individually adapted, the user has to make three consecutive selections by pressing his or her input device once at the triangle, once at the row, and

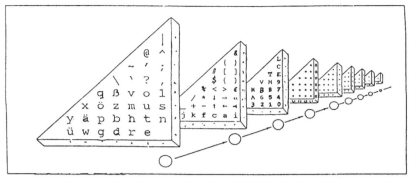

```
strike left switch  2 times = selection of the third triangle
strike right switch 1 time  = activation of that triangle and
                              change to row selection
```

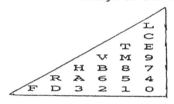

```
strike left switch  3 times = selection of the fourth row
strike right switch 1 time  = activation of that row and
                              change to character (column)
                              selection
```

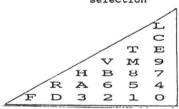

```
strike left switch  1 time = selection of the character "M"
strike right switch 1 time = activation of chosen character
                             and reset to the starting
                             position
```

```
The switches can be replaced by any input device adapted
to the requirements of a special needs user.
```

Figure 13.4. Selection of the majuscule "M" using SIMULA_2.

once at the character level, respectively. When using SIMULA_2, one switch – in Michael's case, the one on his left – is used to move forward within each of the three levels. The other switch – in Michael's case, the one on his right – is used to change the levels: from triangle to row, from row to character within the row, and finally to confirm the chosen character. Figure 13.4 shows the procedure for selecting the majuscule "M" using SIMULA_2.

Letters and specific keyboard characters are distributed according to their frequency in the tetrahedron. Those with a high frequency have a good position, that is, very few strokes are needed to produce them. The basis of this arrangement is a statistical evaluation of the frequency distribution of letters and characters in written German. The corpus comprised 10 million words. The efficiency of the construction according to the frequency can easily be shown: the six most frequent characters represent 50% of any average written text. These have the highest priority within SIMULA.

Last but not least, just as with a normal keyboard, any combination of keys can be produced with SIMULA. Keys that are pressed simultaneously have to be produced in sequence while using SIMULA. Even a full system reset is possible. Thus the user can operate any commercial software with any suitable one- or two-switch input device.

First results concerning the movement patterns

In consideration of Michael's physical abilities and our limited resources, we had simple one- and two-switch input devices constructed. Aside from the initial problems with software and hardware production and testing, the current results of our study are as follows. We started using SIMULA_1 on a regular basis (i.e., two 90-minute sessions per week) in September 1989. By the end of April 1990, that is, within 8 months, Michael learned 26 locations of characters following the tetrahedron structure of SIMULA. Of these 26 characters, 18 represent minuscules, 1 represents a majuscule, 4 are numbers, and the remaining 3 are important keyboard characters.

Michael can identify these characters in two distinct ways. (1) Tests showed that he can produce them accurately on the screen without seeing the triangles, that is, with the triangles covered, using the patterns of head movements depicted in Figure 13.6. (2) He can recall them numerically, indicating with a first set of movements the triangle, with a second set of movements the row, and with the third set of movements

Character	Total	In percent	Accum. in percent	Character	Total	In percent	Accum. in percent
<Blank>	9757782	16.1454	16.1454	U	64499	0.1067	98.9723
e	7745523	12.8159	28.9613	O	63242	0.1046	99.0769
n	4821525	7.9778	36.9391	y	46745	0.0773	99.1542
i	3844148	6.3606	43.2997	9	40776	0.0675	99.2217
r	3545446	5.8664	49.1661	C	39879	0.0660	99.2877
t	2900703	4.7996	53.9657	0	36610	0.0606	99.3483
s	2728829	4.5152	58.4809	3	33985	0.0562	99.4045
a	2546239	4.2130	62.6939	2	33764	0.0559	99.4604
d	2112014	3.4946	66.1885	8	33422	0.0553	99.5157
h	2094722	3.4660	69.6545	)	29135	0.0482	99.5639
u	1751993	2.8989	72.5534	(	28957	0.0479	99.6118
l	1737135	2.8743	75.4277	5	28573	0.0473	99.6591
c	1388043	2.2967	77.7244	;	26220	0.0434	99.7025
g	1290598	2.1354	79.8598	4	25461	0.0421	99.7446
o	1261555	2.0874	81.9472	x	24626	0.0407	99.7853
m	1086896	1.7984	83.7456	?	22913	0.0379	99.8232
b	777282	1.2861	85.0317	6	19493	0.0323	99.8555
f	682066	1.1286	86.1603	7	18974	0.0314	99.8869
'	624619	1.0335	87.1938	/	13085	0.0217	99.9086
k	588197	0.9732	88.1670	Ü	9915	0.0164	99.9250
w	575835	0.9528	89.1198	q	7094	0.0117	99.9367
z	526401	0.8710	89.9908	'	6666	0.0110	99.9477
.	455022	0.7529	90.7437	!	6036	0.0100	99.9577
v	340237	0.5630	91.3067	Ö	5001	0.0083	99.9660
p	334532	0.5535	91.8602	Ä	4934	0.0082	99.9742
ü	316487	0.5237	92.3839	Q	3928	0.0065	99.9807
S	293607	0.4858	92.8697	+	2610	0.0043	99.9850
ä	283617	0.4693	93.3390	Y	2423	0.0040	99.9890
D	227340	0.3762	93.7152	>	1477	0.0024	99.9914
"	221113	0.3659	94.0811	<	1475	0.0024	99.9938
A	218209	0.3611	94.4422	@	1183	0.0020	99.9958
B	194259	0.3214	94.7636	X	921	0.0015	99.9973
M	180564	0.2988	95.0624	&	793	0.0013	99.9986
ß	164506	0.2722	95.3346	^	477	0.0008	99.9994
E	156855	0.2595	95.5941	=	419	0.0007	100.000
G	151927	0.2514	95.8455	#	175	0.0003	100.000
W	150554	0.2491	96.0946	%	133	0.0002	100.000
K	150478	0.2490	96.3436	—	1	0.0000	100.000
P	136075	0.2252	96.5688				
F	134680	0.2228	96.7916	Σ = 60436968 counted characters			
ö	122737	0.2031	96.9947				
R	112234	0.1857	97.1804				
H	112084	0.1855	97.3659				
V	106722	0.1766	97.5425				
-	98957	0.1637	97.7062				
T	94030	0.1556	97.8618				
L	92741	0.1535	98.0153				
I	90648	0.1500	98.1653				
:	77547	0.1283	98.2936				
N	73706	0.1220	98.4156				
Z	69779	0.1155	98.5311				
1	69662	0.1153	98.6464				
J	67229	0.1112	98.7576				
j	65259	0.1080	98.8656				

Figure 13.5. Frequencies of characters in a 10-million-word German text corpus (© 1990 Freie Universität Berlin, Psychologisches Institut, Prof. Dr. Siegfried Schubenz).

the location of the character. The last is especially important since we encountered numerous technical problems with our two-switch input device. This forced us to rely for most of this period on a one-switch input device, that is, on the scanning procedure described earlier.

Despite these additional problems, Michael has not only learned the 26 characters shown earlier but has developed an orientation for finding

Selected Character	Pattern Structure	Total of Movements
Blank	-- C -- C -- C	3
e	-- C -- C 1S C	4
n	-- C 1S C -- C	4
i	1S C -- C -- C	4
r	-- C -- C 2S C	5
t	-- C 1S C 1S C	5
s	-- C 2S C -- C	5
a	1S C -- C 1S C	5
Backspace	1S C 1S C -- C	5
0	2S C -- C -- C	5
d	-- C -- C 3S C	6
h	-- C 1S C 2S C	6
u	-- C 2S C 1S C	6
l	-- C 3S C -- C	6
c	1S C -- C 2S C	6
Return	1S C 2S C -- C	6
1	2S C -- C 1S C	6
4	2S C 1S C -- C	6
g	-- C -- C 4S C	7
m	-- C 2S C 2S C	7
o	-- C 3S C 1S C	7
f	1S C -- C 3S C	7
7	2S C 2S C -- C	7
k	1S C -- C 4S C	8
j	1S C -- C 5S C	9
M	2S C 3S C 1S C	9

C = change level
nS = numbers of steps within the level

Note that the structure of movements is unique for each character.

Figure 13.6. Acquired patterns of head movements for characters.

many more, that is, he understands the logic used in constructing the tetrahedron. Not surprisingly, he learned the most frequently used characters first.

These results seem very promising. It appears that even the use of SIMULA_1 contributed to the acquisition of alternative movement patterns. This led to a higher level of optical and acoustical control – which Michael uses extensively – and may allow for progress on the sensorimotor level, with the ultimate aim of reducing preoccupation with the alphabet to the automatized operations level of activity.

Michael's literacy acquisition is still continuing, and thus new problems that may be encountered along the way must be considered. He has yet to master the whole alphabet, and the letters and characters still missing are harder to learn simply because of their less favorable position within the frequency distribution. Furthermore, even though some encouraging progress in the field of writing can be seen, this has not affected the reading process. However, the fact that reading skills trail somewhat behind writing skills has also been found when teaching methods favor

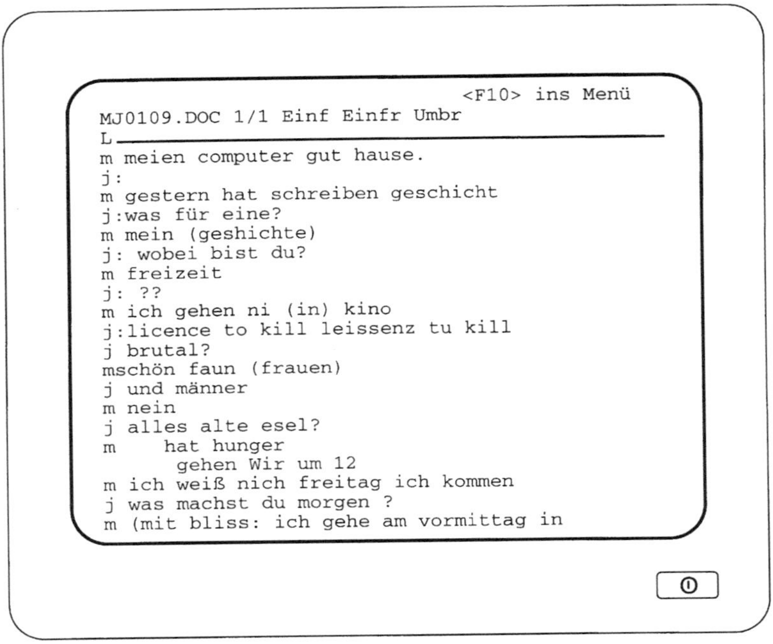

```
                                          <F10> ins Menü
     MJ0109.DOC 1/1 Einf Einfr Umbr
     L _____
     m meien computer gut hause.
     j :
     m gestern hat schreiben geschicht
     j:was für eine?
     m mein (geshichte)
     j: wobei bist du?
     m freizeit
     j: ??
     m ich gehen ni (in) kino
     j:licence to kill leissenz tu kill
     j brutal?
     mschön faun (frauen)
     j und männer
     m nein
     j alles alte esel?
     m    hat hunger
           gehen Wir um 12
     m ich weiß nich freitag ich kommen
     j was machst du morgen ?
     m (mit bliss: ich gehe am vormittag in
```

m: mein computer zuhause ist gut / my computer at home works well

j:

m: gestern habe ich eine geschicht geschrieben / yesterday I wrote a story

j: was für eine? / what kind?

m: meine / about myself

j: wobei bist du? / what's the topic

m: freizeit / leisure

j: ??

m: ich gehen ins kino / I go to the cinema

j: "licence to kill"

j: brutal? / is it violent?

m: schöne frauen / beautiful women

j: und männer? / and the men?

m: nein / no

j: alles alte esel? / only old donkies?
        m. hat hunger / m. is hungry
        gehen Wir um 12 uhr / let's go at 12 o'clock

m: ich weiß nich, ob ich freitag kommen kann / I don't no yet, if I can come on friday

j: was machst du morgen ? / what are you doing tomorrow?

m. changes to Bliss: I go...

Figure 13.7. Part of a written dialogue created by using a computer.

writing in the initial stages of literacy acquisition with vocal children (see Reichen, 1988; May, 1986).

In analyzing the text of Figure 13.7, which is part of a written dialogue, different writing strategies can be seen. There are problems on the orthographic, morphematic, and syntactic levels:

1. Michael often writes down words the way they are depicted in his Blissbook, using a gestalt strategy and disregarding grammatical flexions (conjugation of verbs, etc.).

2. A growing orientation to the phonematic principles may be observed. Michael writes, for example, "betifl wimen" (German = "schh faun"), that is, correctly spelled "beautiful women" (= "schöne Frauen"), where the written sequence of letters more closely resembles spoken everyday German.

3. The beginning of his orientation to morphematic principles can also be seen: "I go to cinema" (= "ich gehe in kino"), that is, "I go to the cinema" (= "ich gehe ins Kino"), and "yesterday had written story" (= "gestern hat schreiben geschicht"), that is, "yesterday I wrote a story" (= "gestern habe ich eine Geschichte geschrieben").

4. More complex syntactic structures are beginning to emerge, though they are not very often used: "Ich weiss nich ich freitag kommen"; "I don't know I come Friday" ("Ich weiss nicht, ob ich am Freitag kommen kann"; "I don't know if I can come on Friday").

This provides an idea of some of the typical problems of text production we are currently dealing with. At this point, it seems appropriate to address the second aspect of our research on literacy acquisition.

Part two: Aspects of personality development in the acquisition of writing and reading

When we started this case study, we did not believe that Michael's long-standing problem of dyslexia could be solved solely by learning alternative movement patterns (hypothesis 1) with assistance from technical aids, hardware, and/or software. We encountered a lot of skepticism in Michael's social environment concerning his ability to become literate. Our own initial doubts went in two directions.

1. How would our relationship to Michael develop as we became more involved with each other? And how would our personal skepticism affect Michael?

2. Would Michael really want to make a new effort after all the failures he had encountered? Would we be able to generate genuine "personal sense" (Leont'ev, 1978), that is, create a positive socioemotional assessment of literacy acquisition? Would increasing literacy competence and the following changes in personal perspectives be tolerated by his social environment, namely, at school and by his family?

Since there was no immediate or easy answer to these questions, we decided to discuss the issues as frankly and openly as possible among ourselves and to involve Michael in these discussions as much as he desired. We agreed that Michael was very interested in new computer technology and highly motivated to take part in a research project at the Free University at Berlin. We thus arranged for him to meet with us at the Psychology Department there twice a week.

In the following weeks and months, our willingness to discuss these issues openly was met by a frankness on Michael's part. This, in turn, helped to establish an intensive relationship between us, leading to our second hypothesis. The evolving communicative contexts provided a full range of topics for our interactions regarding personality, anxiety, and sexuality, to name the most important issues, thus putting the question of literacy acquisition into the general framework that such an undertaking needs to be successful. This means that questions concerning literacy acquisition in the traditional sense often played a secondary role in our weekly sessions.

We were convinced that Michael's task – to master the dyslexia – was so difficult that only a motivating setting engaging him over a long period of time could produce significant changes. For this reason, the computer writing and reading sessions were integrated into a complex system of social relations. These differ significantly from school-type instructional methods. Motivation is not a matter of generating attractive short-term goals that direct some consumptive behavior, but rather is part of a long-term developmental process, that is, a process of personality development.

For our second hypothesis, this means that progress at the micro level of literacy acquisition is influenced strongly by integration of the literacy learning actions and operations into one or more systems of social relations, providing a positive emotional assessment. In activity-theoretical terminology, this integration implies the following two processes:

1. acquisition of successful operations as means for conscious, goal-directed actions;

2. formation of a relationship between personal sense and objective meanings of the activity system(s).

Both processes are socioemotional as well as sensorimotor in character. From an activity-theoretical point of view, personality development is always related to motives and their hierarchy, as well as to the sense-meaning relation, pointing to the more highly valued motives within the whole motivational system. The central question then is: Will Michael be able to integrate the reading and writing task(s) into the structure of his dominant motives, that is, will the task and its context fit into his personal sense dimensions?

It could be that these "old" sense structures constitute one of the major barriers to literacy acquisition. The old motive structure(s) therefore would have to be transformed by integrating them into new activities, thus creating possible new ways to solve contradictions between sense and meaning or creating possible new ways to experience new sense dimensions. This is a therapeutic task.

We are not yet in a position to answer these questions decisively or to decide between the alternatives. We only know that overcoming dyslexia presupposes not only the solution of sense problems but also the solution of competency problems at the sensorimotor level. Metaphorically speaking, we have to solve a "know-how problem" as well as a "know-why problem." According to Leont'ev (1978, 1981), sense cannot be taught; it must be experienced subjectively as emotional relevance and engagement in real life. Within this theoretical framework, the development of new motives or the integration of ongoing needs into old ones must fulfil at least two conditions.

1. The motive must be related to the object of activity. For our purposes, this implies the identification or constitution of a new object of activity as a potential candidate for transformations into a psychologically relevant motive.
2. For the individual, activities exist in the form of action sequences. The realization of these action sequences through operations is governed by conditions. The only road to new motives and new competencies goes through these operational and goal-oriented processes.

The second condition for the creation of new motives has been achieved – at least in part. We divided the complex task of learning to read and to write into operation and action parts that can be handled by the individual. The first hypothesis discussed earlier provided conscious goals, on the one hand, and operative means and technical equipment, on the other hand, allowing an active process of learning letter differentiation. The goal (the communication of words and sentences via computer) had to be cooperatively planned and consciously appropriated. Michael's operations in the form of head movements and the knowledge of working with numbers (mathematical operations) were available, and the technical side was accounted for.

However, an elaboration on the first condition – the objective aspect of motives – has not been theoretically or empirically finalized at this stage of our research (for interpretations of the concept of activity in relation to motives, see Engeström, 1987; Haselmann, 1984; Hildebrand-Nilshon, 1989a, 1989b, 1989c; Hildebrand-Nilshon & Rückriem, 1988, 1989). Here it is sufficient to point out that our position on the interpretation of activity theory varies from positions taken by many psychologists in the Soviet Union. Activity as an object of psychological research (apart from but in relation to action as an object of psychological research) has, in our opinion, to do with sociohistorical systems of activity, that is, with social networks or institutions. These are organized and reproduced interindividually through objects, meanings, rules and roles, interpersonal relations, and values.

We assume that the objective side of motives consists of those social activity systems developed in the history of a society. The objective meanings and features of these systems, the objective interrelations of the people constituting and reproducing the system, are the source of emotional orientations, of personal sense on the part of each participating individual. Crucial for these emotional orientations is the subjective relevance of taking part in the system for the individual and his or her relation to other activity systems. There are contradictions and struggles between the different emotional orientations in regard to the activities the person is involved in. This struggle for priority between the different emotional orientations (symbolized in Figure 13.8 by the flashes between the motives oriented to the different activity systems) is a central aspect of personality development.

Applied to the present case study, the previously mentioned motivation is dependent upon the integration of Michael's actions and operations in an old activity system or the creation of a new one. Both alternatives are possible. Michael's integration into the research project created a spectrum of different activities he could take part in. These are only briefly mentioned here (symbolized by the ovals in Figure 13.8):

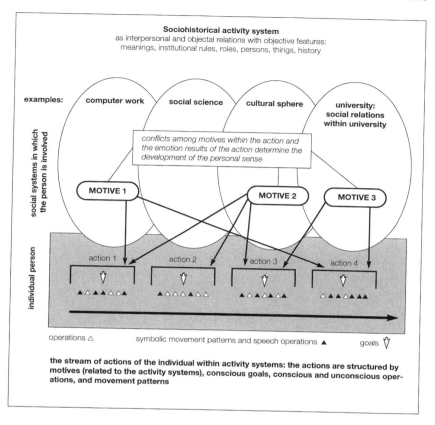

Figure 13.8. Sociohistorical activity systems.

- working on the computer, potentially opening a real employment possibility for severely handicapped people;
- working and interacting with a group of social scientists at the Free University in Berlin;
- taking part in various cultural activities like reading books, going to movies or concerts, and dining in restaurants;
- developing contacts and/or social relations to others marginally connected with the research team, such as computer firms, various institutions for the handicapped, people coming for counseling, and so on.

Each activity system has its own characteristics, its meanings, roles and values, which can produce some kind of emotional orientation in a person acting within the system and taking part in the interactions. The goals, leading to actions in the new systems, can rely on "old motives," that is, on orientations stemming from other activity systems. The new experiences can fit into the old sense system or they can render it questionable. Within new activity systems and their objective aspects, we can follow the old senses in new clothes.

But new activity systems may not only split or alter but also contradict the old sense structure. In any case, the integration and movement into new activity systems is a psychological challenge, provoking contradictions, defense mechanisms, and/or changes in the motivational system.

The actions within our project must therefore be able to create, develop, or solve those contradictions. In other words, Michael must use the new actions and means for change and for dislodging the contradictions between his personal sense and the objective meaning of the new activity systems. Reading and writing must become one of the powerful means to move within these contradictions between sense and meaning. This movement is situated in a triangular structure.

First, there is the conscious goal of learning to read, write, or spell and the search for the means to realize this by means of Michael's own competence, along with help from others and from technical resources. Our first hypothesis was focused on this problem.

Second, there is the activity system (or systems) in which the actions and conscious goals are integrated and confronted with the requirements of the objective structure of this system. The requirements are mediated by the objective meanings of the system – for Michael, for example, the conditions necessary for getting a job involving computer technology. This so-called objective structure is not a dead body. It consists of other subjects having their own emotional and motivational orientations that fit into the system, which may conflict with it or even contradict it. The objective meaning of an activity system constituting the objective requirements for motivational orientation should therefore never be seen as unchangeable. It is reproduced by persons and their actions, that is, by conscious goals and emotional orientations realized in operational sequences under intersubjectively produced circumstances.

Third, there is an emotional orientation that makes some aspects of the activity system attractive for Michael. This attractiveness constitutes the relation to the already existing personal sense in accordance with Michael's personal history, that is, his earlier (sometimes even discarded or closed) activity systems. To initiate learning processes in such a situation implies the intertwining of at least two different manifestations of personal sense: that of Michael's and those of his collaborators. This intertwining cannot happen by imprinting. It has to be experienced in one's own actions and their results, in a process whereby the emotional feedback opens new orientations or reorganizes the old ones in the direction of the new social system – as a sort of incorporation of old sense dimensions and new social relations.

Successful development in this domain is largely dependent upon the existence of personal sense in the actions constituting the activity systems of the other persons Michael is involved with. That is the reason for fashioning our setting as a quasi-therapeutic context.

Michael has to bridge several gaps:

- that between the meanings and objective requirements of the available activity systems and the operational level of his own actions, the movement patterns to develop reading and writing;
- that between the unknown emotional attractiveness of the new activity system, where reading and writing are obvious, and one's own sense system, where reading and writing are almost out of reach or laden with negative values from past experience;
- that between his own sense and the personal senses of his partners concerning his contributions and his personality, that is, he has to examine his relevance as a person in the social system.

Using our two-way approach, we hope to help him bridge these gaps:

1. by looking for goals and means Michael can successfully handle;
2. by providing information and emotional feedback in the different activity systems we are engaged in, so that his operations and conscious actions can be recognized by himself as relevant means for the personal sense dimension – whether in creating a new personal sense or changing an old one by expanding it.

The more reduced the possibilities of development seem to be because of the magnitude of the physical disabilities that complicate any compensatory efforts by the individual, the more important the remaining range of adequate and workable means will become. And the more a person has been disappointed, frustrated, and/or traumatized during development, thus weakening the stability of the self, the more important it will be to integrate the socioemotional processes into an attempt to reorganize personality development in all of its complexity, from the sensorimotor level to motivation and emotion. In our view, activity theory offers the great advantage of being able to model processes of personality development in the full range of their sociohistorical and cultural complexity.

Postscript: 10 months later

Ten months passed since the initial presentation of this chapter. During this period, we continued to work in all the fields described earlier. Michael's writing and reading skills have improved. The usual work schedule during our weekly sessions (as of March 1990, the work sessions took place once instead of twice a week) consisted of a first unit of 90 minutes using SIMULA on a PC, followed by a lunch break of 1 hour in the student cafeteria. Thereafter another hour of work in a more relaxed atmosphere took place (e.g., reading various kinds of literature).

In the spring of 1990, Michael got involved in an occupational learning program at the Berlin Spastic Help Center that is trying to integrate his literacy skills using, among other things, the software developed in our research project. Michael also became involved in a self-help club, participating in the establishment and operation of a computer mailbox.

A simple yet effective two-switch input device for Michael is still being developed. Furthermore, Michael has become more accustomed to the scanning technique and has considerably increased his speed using SIMULA_1 rather than using the more laborious two-switch input device with SIMULA_2. This, in turn, has had adverse effects on the further acquisition of movement patterns for the less frequently used letters and keyboard characters. Thus, further evidence for the effectiveness of the *alternative movement-pattern approach* is difficult to obtain because of the scanning principle of SIMULA_1. To complicate matters further, we have successfully started to use a VOCA (Voice Output Communication Aid) with synthesized speech. Michael uses this to correct his spelling via auditory feedback. With the help of the VOCA, he is transcribing his entire Blissbook into TO by himself.

Learning to write his active, numerically encoded vocabulary in TO enhances his confidence in his writing competence and supports his reading efforts as well. Michael's growing reading and writing competence has enabled him to pass an examination in computer literacy (in Germany called the "PC driving license"). This may serve as an indication of the productivity of our approach. Integration of the micro and macro aspects remains, now as before, the crucial principle of our work.

Note

We wish to thank Ron Coon for his help in translating this chapter into English.

References

Bliss, C. K. (1965). *Semantography.* Sidney: Semantography Publications.

Engeström, Y. (1987). *Learning by expanding. An activity-theoretical approach to developmental research.* Helsinki: Orienta-Konsultit.

Haselmann, S. (1984) *Gesellschaftliche Beziehungsformen und soziale Kränkungen. Eine Tätigkeitstheoretische Grundlegung.* Frankfurt am Main: Campus.

Hildebrand-Nilshon, M. (1989a). Sprachentwicklung des körperbehinderten Kindes. In A. D. Frölich (Ed.), *Kommunikation und Sprache körperbehinderter Kinder.* Dortmund: Verlag Modernes Lernen.

Hildebrand-Nilshon, M. (1989b). Zur Relevanz der Unterscheidung von Tätigkeit und Handlung. In M. Hidenbrand-Nilshon & G. Rückriem (Eds.), *Activity theory in movement: Discussions and controversies. Proceedings of the 1st International Congress on Activity Theory* (Vol. 4.1). Berlin: System Druck.

Hildebrand-Nilshon, M. (1989c). On the difficulties of working empirically with activity theory. *Multidisciplinary Newsletter for Activity Theory, 3/4,* 3–12.

Hildebrand-Nilshon, M., & Rückriem, G. (Eds.). (1988). Workshop contributions to selected aspects of applied research. *Proceedings of the 1st International Congress on Activity Theory* (Vol. 3). Berlin: System Druck.

Hildebrand-Nilshon, M., & Rückriem, G. (Eds.). (1989). Activity theory in movement: Discussions and controversies. *Proceedings of the 1st International Congress on Activity Theory* (Vol. 4.1). Berlin: System Druck.

Kelso, D. P., & Vanderheiden, G. C. (1985). *Talking Blissapple-Benutzerhandbuch.* Düsseldorf: Bundesverband für spastisch Gelähmte u. a. Körperbehinderte e.V.

Leont'ev, A. N. (1978). *Activity, consciousness, and personality.* Englewood Cliffs: Prentice-Hall.

Leont'ev, A. N. (1981). *Problems of the development of the mind.* Moscow: Progress.

Lloyd, L. L. (1985). Augmentative communication: Comments on terminology. *AAC, Augmentative and Alternative Communication, 1,* 95–97.

Lloyd, L. L., Quist, R. W., & Windsor, J. (1990). A proposed augmentative and alternative communication model. *AAC, Augmentative and Alternative Communication, 6,* 172–83.

May, L. (1986). *Schriftaneignung als Problemlösen.* Frankfurt am Main: Lang.

McDonald, E. T. (1980). *Teaching and using Blissymbolics.* Toronto: Blissymbolics Communication Institute.

Musselwhite, C. R., & St. Louis, K. W. (1982). *Communication programming for the severely handicapped: Vocal and nonvocal strategies.* Houston: College-Hill.

Pilz, D., (1982). *Für eine therapeutische Pädagogik.* Berlin: LZ-Verlag.

Reichen, J. (1988). *Lesen durch Schreiben.* Zurich: SABE.

Schlösser, M. (1980). *Narzistisch gestörte Kinder und das Problem erfolgreicher Aneignungstätigkeit bei Sprechen und Handeln.* Osnabruck: OBST, FB 7 der Universität Osnabrück.

Schubenz, S. (1993). *Grundlagen der pädagogisch-psychologischen Therapie. Psychotherapie bei Entwicklungsbehinderung.* Bern: Peter Lang.

Part III

Play, learning, and instruction

14   Play and motivation

Pentti Hakkarainen

Introduction

In this chapter, an attempt is made to redefine the concept of play as a prime example of the complex nature of human motivation. My aim is to show that the social context and social activity individuals are engaged in, rather than individual inner states, are basic determinants of the motivation of children's play.

I first provide an overview of play as a historically developing activity. Next, I employ object orientation and object construction, with their inner contradictions, as basic categories of analysis of motivation. These conceptual tools are then used in the analysis of videotaped play sessions in Finnish kindergartens and reconstructed episodes of the same types of play as they occurred 23 years ago in the lives of educators now working in kindergartens.

Conceptualizing play

Functions of play are defined in different ways, and different functions lead to different explanations of motivation. In Groos's (1922) theory, the main function of children's play is to prepare for adult life. From this viewpoint, the content of play, as well as its relation to the adult world, is important. In other approaches, the essence of play and its main function are defined in terms of independence from the adult world. According to Csikszentmihalyi (1981), we can talk about play only when the rules of reality are suspended. If a girl feeds and dresses a doll in a way that resembles the usual cultural manners, this is not play in the actual meaning of the term because there are no experimental elements exceeding the usual cultural limits. By this definition, for example, Maya children's play is not play in the strict sense of the term (Gaskins & Göncü, 1992).

In some standard definitions, play is described as a unique phenom-enon and is not assumed to produce any concrete results. Cohen and MacKeith (1991, p. 11) compared children's play with the theater: "But nothing remains of their efforts and imagination, except, perhaps, their memory of it. You could argue that it's no accident that we call theatri-cal performance a play. Once the play is over, nothing is left; the players pack up and go. The same is true once children stop playing a particular game."

Play, and children's play especially, is characterized by symbolic ac-tions in imagined situations. Real objects and actions are substituted for by other objects and symbolic actions. One cannot understand substi-tutions and symbolism in play without a broader conceptual framework. Play actions are carried out in imagined situations, and situated actions are part of a role, a script, or a plot. Substitutions and imagined situations obey a certain logic of the development of the script. Bretherton (1984) argues that persons and objects in play can be changed without changing the script. For example, the "mother" in a play situation can feed a baby doll by using a cube if no bottle is available. But play actions cannot be changed at will without changing the script. Scripts are formed from a chain of play actions. The script limits the number and type of possible persons and objects in a play.

An essential feature of play is its place on the border of two worlds: the narrative world of play and the real world. Bateson (1955) talks in this connection about the metacommunicative message "this is play." This metacommunication helps us discriminate play situations from mere de-scriptions of phenomena. In the flow of play, a certain amount of meta-communication and successive movement from play roles to social reality and back is necessary. Scripts and roles cannot be constructed solely by playing the role. Play is interrupted for negotiations, and it can go on af-ter mutual agreement. These two standpoints are necessary in any play.

There are some attempts to operationalize and measure intrinsic mo-tivation in play. For example, van der Kooij (1983) used the following categories: (1) exploratory drive (curiosity, energy, and initiative in play behavior), (2) duration of play (attention directed to play), (3) intensity of play (involvement in play and depth of experiences), (4) joy of play (experience of joy, self-rewarding nature of play), and (5) stability of play (efforts to overcome obstacles met in play). In many cases, the explana-tion of the motivation of play is circular: Play brings joy and satisfac-tion, and this is why people play. Another unsatisfactory explanation is that children are motivated to play because it is possible to solve inner conflicts and reduce anxiety in play (Isaacs, 1930; Sutton-Smith, 1978). The enigmatic nature of play as an intrinsically motivated phenomenon is the reason why the process of play is stressed instead of its contents (e.g., Bruner, 1977).

Attempts to measure intrinsic motivation in play focus on individual play behavior only. The social setting provides only an external context for play, and there are practically no measures for contextual factors. In kindergarten activity, the social and organizational context can be an essential explanatory factor if we want to find out why children play as they play (Hakkarainen, 1991). Kindergarten brings children together, play has its time and space, adults may organize play activities, and certain plays are preferred and others rejected by adults. Individual inner states cannot explain children's play in such a complex setting as kindergarten. Explanations have to be sought in the social space created by organized activity systems. In a broader activity context, intrinsic motivational factors can be explained by indicating how they are related to external factors. But explanation is possible only by revising our notions of what is internal and external in play activity.

Play as an activity type

As noted earlier, different characteristics are used in describing what is essential in children's play. Sometimes roles are used as criteria for differentiating play and not-play; sometimes scripts, symbolic actions, or imagined situations are the criteria. These features, essential as they may be, do not have the integrative potential necessary for organizing an activity system around them. It is the object under transformation that integrates the elements of an activity system (Leont'ev, 1978). This integrative function makes the object of any activity system central in the analysis of motivation.

Different types of activities are distinguished on the basis of their objects. Specific objects are connected to specific needs and motives (see Leont'ev, 1978). Activities are organized and carried out by social subjects in order to change the objects and fulfill needs. Object orientation of activity implies active change and development. Development is the result of dynamic, contradictory interrelations between basic elements in an activity system (Engeström, 1987).

The activity concept is relatively easily applied to processes that deal with concrete changes and results in palpable objects. Children's play is a more complicated phenomenon. What is the object of play? What are the needs explaining the choice of the object of play, and what is the motivation of play?

There have been some interesting attempts to define the objects and needs of play. Play does not change anything visible; thus the object of play must be the process itself (El'konin, 1978; Leont'ev, 1981). There is no necessity to produce any concrete results or attain previously formulated goals in play (Bateson, 1978; Csikszentmihalyi, 1981). Play is oriented to emotions, needs, and motives instead of visible objects. Fein (1987) argues that a child simulates need states, not actual effective needs. For example, a child pretending to sleep in a play is not tired and has no intention of falling asleep. Play can be generally characterized as an activity type dominated by experimenting with potential or virtual objects and motives of human activities.

Leont'ev (1981) explains the social need behind children's play by arguing that its essence is children's desire to act as adults do. Children want to take part in the social life of the adult world, but their skills are not adequate for real participation. The general need to act like adults is directed at the beginning to the use of objects in human life according to their social functions. Later on, needs are directed to the objects of activities in adults' life. According to Leont'ev, the needs of play are in the adults' world, but the motives are in the process of play. This is an essential difference between play and other activity types. Play as an activity type aims at the mastery of mastering. Play does not produce any concrete knowledge about the technology of mastering. It produces general flexibility and a disposition to change one's approach when facing the concrete demands of the situation. Incitements are inherent in the process as intellectual challenges, imagination, fantasies, and emotions.

Satisfaction of a child's vital needs is actually differentiated from the results of the child's activity: a child's behavior does not define satisfaction of her/his needs of nutrition, warmth, etc. There is a vast number of needs independent of concrete results of behavior. In other words, children's activities include their own motives at this stage of development. (Leont'ev, 1981, p. 481)

This is why the general discrepancy between the goals of actions and motives observed in other activity types is not possible in play.

Rubinstein (1989, II, 64–74) stresses that the motives of play reflect an immediate relation to reality. Goals of play actions are always meaningful directly because of their own contents. Different motives of human activities are realized in play actions, but in another mode than in practical activities. Play actions express the meaning of actions and their relation to goals rather than attainment of goals in the form of concrete results.

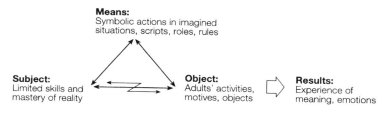

Figure 14.1. The origin of play in classical activity theory.

Children eliminate the contradiction between the need to act like adults and their real skills by cutting off the conditions of real actions from play actions. Thus, according to Leont'ev (1981), play operations do not correspond to real operations, but play actions are like real actions. The main difference is in motivation: Play actions are independent of objective results. Play includes real actions with real objects and real operations, but the operations are carried out in imagined situations. Noncorrespondence between operations and actions in play is the reason for imagined situations. Rubinstein (1989, p. 69) describes the role of imagined situations as follows.

Everything which is essential in play is genuinely real: emotions, wishes and ideas are real and genuine. Genuine are also questions solved in play. . . . Emotions, wishes and ideas are the player's emotions, wishes and ideas, because the role is herself/himself in new, imagined situations. Imagined are only situations in which the player places her/himself, but the emotions experienced are real emotions.

Play actions are always generalized actions. Leont'ev (1981) argues that a child is not imitating any concrete persons in a play; the child is imitating actions (not a concrete driver, but driver and driving a car in general). He supports his argument by comparing the structure of play actions with actions in real situations. If a child masters an action in real life, it is not repeated in identical form in play situations (e.g., the use of a spoon in play takes a symbolic, generalized form).

The arguments presented by El'konin, Leont'ev, and Rubinstein concerning the origin of play are summarized in Figure 14.1. The origin of play is explained by representatives of psychological activity theory, first of all, by the basic contradiction between children's limited skills and adults' activities in the surrounding context. The contradiction is solved by using mediating means: imagined situations, symbolic actions, scripts, roles, and rules. The motivation of play is explained by the object of play.

El'konin (1978) shows how the origin of children's play is connected to the change in children's social status. The motivation of and need for play are societal, not biological. Children's participation in social life is a general explanation for play motivation. Also, the instruments of play have a social nature. They are not results of children's spontaneous intellectual development. Play is socially elaborated and guided by offering materials and toys, scripts and rules. We may have an illusion of spontaneous children's play at home, where adult influence takes the form of mundane everyday situations. Berentzen (1989) demonstrates how different "audiences" affect the cultural and social organization of peer group activities. The impact of the social setting is more visible in kindergarten, where a group of peers gather and play together.

It is easy to agree with the general idea offered by these authors. But it is quite difficult to use this contradiction as a concrete explanation for the motivational mechanism behind children's play. There is a gap between the general conceptualization and explanations offered on the level of concrete play processes. The classic works of activity theory describe contradictions when they analyze the general need giving rise to children's play, but they do not demonstrate how the contradictions manifest themselves at the level of play processes. The general idea of object orientation and cultural contents in play tends to vanish in the analysis of concrete plays. This gap can be filled by showing how children's play is socially and culturally constructed in concrete settings and what are the contradictions of this construction process.

The social construction of play and its motivation

Children's play takes place in different social settings: kindergarten, home, backyard. These settings may transmit quite different pictures of play and its motivation. Play is socially constructed in each setting. It cannot be described or explained properly without analyzing its social construction.

In most cases, the social construction of play is understood at the level of children's mutual co-construction of roles, scripts, plots, symbolic actions, and so on (e.g., Garvey, 1977; Fein, 1987; Nelson & Seidman, 1984; Bretherton, 1984). However, as Bronfenbrenner (1977) points out, the wider social context is of crucial importance in the analysis of developmental processes.

From this point of view, the explanation has to be supposed by a concrete analysis of how play and its motivation are socially constructed in different concrete-historical settings (see Bruner, 1990). The generalization made by Leont'ev, El'konin, and Rubinstein about the origin of play

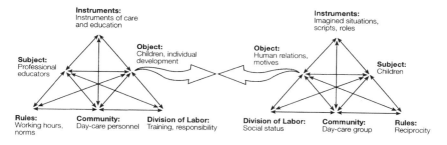

Figure 14.2. The problem of the common object in play.

is still an abstract picture of motivation. Concrete dynamics are missing without an analysis of the social environment in which play takes place. An interesting social setting for the analysis of children's play is day care. The day-care center is a societal institution that cooperates with families and specific societal organizations (municipal administration, special education, health care, psychological services, etc.). There are several simultaneous social worlds (Strauss, 1978) or frames (Goffman, 1974) in day-care institutions.

In day-care settings, children construct play in collaboration with each other. Similarly, day-care personnel organize educational work in cooperation with each other. An essential aspect of the whole enterprise is mutual co-construction between adults and children. This mutual co-construction can be interpreted as cooperation of two activity systems: children's play and adults' educational work in day care. The basic question is whether these activity systems have a common object, that is, in what sense can we talk about co-construction?

The problem of the common object can be described with the help of Figure 14.2.

Play takes place in day care in a situation organized by adults. Space is planned for educational purposes, children follow a daily program, and specific times are dedicated to play, learning, and other purposes. From the children's point of view, there may be a definite time for play in the time schedule, play is not possible in every corner of the institution, and children have not chosen the peers with whom they live every day. So the construction of a common object of play is a problem for the group of children, as well as for the adults working with them.

In my observations in Finnish kindergartens (Hakkarainen, 1990, 1991), I identified a contradiction between adults' and children's conceptions of the common object. Children were constructing the object of their play collaboratively. Adults underlined individual play skills and usually intervened in children's play on the basis of observations of individual play. In this case, one can hardly talk about a co-construction of the object. Children may see adults as outsiders and disrupters of their play. Children's play takes place in kindergarten in a social situation created by adults. Adults' withdrawal from the play situation does not eliminate their influence through the mediation of the social setting.

Co-construction of the object of play depends concretely on the frames that dominate in day care. On the basis of videotapes and observations in Finnish day-care centers (Hakkarainen, 1990), I identified the following frames.

The practical frame

In this frame, child care is stressed and practical results are emphasized. Practical organization and effective accomplishment of tasks defined by adults are important in this frame. In co-construction of the common object, adult logic is dominant and children have to submit to the constraints presented by the adults.

The practical frame is demonstrated in the following excerpt from the organization of play in a kindergarten group by two adults, teacher K and nurse Arja.

K: I'll take a look at what Arja has prepared for you.
Children: I'd like to play home. I'll go to the doctor.
K: I doubt that there will be any doctors today. Is it ready now? Well, well now Arja has prepared things. Who shall I let be the first? Jari, Katariina, Marika, and Joni go over there so Arja will tell you where you can seek your play site. You may seek your play site or Arja will show you.
Arja: Jara and Joni, would you like to play with bricks?
Jari and Joni: No.
Arja: What would you like to do then? Play doctors? What if we do not have it today because . . . .
K: We'll not play doctors today.

The developmental frame

This frame underlines the individual needs of every child. Educational means are selected by considering their developmental potentials. In this frame, the time perspective is important. Immediate practical results are less important than experiences and the possibility for an individual child to mature at her or his own pace. Educational work in this frame is, first of all, the organization of stimulating environments and activities for the satisfaction of individual needs. Co-construction of the common object means offering developmental environments and constructing development in these environments.

The developmental frame was stressed in the interview of teacher K after the play situation described earlier:

Interviewer: You had the idea that a shy and overtidy girl should be involved in sand play in the first place. Why did you choose her?

K: This child is very tidy, overtidy, and shy so that she is upset if her hands get dirty or milk is spilled over or something. I do not know why there is a principle that we should get them to be a little more messy. If we doubt that this is not anymore normal tidiness we try to involve a child in something. These children often cannot do anything because they are so careful. We try to eliminate hysterical reactions if something happens little by little . . .

Interviewer: Did you succeed with Sari?

K: Personally I did not go there, although it was my intention. But I saw the video and I personally think that she felt the sand with her hands quite well. She has been really shy and tidy. She did not tolerate a wrinkle in her skirt. We are not aiming at any untidiness but at getting used to feeling different things. This is our method to initiate play. This is our main task.

The child-centered experiential frame

Children's world and their experiences are central in this frame. Adults try to imagine what the world looks like from the children's point of view. Adults' work is temporarily organizing by taking this into consideration. The child-centered experiential frame is expressed in the following interview excerpt:

Interviewer: There was one boy playing alone with cars for a long time. Did he have a role or was it part of a play? Did you pay attention to him?

K: I would say that he was a truck driver, certainly. He only drove around. I proposed him to take somebody along and play together, because he plays at home a lot alone with cars. He is a single child. There are no playmates around in the neighborhood. But he wanted to play alone. He told later that he has lots of play cars at home and he plays with cars. I did not want to interfere in any way. Joni is quick. Sometimes I would say hyperactive. He is kind of foolish. He overreacts a lot. He has the role of fun maker. With small hand movements he causes laughter and giggling in the group.

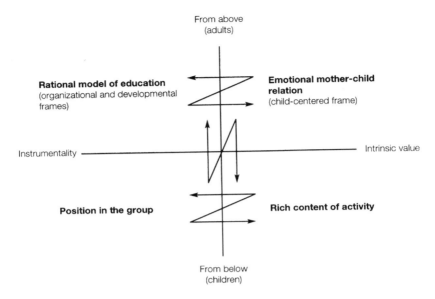

From above
(adults)

Rational model of education
(organizational and developmental
frames)

Emotional mother-child
relation
(child-centered frame)

Instrumentality

Intrinsic value

Position in the group

Rich content of activity

From below
(children)

Figure 14.3. Contradictions in kindergarten play.

Contradictions of kindergarten play

Different frames exist simultaneously in day-care work, and there are tensions between them. The idea of frames and the co-construction of the object of activities in day care may be combined into a comprehensive picture (Figure 14.3).

The motivation of play is jointly constructed by adults and children. Joint construction of the object takes place from two directions: from adults by creating surroundings for children's activity or directly organizing it (from above) and from children through self-initiative (from below). There is a basic contradiction between these directions.

Joint construction is also characterized by another, horizontal dimension. One end of this dimension is instrumentality; the other one is the intrinsic value of the process. Both children's activity and adults' day-care work may be analyzed along this dimension. There are specific inner contradictions in each of them.

The inner contradiction of day-care work is between a rational model of education (organizational and developmental frames) and an emotional model of education (child-centered frame). In children's joint construction, the inner contradiction is between striving for rich contents in activity and striving for a social position in the group. The following excerpt illustrates the latter contradiction in children's construction of play in kindergarten. Children have listened to the fairy tale "The Sleeping Beauty" and want to play it in the presence of adults.

Teacher: What happened then? Anna was the fairy.

Anna: No, I want to be the princess.

Teacher: And Retta was? What happened next? The story goes on.

Anna: We only sit here. Who was the king? You could be the queen and you will be a fairy and Sanna will be a fairy and I will be the princess. We only sit here (stands up). We all stand here like soldiers. You should do something.

Reetta: What then?

Anna: Play the story of course.

Reetta: Of course, but how?

Anna: Have you ever heard the fairy tale "Sleeping Beauty"?

Reetta: Yes.

Anna: Then start now.

Reeta: You start.

Teacher: What happens next?

Anna: You have to sit on the throne (pushes the king toward a chair). This is your throne.

Reeta (to Anna): But you are a small baby. Lay down.

Anna: But who will be the evil godmother? Sanna could be for a while and then she will change back.

Reetta (to Anna): Lie down.

Anna: But this is too big for me.

Reetta: Never mind.

Anna: You will be the queen, you will be the fairy godmother, you the evil godmother.

Reetta: Lie down.

Anna: I have my shoes on (lies down). What are you doing? Do something or I'll turn into a fairy.

Others: What shall we do?

Anna: You wait there, stand there. Then you will give me the presents. Hurry up, give me the presents or I'll fall asleep and will take my afternoon nap and there will be no "Sleeping Beauty." Give me the presents or I'll get mad. Are you afraid? Say something.

Reetta: I give you beauty.

In this example, the play is constructed cooperatively with the help of adults. Before the events described, there was an agreement on the roles.

Anna agreed that she would be the fairy, but then she found out that the role of the princess was the most attractive. Her desire to be the princess governed the construction of the whole play episode. As a matter of fact, Anna dictated the construction of the play.

Motivation of play in kindergarten

In this section, I demonstrate the social construction of motivation in a shopping play (sell and buy) in kindergarten. The basic material was collected in a kindergarten group of 4- to 6-year-old children. At first glance, this play seems to be children's independent play in which adults take part only minimally (they have a coffee break in the kitchen during the play). Besides shopping play, four parallel plays seemed to be going on in different rooms of the building.

There are two kinds of prehistories of shopping play that are essential in the analysis of the social construction process. First, there is a prehistory of the sell and buy play in the childhood of the kindergarten teachers now working at the site. Second, there is a local prehistory of the play in this particular kindergarten group. Interviews of kindergarten teachers showed that shopping play is one of the most popular plays in the childhood of adults working in Finnish kindergartens. There is an indirect link from play experiences 20 or more years ago with educators working in kindergarten at present. Typically shopping play is a yard play organized by children themselves. Shopping play usually has three parts: preparation, selling and buying, and the use of the purchased goods at home. The artifacts used in the play consist mainly of natural materials such as rocks, cones, leaves, sand, and clay.

The common object in each stage of the shopping play is exchange relations between people. This object is constructed from different points of view at each stage. There is a specific contradiction at each stage and a contradictory transition from one stage to another. The stages and their inner contradictions are described in Figure 14.4.

At the first stage, the problem is how the missing properties of available objects are compensated for so that children can agree on their existence in the play situation. The contradiction is solved at the level of shapes, colors, and other properties of play materials. At the following stage, a fair basis for exchange is sought between persons in different roles. The contradiction is solved by using such concrete play actions as weighing to find the correct price, packing, telling the price, and the exchange of

STAGE I   STAGE II   STAGE III

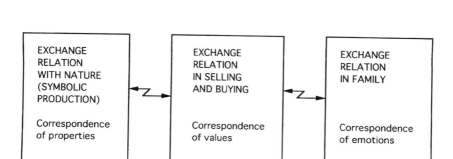

Figure 14.4. Stages of the shopping play.

goods for money (often leaves of different trees in this version). At the last stage, the contradiction is transferred to relations between family members. Food is prepared and meals are served for family members. Caretaking is exchanged for respect, for example.

Play experiences of adult personnel influence the guidance of children's play in kindergartens today. In most Finnish kindergartens there are specific sets of play materials for shopping play (e.g., cash registers, weights, play money). The preparation stage, which was once the main part of the whole play, is now shorter and symbolic production is missing. The play starts immediately with selling and buying.

Hännikäinen (1992) has studied the transition period to role play in kindergarten. In her data there are descriptions of sell and buy play in which the role of adults in the social co-construction is clearly visible. In one videotaped situation there are three children, Hanna (3;2), Anu (1;11), and Mari (2;4), and a teacher, Ritva. At the beginning of the play period, the teacher prepared the sell and buy play by displaying empty packages and shopping bags for the children. The teacher explained what was shown, and the children started to become acquainted with the materials. In the same room, there was a cupboard in which the same children played hide and seek.

There were no clear roles of buyers and sellers in this play. For the children, buying meant gathering packages in shopping bags and carrying them away. The teacher (Ritva) seemed to be worried about the absence of roles. She reacted in the following way to Mari's gathering of packages.

Ritva: What is Mari buying here?
(No answer.)
Ritva: What did you buy, Mari?
(No answer. Ritva shows an empty spice box.)
Ritva: What would this be?
Mari: A box of margarine.
Ritva: Would you like to buy this?
(Ritva hands the box to Mari.)
Ritva: Here you are.
(Ritva starts to pack shopping items into Mari's shopping bag.)
Ritva: Sit down. Otherwise you'll fall.
Mari: You can't take these things (to Anu).
Ritva: There is no room left in this bag.
Ritva: What is this? (Shows an empty egg box to the children.)
Mari with other children: Eggs.
Mari: There is no room for this here. (Takes one item from the shopping bag.)
Marja-Leena: You are right. Buy it next time.
(Mari takes her shopping bag and goes to the cupboard.)

At this transition stage, play motives exist at two levels: Children act on the basis of immediate situational impulses, but there are simultaneously certain roles and situational factors that direct play events. Adults try to introduce actions connected to certain roles. At this stage, children are actually manipulating objects and not playing the roles and scripts offered for them. Children may explain that they are playing a role, but roles and scripts do not organize their play behavior.

Children in the group of 4- to 6-year-olds may have a lot of experience in playing shopping in kindergarten. Episodes of play may look like independent play in which adults have nothing to do. There are, however, historical layers of co-construction of play that are not visible at any given moment. On the other hand, the inner contradictions and contents of today's shopping play are different from those of its historical predecessors. Moral problems are clearly visible in this play type today. Nowadays shopping play is often connected with themes like robbing and arresting the robbers. The object of play is constructed collaboratively between different plots or scripts.

I videotaped a modern shopping play in kindergarten in a group of 4- to 6-year-old children (Hakkarainen, 1990). Children were assisted at the beginning of play time by adults, but adults did not participate until it was time to stop the play. Children constructed five parallel plays in three different rooms: shopping, bank, police and robbers, hairdresser, and library. The most attractive plays were shopping (for girls) and police and

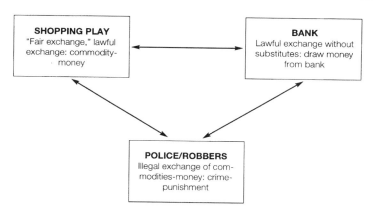

Figure 14.5. Exchange relations as the common object of parallel play.

robbers (for boys). Recording was focused on the shopping play, but the bank was situated in the same room with the shop, and robbers attacked both the shop and the bank. As a matter of fact, different plots were so closely interconnected that one may talk about one complex play with multiple themes. The different themes were variations or aspects of the same object of play: exchange relations between people. The common object of the different plays is described in Figure 14.5.

Exchange relations were constructed carefully in the shop by using a basic script: greetings – "What would you like to have?" "How much?" – choice of items, optical reading of the price tag, paying, and saying good-bye. This was repeated more than 20 times during the play session. Other scripts used in the bank and police and robbers plays were more ambiguous. A common combining factor in all play themes was the use of money in exchange relations. Money was drawn from the bank, it was robbed from the bank and the shop, and it was used in the shop for paying.

Fair exchange is one of the persistent problems in children's play. In this case, the price was usually defined by using the optical reader. But the relation of price to other properties (e.g., weight) of different items was something children tried to figure out in the play. The following excerpt reveals the problem.

Mari: I would like to have toothpaste, too.
Ulla: There! (Seeks the optical code.)
Ulla: Twenty-three two! (Hands the toothpaste to Mari.)
Mari: Weigh this! (toothpaste)
Ulla: She will do it! (Points to Lena, but Lena concentrates on drawing.)

Mari: No, she will not.
(Ulla weighs the toothpaste and drops something.)
Tepa: Are you measuring toothpaste?
Lena: Yes, of course. (Continues drawing.)
Ulla: Three . . . zero, this is zero kilograms! Seven two. I can take from you.
(Takes the play money from Mari.)

The idea of exchange in the bank was not quite clear to the children. Children just came in in order to take money from the bank. An adult (teacher O) tried to explain how money is drawn from an account in the bank.

Mari: Hello. I'll take seven ten-mark notes.
Teacher O: You draw money from bank. (Adult corrects.)
Mari: I'll take . . .
Teacher O: No, you draw money. You draw money from your account. (Adult corrects)
Teacher O: How can you have money? You just came in.
Mari: I gave it back.
Teacher O: Oh, you gave it. That's enough. Now you can go shopping.

Robbers used any possibilities for taking money and goods from the bank and the shop. They fled with the booty, but eager policemen arrested them right away and sent them to jail.

Sauli: Hello. Have you seen robbers?
Seikku: Yes, he came here. We took a walk and came just back to the parking lot.
Sauli: I . . . we have just . . . one robber . . .
Eki: Who was it?
Sauli: Hannu.
Eki: Wow, just him, it was just him.
Sauli: Would you like to have a look at the prison?
Seikku: Yes!!
Tepa: I want to have a look, too. (Leaves the shop.)

In this case, the interconnections of separate plays and their common object reveal the motivation of children's play. Moral problems are present in these episodes in the form of legal and illegal exchanges. This is a new aspect compared to historically earlier forms of the same play. The role of money has changed, too. At the end of the play session, children start to grab the play money for themselves and compare who has the largest amount.

Conclusions

Traditionally children's play is said to be an excellent example of intrinsic motivation because it is internally rewarding and because the play process itself motivates children. The general need for play is explained by naming various general functions of play in individual development, such as preparation for adult life, development of imagination, learning, and so on. There are opposing definitions of play, depending on which aspect of play is chosen, and as a result, opposing ideas about the need for and motivation of play.

My basic argument is that the motivation of children's play cannot be revealed either by describing general, universal functions and developmental needs of play or by carrying out careful, detailed studies of children's play processes. The motivation of play can be revealed only by analyzing the social construction of play in its cultural-historical contexts. Instead of looking for motivation in the inner space of each individual child, it is necessary to turn to the social and cultural space present in activity contexts. There were at least three essential activity contexts in the Finnish kindergarten play described earlier: (1) reconstructed childhood play activity of teachers now working in kindergarten; (2) teachers' day-care work; and (3) children's play activity in kindergarten today.

Motivation is constructed in a complex interplay between these activities. One cannot explain how and why children play only by focusing on ongoing play. There may be long prehistories behind the particular play, as the examples given earlier indicate. Different aspects and elements of the same play theme are repeated in different concrete contexts over many years. What seems to be totally independent play of children at the moment was initiated, guided, and instructed by adults perhaps years ago. The adults' own play experiences influence which play themes are selected and how they are set up and guided. Play motivation has an equally long time perspective. Momentary individual inner states have only subordinate roles in the evolving process. In this sense, motivation is a historical concept that should be studied historically.

The developers of activity theory – Leont'ev, El'konin, and Rubinstein – did not succeed in combining the general methodological approach and analysis of concrete historical data on children's play. The idea of object orientation as the basis for analyzing human motivation was not applied in the analysis of play data. El'konin (1978, 1989) argues that role relations in children's play reflect and refer to the array of social relations in the immediate environment of children. But this methodological tenet is not elaborated into conceptual tools for analyzing concrete play data. Instead, at the level of concrete play, the play process itself is given as the chief motivating factor. In this transition from general methodological tenets to concrete analysis, the idea of contradictions as the moving force behind children's play tends to disappear.

The preceding analysis takes the idea of object orientation as the starting point, reconstructs mutually linked activity systems, and traces basic contradictions in the social co-construction of the object of a specific kindergarten play. Motivation exists in the properties of contexts, as well as in relations between acting partners. Motivation is a relational concept, and contradictions in different relations are essential.

In the play context described earlier, the relational nature of motivation is displayed vividly. Traditional analysis of play would concentrate on one play at a time (e.g., on shopping) by describing scripts, roles, and play actions. In a traditional analysis, motivation is something that can be revealed through the personal interests of individual players. From an activity-theoretical point of view, there is a common object in the seemingly separate plays. The motivating object is not shopping, but symbolic exchange relations between people. The same relations are behind the parallel plays going on in different parts of the center. From the motivational point of view, there is only one play: *symbolic exchange relations.* The essential moving force is the tension between different forms of exchange relations and clashes caused by contradictory interpretations.

References

Bateson, G. (1955). A theory of play and fantasy. *Psychiatric Research Reports, 2,* 39–51.

Bateson, G. (1978). Play and paradigm. In M. A. Salter (Ed.), *Play: Anthropological perspectives.* West Point: Leisure Press.

Berentzen, S. (1989). The interactional context of children's peer group activities. In S. Berentzen (Ed.), *Ethnographic approaches to children's worlds and peer cultures.* Report No. 15. Trondheim: Norwegian Center for Child Research.

Bretherton, I. (1984). Representing the social world in symbolic play. In I. Bretherton (Ed.), *Symbolic play: The development of social understanding.* Orlando: Academic Press.

Bronfenbrenner, U. (1977). *The ecology of human development: Experiments by nature and design.* Cambridge, MA: Harvard University Press.

Bruner, J. S. (1977). Introduction. In B. Tizard & D. Harvey (Eds.), *The biology of play.* London: Spastics International.

Bruner, J. S. (1990). *Acts of meaning.* Cambridge, MA: Harvard University Press.

Cohen, S., & MacKeith, S. A. (1991). *The development of imagination. The private worlds of childhood.* London: Routledge.

Csikszentmihalyi, M. (1981). Some paradoxes in the definition of play. In A. T. Cheska (Ed.), *Play as context.* West Point: Leisure Press.

El'konin, D. B. (1978). *Psikhologiya igry* (*The psychology of play*). Moscow: Pedagogika.

El'konin, D. B. (1989). *Izbrannye psikhologiceskie trudy* (*Collected psychological works*). Moscow: Pedagogika.

Engeström, Y. (1987). *Learning by expanding: An activity-theoretical approach to developmental research.* Hensinki: Orienta-Konsultit.

Fein, G. G. (1987). Pretend play: Creativity and consciousness. In D. Görlitz & J. F. Wohlwill (Eds.), *Curiosity, imagination and play.* Hillsdale: Lawrence Erlbaum.

Garvey, C. (1977). *Play.* London: Open Books.

Gaskins, S., & Göncü, A. (1992). Cultural variation in play: A challenge to Piaget and Vygotsky. *Quarterly Newsletter of the Laboratory of Comparative Human Cognition, 14,* 31–34.

Goffman, E. (1974). *Frame analysis: An essay on the organization of experience.* Cambridge, MA: Harvard University Press.

Groos, K. (1922). *Das Spiel. Zwei Vorträge von Karl Groos.* Jena: Fischer.

Hakkarainen, P. (1990). *Motivaatio, leikki ja toiminnan kohteellisuus* (*Motivation, play and object-orientation of activity*). Helsinki: Orienta-Konsultit.

Hakkarainen, P. (1991). Joint construction of the object of educational work in kindergarten. *Quarterly Newsletter of the Laboratory of Comparative Human Cognition, 13,* 80–87.

Hännikäinen, M. (1992). *Transition to role play as a stage in the development of play. Piagetian point of view.* Unpublished thesis. Jyväskylä: University of Jyväskylä.

Isaacs, S. (1930). *Intellectual growth in young children.* London: Routledge and Kegan Paul.

Leont'ev, A. N. (1978). *Activity, consciousness, and personality.* Englewood Cliffs: Prentice-Hall.

Leont'ev, A. N. (1981). *Problemy razvitiya psikhiki* (*Problems of the development of the mind*). Moscow: IMGU.

Nelson, K., & Seidman, S. (1984). Playing with scripts. In I. Bretherton (Ed.), *Symbolic play: the development of social understanding.* Orlando: Academic Press.

Rubinstein, S. L. (1989). *Osnovy obshtshei psikhologii* (*Foundations of general psychology*) (Vols. I and II). Moscow: Pedagogika.

Strauss, A. (1978). The social world perspective. In N. K. Denzin (Ed.), *Studies in symbolic interaction.* Greenwich: JAI Press.

Sutton-Smith, B. (1978). *Die Dialektik des Spiels.* Schorndorf: Hofmann.

van der Kooij, R. (1983). Empirische Spielforschung. In K. J. Kreuzer (Ed.), *Handbuch der Spielpädagogik,* Band 1. Düsseldorf: Schwann-Bagel.

Drama games with 6-year-old children:
Possibilities and limitations

Stig Broström

Introduction

The cultural-historical understanding of play activity (Vygotsky, 1978; El'konin, 1980; Leont'ev, 1981) has had a growing impact on professional educators during the last decade. Play may be regarded as a subjective reflection of reality. In play the child reproduces observations and experiences in his or her own way. Play is a creative activity. Through play, the child changes his or her surroundings, leaving out something and inventing something. Fiction, imagination, and fantasy are essential. The child works out actions of make-believe and gives new meanings to actions and objects.

Play is voluntary and independent. If you try to force play, children will stop playing. Play is a social activity in which human relations are essential and are expressed together with peers. The motive of play is in the process itself, in the contents of the action, not in the result. The motive of play is unconscious, but the goal is conscious. "Nor does the presence of such generalized emotions in play mean that the child herself understands the motives giving rise to the game" (Vygotsky, 1978, p. 93).

Important changes take place in the preschool child's psyche through play. They pave the way for the child's transition to a new level of development (Leont'ev, 1981, p. 369). The leading function and impact of play activity have a number of causes. In the first place, all three mediating factors, that is, tools, signs, and other people (Vygotsky, 1978, pp. 54–57; Leont'ev, 1978, p. 59), are active in the child's play activity. Children are involved in an interaction with peers and adults; they use tools and artifacts, and represent the culture through signs and symbols. Second, in play children are able to master ideas and to carry through more advanced actions than are possible for them in nonplay situations.

In other words, in play children raise the demand on themselves and with that bring themselves into the *zone of proximal development,* which Vygotsky (1978, p. 86) defined as "the distance between the actual developmental level as determined by independent problem solving and the level of potential development as determined through problem solving under adult guidance or in collaboration with more capable peers." Through this kind of cooperation, children raise their actions to a more advanced level, which initiates new processes of development. According to Vygotsky, not only the independent actions in the zone of proximal development support the development; the child's imitations have a similar effect. Children are able to imitate actions that go beyond their possibilities, but not without limits.

In play a child always behaves beyond his average age, above his daily behavior; in play it is as though he were a head taller than himself. As in the focus of a magnifying glass, play contains all developmental tendencies in a condensed form and is itself a major source of development. (Vygotsky, 1978, p. 102)

In play activity children very often go beyond the current contextual frame. Children not only appropriate the social surrounding world, they also make unexpected creative changes. Observations of play in preschools indicate that children not only adopt to and internalize the local institutional culture but expand beyond it as well. Through this activity new knowledge, skills, and actions often appear. According to Engeström (1987), this kind of activity is dramatic and radical for the future life of the individual; it is a turning point, a revelation. Engeström calls this kind of learning activity *learning by expanding.* It takes shape as if a "voyage through the zone of proximal development" (ibid., p. 175).

My observations in preschools and kindergartens confirm that children's play in its intensive moments can be compared to Engeström's concept of *expansive learning.* Such play changes the situation, and through this change new contents emerge. Although preschool children's play resembles expansive learning, their leading activity is play, not learning. Thus, I choose to call this type of activity – when we speak about preschool children – *expansive play.*

In the following, I first identify general psychological characteristics and potentials of play activity, using a description of a fun fair circus play as the initial example. Then I look more closely into the character of drama games as a specific form of advanced play activity. I analyze examples of drama games and demonstrate the emergence and dynamics of expansive play in them.

A fun fair circus play

After lunch, 6-year-old Peter asks his friends Morten and Danny to play with the circus animals. They start by building some cages of bricks in which they place different animals. Now Peter suggests making a fun fair with "lots of things you can do." Morten accepts and expands the idea, adding a circus project with performing animals. On the basis of this shared plan, Morten starts building a booking office and arranges a line. Peter builds a little lake, places a canoe on it, and declares: "Now you can go canoeing." "Yes," Danny says, "but you have to line up." Now some 5-year-old girls arrive, asking to join in. "Then you can finish the fun fair." The girls construct the seats and the bandstand, which inspires Morten. He grabs a Playmobile figure and bursts out: "I am the man. I am bandmaster." Peter: "Okay, but then I will be your monkey, can't I?" And Peter continues: "And also the man who flings with knives in circus. Is it okay to be two persons at the same time?" "Yes," Morten says while he conducts the band of the circus, which for a while consists only of Danny playing the trumpet.

Soon Danny leaves the band but Morten continues being a bandmaster, still keeping the Playmobile figure in his hand. Then he puts away the figure, plants himself at a table, and begins to color a miniature paper checkered black and white. With great concentration he produces a black-and-white signal flag, which he places in the hand of his Playmobile figure. He returns to the fun fair, where he is all by himself for a lengthy period, absorbed in a play creating a race.

One of the girls asks to be a keeper at the zoo, "and I enter the cages of the animals." She finds a Playmobile figure, puts in some animals, and feeds them. Peter tells her: "Remember, all the animals are inoffensive. They can walk around everywhere if they like." "Yes, and I'm a crocodile, but nobody is afraid of me," Danny says. Now Peter becomes inspired. At the platform he becomes a monkey, shouting: "I'm a wild monkey, and you, Peter, chase me." Peter manages the monkey; it rushes at the other animals and at last falls down in the middle of the ring. Then Peter says: "Now the monkey is tired; let us show him a circus trick."

This play sequence has a happy and cheerful atmosphere. This alone might be a sufficient reason for supporting play. But in addition to this, play is the leading activity of the preschool child, the activity that has the greatest influence on developing new structures in the child's psyche (Leont'ev, 1981, p. 369). How is this manifested in the sequence just described?

Children play in order to cope with their own existence – among other things, experiences of fear. In the preceding play sequence the children are dealing with a harmony–conflict relationship. The wild animals are set free, but they are not dangerous. The monkey shows its wildness, but it is still accepted by the group.

According to El'konin (1980), the most important meaning of play is its influence on the development of motives and needs. Play results in a movement from unconscious motives to more conscious ones. If a 3-year-old girl feeds the animals in this play, she does so just as the keeper at the zoo would, but her motive is unconscious. A girl of 5 performs apparently identical actions, but though the actions seem alike, the child is not content with just doing what adults did. In her consciousness she *is* the keeper of the zoo; she identifies herself with the role and appropriates the actions of the keeper. This is the foundation for developing a new, conscious motive: the wish to be adult and act like adults. Gradually the child realizes that this demands new knowledge and skills. This new understanding eventually leads to the development of a new motive: the learning motive.

In addition, play helps children to overcome their egocentricity. When Morten identifies himself with the role of conductor, he has to take over the motives, feelings, and actions attached to that role. Danny, too, has to understand the motives and actions of the conductor in order to be able to join the band.

Role play also contributes to the inhibition of spontaneous action. In order to be able to play, children have to reflect on and arrange some play actions. Peter suggests playing a fun fair, and Morten suggests doing a circus with performing animals. Play implies that the two boys reflect, then express their thoughts linguistically, and finally carry out the play actions. In other words, there is a gradual movement from unconsciousness and impulsive actions to conscious, willful actions. The order action–speech–thought is changed to the reverse order: thought–speech–action.

Play develops imagination and fantasy. The child can carry out the role play only if he or she is able to imagine the role and the actions. Children have to ascribe another meaning to the play actions and play accessories. For instance, the child has to imagine that a block is a booking office. Otherwise, it is meaningless to wait for a ticket at the block.

Moreover, play develops the social capacity of children. The individual roles demand particular play actions. For example, Morten starts conducting the band, which inspires Danny to blow the trumpet. Because play is an activity children want to do, they enter into an agreement with each other. Play helps children in a meaningful way to subordinate to one another's play wishes.

Finally, in play children often create completely new actions and activities that expand the play and, with that, the children's capacity. The sequence in which Morten became absorbed in coloring the flag illustrates this.

Drama games

At the age of 6, role play gradually changes its character. Children become conscious of their own activity and, as a result, the rules behind the roles become conscious to the children. This forms the basis of mastery of new forms of play. Six-year-old children are able to organize and play games with rules independently of adults.

These are games, whose fixed content is no longer the role and the play situation but the rule and the purpose. Such, for example, is hopscotch; it is necessary to achieve a certain goal set by definite conditions. (Leont'ev, 1981, p. 386)

In this kind of play the rules are relatively specific and arbitrary. They are based on agreement among children about specific actions that are allowed. The rules must be known and understood before the games begin. Awareness of the purpose of the play leads to specific results. In playing tag, for example, it is necessary not just to run, but also to run away from the one who is "it." Still, the motive is in the play process itself. "But that process is now mediated for the child by purpose" (Leont'ev, 1981, p. 387).

Parallel to the growing awareness of the purpose of play, a change concerning its contents and complexity comes into existence. To young children, role play means acting with objects and later carrying out a role. During the period from 5 to 7 years of age, the content of play manifests itself through actions connected to the roles of playmates (El'konin, 1980).

Moreover, 6-year-old children become more conscious of the imaginary play situation, that is, the concrete situation they imagine. Slavina's investigations reported by El'konin (1980) show that the existence of the imaginary play situation ascribes meaning to the play actions. In the previous fun fair sequence, for instance, the 6-year-olds had a joint understanding of the imaginary play situation.

The development of this new level of play makes it possible to introduce new types of play. Leont'ev (1981, p. 389) mentions different *borderline games,* including the development of dramatized and improvised games. Based on Leont'ev's ideas, I developed a new type of play in collaboration with preschool teachers. We call this type of play *frame play* or *drama games*.

Unlike role play, the drama game is a play activity in which the children and the teacher plan together. First of all, they decide on a general theme, such as "What happens in the airport?" or a theme with less social realism. With support from the adults, the children formulate some dimensions of the contents. For example, one child suggested: "Then we pretend there is a catastrophe in the airport." Inspired by various contents, the children plan the setting and discuss the different roles, the rules within the roles, and possible actions attached to some specific roles. Through this shared planning, the frame of the play gradually becomes manifest. Thus, I define *frame* as the participants' conscious and joint plan.

I use the concept of frame with reference to the importance of the imaginary play situation (El'konin, 1980). In role play the imaginary play situation often refers to a situation only within narrow limits. In the fun fair sequence, for instance, Morten as bandmaster and Danny as trumpeter accompany the circus performance. But by creating a frame play along with 6-year-olds, it is possible to generate an extended and common imaginary play situation. It is a shared frame that children use steadily and for a relatively long period of time.

The decisions children make are formulated verbally and also in creative drawings and paintings, which serve as models. As pointed out by Davydov (1990) and Ajdarova (1982), such models help to develop children's self-esteem, awareness of their own activity, and incipient reflective thought. After this planning, the play is carried out.

A drama game thus contains several elements that have been decided beforehand by the children and the adults. Because there is a certain time interval between formulation of the plan and realization of the play, the roles, rules, and actions are prepared thoroughly. Often children produce a lot of accessories for the game. For instance, for a game involving ships, the children may create an engine, a bridge, a wheel, and an anchor, in addition to aprons and money for going shopping at the store and restaurant. In this way, the drama game is more organized and purposeful than role play. The play motive in drama games is different from that in role play. In role play the motive lies in the play itself. In drama games the motive shifts more and more toward the result of the play activity.

In a preschool, we experimented with drama games together with a group of 20 children between 5 and 6 years of age. The children and the preschool teachers worked out play activities with themes such as "Life in hospital," "Railway station," and "On the ferry to Sweden." In the kindergarten class attached to a school, the drama games were organized as projects in the joint teaching of kindergarten classes and Grades 1 and 2. For instance, in the project "We are constructing a town," children between ages 5 and 9 were divided into groups of about six. They turned the classrooms into workshops where they manufactured and sold many products, such as different kinds of toys, portrait paintings, and key racks. Other rooms they converted into a restaurant, a bank, a cinema, and different shops. The children worked in shifts, moving from production to consumption and back. One week the children worked in shops, the restaurant, and the cinema for their wages; the next week they created a play where they spent their wages.

This kind of organization attempts to give the individual child access to roles and actions that correspond to his or her capacity. Nevertheless, many questions were raised: Does the more organized drama game demand too much? Will it cause a storm in the zone of proximal development? Will the children be brought into an activity characterized by motives that, in Leont'ev's (1981, p. 402) words, are "only understandable"? Will the independence, creativity, and voluntary nature of play be spoiled? Will the drama game serve only the function of adjustment?

To illuminate these questions, I observed drama games in preschool and kindergarten settings and subsequently conducted interviews with the children.

"We are constructing a town"

In this drama game, I followed 6-year-old Peter for about 25 minutes. Peter joins a group that is going to town. He goes along with five other children aged 5 to 8 years. Two 8-year-old girls take the initiative: "First, we shall draw our wages from the bank." They walk to the bank, where they receive their wages. Two boys leave the group: "We are going to the movie, and later we are going to the restaurant." Now Peter is alone with the two girls, Brit and Anja. They ask if he would like to go shopping. "We are going to the shop From Head to Foot." Peter nods his head.

In the shop, the girls immediately turn to the beauty salon. Brit says: "We varnish our nails." "Yes, just like pretty ladies," Anja adds. "My sister already has red nails, also when she is at work," Britt says. Now something happens with Anja. In an excited voice she whispers: "Hey, listen! We will enter our own room; then we will be models."

Peter is not involved in this chat, so he does not respond to the girls when they leave the shop. He is looking at T-shirts, ties, and hats that are on display. He takes a tie and turns to a pal who has the role of a sales clerk: "How much does it cost? It can't be very expensive." "Are you mad?" the sales clerk replies. "It is from America; it costs five kroner." "Never mind, I'll buy it," Peter says and fishes out some money, which he hands to the sales clerk. The other boy leaves the role of sales clerk and asks Peter what he is going to do now. "I don't know; maybe I'll go to the restaurant. Yes that is what I want," Peter says resolutely. He walks out, heading in the direction of the restaurant.

At the restaurant the waiter welcomes Peter, shows him to a table, and gives him a menu. He looks at the menu, counts his money, and stares in front of him. Soon the waiter arrives, asking him what he would like to eat. "A glass of water and a bowl of soup," he orders. While Peter is waiting he looks around, following the waiter's work, but he does not say anything. After a few minutes, Peter gets his soup and begins eating.

At first, Peter's play actions do not look like a genuine play activity, characterized in general psychological terms earlier in this chapter. Concerning fiction and imagination, apparently Peter is not able to pretend he is somebody else, that he is playing a role. The role could conceivably be, for example, one of a businessman on a journey who goes shopping, to a restaurant, and so on. It looks as though Peter merely performs the actions the circumstances demand.

Concerning creativity, Peter takes only few initiatives of his own, and these initiatives do not change the situation. For example, he buys a tie and orders some food. He does not change his surroundings.

Concerning human relations, Peter enters into few relations with other children (the girls, the shop assistant, the waiter). He gets no challenges, and he receives little feedback on his own actions.

Concerning the motive, Peter turns his actions to certain goals: buying a tie and ordering a meal. But does his motive correspond to the goals? He looks and moves as if his motive is "they expect me to do this." Or perhaps it is a motive that exists only in consciousness without emotions, an "only understandable motive."

Clearly, this particular drama game did not give Peter the chance to bring out proper play actions. But why was Peter unable to involve himself in this play, to leave out something and to invent something? Why could he not establish relationships and connections to other children? Why did he only adjust himself to the circumstances?

From my point of view, we have to look at two factors. First, the organization of the play was too complex. Peter was not able to survey so many activities and possibilities. He was not engaged in and eager to involve himself in an activity he himself had helped prepare the week before. In other words, he was brought into an activity that went beyond his zone of proximal development.

The second factor I want to point out is the absence of the teacher. Peter was left alone. It was too difficult for him to establish relationships with other children. He waited for the other children's initiative. Even when he received a question from the two girls, he was not able to reply and try to improve the relationship. Because Peter did not receive help, he was forced to be an onlooker instead of taking an active part in the activity.

This example is not an argument against the use of drama games. From the two girls' perspective, probably this play had a positive meaning and influence. In the idea of being models I see an embryo of what I call *expansive play*. But with regard to Peter, the example illustrates some problems and limitations. The success of drama games with 6-year-olds depends on the organization of the play and the children's possibility of shaping their own play actions. When a drama game is organized in another way, it can achieve an expansive character. I demonstrate this with the help of another extract from a drama game in a preschool (Broström, 1992).

"Firemen in action"

In the fire station, fire chief Frederik sits at the control table typing while the drivers, Jesper and Mads, wait eagerly. Nema and Lennon, two firemen, sit in the fire engine, and Nema makes a call on the walkie-talkie.

Nema: I am going to call the chief.
Lennon: What? I will do the same thing. You know something? I will call
              you.
Nema: Lennon, don't. Now it is my turn.
Lennon: I haven't tried.
(Lennon calls to the control desk, where Anders is placed.)
Lennon: Anders, Anders!
Nema: Firemen won't do it like that.
(Frederik picks up the call and turns toward Anders.)
Frederik: Then you will say.

Anders: Hello, hey, fireman.
(Nema accepts that Lennon receives the call.)
Nema: Hurry up! Answer the call.
(Lennon picks up the walkie-talkie.)
Lennon: What's going on?
(Anders thinks they have been out driving.)
Anders: It's okay to return. Return.
Lennon: Oh, well, hey.

After this dialogue, the children sit waiting. Apparently because no alarm comes in, Nema takes the initiative to drive the fire engine.

Nema: We go for a drive, you drive. I call the fire station.
(Frederik picks up the message.)
Frederick: Hello.
Nema: I call you, I want to speak with you, boss.
Frederick: Hey, it's the Fire Department.
Nema: Shall we return?
Frederick: Yes.
Nema: Okay, we will do it, hey.
Lennon: (in a correcting way) Nema, when you do this, don't do it like this.

An observing teacher warns the boys at the control desk that there will soon be a fire. She switches on the bicycle lamp, which she has placed under red tissue paper. The fire chief grabs the phone.

Frederik: Hey, it's the fire station. Return quickly, there is a fire. Bring the fire engine to the scene of the fire.
(Nema and Lennon, sitting in the fire engine, make sounds like a siren, jump off, and drag the fire hose through the room. They uncoil the hose; Nema grabs it and climbs the ladder.)
Nema: Where is the fire?
(While Nema searches for the fire, he observes Anders running around with the bicycle lamp and the tissue paper. Then he climbs off the ladder, hangs the hose on the ladder, and turns, irritated, to Lennon.)
Nema: Now you fix the hose with me.
Lennon: Nema, you will put out the fire all the time.
Nema: (ignoring this objection) I tell you what, we have to hose with water, lots of water.
(Lennon seems to feel too controlled, but before the conflict becomes manifest, a child shouts: "There is a fire in the hospital." Another boy adds: "We only pretend." At the control table Frederik talks to Anders.)
Frederick: Anders, Anders, we have a call. Won't you come? We will take a ride to the hospital.
Anders: I have to tell the man in the hospital.

Frederik: Yes. No, tell the firemen.

(Here Anders gets an alternative idea. Instead of calling the two firemen, he places himself in the center of the room, pointing to Nema and screaming: "Stop the thief. He stole the policeman's gun. He is a holdup man." Nema catches the change to a robber and runs away. Now everybody runs around yelling while Anders chases the robber for a long time.)

Here I stop the description. It should be pointed out that parallel to the processes centered on the fire station, others are going on in the emergency room, the waiting room, and the sickroom. The house is humming with activity.

Play often seems to consist of strings of isolated actions: The firemen respond to a fire, the doctor examines the patients, and the cleaner mops the floor. But we also witness coordinated play actions: The teacher initiates a fire, after which the children set off the alarm, the fire chief answers the phone and turns on the red light on the control desk, and the firemen go into action. Similarly, the patients move from the waiting room into the hospital and later enter the sickroom.

In the preceding episode, the firemen, Nema and Lennon, took the initiative themselves. First, they made a call to the fire chief, and subsequently they arranged a ride. Apparently the play actions were based on genuine feelings, motivated by what Leont'ev (1981, p. 402) calls "really effective motives." For example, Nema took a number of initiatives: He called the chief and climbed up the ladder in order to put out the fire. He placed himself in the center of the events, created exciting action strings, and presumably saw himself as an active subject. He was a fireman, and for him it was meaningful to put out a fire. Using Leont'ev's (1981, pp. 399–400) terms, the object of the process coincided with the objective that stimulated the subject to his activity.

But what about Lennon, who is one year younger than Nema? He complained that Nema put out the fire. Was he so dominated by Nema and others that the role of fireman was less meaningful to him? This seems unlikely. Though Nema initiated the call to the fire chief, Lennon actually carried out the call, and later, when they took a ride, Lennon drove the car. So Lennon was involved in the play.

In "Firemen in action" the boys were conscious of the coherent play pattern: call to the fire chief, alarm, firemen on their guard, response, firefighting, and back again. Nema demonstrated this awareness. He was eager to put out the fire, but he controlled his impatience. He knew he had to wait for instructions from the fire chief, so he used the waiting time making walkie-talkie calls and taking a ride. He was conscious of the rules of reality and play, and he accepted them.

We see a corresponding consciousness in Frederik when Nema asked him whether they should return. "Yes," Frederik replied because he thought the fire engine ought to be in its place. This consciousness was manifest in the command "It's the fire station. Return quickly, there is a fire." And later, when there was a fire in the hospital and Anders asked if he should tell the man in the hospital, Frederik rationally responded: "No, tell the firemen."

In play, children reflect their experiences and take independent initiatives. They play up to each other and understand how to make use of these challenges. They bring each other into a zone of proximal development. But they do not exceed the zone even when the teacher enters into the play. When the teacher started the fire, she acted in agreement with the children's capacity. The teacher enriched the play, but on the children's premises and without going beyond their zone of proximal development.

Most of the play actions were worked out in agreement with the children's experiences and the frame of the play. Nevertheless, within the described play sequences we see some new actions come into existence. In the fun fair, we see Morten deeply involved in painting. When Anja and Brit left the shop From Head to Foot to perform as models, they expanded beyond the current given context. Finally, in taking up the thief and police idea, Anders and Nema acted contrary to the expectation of fireman's work and activity.

Through these play activities, the children brought themselves into the zone of proximal development. Such play activities are characterized by changes and by the appearance of new contents. If the teachers make room for children's creative activities, they themselves will generate such expanding elements. The opposite will occur if the teachers put too much structure into the play. Expansive play will not appear.

The drama game also forms a basis for the emergence of new games when the concrete drama game ends. Children may use the equipment and costumes to develop a completely new play.

Educational implications of drama games

In a successfully organized drama game, the child's motive corresponds to the object. Consequently, the activity is meaningful. Children are engaged in the activity and express genuine feelings. This indicates that their motives have the character of "really effective motives."

Children need to understand the whole play and to see the connections between the various play actions. The contents and elaboration of the play challenge the children but should not go beyond their zone of proximal development.

The theme of the drama game has to be formulated on the basis of children's interests and motives. The themes may arise as extensions of earlier project work, as joint excursions, or as continuations of children's own stories and imaginations. In order to build up the common frame and to play on the basis on the theme, the children must have insight into and experiences in connection with the topic of the play. The best foundation is children's own physical experience, gained, for example, through a visit to the hospital, to the harbor, or to the airport, where the children have an opportunity to observe firsthand the relations between people engaged in a practice (Launer, 1968). Naturally, a drama game can be established on the basis of a story or a movie, but 6–year–old children prefer firsthand experience.

In the arrangement of the drama game, the teachers are responsible for encouraging and supporting the children and for promoting a good atmosphere. The children have to formulate the frame of the drama game themselves. The teachers should support and guide, but they have to be very gentle in the way they make suggestions and introduce play scenarios and ideas for the frame of the play activity. In order to inspire the children to play, the teacher has to take an active part in the play and be genuinely involved. The teacher's role in play is to support, enrich, and expand the play – but without exceeding the zone of proximal development. On these premises, the organized drama game has the potential to contribute to the development of qualitatively new structures in the child's psyche and activity.

References

Ajdarova, L. (1982). *Child development and education.* Moscow: Progress.

Broström, S. (1992). Quick response: An ethnographic analysis of a drama-game in a Danish preschool. *Quarterly Newsletter of the Laboratory of Comparative Human Cognition, 14,* 17–25.

Davydov, V. V. (1990). *Types of generalization in instruction: Logical and psychological problems in the structuring of school curricula.* Reston: National Council of Teachers of Mathematics.

El'konin, D. B. (1980). *Psychologie des Spiels.* Berlin: Volk und Wissen.

Engeström, Y. (1987). *Learning by expanding. An activity-theoretical approach to developmental research.* Helsinki: Orienta-Konsultit.

Launer, I. (1968). *Persönlichkeitsentwicklung im Vorschulalter bei Spiel und Arbeit.* Berlin: Volk und Wissen.

Leont'ev, A. N. (1978). *Activity, consciousness, and personality.* Englewood Cliffs: Prentice-Hall.

Leont'ev, A. N. (1981). *Problems of the development of the mind.* Moscow: Progress.

Vygotsky, L. S. (1978). *Mind in society.* Cambridge, MA: Harvard University Press.

16 Activity formation as an alternative strategy of instruction

Joachim Lompscher

Introduction

Teachers' experiences and countless studies show that in the majority of classrooms real learning results do not correspond with either the expectations of society or the efforts of most of the teachers and learners. High rates of forgetting, low levels of applicability of knowledge and skills, insufficient quality of problem finding and problem solving, and aversion to school learning are often demonstrated in discussions and reports.

Results from one of our studies illustrate this point. Fourth-grade pupils (10 to 11 years of age) had to solve two text problems. Both problems had the same mathematical structure but were different in content. The mathematical structure of both problems corresponded with the students' available mental preconditions. In both cases, the same operations (addition and multiplication of whole numbers) had to be used. The first problem referred to familiar things often used in such tasks. The second problem, however, was about liquids, a type of problem with which the children had little calculatory experience.

The study was part of a larger investigation performed in normal classrooms in several schools (Reinhold, 1988). Earlier results obtained with different methods allowed us to select pupils as representatives of relatively homogeneous performance groups (high, average, and low performance). The difficulties in uncovering the mathematical structure and in finding necessary operations increased sharply from performance group I (high) to group III (low) (Figure 16.1). Students with similar psychological characteristics but taught on the basis of another instructional strategy reached significantly higher results, although differences between the performance groups show the same trend that occurs in the classes that received traditional instruction.

264

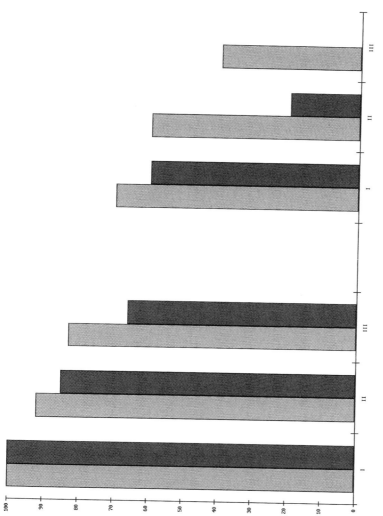

Figure 16.1. Solution of two text problems with the same structure but different content. Darker columns: familiar content; lighter columns: unfamiliar content; I, II, and III: performance groups; left half: experimental classes; right half: control classes.

The findings demonstrate, on the one hand, the insufficiency of normal instruction and difficulties in problem solving for almost all the learners, especially the average- and low-performance groups. On the other hand, they demonstrate the learners' great potential when an adequate instructional strategy is found (see also De Corte, 1990; Van Oers, 1990).

There are several different intertwined causes underlying these facts. One of the main reasons is the theoretical background of instructional strategies usually implemented in schools. Despite declarations about the learner's position as an active subject, in most classrooms students are objects of didactic actions aimed at the transmission of knowledge and skills (and norms and values, as well) from the teacher's head (or from the textbook) to the pupils' heads. This dominant *transmission strategy* is oriented, first of all, toward the material to be learned and much less toward the learners' activity necessary for the acquisition of that material. Therefore, teachers are more interested in their own actions and tools necessary for the transmission than in the learners' actions and the psychological characteristics necessary for the acquisition. When these characteristics do play a role, they are analyzed very globally and often only in terms of what should be already known (what was transmitted), not what is actually known and which psychological prerequisites are necessary to reach a higher level, to enter a new domain, and so on.

The gap between the necessary prerequisites and the actually existing psychological qualities is one of the main contradictions arising again and again in the learning process. This gap can be overcome by permanently changing the organization of the learners' own activity aimed at the formation of psychic conditions undeveloped or insufficiently developed for further progress in learning. Thus, the *zone of proximal development* (Vygotsky, 1978) can be transformed into a *zone of actual performance,* opening a new zone of proximal development. These transformations depend, first of all, on the learners' own activity.

Our alternative for the transmission strategy may be called the *activity formation strategy.* It is oriented to the learner's personality and development. Therefore it cannot be restricted to isolated aspects of knowledge or skill.

With this strategy, one has to consider the full complexity of activity regulation (cognitive, emotional, motivational, and other components and their interrelations). At the same time, one has to consider the real conditions under which learning activity is performed and may be brought about according to societal and individual prerequisites, goals, and opportunities. This way a claim is formulated that can be tested and realized only in the course of a long process and with joint efforts involving researchers, teachers, parents, communities, authorities, and, of course, learners themselves.

The opposition between the instructional strategies of transmission and activity formation is stated here in absolute terms for the sake of clarity. There are, of course, many variations occurring more or less on one side or the other.

Contradictions in learning activity

Learning activity differs from other kinds of activity in that it aims, above all, at psychic transformations of the subject itself (Davydov, 1988a; El'konin, 1989; Lompscher, 1988). Other kinds of activity (play, labor, everyday communication, etc.) may have learning results, too, but they are not consciously aimed at by the subject (though possibly by other persons, e.g., teachers). It is an essential feature of learning activity that the acquisition of new knowledge and skill requires certain prerequisites in terms of abilities, motivation, and memory structures that are only partially developed to the necessary degree at a certain moment. If they were fully developed, learning would not be necessary; if they were not developed at all, learning would not be possible.

The contradiction between the objectively necessary prerequisites for the acquisition of certain material and the existing prerequisites – the real state of psychic development – must be solved continuously, time and again, in the course of learning activity by performing appropriate learning actions (ranging, for example, from such elementary actions as relating objects to samples and pronouncing words to such complex actions as text comprehension and problem solving). But the problem is that these learning actions necessary to reach certain goals are often not yet available to the learner or are available only at an insufficient level. At first, they have to be formed systematically; only then can they serve as essential means for learning.

Another contradiction arises here. Learning actions are prerequisites for acquisition of certain material, but they cannot be formed (acquired, learned) without being engaged in the corresponding material. It is impossible to learn the appropriate learning actions first and then to learn the material itself. The actions' content, structure, and course are determined by the object; there is no contentless or objectless formal action to be transferred to different materials.

Of course, there are different degrees of generality – actions applicable only in a narrow domain or for specific ends, on the one hand, and actions with a broad field of application, on the other hand (e.g., heuristics). The relationship between domain-specific and more or less general actions is complicated and full of contradictions and transitions from one degree of generality to another. In recent literature, one can find very different results and positions on this topic (see, e.g., Klauer, 1989; Detterman & Sternberg, 1993). But even very general actions are not independent of any content or object; they correspond, for example, to highly generalized problem structures. How can these contradictions of learning activity be solved in such a way that learners' psychic development is promoted and high learning efficiency as a relation between learning efforts and learning results is ensured?

A proposed solution

Our solution of the contradiction mentioned earlier consists of an arrangement of learning activity in which the acquisition of the learning material is organized, first of all, as *formation of the learning activity itself* (Davydov, 1988a, 1988b, 1991; Hedegaard, 1990; Hedegaard & Chaiklin, 1993; Lompscher, 1982, 1984, 1985, 1988, 1989a, 1989b, 1992). This *activity formation strategy* may be briefly characterized by the following features.

1. Whereas the transmission strategy, as a rule, emphasizes goal orientation in the sense of presenting learning goals in a ready form, explaining them, if necessary, and expecting or demanding an appropriate learning behavior, our orientation is directed to *goal formation*. We confront the learners with phenomena, situations, and tasks going beyond their actual possibilities to such a degree that a problem situation can arise. The learners' available knowledge and skills are not sufficient for an immediate solution, but they are sufficient for understanding and accepting the problem. This is a question not only of cognitive prerequisites but of emotional and motivational ones as well. An active and productive learning process will start and go on if there is appropriate motivation. In the study mentioned earlier, we gave fourth-grade students relatively complex mathematical problems – compared with those solved so far – and with thought-provoking contents, so that the children were interested and tried to solve the problems but failed to do so.

Pedagogical guidance in this situation consisted of stimulating and instructing the learners to analyze the new learning task in such a way that they related it to their own prerequisites and assessed the latter with respect to what they did *not* know or could not do yet. This is possible only in a more or less general form. On this basis, learning goals are formed showing a certain learning prospect by indicating *what one has to acquire in order to be able to solve a certain class of problems.* General learning goals may be subdivided into partial ones to be put into practice step by step. This is also the basis for permanent, increasingly independent self-control and self-assessment of the course and the results of learning, for increasing awareness, responsibility, and independence of learning activity.

2. In order to put into practice a certain learning goal, the learner has to know *how* to do it, that is, which actions have to be performed and in what way. In the case of transmission strategy, this knowledge and the corresponding methods are usually given in a ready-made form related to particular tasks or phenomena; in some cases, learners have to find the appropriate methods more or less by trial and error. The learners' orientation is limited by the particular tasks they solved or by the particular objects they studied. As a rule, generalization in such situations is based on superficial similarities that may not correspond to the essence (structure, content, features, etc.) of the relevant object or task classes. In epistemological and psychological literature this kind of generalization is called *empirical* (Davydov, 1990). It is useful for orientation in everyday conditions but insufficient for orientation in complex problem situations and for the transfer of knowledge and methods to unknown domains and subjects. Here a different type of generalization is called for: *theoretical* generalization characterized by orientation toward the revelation of the inner structure of the object, of its essential features and relationships, independent of its outward appearance (Davydov, 1990). Such a theoretical approach can be formed if the orientation basis[1] is elaborated by the learners themselves in the course of *actively transforming the object to be studied.* For example, orientation toward the mathematical structure of text problems (and not toward isolated numbers or words, as many students do) was formed by studying real transformations (e.g., relations between the lengths of different spring tensions and the weights of objects fixed to them), by transforming the quantities in text problems and controlling the change of the outcomes, by transforming unknown quantities into given ones, and vice versa. Thus the students learned to analyze unknown quantities, to discover the functional interrelations between

unknown and given quantities, and to reveal the mathematical structure hidden behind different text formulations and contents. This approach demands differentiated pedagogical guidance and close cooperation between teacher and students, precise knowledge of students' characteristics, and a good psychological touch.

3. A more or less generalized and complete orientation basis is a necessary prerequisite for the acquisition and conscious, rational performance of certain learning actions. But this is not enough. Actions must be *mastered*, and this means that they have to be *formed systematically*. A differentiated theoretical analysis has to determine which actions are necessary for the acquisition of certain knowledge and skills and for the formation of certain competencies, approaches, and so on. This analysis has to bridge the gap between the learners' existing preconditions and the necessary psychic prerequisites related to the objective requirements of the learning material, as well as the educational goals of an instructional process or experiment. The transmission strategy is not much concerned with such an analysis and formation because of its orientation toward the material to be transmitted in ready-made forms.

In our example of mathematical text problems, we tried to develop a generalized solution method applicable to different task structures and contents (*goal–means–conditions analysis*, as we called it). We determined an action structure to be formed consisting of:

- Analysis and modellike representation of the respective task structure. Beginning with analysis of the unknown quantity and the quantities necessary for its determination, the interrelations between the quantities given in the text have to be uncovered step by step, and a chain of partial goals has to be derived (backward chaining and the strategy of global optimization). First, quantities and their interrelations are characterized in general terms; then they are specified according to the task content. In solving different problems, varying forms of the general structure model emerge, depending on the respective relations between unknown and known quantities.
- Derivation of mathematical equations on this basis and execution of corresponding operations (mostly by forward chaining and local optimization, including resources to, control of, and correction of already performed steps).
- Reflection on performed or required actions. The achieved result has to be related to the quantity sought, the solution path

has to be justified, causes of mistakes have to be revealed and discussed, and so on.

The formation of such a complex action structure needs time and a variety of tasks and exercises. The complex action has to be practiced as a whole, but partial actions may be formed at first as relatively independent objectives, if necessary, and then integrated, step by step, into the whole structure. Usually, new actions are formed first in practical forms and then transferred, step by step, to verbal and mental forms. The modellike representation is an important means for the transition from practical to mental action forms and for the abstraction of essential features and relations of the object or task classes from particular contents and structures. During the formation process, the action structure is continuously changing. Certain parts or components are reduced, automatized, or otherwise modified; the action as a whole becomes more flexible and adjusted to different conditions (e.g., a flexible combination of global and local optimization).

4. An instructional strategy directed toward the learners' own activity and its systematic formation (or enabling the learners to learn more and more independently and efficiently) has to pay attention to the fact that, on the one hand, learning activity is based on individual reproduction of societal knowledge and skill, but that, on the other hand, as a rule it is embedded in and depends on social interaction. *Learners cooperate* with the teacher and with peers. The learning group is part of larger groups and organizations of the society as a whole (see Rubtsov, 1987; Jantos, 1989; Mevarech & Light, 1992; Perret-Clermont & Schubauer-Leoni, 1989; Webb, 1989). Cooperation and communication are essential conditions of learning activity, and their systematic arrangement and formation contains very strong impulses for effective learning. Nguyen Danh Moc (1989) investigated specially organized dyadic work (mutual control and support, assessment and explanation, common planning and division of labor in action performance, etc.) of third-grade students in mathematical text problem solving. He obtained significantly better learning results compared to those achieved with predominantly individual work. Köster (1985) formed heuristic strategies in dyadic cooperation among fourth-grade students, the results of which differed significantly, depending on the concrete forms of cooperation (see Figure 16.2). The subjects' functions were divided between "problem solver" and "controller" (groups 1 and 2) or "problem solver" and "opponent" (groups 3 and 4), and this division was either stable (groups 1 and 3) or constantly changing (groups 2

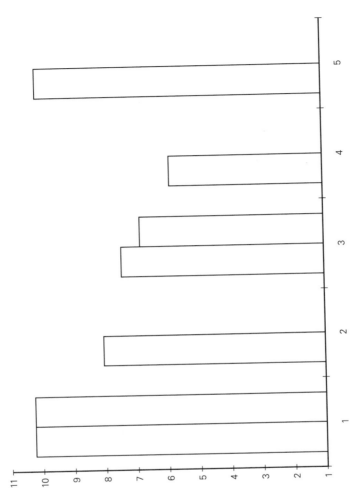

Figure 16.2. Problem–solving dyads (number of steps to solution). (1) problem solver and controller – stable division of functions; (2) problem solver and controller – changing division of functions; (3) problem solver and opponent – stable division of functions; (4) problem solver and opponent – changing division of functions; (5) control groups.

and 4). The change of functions and the problem solver–opponent division was the most effective variant in this experiment. This was true not only with regard to the number of steps necessary until a solution was found but also with regard to the quality of the strategies.

5. All the aspects mentioned so far were integrated into a special instructional strategy called *ascending from the abstract to the concrete*. Its philosophical, psychological, and pedagogical prerequisites and consequences, as well as the experience with and results of its implementation in instructional experiments, are described in detail in the literature (in particular, see Davydov, 1988a). Its main difference from the transmission strategy consists of the following: In the first phase, the most essential constitutive features and relations of a learning object or domain are abstracted on the basis of the learners' own practical and/or mental actions and fixed in easily manageable models in graphic or symbolic forms. This is the process of transition from the concrete to the abstract. This abstraction is based on theoretical generalization (see the earlier discussion), though in very elementary forms, considering the developmental level of the students (mostly third to sixth graders, but the strategy is not restricted to these age groups). We call these abstractions *initial* or *starting abstractions* because the most important phase or part of the acquisition process is only beginning now: Ascending from the abstract to the concrete[2] depends decisively on the quality of that starting abstraction. It now becomes a means of further mental penetration of the learning object, a means of orientation, planning, and analysis in the ongoing learning activity.

The initial abstraction serves as a conceptual macrostructure that offers a general framework for analysis of the many concrete phenomena and their fixation in appropriate memory structures. The initial abstraction fosters a mental grasp of the concrete by tracing back to the basic relations and features of the learning domain, and in turn, it is gradually enriched in content by means of the production of many links while analyzing the concrete phenomena. This learning process may be continued until the explorative potential of a starting abstraction is exhausted and a higher or different abstraction is needed to further penetrate the object, if necessary or desirable. In any case, determination of the content and structure of a starting abstraction, its modellike representation, the ways and conditions of the transition from the concrete to the abstract, and then the ascent from the abstract to the more and more mentally penetrated concrete presuppose serious theoretical work and, of course, much empirical research. On this theoretical basis, we conducted instructional experiments in different domains (e.g., language, mathematics, physics, history).

Selected examples and results

The initial abstraction elaborated and used for mathematical text problem solving was the general concept of task structure and the general strategy of goal–means–conditions analysis. In ordinary classes, a general strategy is formed, too, but it orients students toward given quantities and operations. Many mistakes and incorrect operations are the consequences of that kind of orientation very often found in schools.

Reinhold (1988) asked students in experimental and control classes in individual sessions to describe the procedure they used when confronted with text problems. The reproduction of corresponding procedural knowledge showed minimal differences, but its application to the solution of a rather complicated word problem (including both relevant and irrelevant data) yielded significant differences between the experimental and control classes: In the latter, only about 50% approached the task according to the strategy reproduced a minute before (Figure 16.3). The difference between the experimental and control classes increased even more when Reinhold checked whether they obtained the right numerical result. The whole sample had to write a solution plan for another text problem without performing the calculatory operations. In experimental classes ($n = 34$) only 12% could not solve this task, in control classes ($n = 96$) 80%. Findings such as these, as well as other evidence obtained over several years, demonstrate the efficiency of the activity formation strategy, especially that of ascending from the abstract to the concrete. This is true for different performance groups, too, though the progress of low-performance students cannot be interpreted as satisfactory.

Similar results were obtained in other investigations as well. Average-performance students in experimental classes often reached the same level as high-performance students or even higher. Low-performance students correspondingly reached the level of average-performance students or better. High-performance students in experimental classes reached a higher level than those in control classes, too, but we did not analyze and compare this in particular.

In an experiment in science in fourth-grade classes repeated several times, we found some students in each class who had little or no gain from this experiment (against the background of remarkable progress in the experimental classes as a whole, considering concept and strategy

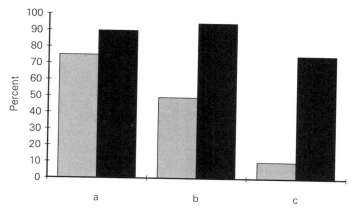

Figure 16.3. Efficiency of different strategies for the solution of text problems. (a) Reproduction of procedural knowledge; (b) application of procedural knowledge; (c) correct solution. Lighter columns: control classes; darker columns: experimental classes.

formation, cognitive motivation, etc.). We wondered whether the failure in systematically forming the learning activity of these students depends, above all, on the instructional strategy itself or on its performance under classroom conditions. Therefore, Böhme (1990) conducted an instructional experiment with small groups of low-performance students only. The teaching program was the same as in the corresponding classroom experiments, but students' cognitive and motivational characteristics were considered in a more differentiated way. This meant in particular:

- intensive, detailed goal formation by making conscious what is unknown, why it is worthwhile to uncover the unknown, and which methods are available to reach this goal;
- individualized motivating, detailed assessment and assistance, emphasis on each (even very small) success, and formation of trustful interpersonal relations;
- arrangement of a variety of learning actions to compensate for negative peculiarities of the students' learning activity;
- detailed orientation and guidance of the relevant action execution, decomposition of complex tasks into partial tasks, and systematic formation of appropriate partial actions and their step-by-step integration;
- broad, manifold use of external, materialized forms of actions and intensive work on discrimination and systematization of relevant concepts in order to guarantee the acquisition of necessary

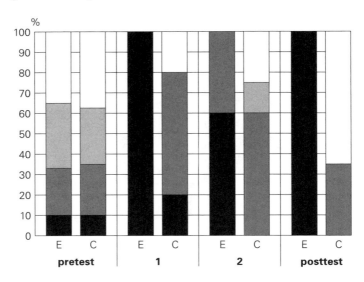

Recognition of causal relations by low performance pupils

E experimental groups
C control groups
1 after the 1st learning phase
2 after the 2nd learning phase
☐ **no answer**
▨ **inadequate**
▦ **partially correct**
■ **correct**

Figure 16.4.

knowledge and methods, as well as the formation of necessary cognitive operations and verbal formulations;

• intensive work for elaboration and use of the model of natural processes in order to make it a means for further exploring and explaining concrete phenomena and processes;

• consideration of the slower learning pace, guarantee of permanent feedback, repetition, and so on.

Under these conditions, low-performance students reached the same or higher level of concept and strategy formation, problem solving, and cognitive motivation as average-performance students (Group II) in the classroom experiments (Figure 16.4). In a problem situation, 83% of low-performance pupils were able to use the model as a cognitive means, 67% stated partial problems after having understood the contradiction in the problem, and only 33% needed the visual support of the model to find the relationship between the initial abstraction and a concrete phenomenon. These and similar results were obtained even though the time used for the instructional experiment with small groups was approximately the same as with whole classes.

Unresolved problems

The activity formation strategy has strong potential for both analysis and promotion of personality development and its psychic components. These two aspects – the differentiated analysis of developmental states and processes and the goal-oriented, theory-based transformation from a given state to a more advanced one – are often opposed to each other in the literature and in research practice. In our opinion, the main problem consists of how to bring them together.

Formation is both an end in itself and an important means of psychological analysis. On the one hand, by changing objects, conditions, and means of activity, creating new ones or managing them in new ways, and so on, we can reveal hidden potential in psychic development and demonstrate what can be reached in cognitive, motivational, emotional, and other relations in a certain age group or in a certain learner category. On the other hand, by constructing theoretical hypotheses about the psychic substance and the regulation structure of learning activity phenomena, by designing and managing concrete conditions, steps, and means in order to produce these phenomena and psychic features, structures, and so on, we can test and verify our hypotheses.

Thus the formation process serves as a means of analysis. This is much more than the intention of many training studies. As Rubinstein (1940) and Vygotsky (1934) pointed out long ago, we analyze psychic development or certain components of it in the process of its formation. If we are able to form psychic phenomena with defined qualities and under defined conditions according to our hypotheses, we can explain them to a certain degree. But, of course, this is easier said than done. One of our main tasks today and in the future is to develop further the methodology of formative experiments and to improve the analytic methods within the process of formation, as well as formation methods and organizational forms themselves. The necessary degree of complexity and ecological validity in the organization of the content and form of the formation process has to be combined with a high level of differentiation and solidity of empirical analyses.

Another central problem in our domain – and in other ones as well – has to do with the interrelations between cognition, emotion, and motivation in learning activity. Very often the psychological analysis was and is directed only toward one of these aspects or they are simply added to one another. But the main problem here is the interdependence, for example, between the concrete motivation and processes of goal setting, cognitive operations, and modes of thinking. Another problem lies in the differences and connections between cognitive and social motivation, their conditions of emerging, and their impact on the process of learning goal realization or, last but not least, the interrelations of emotional processes and states with cognition and motivation in the course of learning activity. Recently, these problems have begun to play a greater role in theorizing and empirical research (Boekaerts, 1988, 1992; Heckhausen, 1991; Mandl & Huber, 1983; Markova, 1983; Scheibe, 1989; Tikhomirov, 1988). If we seriously want to analyze and further promote learning activity (and personality development under this condition), the interfunctionality (Kovac, 1990; Lomov, 1984; Vygotsky, 1985) in structures of psychic regulation and in developmental processes is one of the crucial problems.

This leads to a closely related problem: individual differences in learning activity. Although this is an old problem in educational and learning psychology, there are more questions than answers. The list of unsolved or insufficiently solved problems could be extended. I will mention only one more problem: the interrelation between learning and instruction. A certain concept of learning activity and its formation leads to certain instructional strategies – for example, to the strategy of ascending from the abstract to the concrete. Which aspects of learning activity have to be considered, and how, when elaborating and managing an instructional strategy according to certain goals, object domains, and other determinants? How shall we define and analyze the main lines of the impact of an instructional strategy on learners' activity and development, and vice versa? How shall we differentiate, for instance, between strategy effects and teachers' personality effects? What kinds of psychic transformations are possible in the course of formative experiments, and which ones are desirable or necessary in terms of personality development? We interpret these problems and questions as strong challenges for more intensive research and closer international collaboration and communication in this field.

Notes

1. This concept, originated by Galperin (1967, 1969, 1982), refers to the representation of essential features and relations of an object or task domain and of the relevant conditions, phases, checkpoints, necessary means, and possible consequences of the actions to be executed in order to reach a certain goal.
2. This phase gave the name to the whole strategy because of its importance and role. But this does not mean that abstractions arise out of a vacuum.

References

Boekaerts, M. (Ed.). (1988). Emotion, motivation and learning. *International Journal of Educational Research, 12*(3) (whole issue).

Boekaerts, M. (1992). The adaptable learning process: Initiating and maintaining behavioral change. *Applied Psychology: An International Review, 41*, 377–397.

Böhme, B. (1990). *Besonderheiten leistungsschwacher Schüler 4. Klassen bei der Ausbildung von Lernhandlungen zum selbständigen Erkennen von Ursache-Wirkung-Zusammenhängen.* Dissertation A. Berlin: Akademie der Pädagogischen Wissenschaften der DDR.

Davydov, V. V. (1988a). Problems of developmental teaching: The experience of theoretical and empirical psychological research. *Soviet Education,* Part I: *30*(8), 15–97; Part II: *30*(9), 3–38; Part III: *30*(10), 3–77.

Davydov, V. V. (1988b). Learning activity: The main problems needing further research. *Multidisciplinary Newsletter for Activity Theory, 1*, 29–36.

Davydov, V. V. (1990). *Types of generalization in instruction: Logical and psychological problems in the structuring of school curricula.* Reston: National Council of Teachers of Mathematics.

Davydov, V. V. (1991). The content and unsolved problems of activity theory. *Multidisciplinary Newsletter for Activity Theory, 7/8*, 30–35.

De Corte, E. (1990). Acquiring and teaching cognitive skills: State of the art of theory and research. In P. J. D. Drenth, J. A. Sergeant, & R. J. Takens (Eds.), *European perspectives in psychology* (Vol. 1). London: Wiley.

Detterman, D. K., & Sternberg, R. J. (Eds.). (1993). *Transfer on trial: Intelligence, cognition, and instruction.* Norwood: Ablex.

El'konin, D. B. (1989). O strukture ucebnoj dejatel'nosti. In *Izbrannye psichologiceskie trudy.* Moscow: Pedagogika.

Galperin, P. J. (1967). On the notion of interiorisation. *Soviet Psychology, 5*, 28–33.

Galperin, P. J. (1969). Stages in the development of mental acts. In M. Cole & I. Maltzman (Eds.), *Handbook of contemporary Soviet psychology.* New York: Case Books.

Galperin, P. J. (1982). Intellectual capabilities among older preschool children: On the problem of training and mental development. In W. W. Hartup (Ed.), *Review of child development research* (Vol. 6). Chicago: University of Chicago Press.

Hedegaard, M. (1990). The zone of proximal development as basis for instruction. In L. C. Moll (Ed.), *Vygotsky and education: Instructional implications and applications of sociohistorical psychology.* Cambridge: Cambridge University Press.

Hedegaard, M., & Chaiklin, S. (1993). Foundations for investigating the role of culture in Danish school teaching. In N. Engelsted, M. Hedegaard, B. Karpatschof, & A. Mortensen (Eds.), *The societal subject*. Aarhus: Aarhus University Press.

Heckhausen, H. (1991). *Motivation and action*. Berlin: Springer.

Jantos, W. (1989). Kooperation und Kommunikation in der Lerntätigkeit. In J. Lompscher (Ed.), *Psychologische Analysen der Lerntätigkeit*. Berlin: Volk und Wissen.

Klauer, K. J. (1989). Teaching for analogical transfer as a means of improving problem solving, thinking and learning. *Instructional Science, 18*, 179–192.

Köster, E. (1985). Problemlösen als Lernhandlung betrachtet. *Psychologie für die Praxis, 3*, 239–247.

Kovac, D. (1990). *Theoretische Fragen der allgemeinen Psychologie*. Berlin: Volk und Wissen.

Lomov, B. (1984). *Methodologische und theoretische Probleme der Psychologie*. Berlin: Volk und Wissen.

Lompscher, J. (1982). Conditions and potentialities of the formation of learning activity. In R. Glaser & J. Lompscher (Eds.), *Cognitive and motivational aspects of instruction*. Berlin: Deutscher Verlag der Wissenschaften.

Lompscher, J. (1984). Problems and results of experimental research on the formation of theoretical thinking through instruction. In M. Hedegaard, P. Hakkarainen, & Y. Engeström (Eds.), *Learning and teaching on a scientific basis: Methodological and epistemological aspects of the activity theory of learning and teaching*. Aarhus: Aarhus Universitet, Psykologisk Institut.

Lompscher, J. (1985). Formation of learning activity – a fundamental condition of cognitive development. In E. Bol, J. P. P. Haenen, & M. Wolters (Eds.), *Education for cognitive development*. Den Haag: SVO/SOO.

Lompscher, J. (Ed.). (1988). *Persönlichkeitsentwicklung in der Lerntätigkeit*. Berlin: Volk und Wissen.

Lompscher, J. (1989a). Formation of learning activity in pupils. In H. Mandl, E. de Corte, N. Bennet, & H. F. Friedrich (Eds.), *Learning and instruction – European research in an international context* (Vol. 2.2). Oxford: Pergamon Press.

Lompscher, J. (Ed.). (1989b). *Psychologische Analysen der Lerntätigkeit*. Berlin: Volk und Wissen.

Lompscher, J. (1992). Concept and strategy acquisition in pupils – intergroup differences in the formation of learning activity. *Multidisciplinary Newsletter for Activity Theory, 11/12*, 8–12.

Mandl, H., & Huber, G. L. (Eds.). (1983). *Emotion und Kognition*. Munich: Urban und Schwarzenberg.

Markova, A. K. (1983). *Formirovanie motivacii ucenija v skolnom vozraste*. Moscow: Prosvescenie.

Mevarech, Z. R., & Light, P. H. (Eds.). (1992). Cooperative learning with computers. *Learning and Instruction, 2*(3) (whole issue).

Nguyen Danh Moc (1989). *Ausbildung kooperativer Lerntätigkeit durch das gemeinsame Lösen von Sach- und Anwendungsaufgaben im 3. Schuljahr*. Dissertation A. Berlin: Akademie der Pädagogischen Wissenschaften der DDR.

Perret-Clermont, A. N., & Schubauer-Leoni, M. L. (Eds.). (1989). Social factors in learning and instruction. *International Journal of Educational Research, 13*(6) (whole issue).

Reinhold, J. (1988). *Ausbildung der Lerntätigkeit im Mathematikunterricht des 4. Schuljahres zur Befähigung zum Lösen mathematischer Sach- und Anwendungsaufgaben.* Dissertation A. Berlin: Akademie der Pädagogischen Wissenschaften der DDR.

Rubinstein, S. L. (1940). *Osnovy obscej psichologii.* Moscow.

Rubtsov, V. V. (1987). *Organizacija i razvitie sovmestnych dejstvij u detej v processe obucenija.* Moscow: Pedagogika.

Scheibe, I.-P. (1989). Entwicklung kognitiver Lernmotive. In J. Lompscher (Ed.), *Psychologische Analysen der Lerntätigkeit.* Berlin: Volk und Wissen.

Tikhomirov, O. K. (1988). *The psychology of thinking.* Moscow: Progress.

Van Oers, B. (1990). The development of mathematical thinking in school: A comparison of the action-psychological and information-processing approaches. *International Journal of Educational Research, 14,* 51–66.

Vygotsky, L. S. (1934). *Myshlenie i rech. Psikhologicheskie issledovania.* Moscow-Leningrad: Gosudarstvennoe Social'no-Ekonomicheskoe Izdatel'stvo.

Vygotsky, L. S. (1978). *Mind in society: The development of higher psychological processes.* Cambridge, MA: Harvard University Press.

Vygotsky, L. S., (1985). *Ausgewählte Schriften: Band 1. Arbeiten zu theoretischen und methodologischen Problemen der Psychologie.* Berlin: Volk und Wissen.

Webb, N. M. (Ed.). (1989). Peer interaction, problem solving and cognition: Multidisciplinary perspectives. *International Journal of Educational Research, 13*(1) (whole issue).

17   Activity theory and history teaching

Mariane Hedegaard

Introduction

Why is teaching history part of elementary education, and how does it become useful for children outside the school context? How can concrete events and abstract principles be related in history teaching, and how can history be a means of relating to the past and orientating toward the future? How can the child become explorative and active in history teaching? These questions are central for history teaching and have been approached in different ways within various traditions of instructional theory.

In this chapter, I argue for an activity-theoretical approach to history teaching. The activity approach is characterized with the help of four principles. In the last part of the chapter, I use these dimensions to describe and analyze a history teaching experiment we conducted in Grades 4 and 5 in a Danish comprehensive school. In this experiment, historical knowledge was viewed as a tool for understanding the societies of today.

The objective of history teaching has changed over time (Engelund, 1988; Sødring Jensen, 1978; Manifest, 1983). In Denmark schools became public in 1814 and in Sweden in 1842 (Ramirez & Boli, 1987). From the beginning, history teaching in the Scandinavian countries had the task of developing students' national identity and moral character. This last task coincided with the ideals of the obligatory teaching of religion, and the two were the main objectives in public school teaching besides teaching reading (Sødring Jensen, 1978). The task of history teaching was transformed in the late 1950s. In Denmark, a new school law was confirmed in 1958. The change in the objectives of schooling influenced history teaching. It became a descriptive subject with the task of imparting objective knowledge. In the 1980s there was a return to a discussion of the importance of history teaching for the formation of the child's national consciousness (Skovgaard-Nielsen, 1985; Karlegärd, 1983, 1985, 1986; Castrén, 1985, Engelund, 1988; Sødring Jensen, 1988). Recent instructional approaches seem to be leaving the ideal of "the rational man" and turning to the ideal of "critically morally conscious human being."

The relationship between the science of history and the school subject of history has been another persistent topic in the instructional debate. The British educators Dickenson, Gard, and Lee (1978) asked whether the task of school teaching is to mediate the findings of scientific history based on chronology or to focus on themes or topics in which children should learn to ask questions like real historians.

These two issues, the question of the character-forming mission of history teaching and the question of the relationship between historical research and history teaching, are challenges to any new approach to history instruction. The relevance of activity theory in history teaching depends on its ability to contribute something significant to these two persistent issues.

An activity-theoretical approach to history teaching

The goal of history instruction, as I see it, is to help children acquire a synthesizing approach to the central concepts of history that gives them a tool for understanding and analyzing living conditions in past and present societies. This formulation is based on Vygotsky's (1978) characterization of the relation of humans to their environment, as mediated by tools (physical and psychological), and on Wartofsky's (1990) characterization of perception and cognition as formed by the cultural and historical traditions of representation.

Knowledge of history can therefore be seen as a psychological tool that is effective if it can be used to analyze the phenomena persons confront in their lives from a societal and historical perspective. In my view, the objective of history teaching is to give students an understanding of the connection between differences in living conditions, resources, and societal characteristics in different historical periods so that they can gain insight into how the living conditions and societies of today have developed throughout several periods. This insight enables a child to understand and relate to the living conditions of different people, both in the child's own society and in different societies today. The students develop the possibility to understand that, for example, the Danish society of today is historically developed, that it is not stable and unchangeable but will go on changing.

Furthermore, I want to give children a conceptual basis synthesized in models so that they have a tool for analyzing societies, especially their own, and at the same time a conceptual basis that can be expanded and form a basis for new knowledge construction and acquisition. The use of models in history teaching for developing a tool character of knowledge is inspired by Davydov's theoretical approach (1982, 1990) and by Markova's (1979), Aidarova's (1982), and Lompscher's (1984; Lompscher, 1988) research on language and biology instruction.

One of the problems in history teaching is to select what is relevant as themes for teaching. It is important that the students gain insight into the relation between national history and world history as part of an integrated world view. It is also important for them to understand how we, in the concrete national setting, create our own history as part of a larger world history, that is, that the national history is dependent on and connected to world history. It is important that the students acquire an understanding of historical narratives as centered on themes and based on historical methods. Historical knowledge is interpretative; to get the connection between facts and theory, interpretations have to be focused on themes. Thus children should come to understand that the foundation of historical knowledge is historical materials (objects, documents, pictures, etc.) but that, by themselves, these materials do not make up historical narratives. Historical knowledge will not appear until the objects and facts become interpreted (Nevis, 1962).

Our application of activity theory to history teaching was based on the following four principles:

1. Development of conceptual models as tools for analysis: formulating and modeling conceptual relations of historical knowledge.
2. Conceptualization of a time line and periodization of historical events.
3. Practicing skills in historical methods: interpretation of historical materials, use of analogy, critical evaluation of source materials.
4. Use of conceptual relations of history in analyzing societies of today.

The meaning and relevance of these four principles will be illustrated in the following thorough description of how they were applied in the teaching experiment we conducted.

A teaching experiment

The aim of our experimental instruction was to remediate the students' historical thinking by means of theoretical knowledge. We wanted to achieve a change in which empirical knowledge would become subordinated to theoretical thinking. This aim was based on Davydov's (1990) distinction between these two kinds of thinking and societal knowledge. Theoretical thought and knowledge deal with dialectically interconnected systems of categories that evolve through a historical process of knowledge formation.

Theoretical knowledge of a subject matter area is founded on a few basic categories that define each other and, at the same time, depict the contradictions in the subject area. These basic relations may be seen as the "germ cell" of the subject area and can be represented in the form of graphic models. Empirical knowledge deals with external differences and similarities in categories or phenomena abstracted from their development and context.

We generated an instructional plan for 2 school years on the basis of a germ-cell model. This plan was then modified through detailed planning and evaluation of each lesson in cooperation between the researcher and teacher. The experiment was conducted in one class with 19 students, using 3 school hours each week through fourth and fifth grades in a Danish comprehensive school. The research intervention was finished at the end of fifth grade. However, the same teacher continued to teach this class through sixth and seventh grades. The instructional principles of our experiment were used by the teacher throughout those years, and I observed the class several times after the research project had officially been brought to an end.

The instructional strategy of the teaching experiment may be characterized as a double move from the abstract to the concrete and from the concrete to the abstract. The teacher conducted the instruction on the basis of the general conceptual relations depicted in the germ-cell model (see Figure 17.1).

The conceptual system we used was developed as part of a broader attempt to integrate history with biology and geography. The broader experimental curriculum followed the problem sequence: the evolution of animals → the origin of humans → the historical change of society. The first part of the experiment dealt with the evolution of animals and was described earlier (Hedegaard, 1988, 1989, 1990).

The students learned through explorative and investigative tasks in practical or visual contexts such as museum visits, films, and pictures. In the class dialogue, core examples were then formulated to establish the basic germ-cell model. The teacher formulated tasks and action sequences that were based on the abstract principles of the problem area, as well as on the knowledge we had of the children's conceptual frames and experiences.

At the beginning, the tasks were to provide experiential grounding for concepts. Core examples were used to establish the basic germ-cell relation of tool use and tool production as a mediating link between nature and societal living. The teacher provoked the students to formulate the relation through contrasting examples, and by asking the children to reflect on and analyze the conflicts and contrasts that could be experienced through different materials. The first core example was based on a film about the !Kung people's way of living in the desert. Their living style was found to be analogical to that of Stone Age people. The contrasting example was Iron Age people's production and use of tools to create living conditions in a cold environment. The experiencing of Iron Age people's living conditions, tool use, and production was created through participation in a workshop at an outdoor museum. The teacher provoked the children to formulate the relations through this contrast.

The contents of the experimental teaching over the 2-year period were characterized by different learning actions: problem formulation, practicing research methods, model formulation, model use, creation of tasks, model extension, and evaluation. An overview of the different phases and their contents is presented in Table 17.1.

Development of conceptual models

In instruction based on activity theory, the historical development of the given field of knowledge is the basis for selecting curricular contents. The development of science is seen as interwoven with the evolution of the society. Thus, there is a close correspondence between the societal and the scientific relevance of concepts in a subject area (Il'enkov, 1982; Davydov, 1990; Wartofsky, 1979; Hedegaard, Hansen, Engeström, & Juul-Jensen, 1985; Hedegaard, 1988).

One of our first tasks in the history teaching experiment was to create a connection between children's conceptions of nature and of societal conditions. Especially in the prehistoric periods this connection was obvious,

Table 17.1. *Overview of experimental teaching in history and anthropological geography*

4th grade	
Goals and concepts of teaching	Learning actions
Problem formulation	
Exploration of different cultural societies of today and differences in historical periods in Denmark	Picture analyses of different historical periods and different societies of today
(Focus on types of work, living conditions, and division of labor)	
The general research method	
Paralleling to researchers' working methods	Construction of a goal result board based on the children's ideas of how researchers work in general
	Role play of researcher at work
Model use	
The concepts of nature, form of living, collective tool use and division of work	Analyses of the !Kung people's way of living from a film presentation; analyses of the Stone Age people's way of living from reading a text
The historical dimension	A child's model is discussed and used.
Model extension	
1. Collecting experiences	
Model formulation for human's way of living with focus on tool production	Analogy between the !Kung people's way of living and the Stone Age people's way of living
The nature–human relation differs from the nature–animal relation in terms of tool production and tool-based interaction.	Two-day excursion to an open-air museum, with activities in tool use in the Iron Age and visiting farms at an open-air museum
Use of the model to analyze differences in tool use in different time periods	
2. Formulations of the relations in the model	
Differentiation and change of the animal–population relation to the relation between ways of living and society	Model making of historical periods
	Dramatic play making and performance showing different ways of living, with focus on differences in tools in the Stone Age, the Iron Age, and the Viking Age
	Performing written tasks about the Iron Age, with focus on ways of living, tools, division of work, beliefs, and society in the Iron Age
Problem formulation again	
What did we investigate last year? What do we investigate now? What do we plan to investigate?	Cooperation in model making on posters of the four themes. Themes the children have worked with in third grade and themes they are going to work with in fourth grade:

Table 17.1 *(cont.)*

4th grade

Goals and concepts of teaching	Learning actions
	the evolution of animals; living conditions for humans; development of human societies
Model use – variation – extension Model use on Stone Age and Iron Age: Introduction of concepts, beliefs/rules, and focus on tool use	Cooperation in model making on posters: the Stone Age, the Iron Age, the Viking Age, the Middle Age. The class library is used as an information source.
Model use on the Viking Age and Middle Age, with focus on concepts, beliefs/rules, and tool use	
Creation and evaluation of tasks and of own skills Model use and extension: Introduction to division of work as a concept in the model	Formulation of tasks in small groups for the four periods: One group formulates for the Stone Age; the other groups should perform these tasks, and so on.
Evaluation of own capacities	Class dialogue about creation of good and bad tasks for the different periods
Model evaluation	Visiting an exhibition of the Viking Age: The tasks are to create good questions about the Vikings' ways of living, division of work, beliefs, and society, and to create a play with a focus on these topics.

5th grade

Goals and concepts of teaching	Learning actions
Problem formulation – model extension Exploration of variation of societies of today and in historical periods in Denmark	Resumé of children's activities before the summer holiday
	The children draw models for the problem formulations.
Focus on division of work	The models are expanded by division of work and beliefs/rules, and the category of society is formulated.
	Dramatic play about division of work in four historical periods
The general research method Used together with the formulation of models	Creation of posters with models about: what we know; what we do not know; what we are investigating

Table 17.1 *(cont.)*

5th grade	
Goals and concepts of teaching	Learning actions
Model use	
The concept in the model is used on the problem: How can it be that people live differently in different historical periods?	Comparison and evaluation of museum tasks with own produced tasks about the Viking Age
Investigation of differences in living conditions	Analyses of the effects of change in societal living from a novel on division of work and rules in the Viking Age
Historical method	
Interpretation of archaeological discoveries	Analysis of archaeological discoveries of a Middle Age ship from a movie presentation
Model extension	
The concept of society is defined based on its institutions. In the Middle Ages these are the church, the village, the town, and the castle.	The children have to write an essay about the structure of society in the Middle Ages from text about the four institutions in the Middle Ages.
Ways of living are defined in relation to people's needs.	Communication to other children in New York about their models by making a book about the institutions in the Middle Ages
Division of work is defined in relation to results of work.	Essay about what determines society's development from the Middle Ages to the New Age (exploration of the New World)
Focus on explanations of the development from the Middle Ages to the New Age (exploration of the New World) by using the concepts of the model	
Use of the model for communication	
Differences in the Danish society	Letters to the children in New York with models showing the changes from the Middle Ages to the society of today
Model evaluation – model extension	
The New Age (exploration of the New World)	Movies about exploration of the New World and analysis of the changes in the historical periods
Extension of the concepts: 1. Beliefs $\Rightarrow$ power 2. Tools $\Rightarrow$ academic knowledge 3. Division of work within classes	
Planning from the conceptual relations of the model	
Focus on the concepts of power and class	Planning a dramatic play about the New Age (exploration of the New World)
	Formulations and use of own tasks at a visit to the museum of craft and industry

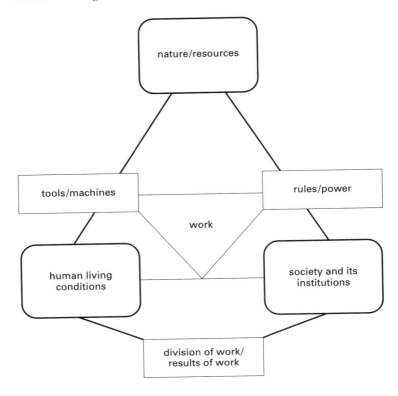

Figure 17.1. Model for analyses of historical change in society.

as indicated by the core example of the contrast between the !Kung people and the Iron Age people.

In this chapter, the focus is on the treatment of historical change in society, with special emphasis on Danish society. Danish history is an obligatory subject in the Danish elementary school.

We chose to work with models that integrate the development of nature and society (see Hedegaard, 1988). It is important to stress that the conceptual relations we used to describe and explain the evolution of animals were not replaced but incorporated into the following models so that concepts of nature became related to concepts of society.

The basic relations that make up the model for the evolution of animals are species, population, and nature, which define each other (Mayr, 1976, 1980; Gould, 1977). These concepts became extended and specified for the model of the origin of humans, so that the concept of species was transformed into the concept of human individuals, the concept of population was transformed into the concept of group, and the concept of nature was transformed into the concept of surroundings. Tool creation, division of work, and beliefs became the mediating concepts between the central concepts of individual, surroundings, and group (see Leont'ev, 1978; Leakey & Lewin, 1978; Engelsted, 1984). These concepts were further developed and transformed into subjects' needs and living conditions, society and its institutions, and human–made reality with its resources. Again, the mediating concepts of tools (both physical and psychological), work functions/division of labor, and beliefs/rules were incorporated into the model. This last model is depicted in Figure 17.1.

It is important to point out that the models were changed and developed as part of the teaching experiment. Both theory and pedagogical practice influenced the models. Professionals in the fields of biology, geography, and history were consulted.

The functions of the models were to organize and differentiate the problem area and to guide the teacher in his or her interaction with the children in the teaching situation. Through tasks and actions in the experimental instruction the children came to develop their own models, which gradually became differentiated and more complex. Examples of the evolution of children's own models are presented in Figures 17.2a and 17.2b.

The historical changes of societies were divided into subproblems guided by the concepts in the models. The subproblems the children came to work with during the 2 years of experimental history teaching were derived from the following question: How can it be that humans have lived differently at different places in the world and in different historical periods in Denmark?

The teacher started by introducing problem formulation and some of the conceptual relations of the model through specific tasks. The children were given the task of sorting and discussing two sets of pictures. They were divided into groups of four, and the members of each group were supposed to help and discuss the pictures with each other. One series of pictures showed episodes from different societies of today (industrial as well as nonindustrial). The other series of pictures showed episodes from Danish society in different historical periods. The episodes chosen focused on themes that were connected to the

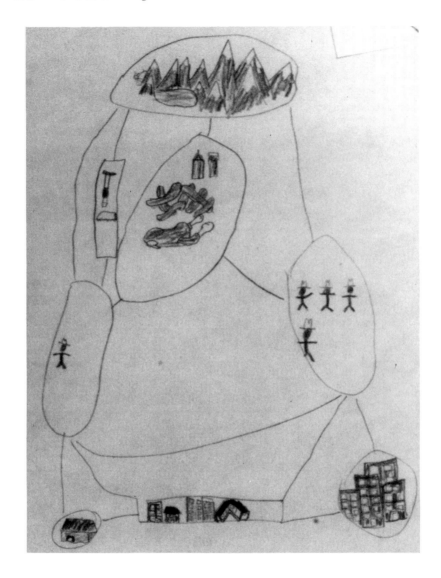

Figure 17.2a. A fourth-grade child's model of society's basic relations.

concepts of the model of society, such as development of tools and division of labor. For example, some pictures showed tool use in farming and carpentering in different areas of the world and in different historical periods.

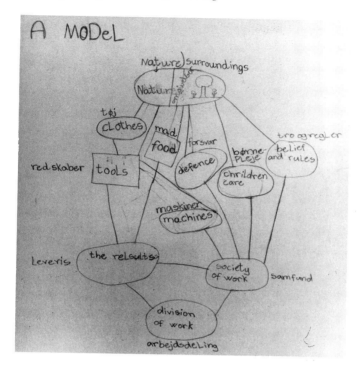

Figure 17.2b. A fifth-grade child's model of society communicated to children in a class in New York.

Historical timeline and historical periodization

Along with the germ-cell model of society, we worked with and structured the children's activity around the construction and use of a historical time line and periodization of history. During the first year, we worked with the prehistoric periods: the Stone Age, the Bronze Age, the Iron Age, and the Viking Age. During the second year, we extended the teaching to include the historical periods: the Middle Ages, the New Age or the Age of Exploring the New World, and Early Industrialism. In all periods, we worked with the conceptual relations of the germ-cell model, differentiating and integrating new concepts into the model as we went along.

We focused on different relations of the model when we worked with different periods. Differences between the periods were characterized by the different forms of tool use, as well as by the different forms of division of labor and of rules and beliefs. In the Stone, Bronze, and Iron ages, we focused on differences in tool use and on what this meant for changing people's living conditions from one period to the next. But in the Iron Age we also found that the development of new types of tools changed people's relations to nature. The population of Denmark started to become settled, and a more clearly differentiated division of labor evolved. In the Viking Age, differentiation in the division of labor meant the beginning of classes, slaves, and free-born men and women. The free-born (the Vikings) went out on expeditions, which led us to focus on rules for living together among the two classes. We compared the Viking Age with the Middle Ages and saw that religion acquired a special status in relation to classes. The clergy became a class of its own in the Middle Ages, with the Church as a strong, all-encompassing institution.

We differentiated the society of the Middle Ages into four key institutions: (1) the Church (priests and monks), (2) the town (mostly craftsmen), (3) the castle (the nobility), and (4) the village (the peasants). We explored how these groups lived together. Rules for distribution of resources and beliefs (relation to nature and its resources) came into focus. In the New Age, the focus extended to rules for classes and countries. The distribution and exploitation of resources and the concept of ownership became central in the analyses of this period. The exploration of the New World led us back to tool use and tool invention by focusing on the development of skills such as navigation and knowledge about the world and the universe, as well as extension of the knowledge of writing and reading. The study of the exploration of the New World led to transcendence of the Danish borders and to looking at history as a world history.

Skills in historical methods

One aspect of our goal was to develop children's skills in the use of scientific methods, with a focus on the specific methods developed for the investigation of prehistoric periods. We used a general research procedure with the following steps:

1. Formulation of the research topic.
2. What do we know and what do we not know about this topic?
3. How can we relate the known to the unknown in a model?
4. What means do we have for exploring this model?
5. How are the results of exploration related to the research problem?

This procedure was used both to guide the children's research actions and to guide the teacher's structuring of the class periods. The children made a role play about historical research, and we showed them research methods in use by taking them to a prehistoric museum to see and participate in historians' work on reconstruction of work in different workshops and at a farmhouse. The children were shown films about rescuing historical materials and determining their age. Afterward they were given tasks and had discussions on how historical evidence is used in dating and interpreting archaeological findings.

Use of conceptual relations of history to analyze today's society

The forward-oriented aspect of the teaching was realized after the official conclusion of the teaching experiment, in sixth and seventh grades. The students applied their knowledge of biology and history to the society of today. They used their models of evolution and historical change of societies on a range of different themes that they negotiated among themselves. These themes included the relation between the fishing industry, ecological problems, and geographical characteristics of the places where fishermen live. In this theme, the students compared the Faroe Islands and Chile – their nature, living conditions, and cultural and political characteristics. Another theme the students selected to research was the rain forest. Here they developed an ecological model for analyzing the evolution of plants, which they subsequently applied to the tundra in Lapland.

In the sixth and seventh grades, the children demonstrated that *they had acquired biological, geographical, and historical concepts as tool-using capacities,* which they could use to understand today's societal problems (Hedegaard & Sigersted, 1992a, 1992b).

Conclusion

I have argued for the relevance of an activity-theoretical approach to history teaching. The main characteristic of our approach is the *modeling of basic historical-conceptual relations.* The continuous elaboration and use of the conceptual models gradually gives the subject matter of history a *tool character.*

This characteristic has been used in other experimental teaching programs based on activity theory (e.g., Davydov, 1982; Aidarova, 1982;

Lompscher, 1984). In history teaching, two earlier experiments have been reported (Engeström, 1990, pp. 25–47; Hedegaard et al., 1985). A lot is still missing, both in the theoretical argument and in the experimental research. However, the emergence of historical concepts as tools for students is a strong argument for the revitalization of history as a school subject.

The main contribution of activity theory to history teaching consists in turning history into a toolkit for children, both to relate to their past and to orientate toward their future. This point has obvious potential implications for the development of children's cultural and historical identity, particularly among ethnic minorities (for a beginning in this direction, see Chaiklin, Hedegaard, & Pedraza, 1991).

References

Aidarova, L. (1982). *Child development and education.* Moscow: Progress.

Castrén, M. (1985). Den nationale identitet i historieundervisningen i en småstat. In *Historieundervisning i Norden 2.* Copenhagen: Danmarks Laererhøjskole.

Chaiklin, S., Hedegaard, M., & Pedraza, P. (1991). *Building the identity of minority children through social studies.* Aarhus: Aarhus University, Institute of Psychology.

Davydov, V. V. (1982). Ausbildung der Lerntätigkeit. In V. V. Davydov, J. Lompscher, & A. K. Markova (Eds.), *Ausbildung der Lerntätigkeit bei Schülern.* Berlin: Volk und Wissen.

Davydov, V. V. (1990). *Types of generalization in instruction: Logical and psychological problems in the structuring of school curricula.* Reston: National Council of Teachers of Mathematics.

Dickenson, A. K., Gard, A., & Lee, P. J. (1978). Evidence in history in the classroom. In A. K. Dickenson & P. J. Lee (Eds.), *History teaching and historical understanding.* London: Heinemann.

Engelsted, N. (1984). *Springet fra dyr til menneske.* Copenhagen: Dansk Psykologisk Forlag.

Engelund, T. (1988). Historieemnets selektive tradition set ur ett legitimitetsperspektiv. In *Historiedidaktik i Norden 3.* Malmö: Lärarhögskolan i Malmö.

Engeström, Y. (1990). *Learning, working and imagining: Twelve studies in activity theory.* Helsinki: Orienta-Konsultit.

Gould, S. (1977). *Ever since Darwin.* London: Penguin.

Hedegaard, M. (1988). *Skolebørns personlighedsudvikling, set gennem orienteringsfagene.* Aarhus: Aarhus Universitetsforlag.

Hedegaard, M. (1989). Undervisningens betydning for børns opfattelser af evolution. *Psykologisk Skriftserie Aarhus, 14*(3) (whole issue).

Hedegaard, M. (1990). The zone of proximal development as basis for instruction. In L. Moll (Ed.), *Vygotsky and education.* Cambridge: Cambridge University Press.

Hedegaard, M., Hansen, E., Engeström, Y., & Juul-Jensen, U. (1985). Fagundervisning – Elevundervisning og udvikling af teoretisk taenkning. *Psykologisk Skriftserie Aarhus, 10*(1) (whole issue).

Hedegaard, M., & Sigersted, G. (1992a). Experimental classroom teaching in history and anthropological geography. *Multidisciplinary Newsletter for Activity Theory, 11/12,* 13–23.

Hedegaard, M., & Sigersted, G. (1992b). *Undervisning i samfundshistorie.* Aarhus: Aarhus Universitetsforlag.

Il'enkov, E. V. (1982). *The dialectics of the abstract and the concrete in Marx's Capital.* Moscow: Progress.

Karlegärd, C. (1983). *Varför historia? Några didkatiska spörsmål.* Rapport 4. Malmö: Lärarhögskolan i Malmö.

Karlegärd, C. (1985). Vad är det at vara svensk? In *Historiedidaktik i Norden 2.* Copenhagen: Danmarks Laererhøjskole.

Karlegärd, C. (1986). Varför historia? Historiedidaktikens kärnfråga. In F. Merton (Ed.), *Fackdidaktik* (Vol. 1). Stockholm: Liber.

Leakey, R., & Lewin, R. (1978). *People of the lake: Mankind and its beginnings.* Garden City: Anchor Press.

Leont'ev, A. N. (1978). *Activity, consciousness and personality.* Englewood Cliffs: Prentice-Hall.

Lompscher, J. (1984). Problems and results of experimental research on the formation of theoretical thinking through instruction. In M. Hedegaard, P. Hakkarainen, & Y. Engeström (Eds.), *Learning and teaching on a scientific basis: Methodological and epistemological aspects of the activity theory of learning and teaching.* Aarhus: Aarhus Universitet, Psykologisk Institut.

Lompscher, J. (Ed.). (1988). *Persönlichkeitsentwicklung in der Lerntätigkeit.* Berlin: Volk und Wissen.

Manifest '83. (1983). *Historie i folkeskolen.* Copenhagen: Centrum.

Markova, A. K. (1979). *The teaching and mastery of language.* White Plains: M. E. Sharpe.

Mayr, E. (1976). *Evolution and the diversity of life.* Cambridge, MA: Harvard University Press.

Mayr, E. (1980). Some thoughts on the history of the evolutionary synthesis. In E. Mayr & W. B. Province (Eds.), *The evolutionary synthesis.* Cambridge, MA: Harvard University Press.

Nevis, A. (1962). *The gateway to history.* Garden City: Anchor Books.

Ramirez, F. O., & Boli, J. (1987). The political construction of mass schooling: European and worldwide institutionalization. *Sociology of Education, 60,* 2–17.

Skovgaard-Nielsen, H. (1985). Historie, historieundervisning og moral. In *Historiedidaktik i Norden 2.* Copenhagen: Danmarks Laererhøjskole.

Sødring Jensen, S. (1978). *Historieundervisningsteori.* Copenhagen: Christian Ejlers's forlag.

Sødring Jensen, S. (1988). Den historiske roman, den historiske fortaelling og den historiske bevidsthed. In *Historiedidaktik i Norden 3.* Malmö: Lärarhögskolan i Malmö.

Vygotsky, L. S. (1978). *Mind in society.* Cambridge, MA: Harvard University Press.

Wartofsky, M. (1979). *Models: Representation and the scientific understanding.* Dordrecht: Reidel.

Wartofsky, M. (1990). *Readings in historical epistemology.* Seminar in historical epistemology. New York: Department of Philosophy, Graduate Center, City University of New York.

18 Didactic models and the problem of intertextuality and polyphony

Jacques Carpay and Bert Van Oers

Introduction

Some time ago, the psychologist Kurt Koffka made a short reference to a peculiar snatch of conversation he once overheard (Koffka, 1921, 1935). Four men were sitting at a table, and one of them – a German – was trying to prove that his native language was the best. He picked up a knife and argued as follows: "Look, the French call this 'couteau,' the English 'knife' and we Germans call it 'Messer.' Na, und ein 'Messer' *ist* es eben auch." (And that's just what it is – a "Messer.")[1]

This anecdote has an impact only if the addressee is able to make a clear distinction between two modes of thought: functional reasoning, on the one hand, and metalinguistic reflection, on the other. In the argument put forward in the "Messer debate," both modes of reasoning clearly conflict with one another. In the noun phrase (i.e., the topic) of the argument, the *functional classification* of the referent "knife" as a thing "in and for itself" is reflected, whereas in the verb phrase (i.e., the comment) the *everyday reference* "Messer" is discussed and evaluated. The latter appears primarily to be a thing "for us Germans."

This reference to the sociocultural valence of the artifact called Messer indicates that it is not the functional use as such, but the *actual usage* and the *personalization of knowledge* that are discussed here. The everyday meaning (i.e., the practical value) of the object "knife" is compared by juxtaposing three different word forms. At the same time, the sociocultural classification in question is made into *a problem* because the speaker makes a clear-cut demarcation between "us" and "them." Apparently, in the frame of reference actualized here, everyday meaning and sense are intrinsically interwoven. (*Sense* in Leont'ev's definition refers to *meaning for oneself* and is put on a par with *meaning for others*.) As a matter of fact, the actualization of the sociocultural classification involved emerges not by means of an intentional act of reflection, but in a more or less spontaneous manner (for further discussion, see also Tolman, 1992).

What is the point of this anecdotal introduction? What matters in our argument is that humans in their sociocultural environment (i.e., in their private "microclimates") apparently deal not only with material objects that they can manipulate physically but also with word forms and concepts that can be put into action in any given *language game* (Wittgenstein, 1953), whereby meaning is seen to vary according to context. In such language games, *reference* is not treated as a universal category, but rather as a common denominator in certain sociocultural activity settings (see Walkerdine, 1988; Wertsch, 1991). We assume that linguistic and cultural *pluriformity* is a distinctive feature of communicative activity (see also Foucault, 1972; Wittgenstein, 1953; Peirce, 1958).

So the thorny question arises as to which *explanatory framework* and which *conceptual inventory* should be chosen as a basis on which to carry out a culturological analysis of certain discursive practices. Moreover, if a given set of convictions and conceptual inventories indeed reflects a long articulated mode of reflection on the (speech) culture involved, then we cannot start philosophizing from the linguistic tabula rasa that the Cartesian method may seem to suggest. Actually, this key issue turns out to be even more complicated if we concentrate on the "cultural scripts" involved in classroom-bound communicative activity, which takes shape within the context of formal education. We assume that Vygotsky's seminal work and that of his followers fits in here as a heuristic framework for research on the varieties of speech and thinking in the context of everyday shared conventions of classroom discourse. In our own research over the last decades (Carpay, 1975, 1987; Van Oers, 1987, 1990), we have found ample evidence of the explanatory power of a Vygotskian approach in analyzing the contribution made by formal education to the quality of cognitive and moral development of the (model) *personality.*

Within this epistemological framework, however, two ethically sensitive topics have emerged, which present a serious obstacle to an extension of the Vygotskian heritage (at least in Western Europe).

The first issue is *the evaluative standard* being used in straightforward comparisons of the *intended outcomes* of the different teaching strategies proposed. All strategies use certain value-loaded standards and discourse modes, and require a careful and critical assessment of both disadvantages and advantages regarding the educational and political claims involved. This is especially the case, as previously mentioned, when the educational research in question is done according to a Vygotskian mode of thought in our Western comprehensive schools. We shall return to this touchy point later when we discuss the attitude in the West toward a "thinking curriculum," as propagated in the Davydovian approach to developmental teaching (Davydov, 1988).

The second sensitive topic is *cultural relativism*. Here the key issue is that if we reduce certain modes of thought to a common denominator that is regarded as psychologically and morally equivalent to our own, we discard all the epistemological claims worshiped since the early Enlightenment – or at least our declared confidence in scientific progress and emancipation. It is for this reason that we introduced the Messer debate, for this phenomenon places us at the heart of the problem. In this debate we notice that the interlocutors are sincerely concerned with the "basics" of the sociosemiotics of their own culture, even though their line of reasoning is somewhat puzzling, at least from a cross-cultural psychological point of view.

We have, however, decided to exclude both intriguing questions from the present argument. In the rest of this chapter we discuss, from a strictly Vygotskian perspective, one of the key issues of the quest for meaning in the context of formal education. According to our sociosemiotic approach to education, *learning activity* is the process of searching for meaning within discursive practice. To begin with, we would like to make some additional remarks from an educational point of view on the much-disputed area of *teaching* discursive thinking, conceived as a problem of shared understanding on the interindividual plane, that is, between partners standing in an *asymmetric* relation to each other. According to Yaroshevsky (1989) and Kozulin (1990), Vygotsky's research program was primarily focused on the developmental change (or transition) that takes shape on this plane.

Polyphony and the process of semiosis

The Russian semiotician Yuri Lotman calls the universe of social-cultural conceptual inventories the *semiosphere*. He distinguishes this universe of meaning from both the biosphere and the noosphere. Lotman associates the latter with the rational, scientific (and mostly detached) research activities of humanity (Lotman, 1989). The reproduction of sociocultural meaning (*semiosis*) is regulated by culture-bound – and as such contestable – values and rules.[2] Modes of contrafactual and hypothetic discourse are examined in sociosemiotic research *in vivo* and conceived as "deep structures" for conceptualizing and making sense. According to Bruner (1986; also Bruner & Haste, 1987), *making sense* is a sociocultural process. It is an *ongoing activity* that is always situated within a certain socioecological context. Semiotic multivoicedness (or *polyphony*, as Bakhtin [1963] calls it) is a distinctive feature of any "life form." Multivoicedness refers to culture. The same holds true for cultural pluralism, which some authors consider a necessary condition for *sociogenesis* (Asmolov, 1986; Elias, 1991). Paraphrasing the Russian poet Mandel'sthan, "a nostalgia for world culture" is also involved.

In this polyphonic discursive practice the limit is not "I" but "we." Speakers project their own views, attitudes, and convictions on their interlocutors and look for their own reflections in others. However, the inverse process also takes place: Speakers anticipate the interpretations of their interlocutors and integrate these expected outcomes into their own orienting basis. Consequently, the *unit of analysis* in the process of producing meaning is the social unit of the joint coordination of polyphony, that is, the negotiation of meaning and its context of reconstruction. No doubt negotiation and an intersubjective search for meaning were at stake in the Messer debate. Hence negotiation and management of meaning is the core process in sociocultural activities, from early childhood (Walkerdine, 1988; Lisina & Kapcel'a, 1987; Podd'jakov & Michailenko, 1987), up to and including school age (Davydov, 1988), after which it continues in all life forms (Leont'ev, 1978; Mead, 1934; Peirce, 1958; Wittgenstein, 1953).

The phenomena discussed in this section can be considered as a form of *public metalinguistic commentary* on sociocultural classification and naming practices. From a Vygotskian perspective on the *psychosociology* of communication,[3] thinking and learning, the activity involved in the Messer debate, can be classified as a vivid illustration of what Nuttin (1984) called *communicated thinking,* what Gal'perin, El'konin, and Davydov in their theory of mental actions conceived of as *disputation by speaking and thinking aloud.*

It is obvious, with regard to the speech intention involved, that our speaker from Germany takes a firm stance in the Messer debate. As exemplified in this case, the joint attempt to produce meaning and sense is no doubt an instructive instance of what the Estonian cross-cultural psychologist Tul'viste (1991) characterizes as *heterogeneity of human thinking.* This kind of heterogeneity is, first and foremost, a distinctive feature of educational discourse practices. The most complicated task facing the teaching profession today is managing this polyphony in the various activity settings that constitute the prevailing classroom discourse.

The asymmetry in educational activity settings

Let us sum up briefly the points made so far. We have argued that there is a special register of speech called *discourse,* which should be considered the essence of sociogenesis and notably of education as an activity sui generis. Along the Vygotskian line of reasoning, we use the term *discourse* to refer to a genre of communication in which the utterances of each of the interlocutors are *determined by the position they occupy in a certain specific social formation, not just by the speech content to which they refer.* The primary function of the symbolic inventory used in discourse is *not to label objects, but to categorize people's activities* with respect to their particular social positions and the speech registers they use. *This very process makes educational sociosemiotic practices different from any other communicative activity.* Education is a finite province of meaning, as Goethe once remarked.

The first key issue that comes up in this context is the demarcation between *scientific* and *everyday concepts,* as described by Vygotsky and his followers, and, consequently, between scientists (experts) and laypersons (novices). Education is essentially characterized (more than any other kind of human interaction) by the contrast between scientific and everyday concepts, by *a clash* between experts and novices, respectively.

The second issue concerns the problem of *decentration,* as Piaget calls it (or *recentration*; see Raeithel, 1990). Indeed, without this notion, it is impossible to conceptualize adequately either discursive communication or communicated thinking in terms of activity theory.

Third, in conducting psychosociological studies (but especially research on the practice of upbringing and education), it is necessary to distinguish two levels: the *actual standards* by which the subject is measured (or measures personally) and *the mental standards the subject establishes* when trying to pursue a personal or social identity or adopting a zone of individual responsibility. "As long as a man is alive, he lives from the fact that he is not yet perfected, and has not yet said his last words," as Bakhtin (1963, p. 78) aptly remarked. According to Bakhtin, "to live is to communicate." (For an analysis of Bakhtin's legacy, see Wertsch, 1991.)

The points made so far show the fundamental difference between the *social position* of an educator and that of an average conversation partner. This brings us to the core issue of our present argument, namely, the *unequal status of interlocutors.* In educational practice, it is necessary to assume that learners and teachers are equal in their human essence but *not* in their particular existence. At best, the educator's role is that of *a sparring partner,* that is, an individual from whom the pupil can learn on the basis of "loaned consciousness," as well as efficient didactic and social support. Not only *heterogeneity* but also *asymmetry* appears to be the fundament underlying any educational discursive practice. How can this interindividual relationship be managed by the teacher in orchestrating the classroom-bound communicative polyphony?

Intertextuality and the aims of education

We hope that the conceptual framework we have sketched so far has sufficiently outlined the semantic makeup of the psychosociological structure of *the teacher–learner unity* in *settings* in which the learning of hypothetical and critical thinking is conceived of as a discursive activity and in which the teacher's job is to try to teach worthwhile sociosemiotic activities.[4] Thinking and making sense (in society as well as in schools) has to be conceived of as a *sociosemiotic process* in which oral and written *texts* (i.e., utterances, not propositions) constantly interact in order to bring about improved texts on the part of interlocutors or even to merge into a revised text as a final product of the whole group. In essence, learning activity as conceived in a Vygotskian framework depends strongly on *intertextuality.* The teaching strategy that leads to learning activity is based on the joint activity of teacher and students focusing on the production of new personal meanings by constructing improved personal texts in the interaction between canonical (scientific) texts and a subjective text (Davydov, 1988).

Later in this chapter, we shall return to this intertextual conception of discursive learning activity in our discussion of the research done in the scientific community centered on Gal'perin and Davydov. We shall refer to the issue of *change* in the structures of attitude and motivation, depending on whether the emphasis is placed on the *relational* or on the *epistemological* dimensions. However, before moving on to this topic, we would like to deal briefly with the problem of intentional search for meaning, especially in relation to the problem of educational aims.[5] The scope of this chapter does not permit comprehensive discussion of this issue, so we must confine ourselves to the following remarks.

When we say that a person is a good thinker, we mean one of two things: that the person is *intelligent* or that the person is *thoughtful.* A person may be clever without being thoughtful and vice versa. In the first sense, we mean a skill or competence. In the second sense, we mean something more like an intellectual virtue or character trait. Educators should focus on the development of thoughtfulness as a virtue. A person may be unable to perform a certain activity due to lack of skill. Such an inability may be attributed to technical problems. In this case, teaching and learning are the obvious means by which certain techniques can be mastered. Virtues, however, are not acquired by mastering techniques. Some virtues may indeed involve being able to do difficult things, but these difficulties are due to problem situations, not to technical difficulties arising from the actions themselves (Gal'perin, 1989).

The distinction we have made between skills and virtues is certainly not beyond challenge. However, we do not think it necessary to consider all the subtleties here. Our reason for making this demarcation is that is has a certain bearing on the way *educational aims* are conceived. An educator whose primary interest lies in the development of the learner's *personality* must be sensitive to the perfectibility of intellect, namely, the development of good thinking as an intellectual virtue.

Later on, we shall refer briefly to some new and promising teaching strategies that might be of help in making this educational aim attainable. It is clear by now that attention should be focused on the various activity settings in which school learning takes place. The teacher, therefore, must give serious consideration to the aspect that Wallon (1942) aptly called "le rôle capital de l'ambiance." It is even more important, however, to recognize the following: Good thinking develops in social bodies (units, formations) that cherish specific goals and beliefs about the importance of thought and heterogeneous thinking. It is necessary, therefore, to develop and implement a "thinking curriculum" in our schools.

The institutional context of learning activity

So far, our discussion has been a kind of play on words. We wanted to illustrate that the Vygotskian line of thought, as it has been explored and extended worldwide over the last 30 years, has brought about necessary changes in educational thinking. But we also wished to make serious note of what occurs as the beginning of a new paradigm: *Mass education* in our comprehensive schools can be truly effective only if students develop themselves through authentic and efficient interindividual interaction. This interaction would have to take place not only with *generalized others* (primarily teachers) but especially with *significant others* who can offer the necessary social support and serve both as purveyors of culture and sparring partners with whom the learner can *identify.*[6]

The Russian psychologist Stetsenko (1989, pp. 15–16) pointed out that it is a mistake to think of identity development as an *individual* process because "it is not the child who really exists and develops, but the child–adult unity, from which the child is only gradually and partially differentiated as an independent *formation.*" The assumption that identity development is more than a dialectic between ontogeny and phylogeny is crucial to this argument: It is *a triadic interaction* in which ontogenetic and phylogenetic influences are constantly refracted and reconstructed through and in socioculturally mediated joint interaction. A major consequence of this argument is that the student does not have to be burdened with the responsibility for creating a new, meaningful "image of the world" from scratch. Possible worlds (Bruner, 1986) already exist in the way that "life forms" structure the sociocultural and societal dimensions of the prevailing educational system. These, in turn, shape to a high degree the activity settings and learning experiences of both students and teachers.

We live, according to Stetsenko's view, in a *five*-dimensional world (the three spatial dimensions, plus time and sociocultural meaning as contained in the prevailing semiosphere).[7]

Experts on Russian psychology have presumably already noticed that the perspective outlined here is congruent with the outlook of the late A. N. Leont'ev (1978). He and his associates viewed identity development and learning to learn primarily as a matter of *becoming* acquainted with already existing conceptual inventories and "cultural scripts." Although Leont'ev paid obligatory lip service to the making of personal sense, he never (at least to our knowledge) devoted a serious study to the critical distinctive features of the conditions in which making sense emerges (or is achieved) in *differently* structured activity settings where various expressive orders exist and are used juxtaposed next to, or interwoven with, one another. Hence, for the study of the semiosis from meaning to sense, we can only partly rely on Leont'ev because he does not take the whole picture of the *social other* into full account (Kozulin, 1990, p. 251). A clear view of the *macrogenetic direction* of development as an educational construct (or, as Heinz Werner [1957] has called it, of an *orthogenetic* principle) is remarkably absent in Leont'ev's argument.

So the picture becomes complicated when we seriously embark on the task of trying to develop social and personal identity. In discussions on this topic, proper emphasis has been placed on the *problems and prospects* involved in adopting the view that socioculturally mediated joint activity is the basic starting point for a scientific analysis of human nature.

We think that the answer to this tricky question should be looked for in constructs like *socium, contextuality,* and *intersubjectivity.* The development of social and personal identity is a process in which individuals adopt *moral value orientations* and renounce unrestrained self-fulfillment for the sake of others they have accepted as being just as real as the self, or (in Marxist terms) as two sides of a single social formation. This is the reason why we emphasized hypothetical and critical thinking, as well as contrafactual discussion, when we discussed the Messer debate. But how can individuals be motivated to cooperate in such a way at an interindividual level? What are the sources of reciprocal social relationships that teachers and pupils should be aware of?

We are only beginning to conceive the importance of *the educational explanatory frameworks* and the *conceptual inventories* they involve within a Vygotskian research program. We are still left with the problem of having to know precisely *what* is to be taught before we can orchestrate classroom learning in such a way that it promotes the development of critical thinking combined with moral value orientations. What are the optimal activity settings that make this reciprocal teaching and learning possible?

Learning activity and intertextuality

In the foregoing sections, we argued that students need to have not only efficient interaction with but also a more *constructive* social relationship with a *model for growth.* The need for active functioning has two important characteristics: it is both selective and socially oriented.

We agree with many other researchers who follow the Vygotskian line of thinking that cooperative, productive learning activity has to be implemented in the thinking curriculum we are aiming to establish (Davydov, 1988; Engeström & Hedegaard, 1985; Engeström, 1990; Hedegaard, 1990; Carpay, 1990; Van Oers, 1990, 1992). In this conceptual framework we should also mention Amonashvili's work (1984) and his view on "the pedagogics of collaboration." His perspective on cooperation is especially important in activity settings where the outcome of a learning task depends not only on the individual but also on interindividual interaction, as is the case in small groups or in whole classes. Reciprocal coordination characterizes many activity settings, notably those involving negotiations and transactions in school classes. As we have said, the issue of sociocultural embeddedness motivation in relation to the schematic or script-like makeup of the learning tasks, the lesson formats, and the classroom procedures contained in a variety of Davydovian teaching strategies has only recently been studied (Davydov, 1988; Hedegaard, 1990; Engeström, 1990). However, in order to make the teaching of hypothetical and critical thinking effective at all, students must be confronted with certain shared conventions of discourse (i.e., images of the world) that are contrafactual with whatever they have believed in so far (contrast teaching).

In addition to all of this, however, we have come across yet another aspect of learning activity that has been studied, though to a much lesser extent. We argued that the main challenge in modern education is the orchestration of *polyphony* by means of introducing students to the activity of shared meaning construction in which the sociocultural canon (as represented by the teacher) plays a central role. It is here that didactic models come into the picture. The core function of *didactic models* is basically to represent the cultural heritage and the perspectives involved (e.g., scientific ideas) and bring them home by means of the discursive activities of the students (Davydov, 1988). As such, productive learning activity should essentially be *multiperspective* activity, including the belief systems of the participants in question and the historically constructed representations of the given sociocultural curriculum content. As Davydov once remarked, the essence of learning activity is *polylogue,* that is, discourse with actual contemporary and historically prominent people (see also Wertsch, 1991, on the Bakhtinian notion of *voices*; also Elias, 1991).

However, to make the concept of polylogue useful for educational purposes, we must first find an adequate materialization (i.e., a cultural script) of sociocultural contents. A didactic transformation of the concept of polylogue, then, is a *conditio sine qua non*. In our opinion, polylogue at the classroom level should be conceived of as an interaction of texts (see also Freinet, 1993, on intertextuality based on what he calls *text libre*). Learning activity, then, is in essence a text-composing activity. Students should be encouraged to compose their own (written or oral) "scientific" texts (utterances) according to a particular body of knowledge as embodied in didactic models. Moreover, they should learn to feel obliged to defend their text against other public texts on the same topic. As such, didactic models (as an analogue of scientific models) should never be introduced into the learning process as "models to copy," but only as "learning models." The ultimate goal of any learning activity should be to establish *a new personalized* mode of speaking about the world (i.e., a new "narrative").

Concluding remarks on teaching strategies

In our argument so far, we have tried to provide what might be called a mini-conceptual analysis of learning activity as a teaching strategy in a multiperspective world. Much more research is needed on personalized and social construction of intersubjective cognitive representations in elementary and secondary schools. This is especially true if the contents of the core curriculum are no longer to be selected exclusively from the sciences but also from the humanities, and if long-term aims and purposes such as the development of thoughtfulness are also to be taken into serious account. Even more complications emerge if the focus of educational research is shifted to the development of personal and social identity and social bodies within average classrooms of 25 or more students. Finally, more research is needed on the provision of thoroughly tested prototypes of multiperspective and integrated curricula, as well as the necessary overt and covert cultural scripts involved.

Certain proposals concerning the use of the cultural script concept, put forward by Hedegaard (1986, 1987, 1990) in Denmark and by Markova (1979) in the former Soviet Union, appear to be worth investigating (on this point, see also Cole, 1990; Tharp & Gallimore, 1988). The same is true of discussions on such heuristic concepts as *making sense* (Bruner, 1986), *language games* (Wittgenstein, 1953), *social construction* (Garai & Köcski, 1989), *human projects* (Nuttin, 1984), or *images of the world* (Stetsenko, 1989). A common denominator of these concepts is that they all refer to value orientations in the world of sociocultural reality, that is, in the world of people for people, and the issues of identity and morality involved in it.

Our students undoubtedly need "cultural toolkits" (Bruner, 1986; Cole, 1990; Wertsch, 1990), as well as other mental equipment to enable them to manage the heterogeneity of speaking and thinking and to guide processes of human (inter- and intraindividual) value orientations in order to make this world a better place to live in (Asmolov, 1986; Nuttin, 1984; Zinchenko, 1989; Wertsch, 1990; Tul'viste, 1991).

It is possible to advocate or explain the educational pivotal concepts described previously to teachers. In our research, we have done so in the past decennia. However, it became more than clear to us that talking *to* teachers has restricted impact in bringing about a radical change in the teaching profession (as William James [1899] already noted). Instead, educationalists should learn to talk *with* teachers to help them adapt to their new social position in modern classrooms. Both teachers and researchers should get accustomed to the actual heterogeneity in our culture and adapt their habitus according to that insight. They should accommodate their teaching routines to this new conception of developmental teaching and take up the role of a sparring partner for the students. Subsequently, teachers should redefine their professional authority within this multiperspective context with regard to the issue of the heterogeneity of thinking. This is not an easy job, as our own studies have shown (see also Bernstein, 1977; Tharp & Gallimore, 1988; Wardekker, 1991).

Looking at the future

In this chapter we have tried to outline a Vygotskian approach to classroom discourse, stressing the necessity to focus more on the characteristics and the formation of particular interindividual relations, on the devotion to inquiry and mental elaboration of cultural scripts, than on specific predetermined outcomes in terms of learning contents. We cannot stress this final point too strongly: Pursuing intellectual and communicative virtues and skills is essential to important aims of identity development and moral conduct. The concepts of both social relations and the shared construction of meaning constitute the foundation for the idea of socially based human individuality. Identity development is achieved through discourse taking place in a specific (speech) community. The concept of communicated thinking, therefore, must also be studied within the framework of specific sociocultural activity settings and the social relations involved.

In our discussion, we outlined a conceptual analysis of the main assumptions and principles of our research program in order to provide a conceptual framework for an implementation strategy in Vygotskian "school-bound" educational research. In our own research program, we gradually shifted away from the strategy of *talking to teachers* in order to explore and extend an implementation-oriented perspective on teaching and learning activity. We decided to do so because we came to the conclusion that realizing that something is true and understanding *why* it is true are not necessarily the same thing. Indeed, clarity before commitment remains our motto, especially nowadays when there is such a strong tendency to elbow one's way through life. However, clarity of understanding should never be mistaken for clarity of vision, as is often the case in social studies. We still have a long way to go before the "learned discourse" advocated by many educationalists becomes common practice in classrooms. This mode of thinking represents a qualitatively different form of classroom discourse because words act not only as a *means of communication*, as they do in everyday discourse, but also as *an object of study* (Davydov, 1988; Wertsch, 1991). It is obvious that Vygotsky was not only ahead of his time, but that in many respects he was also very much ahead of our time.

Notes

1. In an article titled "The Genesis of Higher Mental Functions," Vygotsky refers to the same anecdote. In Vygotsky's story, however, a Russian soldier argues with a German about the word *nozh*, which is juxtaposed to *knife, Messer*, and *couteau*. Vygotsky borrowed the example not from Koffka, but from a book by Fedorchenko (Vygotsky, 1981).

2. According to Aristotle's *Ethics*, true and fair reasoning requires both intellectual and moral virtues.

3. We use the term *psychosociological* here and elsewhere in this chapter to refer to a communitarian ideal in the sense described in John Dewey's *Democracy and Education* (1916). We are of the strong opinion that the topic of community is a central value orientation in Vygotsky's perspective on communicated thinking and discursive speech.

4. We prefer the adjective *critical* (or *contrafactual*) to *scientific* or *theoretical*. The former refers to a mode of thinking; the latter also implies an epistemological stance. For further elaboration on the issue of critical thinking as an aim of education in elementary and secondary schools, see Wardekker (1991).

5. We consider the following aims to be essential in any form of education geared to identity development: promotion of thoughtfulness, reflectiveness, and field-independent (i.e., rational and flexible) thought, these being the hallmarks of cognitive maturity for the informed citizen in the Piagetian as well as the Vygotskian paradigm. In addition to these intellectual virtues, the pursuit of *communicative virtues* (e.g., patience and willingness to listen) is also essential.

6. According to Mead (1934), the *generalized other* in the psyche monitors and censors thought, reflecting the laws and axioms of the universe of discourse, constraining what utterances and what topics are permitted or impermissible.

7. In his last (posthumous) publication, the well-known sociologist Norbert Elias also discerns a fifth, that is, the *symbolic* dimension in which humans live (see Elias, 1991). Through this dimension we struggle to orient ourselves to others in a certain sociocultural community and struggle for conscious control over our actions. Although what Elias says regarding the social and personal function of symbols is congruent with the basic tenets of the cultural-historical school, there is no evidence that he was familiar with the Vygotskian paradigm.

References

Amonashvili, S. A. (1984). Development of the cognitive initiative of students in the first grades of elementary education. *Voprosy Psychologii, 5,* 36–41 (in Russian).

Asmolov, A. G. (1986). The historical-evolutionary approach to the understanding of personality: Research problems and perspectives. *Voprosy Psichologii, 1*, 28–40 (in Russian).

Bakhtin, M. M. (1963). *Problems of Dostojevsky's poetics.* Moscow: Sovetskii Pisatel (in Russian).

Bernstein, B. (1977). *Towards a theory of educational transmissions. Class, codes and control* (Vol. 3). London: Routledge & Kegan Paul.

Bruner, J. (1986). *Actual minds, possible worlds.* Cambridge, MA: Harvard University Press.

Bruner, J., & Haste, H. (Eds.). (1987). *The child's construction of the world.* London: Methuen.

Carpay, J. A. M. (1975). *Instructional psychology and the development of foreign language curricula.* Groningen: Wolters-Noordhoff (in Dutch).

Carpay, J. A. M. (1987). The meaning of Vygotski's work for the educational sciences. *Handelingen, 3,* 5–24 (in Dutch).

Carpay, J. A. M. (1990). *Cognitive mastery of grammar rules in foreign language teaching: Some experimental work based on the Vygotskian model.* Paper presented at the 2nd International Congress for Research on Activity Theory, Lahti, May.

Cole, M. (1990). Cultural psychology: A once and future discipline? In J. J. Berman (Ed.), *Cross-cultural perspectives.* Nebraska Symposium on Motivation (Vol. 37, pp. 279–335). Lincoln: University of Nebraska Press.

Davydov, V. V. (1988). Problems of developmental teaching: The experience of theoretical and empirical psychological research. *Soviet Education,* Part I: *30*(8), 15–97; Part II: *30*(9), 3–38; Part III: *30*(10), 3–77.

Dewey, J. (1916). *Democracy and education: An introduction to the philosophy of education.* New York: Macmillan.

Elias, N. (1991). *The symbol theory.* London: Sage.

Engeström, Y. (1990). *Learning, working and imagining: Twelve studies in activity theory.* Helsinki: Orienta-Konsultit.

Engeström, Y., & Hedegaard, M. (1985). Teaching theoretical thinking in elementary school: The use of models in history/biology. In E. Bol, J. P. P. Haenen, & M. A. Wolters (Eds.), *Education for cognitive development* (pp. 170–193). Den Haag: SVO/SOO.

Foucault, M. (1972). *The archaeology of knowledge.* London: Tavistock.

Freinet, C. (1993). *Education through work: A model for child-centered learning.* Lewiston: Mellen.

Gal'perin. P. Ya. (1989). Mental actions as a basis for the formation of thoughts and images. *Soviet Psychology, 27*(3), 45–64.

Garai, L., & Köcski, M. (1989). The principle of social relations and the principle of activity. *Soviet Psychology, 27*(4), 50–69.

Hedegaard, M. (1986). Instruction of evolution as a school project and the development of pupils' theoretical thinking. In M. Hildebrand-Nilshon & G. Rückriem (Eds.), *Workshop contributions to selected aspects of applied research. Proceedings of the 1st International Congress on Activity Theory* (Vol. 3). Berlin: System Druck.

Hedegaard, M. (1987). Methodology in evaluative research on teaching and learning. In F. J. van Zuuren, F. J. Wertz, & B. Mook (Eds.), *Advances in qualitative psychology: Themes and variations* (pp. 53–78). Lisse: Swets & Zeitlinger.

Hedegaard, M. (1990). The zone of proximal development as basis for instruction. In L. Moll (Ed.), *Vygotsky and education: Instructional implications and applications of sociohistorical psychology* (pp. 349–371). Cambridge: Cambridge University Press.

James, W. (1899). *Talks to teachers on psychology.* New York: Norton.

Koffka, K. (1921). *Die Grundlagen der psychischen Entwicklung.* Osterwieck: A.W. Zickfeldt.

Koffka, K. (1935). *Principles of Gestalt psychology.* London: Routledge & Kegan Paul.

Kozulin, A. (1990). *Vygotsky's psychology: A biography of ideas.* New York: Harvester.

Leont'ev, A. N. (1978). *Activity, consciousness, and personality.* Englewood Cliffs: Prentice Hall.

Lisina, M. I., & Kapcel'a, G. I. (1987). *Communication with adults and the psychological preparation of children for school.* Kisinev: Stinica (in Russian).

Lotman, Y. M. (1989). The semiosphere. *Soviet Psychology, 27*(1), 40–62.

Markova, A. K. (1979). *The teaching and mastery of language.* White Plains: M. E. Sharpe.

Mead, G. H. (1934). *Mind, self and society, from the standpoint of a social behaviorist.* Chicago: University of Chicago Press.

Nuttin, J. (1984). *Motivation, planning and action: A relational theory of behaviour dynamics.* Hillsdale: Lawrence Erlbaum.

Oers, B. van (1987). *Activity and concept.* Amsterdam: VU-uitgeverij (in Dutch).

Oers, B. van (1990). The development of mathematical thinking in school: A comparison of the action-psychological and information-processing approaches. *International Journal of Educational Research, 14*(1), 51–66.

Oers, B. van (1992). The dynamics of school learning. In J. Valsiner & H.-G. Voss (Eds.), *The structure of learning.* New York: Ablex.

Peirce, C. S. (1958). *Charles S. Peirce selected writings* (P. Weiner, Ed.). New York: Dover.

Podd'jakov, N. N., & Michailenko, N. J. (1987). *Problems of young children's play.* Moscow: Pedagogika (in Russian).

Raeithel, A. (1990). Production of reality and construction of possibilities. *Multidisciplinary Newsletter for Activity Theory,* No. 5/6, 30–43.

Stetsenko, A. P. (1989). The concept of an "image of the world" and some problems in the ontogeny of consciousness. *Soviet Psychology, 27*(4), 6–23.

Tharp, R. G., & Gallimore, R. (1988). *Rousing minds to life: Teaching, learning and schooling in social context.* Cambridge: Cambridge University Press.

Tolman, C. W. (1992). Meaning, sense and common sense. *Multidisciplinary Newsletter for Activity Theory,* No. 11/12, 55–59.

Tul'viste, P. (1991). *Cultural-historical development of verbal thinking.* New York: Nova.

Vygotsky, L. S. (1981). The genesis of higher mental functions. In J. V. Wertsch (Ed.), *The concept of activity in Soviet psychology* (pp. 144–188). Armonk: M. E. Sharpe.

Walkerdine, V. (1988). *The mastery of reason: Cognitive development and the production of rationality.* London: Routledge.

Wallon, H. (1942). *De l'acte à la pensée. Essai de psychologie comparée.* Paris: Flammarion.

Wardekker, W. (1991). Meaning and context in education. *Multidisciplinary Newsletter for Activity Theory, 9/10,* 36–41.

Werner, H. (1957). The concept of development from a comparative and organismic point of view. In D. B. Harris (Ed.), *The concept of development: An issue in the study of behavior* (pp. 125–148). Minneapolis: University of Minnesota Press.

Wertsch, J. V. (1990). *Voices of the mind.* Cambridge, MA: Harvard Univesity Press.
Wertsch, J. V. (1991). The problem of meaning in a socio-cultural approach to mind. In A.
    McKeogh & J. L. Lupart (Eds.), *Towards the practice of theory-based instruction*
    (pp. 31–49). Hillsdale: Lawrence Erlbaum.
Wittgenstein, L. (1953). *Philosophical investigations.* London: Basil Blackwell.
Yaroshevsky, M. (1989). *Lev Vygotsky.* Moscow: Progress.
Zinchenko, V. P. (1989). Psychology-perestroika. *Soviet Psychology, 27*(5), 5–28.

19　Metaphor and learning activity

Bernd Fichtner

Introduction

The novel *Ardiente paciencia* by the Chilean writer Antonio Skarmeta is actually a novel about metaphors. The plot centers on the story of a friendship between Mario Jimenez, the son of a fisherman in Isla Negra, and the poet Pablo Neruda. Mario, a young man who does seasonal work as a postman, delivers the mail to Neruda daily and always brings his problems along. At the first encounter of the two, a dialogue concerning the question of what a metaphor really is ensues:

Mario placed his hand over his heart in an attempt to control the wild palpitations. He was sure his chest would burst open right there. But he pulled himself together, and with one impertinent finger shaking just inches away from his emeritus client's nose, said, "Do you think that everything in the world, I mean *everything,* like the wind, the ocean, trees, mountains, fire, animals, houses, deserts, the rain . . ."

"Now you can say 'etcetera.' "

". . . all the etceteras. Do you think the whole world is a metaphor for something?"

Neruda's mouth gaped and his robust chin seemed ready to drop right off his face. (Skarmeta, 1987, pp. 15–16)

Here the metaphor is not a stylistic embellishment of rhetoric. Nor is it an abnormal grammatical expression or phrase. On the contrary, the entire world itself is a metaphor for something. The basis of this view of metaphors is the ability to see something as something else. In this chapter, I concentrate on this ability. First, I outline a philosophical conception of metaphors – not a linguistic one or one from the standpoint of literary criticism. Then I consider the question of how metaphors can be understood as "modeling ideas" with reference to learning activity.

314

Metaphors, metaphorical principle, and metaphorical process

The following assumptions form the basis of my reflections.

- Metaphors are fundamental for our conception of reality in general. We structure the various ranges of our experiences in a systematic manner with the use of metaphors. With the metaphor, we construct ideas as "visual images" that create manifold relationships between very different and contradictory spheres, phenomena, and processes and form these into a coherent system.
- In daily life, art, and science, metaphors are instruments for forming systems. Here they function in various ways as models that orient our activities and cognition.
- The basis of the metaphor, as well as of the metaphorical process in the sense of understanding and producing metaphors, is the metaphorical principle. This manifests itself in the fundamental competence to see something as something else. This competence requires the structuring of a particular phenomenon, sphere, or process in a certain mode in accordance with the pattern of another.
- The metaphorical principle is not only fundamental for the systematization of experience; it also plays an innovative role in experience's alteration or expansion, or, to put it briefly, in the generation of something new. The limits of a certain range of experience can be altered, expanded, or burst by discovering new systematic relations. In this way, a standardized and mechanical relation to reality can be upset. Metaphors do not change reality, but they make it changeable.

All of this must be explained in a more concrete fashion. The metaphor "The night is a blue satin blanket" is neither a comparison nor a mere visualization. Nor does it illustrate any similarities between "night" and "blue satin blanket." According to Aristotle, a metaphor proclaims: "This is that" (Rhetoric, III, 2, 10). In every metaphor, one element becomes the predicate of another. H. Weinrich calls these elements *Bildspender,* the "donor" of the visual image, and *Bildempfänger,* the "recipient" of the image (1963, p. 325). The donor – in this case the "blue satin blanket" – as the actual metaphorical element functions as a predicative scheme for the recipient, that is, for the "night."

In essence, the metaphor is not concerned with understanding the recipient with regard to a certain cognitive aspect, but rather with perceiving, imagining, and experiencing it within a certain perspective that embraces an entire system of aspects. This perspective cannot be reduced to an assigned, standardized lexical meaning. Max Black calls this the *system of associated commonplaces* of a speech community (1962, p. 40).

By calling the night a blue satin blanket, one evokes the entire "satin system" of corresponding commonplaces such as mystery, splendor, costliness, infinite depth, luxury, and much more. While actuating these commonplaces, the person who attempts to understand the metaphor constructs a subjective system of manifold implications corresponding to the satin system with regard to the recipient. What is activated in a particular case depends on the concrete situation, the context, and the personal significance of the individual. The satin metaphor organizes in a certain mode that is still to be further explicated: our perception of night itself. Black describes this function as follows:

A memorable metaphor has the power to bring two separate domains into cognitive and emotional relation by using language directly appropriate to the one as a lens for seeing the other; the implications, suggestions, and supporting values entwined with the literal use of the metaphorical expression enable us to see a new subject matter in a new way. The extended meanings that result, the relations between initially disparate realms created, can neither be antecedently predicted nor subsequently paraphrased in prose. We can comment upon the metaphor, but the metaphor itself neither needs nor invites explanation and paraphrase. Metaphorical thought is a distinctive mode of achieving insight, not to be construed as an ornamental substitute for plain thought. (1962, pp. 236–237)

With the metaphor, recipient and donor do not somehow become mixed or amalgamated. Rather, the metaphor asserts that "this is that." At the same time, we realize that "this is not that." In this way, an equation (The night is a blue satin blanket) and, at the same time, a disparity are asserted. Anyone who understands this metaphor is conscious of the fact that the night is not at all a blue satin blanket. Because of this simultaneous equation and disparity, we often say: "This is only a metaphor."

This semantic incongruence is not dissolved or neutralized, but rather remains present as a source of tension and contradiction. The metaphor can be understood as the result of a tense interaction between heterogeneous and contradictory elements. Within the realms of this interaction, the relationship of the individual elements to one another is not fully arbitrary; they do not supplement each other in some undefined manner. The metaphor is strictly complementary, that is, the individual elements are presuppositions of each other as far as their tension and contradiction are concerned.

With the following remarks, I can discuss only those aspects of this complementary relationship that are of particular importance for epistemology and didactics, namely, the complementary relationship between visual image and concept and between subject and object. I can only refer in passing to the relations between coherence and incongruence, cognition and emotion, visualization and reflection, and intuition and knowledge.

The complementary relationship between visual image and concept

Metaphors cannot be reduced to a visualization, to an elaboration, or to the function of an example. When Aristotle says that the metaphor "sets [a thing] [. . .] before our eyes," he means a productive process. In understanding as well as in producing metaphors, we actively take part in the development of a new dimension of meaning that proceeds from the interaction of heterogeneous and contradictory elements. Within this process, the picturesque, vivid, visual aspect – which can be termed the *iconic aspect* – plays a decisive part.

The iconic aspect enables us not only to maintain the contradiction of the heterogeneous elements, but also to let this contradiction become productive. In this way, the heterogeneous meanings "night" and "satin blanket" remain in such a tense relation to each other that a picturesque structure – the iconic aspect – is developed, which, in turn, supports and sustains the conceptual–semantic incongruence. The diversity of a metaphor depends on the quality of the iconic aspect. The donor "blue satin blanket" develops sense-related, aesthetic, but also emotional correspondences and connotations. These guarantee and ensure the similarity and thus support the heterogeneity with regard to meaning.

Thus, the metaphorical process can be understood as an essentially imaginative act. It realizes a similarity on the visual level that sustains the incongruence on the level of meaning.

By no means does the iconic aspect forfeit its aesthetic and sense-related quality, its material and formal independence, to the recipient during this process. This was demonstrated in an ingenious manner by Picasso's collages.

The artist understood especially his sculptures as plastic metaphors. Instead of forming his figures from traditional materials like plaster, he fashioned them primarily from such rubbish as old baskets, vases, bicycle parts, and so on. In his study "Visual Metaphor," V. C. Aldrich notes that metaphors in a work of art are made more apparent by compositions of which the individual parts are objects with their own identity and qualities. According to Aldrich, the metaphor is aimed in two directions if, for example, instead of molding plaster into the chest of a goat, a wicker basket is placed where the ribs would normally be. The result is a wicker basket that is to be regarded as the goat's chest. In the reverse manner, if the entire body of the goat is examined, its ribs can be seen as a wicker basket – thus, a compound metaphor with two lines of sight. If the ribs were made of plaster, the view would go only in one direction. Molded plaster would be seen as the chest of a goat (Aldrich, 1983, p. 73). And Picasso himself remarked that he traced the way back from the basket to the chest, from the metaphor to reality. He maintained that he made reality visible because he used the metaphor (Gilot & Lake, 1964).

The iconic aspect of the metaphor is fundamental for the analogy, for the similarity that the metaphor employs in order to evoke precisely the incongruence. The tension between visual image and concept becomes productive for the development of something new, of a new dimension of meaning.

The complementary relationship between subject and object

Metaphors refer to the priority of content in a specific way. At the same time, they focus radically on the subject as the subject of the activity.

Their assertions are apodictic and cannot be dissolved in a discoursive manner. The truth of a metaphor is spontaneously acceptable and intuitively convincing. Its assertion is not extensional in the sense of formal logic, but rather is always intensional, aimed at essentials.

Thus, a metaphor cannot be replaced by expressions that state what is actually meant. We can, of course, attempt to explain the statement about the night in the metaphor "The night is a blue satin blanket" with the use of paraphrasing, examples, and comparisons. At best, this would be an approximation but never the semantic basis of the metaphor. Exactly because of its intensionality, the metaphor can provide much food for thought without becoming totally arbitrary. The intensionality is especially apparent in metaphors we use for acoustic, visual, and taste-related phenomena in order to articulate experiences of synaesthesia, for example, "dark tones," "warm colors," "dry wine," and so on.

The intensionality of metaphors has a fundamental theoretical function in the history of science. *Field, power, wave, inertia,* and *atom* have become widely accepted theoretical concepts; their metaphorical quality is effective now only below the surface, but it still determines the further development of theory (Kuhn, 1979; Boyd, 1979; Ortony, 1979).

Furthermore, the intensionality of the metaphor establishes its indirect relation to the object involved or to reality. The metaphor organizes a broad, active perspective of a scope of matter and never dissolves into a direct reference. Only by activating its inner system of tensions and contradictions can the content of the metaphor be generated as a new dimension of meaning. In this way, it provides an important link to so-called theoretical concepts, for which the indirect relation to reality is also fundamental. The content-related core of a theoretical concept functions as a means of its own development and differentiation. It can be related to a particular sphere of reality only in combination with systematic connections to other concepts (Dawydow, 1977).

The priority of content as the object-related part of the metaphor places certain demands on the subject and his or her activity. In his *Rhetoric,* Aristotle considers the metaphor as a sort of syllogism of which the middle term must be found, developed, or constructed by the listener (or observer) in order to understand the metaphor. Thus, the metaphor requires a maximum of intellectual activity: If A is B in a metaphorical sense, then there must be some middle term, T, so that A is to T what T is to B. Where Shakespeare lets Romeo cry out: "Juliet is the sun!", this T is inexhaustible in the abundance and diversity of its aspects of meaning – life-bestowing warmth, glowing embers, a light in the darkness (Danto, 1981).

A metaphor must not be confused with a complete, static picture. It organizes seeing as an activity that creates a special relation to the world. In contrast to the other senses, vision allows perception from a distance. The ability of the sense of sight to cover distances caused Kant to designate it as the noblest of all the senses because it is "the farthest removed from the sense of touch, the most limited condition of perception" (Kant, 1963). With sight, we not only have a certain relation to the objects around us, but we also view this relationship itself.

In summary, one could say that the metaphor is objective and subjective at the same time. Its objectivity has to do with the intensionality of its assertion. By means of this priority of content as a matter to be developed, the metaphor involves the subject and his or her subjectivity. Here subjective does not mean left to the will of the individual, but rather concerns the subject of the idea, experience, and cognition.

The metaphorical competence of seeing something as something else implies the development of a perspective of a scope of reality and thus presupposes consciousness of this standpoint. With the complementary relationship of subject and object, the metaphor can be considered as a classic example of that "subjective universality" that Kant describes in his "Critique of Judgment" (Fichtner, 1977).

With its complementary relationships, the metaphor corresponds to the diversity of reality and, at the same time, to the manifold intentions and perspectives of this reality.

The metaphor as a "modeling idea" in learning activity

Usually, we associate with learning the idea of a process that unfolds over time and can be divided into phases or segments. From this point of view, an inner determination results from the relationships and regularities among the segments, whereas the totality of the process can be established only from the outside. It is then a result of the reciprocal action between this process and something else. With regard to the specific quality of learning itself, above all with regard to its content, this process scheme remains peculiarly abstract. On the basis of this scheme, learning cannot be comprehended as an activity. This is due to the fact that temporal succession bears no essential meaning for the entirety of the functional components of an activity. Here quite different circumstances are important.

The Soviet philosopher and system theorist Judin attempts to clarify the functional components of an activity with the role of the means employed. According to Judin, the analysis of an activity with regard to its means focuses interest on the object of the activity. Furthermore, the importance of the historical, concrete context for the activity can become a subject of investigation as a result of a precise description and specification of the means. In addition, Judin stipulates that only from an examination of the means can activity be described as activity of a concrete individual whose characterization can then no longer be neglected (Judin, 1978).

Judin describes the means employed in an activity with reference to their systematic relationship with the use of a hierarchy of levels or functions. These include:

- theoretical arguments,
- modeling ideas,
- and procedures.

Their relationship to one another is one of mutual effect. Here hierarchy means that the means of a higher level direct the lower ones, but that the former can be produced and corrected by the latter. Within this hierarchy, modeling ideas operate in an important way as a sort of hinge. They ensure the totality, the content-related connection of procedures, operations, and active processes by being founded on "generalizations," "theoretical arguments," or aspects thereof. A modeling idea is, however, always the idea of a concrete individual. It tells us something about how theories and their contents appear to this individual and how important they are with respect to his or her activity. A modeling idea is linked to practice as well as to theory.

What does it mean to understand the metaphor as a modeling idea for learning activity? Current research on the ontogeny of metaphorical competence can be instructive in answering this question. Within the scope of psycholinguistics, this has developed into an important field of research (see the overview by Augst, Kaul, & Künkler, 1981). If metaphorical competence is comprehended as the ability to understand, produce, and explain metaphors, then only the assumption that a child does not fully attain the ability to explain metaphors until the age of 11 has gained wide acceptance by researchers.

Statements about when children can understand and produce metaphors are very controversial. Many American researchers assume that even children aged 2 or 3 can form metaphors (Gardner, Kircher, Winner, & Perkins, 1975; Leondar, 1975; Billow, 1975; Smith, 1976; Winner, 1979). Usually, all nonliteral designations attributed to things by children are regarded as metaphors from this point of view. But when a child uses a toothbrush as a car in play and names it accordingly, then the toothbrush is a car to this child and by no means a metaphor (Augst et al., 1981).

I doubt very much that small children can master the complexity of a metaphor. This skill presupposes a full reorganization of the lexicon, a metalevel, or a particular perspective that allows the simultaneous equation and disparity of two meanings to become accessible. Every metaphor has a certain "theoretical potential." This does not develop naturally and automatically in learning.

Empiricist theories of learning assume that learning is a process that leads from the concrete, something given and perceptible, to something imperceptible and abstract. Here pictures are simply stations along the way to real knowledge, which, however, must be made concrete by means of visualizations. This standpoint is based on a problematic understanding of generalization because it presupposes that something concrete can be perceived in isolation from something in general and that the former must even become the basis of the latter. However, the mediated character of human insight consists in the mediation between concrete and abstract.

For learning activity, this mediation between concrete and abstract presents itself as the general tension between "empirical" and "theoretical" concepts (Dawydow, 1977). Precisely here, metaphors exercise a particular function if they are not simply reduced to pictures or parables, that is, to visualizations: They relate the mediation between abstract and concrete to that between subject and object in learning activity. In this way, metaphors exhibit theoretical potential. This potential will be further elaborated in the following concluding arguments.

Metaphor and the selection of one's own standpoint

Common sense presupposes a fixed and assigned relation between object and description, between meaning and sign. The acquisition of a theoretical concept in learning activity requires that learners dissolve this fixation and develop a personal attitude with regard to the knowledge to be attained, that is, the selection of their own standpoint and thus real initiative on their part (*Selbsttätigkeit*). As a perspective, every metaphor is centered on the subjectivity of the individual. My argument is that, for the acquisition of theoretical concepts, metaphors have a particular potential for the development of perspectives on the object of the concept involved – the metaphor as a modeling idea that avoids the naive and direct reification of knowledge that common sense undertakes.

Metaphor and indirectness

A metaphor cannot be reduced to a simple view or a simple perspective. Its meaning is not directly exhausted in some momentary usage. The metaphor is a perspective that removes itself from its object in an explicit manner. Its indirectness can provide a link to the acquisition of theoretical concepts. These concepts are never directly related to an object. They are formal structural systems, explications of a particular way of relating to reality. Theoretical concepts can never be fully dissolved into elements of their employment, that is, into procedures, operations, and algorithms.

Metaphor and totality

As a modeling idea, the metaphor orients the learner to totality. Two heterogeneous spheres are transformed into components of a new, systematically organized total meaning. This involves a connection between visual image and concept. Metaphors are not illustrations of empirical facts, but rather visual images of theoretical relationships and, thus, means of reflection. With metaphors, perception is closely connected to reflection. In the mediation between object and subject, metaphors also connect emotion to cognition, seeing to thinking, and insight to intuition. The dominance of content of the metaphor is always somehow compelling. A metaphor must be spontaneously acceptable and intuitively so convincing that thinking can proceed from it.

Note

This chapter is dedicated to Maria Benites Moreno.

References

Aldrich, V. (1983). Visual metaphor. *Journal of Aesthetic Education, 2*, 73–86.

Aristotle. (1946). Rhetoric (W. D. Ross, Ed.). *The works of Aristotle* (Vol. III). Oxford: Clarendon Press.

Augst, G., Kaul, E., & Künkler, H. H. (1981). Zur Ontogenese der metaphorischen Kompetenz – erste Ergebnisse eines Forschungsprojektes. *Wirkendes Wort, 6*, 363–377.

Billow, R. M. (1975). A cognitive development study of metaphor comprehension. *Developmental Psychology, 11*, 415–423.

Black, M. (1962). *Models and metaphors*. Ithaca: Cornell University Press.

Boyd, R. (1979). Metaphor and theory change: What is "metaphor" a metaphor for? In A. Ortony (Ed.), *Metaphor and thought* (pp. 356–408). Cambridge: Cambridge University Press.

Danto, A. C. (1981). *The transfiguration of the commonplace: A philosophy of art*. Cambridge, MA: Harvard University Press.

Dawydow, W. W. (1977). *Arten der Verallgemeinerung im Unterricht*. Berlin: Volk und Wissen.

Fichtner, B. (1977). Ästhetik und Didaktik. Baumgartens "Aesthetica" und Kants "Kritik der Urteilskraft" als Paradigmen der Erfahrung und ihre didaktische Relevanz. *Pädagogische Rundschau, 31*, 603–625.

Gardner, H., Kircher, M., Winner, E., & Perkins, D. (1975). Children's metaphoric production and preferences. *Journal of Child Language, 2*, 125–141.

Gilot, F., & Lake, C. (1964). *Life with Picasso.* New York: McGraw-Hill.

Judin, E. (1978). *Systemnyi podhod i princip dejatelnosti. Metodologicheskie problemy sovremennoj nauki.* Moscow: Nauka.

Kant, I. (1963). *Kritik der Urteilskraft* (K. Vorländer, Ed.). Hamburg: Meiner. (Original work published 1790)

Kuhn, T. S. (1979). Metaphor in science. In A. Ortony (Ed.), *Metaphor and thought.* Cambridge: Cambridge University Press.

Leondar, B. (1975). Metaphor and infant cognition. *Poetics, 4,* 273–287.

Ortony, A. (Ed.). (1979). *Metaphor and thought.* Cambridge: Cambridge University Press.

Skarmeta, A. (1987). *Burning patience.* New York: Pantheon Books.

Smith, J. W. A. (1976). Children's comprehension of metaphor: A Piagetian's interpretation. *Language and Speech, 19,* 236–243.

Weinrich, H. (1963). Semantik der kühnen Metapher. *Deutsche Vierteljahrsschrift für Literaturwissenschaft und Geistesgeschichte, 37,* 324–344.

Winner, E. (1979). New names for old things: The emergence of metaphoric language. *Journal of Child Language, 6,* 469–491.

20 Transcending traditional school learning: Teachers' work and networks of learning

Reijo Miettinen

Introduction

It has been argued that school as an institution has been dominated by a historically specific type of learning called *school learning* or *school-going activity*. The theory of school learning advocated in this chapter provides a historically based conception of the essential problem of teaching and learning in the modern school. School learning is characterized by memorization and reproduction of school texts. It is accompanied by an instrumental motivation of school success that tends to eliminate substantive interest in the phenomena and knowledge to be studied. The fundamental problem is that knowledge learned in such a way is difficult to use and apply in life outside the school.

If we want to transcend the limitations of traditional school learning, it is important to analyze the nature and conditions of school learning and the germs of qualitatively new kinds of teaching and learning within the school. This chapter discusses the problem of learning at school both theoretically and with the help of empirical data. It contributes to an ongoing theoretical discussion on learning activity by analyzing the object and the subject of learning at school. The discussion is grounded in results of the author's study of business teachers' work at the Finnish Businessmen's Commercial College (SLK). In addition, the chapter draws on other examples of new forms of teaching in Finland, Sweden, and England.

The nature and persistence of traditional school learning

Bernd Fichtner (1984) and Yrjö Engeström (1987) have analyzed the cultural and social history of learning from an activity-theoretical viewpoint. Fichtner demonstrates how the emergence of the phonetic

325

alphabet gave birth to the school and at the same time to the most important artifact of the school institution: decontextualized, independent text. Fichtner analyzes how memorizing, repeating, and reproducing the text became the essence of learning at school. This was connected to the conception of knowledge during the Middle Ages: "Knowledge is understanding text. Getting to know reality means to learn what the authorities wrote about it" (Fichtner, 1984, p. 53). Fichtner argues that the birth of modern science and the universal school system involves a change in the general attitude to reality. Cognition can now be seen as knowledge construction.

Engeström further specifies the nature of school learning with the help of Leont'ev's concepts. The nature of activity is determined by its object and motive. According to Engeström (1987, p. 101), the essence of school learning (or school-going) is "the strange reversal of object and instrument."

> In school-going text takes the role of the object. This object is molded by pupils in a curious manner: the outcome of their activity is above all the same text reproduced and modified orally or in written form. (Engeström, 1987, p. 101)

The reason for this reversal is the historical isolation of school from other societal activities. As a result, the text to be studied is isolated from the life activity of the students as well. The motive to reproduce the text is primarily to succeed in examinations and to get high grades. According to Engeström (1987, p. 100), the transition to modernity and public schooling has not been a qualitative breakthrough to a new kind of learning activity.

Many critics of the modern school still regard the passive reception of texts as the main problem of learning at school. John Dewey analyzed the problem in the school at the turn of the century. For him, it was a problem of "book school." Passive reception and memorization produce the paradoxical combination of slavish dependence on books and a real inability to use them. Students lose their capacity to observe and analyze objects and phenomena themselves.

> Their first reaction is that of helplessness when they are told that they must go to the object itself and let it tell its own story. It seems much simpler to occupy the mind with what someone else has said about these things. (Dewey, 1898, p. 324)

Dewey saw the causes of the situation in the same way as the activity-based theory of school learning: the separation and isolation of school from other activities of society and the decontextualization of the school text. In his 1933 essay written with John Childs, Dewey argued: "The essential point of the social conception of education is, however, that these subjects be taught in and with definite reference to their social context and use; taken out of their social bearing they cease to have social meaning, they become wholly technical and abstract" (Dewey & Childs, 1933, p. 51). In *Aims of Education*, A. N. Whitehead (1929) concluded that when taken out of its movement, its generation and use, knowledge becomes inert – dead structure. He maintained that the central problem of all education is the problem of keeping knowledge alive, of preventing it from becoming inert.

In his recent analysis, Howard Gardner (1990) refers to numerous studies suggesting that there is a surprising disjunction between the intuitive knowledge individuals have about the physical world and the kind of knowledge acquired in school. He goes on to suggest the basic difficulty of school:

> Here, then, we confront directly the major, though hitherto ignored, difficulty of school. "School knowledge" is typically presented and apprehended in a way remote from the manner in which that knowledge is customarily mobilized to solve problems and fashion products outside of a scholastic context. So long as testing is geared exclusively to "school knowledge," this disjunction can be ignored; but once researchers begin to probe the flexibility and depth with which such knowledge has been acquired, we encounter a most unsettling conclusion. By and large, knowledge acquired in school helps one to progress in school, but its relation to life outside the school is not well understood by the student, and perhaps even by the teacher. The credentials provided by the school may bear little relevance to the demands made by the outside community. (Gardner, 1990, p. 93)

Studies over the past 30 years have demonstrated the unique inertia and conformity of classroom teaching and interaction. Lecturing and the question–answer method still seem to be the dominant forms of work in classrooms. Teacher talk dominates, and students' activity is largely limited to answering questions formulated by the teacher. Students seldom ask questions spontaneously. This pattern was found in studies based on data from the United States (e.g., Cuban, 1982), Sweden (Lundgren, 1979), and Finland (Leiwo, Kuusinen, Nykänen, & Pöyhönen, 1987). Historical reviews demonstrate the persistence of this pattern (Hoetker & Ahlbrand, 1969; Cuban, 1984). John Goodlad and his colleagues summarized the results of their observations of 150 classrooms in 13 different states in the United States as follows:

> Our observers had grave difficulty gathering evidence regarding what teachers were endeavoring to accomplish in the classroom apart from coverage of the topics selected largely by courses of study and textbooks. . . . Even when using the materials of curriculum projects . . . emphasizing "discovery methods," pupils appeared to bet on covering the content of textbooks, workbooks and supplementary reading material. . . . We do conclude that telling and questioning were the predominant characteristics of instruction in our sample classrooms. . . . Textbooks and workbooks dominated the teaching-learning

process. . . . We conclude that the prime medium of instruction in our sample of schools was the textbook, supported by textbooklike related reading and workbooks. (Goodlad & Klein, 1970, p. 78)

At least two explanations have been presented as causes of the persistence of this pattern. Reproduction theories and the hidden curriculum tradition maintain that the roles and relations in the classroom prepare students for the obedience necessary in the hierarchical power relations in work life and society (e.g., Bourdieu & Passeron, 1990; Bowles & Gintis, 1976). Another explanation refers to the so-called frame factors of teaching and the teacher's socialization into them. *Frame factors* are institutional and physical factors such as curriculum, time, number of pupils, and the classroom as a physical space. These frame factors, taken as practical necessities, are said to determine teachers' behavior. The traditional model of teaching and classroom interaction is a necessary "habit" or "theory in use" by means of which teachers control the turbulent life of the classroom. According to Martin Denscombe (1982, p. 255), the universality of this model "remains remarkably unchanged from generation to generation of teachers because the basic structural features of classroom experience have remained unaltered."

Denscombe's explanation seems reasonable. The traditional model of classroom instruction is a historically formed adequate habit to master this definite context, the classroom and the school day divided into lessons. If that is true, overcoming the prevailing form of teaching and learning requires breaking this context.

The influence of rationalized curriculum practice and the standard textbook

To understand the persistence of school learning, control mechanisms used by school authorities must be analyzed as well. Curriculum theories and procedures have been an important general instrument in unifying and controlling the content of teaching. Samuel Haber (1964) and Herbert Kliebard (1986) have demonstrated how school administration and early curriculum theory in the United States adopted Taylor's scientific management as their basic model. The psychological basis for this model was supplied by Thorndike's (1962) psychology, connectionism.

The essential characteristics of this model were the control of schoolwork by means of specified goals and a clear division between planning and execution. Specialists (curriculum planners and authorities) were to decide the goals and contents. Teachers were to execute the plans.

This model, refined with taxonomies of instructional objectives, was later commonly characterized as *educational* or *instructional technology*. It became dominant in the 1960s and 1970s in the United States (Apple, 1983; Kliebard, 1971; Wise, 1977). It also exerted considerable influence on major school reforms in Sweden and Finland in the 1960s and 1970s. Curricula became centrally prepared, and the schools were supposed to implement them, which meant that teachers were supposed to cover the lists of content titles and objectives of the official curriculum documents.

Another, perhaps stronger instrument for unifying and controlling the classroom was also introduced: the officially approved, grade-specific standard textbook package. Textbooks were checked by the authorities and tied to the content lists of the official curriculum. Instead of textbooks that covered several grade levels, series of grade-level-specific textbooks were introduced. The package also included workbooks and teacher manuals. It was designed to be a complete teacherproof vehicle for standardized teaching of the curriculum. The textbook was divided into lessons, with corresponding tasks in the workbook. Michael Apple assesses the meaning of the textbook in school work as follows:

How is this "legitimate" knowledge made available in schools? By and large it is made available through something to which we have paid far too little attention – the textbook. Whether we like it or not, the curriculum in most American schools is not defined by courses of study or suggested programs, but by one particular artifact, the standardized, grade-level-specific text in mathematics, in reading, social studies, science (when it is even taught), and so on. The impact of this on the social relations of classroom is also immense. It is estimated, for example, that 75 percent of the time elementary and secondary students are in classrooms and 90 percent of their time on homework is spent with text materials. Yet, even given the ubiquitous character of textbooks, they are one of the things we know least about. (Apple, 1986, p. 85)

One important aspect of the influence of textbooks is the consequences of the decontextualization of language, its removal from the human life-world. David Olson (1980, p. 189) compares textbooks to ritualized oral language. "They are used in a particular context (the school), have a particular linguistic form, explicit logical prose, and a particular type of interpersonal relation – that between the author and reader." Olson points out that writing provides a means for separating the speaker/writer from the text. It thus encourages the differentiation of intention (what was meant) from the expression (what was said) and puts the emphasis on the latter. The distinctive linguistic form Olson refers to is expressed in many ways in school work. In ordinary oral language, questions are used to request information and action. In schools, questions are asked to which the teacher already knows the answers. Indeed, the teacher has commonly just provided the information needed by means of teaching or having the students read the text. Questions within school-going are evaluative "test questions."

Textbooks have become compendiums of topics, none of which are treated in much depth (Tyson & Woodward, 1989; Elliot & Woodward, 1990). To avoid learning problems, difficult words and abstract concepts are avoided and colorful pictures are included (Tyson-Berstein, 1988). Piagetian theory is used to evaluate what is not possible to teach at different age and grade levels. As a result, repeating and remembering of superficial and scattered material easily becomes the only viable course of action for the pupil.

Workbooks commonly require trivial intellectual operations such as recognition and transfer of information from textbook to workbook. Teacher manuals often give detailed – and conservative – instructions based on "teacher efficiency" studies (Zumwalt, 1988). Thus, it may be argued that the rationalized curriculum practice, including officially approved standard textbooks, has formed a new kind of infrastructure that maintains and consolidates traditional school learning.

It has also been argued that the rationalized control has made receptive school learning more technical (e.g., Wolcott, 1977; Popkewitz, Tabachnick, & Wehlage, 1982). The ever more abundant material in packages no longer has the status of "truth" in the eyes of teachers and students. It has the status of an officially approved "standard."

The object and motive of learning activity

School learning is a specific historical type of learning. Where, then, can the possibility of a qualitatively new, productive type of learning emerge? A dialectical viewpoint calls us to seek the new within the old, as an emergent consequence of the evolution of internal contradictions in existing activities. Thus, preconditions and initial forms of a new type of learning must develop within the basic activities in society, that is, within labor, science, and art, and also within school-going activity itself. In activity theory, this issue has been analyzed as the problem of learning activity (Davydov, 1982, 1988).

According to Leont'ev (1978), an activity is defined by its object. In his analysis of learning within school-going, Engeström (1987, p. 103) argues that the object of genuine learning activity cannot be reduced to text. What then could be the alternative object of learning at school? For Engeström, the forces leading to a new kind of learning activity cannot be found exclusively within school-going. According to him, "the symptoms of deeper qualitative change in school learning are still premature" (1987,

p. 104). He maintains that the conditions of learning activity are maturing within work activities because of the radically increased societal character and productivity of work. There is an objective pressure, manifesting itself in various forms, toward radically enlarged mastery of the entire work activity among those who perform the work. This expanded mastery can be attained only by means of a new type of learning. Engeström characterized the object of such new type of learning activity as follows:

> The object of learning activity is the societal productive practice, or the social life-world, in its full diversity and complexity. The productive practice . . . exists in its present dominant form as well as in its historically more advanced and earlier, already surpassed forms. Learning activity makes the interaction of these forms, i.e., the historical development of activity systems, its object. (1987, p. 125)

Learning activity cannot be realized within any single societal activity alone. It is realized within a network of interconnected activities. In the network, learning activity will mediate between other activity systems, such as science (production of new models and instruments) and labor.

What could this mean for the school? John Dewey's attempt to resolve the problem of schooling in industrialized society may be relevant here. Many features of Dewey's pragmatism are closely related to the central tenets of activity theory. Thus, it is not altogether surprising that his educational vision proves to be a rich source of insights for activity-theoretical attempts to analyze and resolve contradictions of current school learning.

When Dewey formulated the principles of his progressive school, it was very clear to him that the possibility of teaching the use of the scientific method (or, more specifically, the "experimental method") was tied to the use of science in society. He characterized our century as the century of applied science. Science, through its applications, "permeates every nook and corner of life: nothing in the domain of human relations remains what it was" (Dewey, 1938, p. 483). But – he goes on – "the bearing of all these changes upon the work of the school in promoting understanding of method and of the forces, problems and needs of social life have received relatively little attention" (p. 483). V. V. Davydov makes the same point, emphasizing that the investigation of reciprocal relations between learning activity and productive labor would be of great value. "This problem has received precious little attention by developmental and pedagogical psychology in the Soviet Union, although the development of learning activity is closely tied precisely to productive activity" (Davydov, 1988, p. 34).

For Dewey, the task of education was to prepare individuals to take part intelligently in the management of the conditions under which they live, to make them understand the forces that are moving them, and to equip them with intellectual and practical tools by which they themselves can chart the direction of these forces (Dewey & Childs, 1933, p. 69).

Education has the responsibility for training individuals to share in this social control instead of merely equipping them with an ability to make their private way in isolation and competition. The ability and desire to think collectively, to engage in social planning conceived and conducted experimentally for the good of all, is a requirement of good citizenship under existing conditions. Educators can evade it only at the risk of evasion and futility. (Ibid., p. 71)

Dewey stated that new industrial technology is based on science and, accordingly, "industrial occupations have indefinitely larger cultural possibilities than they used to possess" (Dewey, 1961, p. 314). The deep division between planning and operating is no longer necessary. The task of occupational education is to develop "general industrial intelligence." This kind of education "would include the historic background of present conditions, training in science to give intelligence and initiative in dealing with material and agencies of production" (ibid., p. 318).

Dewey wrote that the organizing unit of school work should be an occupation of the child. He defined it in two ways. First, it is a meaningful activity in which intellectual and practical aspects are united. Second, it is a "mode of activity on the part of the child which reproduces, or runs parallel to, some form of work carried on in social life" (Dewey, 1906, p. 81). Thus, Dewey's solution was to construct activities or occupations (projects) at school that reproduce or run parallel to work activities and in which the contents are taught "in and with definite reference to their social context of use" (Dewey & Childs, 1933, p. 51).

Dewey's ideas are very timely today. Lauren Resnick analyzed educational programs claiming to teach higher-order thinking skills or cognitive performances. She found certain key features in successful projects.

First, most of the effective programs have features characteristic of out-of-school cognitive performances. They involve socially shared intellectual work, and they are organized around joint accomplishment of tasks, so that elements of the skill take on meaning in the context of the whole. . . . This suggests a general need to redirect the focus of schooling to encompass more of the features of successful out-of-school functioning. . . . Realizing this vision will require a civic consciousness that goes beyond the individualist one of current classroom learning models and draws on models of shared intellectual functioning such as we see in our best work organizations. (Resnick, 1987, pp. 18–19)

But what are the societal activities that should be represented in schools or taken as models when reorganizing school work? Resnick refers to shared intellectual functioning such as we see in our best work organizations. On the other hand, research activity or scientific activity is often regarded as an ideal model for learning (e.g., Driver, 1983). Evidently,

Engeström's idea of learning activity situated within a network of societal activities is important in this context. As pointed out earlier, learning activity may be seen as something between science and labor. The object of learning activity thus includes both the creation of theoretical concepts and their practical application in society.

In sum, the object of learning activity is other societal activities. More precisely, the object of learning activity is the generation and use of knowledge in solving vital societal problems. This kind of redefinition of the object of learning at school implies a program of recontextualizing the knowledge, of bringing the knowledge back to the contexts of creation and use. What could this mean practically? If learning is to reproduce or have common features with work and research activities, how is it to be interconnected with these activities?

How teachers at SLK tried to bridge the gap between school and society

In this section, I describe and analyze attempts by supervising teachers of the Finnish Businessmen's Commercial College (SLK) to resolve the problem of relating schoolwork to society. Because SLK is a vocational college, the connection between teaching and learning to work is a problem often discussed among the teachers. How can school follow the rapid developments in the world of work?

To identify teachers' attempts, 11 supervising teachers of the SLK were interviewed twice in the spring of 1986. The data show that they had used basically three different ways of developing a connection with work practices in the teaching-learning process. The first way consists of attempts to bring reality into the school in the form of materials and tasks taken from work activities. The second way is to have the students study objects and activities outside the school. The third way is to apply models studied in school in resolving real or realistic planning and problem-solving tasks outside the school. Each of these types consists of two or three subtypes, which will now be presented. These forms may be seen as "germs" or "buds" on the basis of which more advanced forms of teaching and learning can be developed.

1. Bringing reality into the school

In this category, three subtypes were identified: (a) taking materials for tasks and exercises from real organizations and activities; (b) making the teaching-learning process simulate, in a concise form, an ongoing planning or decision-making process of some organization; and

(c) asking practitioners of different organizations to teach and discuss issues with students.

Three of the teachers said that they always try to get the material for exercises and tasks from real organizations. They had two reasons for that decision. First, they argued that this procedure makes possible a discussion about the meaning of the results and figures included.

We make real exercises, we aim at as realistic exercises as possible. Sometimes we make a calculation which is based on information obtained from some company. The relations of figures and data are correct and you can maybe explain the real circumstances of the case. If it's done according to the real figures . . . there is a sense of real work in it. (Teacher 10)

Knowledge of the real organization permits teachers to go behind the figures, referring to real conditions and circumstances. The other purpose of this acquisition of real materials was to stay in contact with the development of activities in different organizations. There was an attempt to make this task a permanent part of the teacher's work. As part of teacher education, student teachers were asked to prepare "packages" on new and problematic subject matter areas by visiting companies and studying the problems and practices in question. For instance, one package dealt with the accounting of service organizations. It included an analysis of seven pages on the special features of internal and external accounting of service organizations (the theory), as well as two cases with tasks.

One of the student teachers had developed in his school a course on the selection of information systems. He organized the course so that the teaching followed a real process of selecting an information system for an organization. The documents, including the real offers made by vendors, were used as material during the course. A representative of the organization came to give additional information and to discuss the situation with the students.

There are problems in this procedure of bringing reality into the school. The students are not in direct contact with the real object. The real experience is tied to the teacher who has prepared the task. It is difficult to transfer this experience in written form without losing the authenticity and the "sense of work." And it is not at all clear how these materials should be used as a meaningful part of the learning process.

2. Students' independent study of objects and activities in society

In this category, I found two subtypes: (a) comprehensive student assignments that require independent gathering of mainly textual information, resulting typically in a written presentation, and (b) comprehensive student assignments that require the study of an object or an activity by means of observation and interviewing, again typically resulting in a written analysis.

One teacher gave students the task of collecting material about certain product groups during one school semester. The goal was to compare the results in order to form a more comprehensive idea of how to analyze a certain type of product family. In the minimal case, the student uses only textbooks in the task. More advanced sources consist of materials from newspapers and periodicals. Still more demanding sources consist of original documents and artifacts produced in the activities to be studied.

A more important distinction, however, is whether the acquisition of information includes observation of real activities and interviews with practitioners of these activities.

One thing that I have used nowadays quite often – and it is a little bit different and new but very good feedback has been received from it – is that I send pupils in groups of two or three to business enterprises to complete some kind of a task. They may be there for one day, sometimes two. For instance, when the export transaction was taught in the export line, each of the groups went to an enterprise to make a description about the export of that enterprise. Then they reported it – and they were just enthusiastic. These kinds of tasks I have given quite often. And I will do it considerably more. One class will go and clarify the organizational models of the enterprises after they have been discussed. . . . It has occurred to me that the classroom is not necessarily the best place to learn. (Teacher 4)

One of these tasks concerned the concept of business idea. A business idea is a systemic way of analyzing and modeling the basic strategy of a business enterprise, developed by the Swedish economist Richard Normann (1983). This conception was widely used in the SLK. The teacher describes how the business idea was studied.

During the winter of 1985–86, the class had a task that concerned the business idea. . . . The students went to the enterprises to search for their business ideas. Enterprises define their business ideas in very different ways. Some formulate them more imprecisely and on a very insufficient basis. Others do it more carefully. In this task, the significance of the business idea and the way it is used in the field became obvious. The comparison of several analyses and the comparison to the theory of business idea, on the other hand, enriched and concretized the matter. . . . The assignment was accepted in a very positive way. I don't know whether this was the reason, but three students of that course founded their own enterprise during the same year. (Teacher 4)

It would not be possible to understand the real societal meaning of the model of business ideas without studying how it is used and understood by practitioners in different organizations. In this type of teaching, the model can be analyzed in the context of its use, "in movement." In this process, the limits of the model can be analyzed as well.

3. Application tasks

In this category, two subtypes were found: (a) making an analysis or plan that is not realized in practice and (b) making an analysis or a plan that is utilized by somebody outside the school. This category includes tasks that are at the same time parts of some larger cooperative research or planning project.

A group of students was supposed to make a plan to start a service enterprise (a barber shop, a car repair shop, a local branch of a bank, etc.) in a suburb near the college. The students were expected to acquire all of the knowledge needed to formulate a realistic business idea and to evaluate the chances of the new unit's success.

In some tasks, the result was utilized by practitioners or organizations outside the school. In the classes of one teacher, the students did marketing research as a final paper. The research was done, for instance, for an entrepreneur from a nearby suburb. Another study was made for the Ornithological Association of Finland to improve the delivery of their great achievement, the *Bird Atlas of Finland,* to customers. Another teacher told the student groups to analyze the quality of local shops. Shopkeepers paid a small fee for the resulting reports. Both of the teachers regarded these tasks as limited in the sense that in general a ready-made formula or procedure was used to complete them.

Conditions for restructuring the object of learning

The teachers had one repeated experience with tasks dealing with real objects. They reported that the students were very motivated, in many cases enthusiastic. This motivation may, of course, have been just a result of the fact that these tasks differ from routine forms of schoolwork and hence are more exciting. Another possibility is that there is something more deeply engaging in the object of learning as presented in these tasks.

This problem requires, once again, a comparison between the new object and the traditional school text. Olson describes the special character of school text as follows.

Both ritual speech and written text serve an important archival function in preserving what the society takes to be "true" and "valid" knowledge, knowledge from which rules of thought and action may be derived. . . . Textbooks, nonetheless, constitute a distinctive linguistic register involving a particular form of language (archival written prose), a particular social situation (schools), and a particular form of linguistic interaction (reading and study). Any archival form, being traditionally or historically grounded, calls for comprehension and production strategies somewhat different to those employed in everyday speech, skills that may require sustained "education" for their acquisition. Basic [to] those strategies is the displacement of that speech from the speaker and context of its production. That separation, I have suggested, produces an alteration in the illocutionary force and in the preparatory conditions of utterance, with the result that the child's role is changed from that of participant to that of recipient of language. (1980, p. 194)

How can we characterize the object of learning when societal activities are the object of study? In the tasks of type 2 and 3 just described, the students are immersed in a new way in the context of knowledge use. This is most evident when they must communicate actively with practitioners of activities under study. Language is "returned" to the context of speech concerning the problems of activity. The active subjects of those activities are transmitting not only knowledge and problems of its application, but also its meaning and significance in their activity. They transmit their motives, hopes, and suspicions as well. The object includes the intentions and hopes of living subjects. In addition, in the SLK, the activities selected to be the objects of study were at the same time work activities that the students are supposed to perform in the years to come. The decisive cause of the intense motivation in these tasks is evidently the nature of the object of learning, that is, the societal activities with living subjects.

Two questions may be raised. First, does this kind of restructuring of the object generate better learning, "profound learning" or theoretical thinking? Second, is the significance of the attempts described earlier limited to vocational education alone, in which the idea of applying knowledge to work processes is natural?

It is essential to consider carefully what kinds of activities are chosen to be objects of study. If they are just limited techniques or actions, separated from the activity system, no theoretical understanding is needed or presupposed. This is often the case in vocational education, which is heavily influenced by the traditions of Taylorism and educational technology. But the situation is different if broader systemic objects and activities are selected, including their problems and transitions.

The business idea task is a case in point. It represents an attempt to understand the changing interactions between the business enterprise and its environment, as well as the different functions within the firm. Such an object calls for studying change and functional relationships. Most organizational functions (e.g., the operations of accounting) can be constructed as objects of learning, either as separated functions or in their connection to the whole activity system. Moreover, the object may be constructed either as a fixed entity or to highlight the developmental aspect, the contradictions between the new and the old in the activity.

Is the idea of activity systems as objects of learning limited to vocational education? Could it be applied in primary schools? I take an example from the work of two teachers in the Pukinmäki Comprehensive School in Helsinki. The description is based on an interview with the teachers in April 1990. The teachers were planning how to teach and study meaningfully the curriculum unit "water." One of the teachers found a good book on water in a public library. She called the author, who happened to be the director of the Finnish Game and Fisheries Research Institute. The Institute was interested in informing the larger community of the measures and activities used to recover the Vantaa River and the results of an ongoing research project on the status of the river. The Pukinmäki Comprehensive School is situated on the riverside. A collaborative project was launched between the teachers and the Institute.

With two of the researchers from the Institute, the teachers developed a study program on "Water and the Vantaa River." The students of two third-grade classes learned to use certain methods used by the researchers in their work. They learned, for instance, how to determine the age of the fish from their scales. They participated in the inventories of the stock of fish in the river by electric fishing. They learned how to study the small and microscopic organisms in the water. In a way, the teachers and students studied water and the river with the research methods used by researchers. Evidently they studied the "context of research" as well, that is, the problems and goals of research activity on the Vantaa River and the overall measures used to recover the polluted river.

The connection between the curriculum unit of the school and the research activity was made in at least five ways. First, in lectures and discussions, the researchers presented the concepts and ideas on the basis of which the children's projects were formed. Second, the children used mainly the methods used and taught by the researchers. Third, teachers, students, and parents participated in certain phases of the field research of the Vantaa River project. Fourth, the research reports on the Vantaa River's state were studied and used in instruction. Finally, the teachers, as well as the pupils and parents, followed up the results of the research project. The teachers planned to return to this object of study at a more advanced level. Dewey's notion of learning as "reproducing" or "running parallel" to work carried out in social life is quite appropriate in this case.

The connection to research work, however, does not guarantee that the students will learn the essential theoretical concepts relevant to the object. In this case, one such concept is that of a river system under the influence of human activities. Such basic concepts are not "visible" in the researcher's work. The models needed cannot be experientially extracted directly from research activities or reports. They must be created in planning the learning project and during the study process itself. Although learning may be parallel and connected to research activity, it is by no means equal to the latter. It has its own requirements and its own unique contribution. The teaching-learning process can transform the results of research activity into models needed by citizens to understand the object of study as an ecological system under the influence of culture.

The need for cooperation: Networks of learning

All the methods used by the teachers of SLK to bridge the gap between school and society included collaboration with practitioners from different activities and organizations. Most of the methods described earlier imply such cooperation. By definition, if the object of the learning is an activity system, some form of cooperation with practitioners of the activity must be included. The first method employed by the SLK teachers (bringing reality inside the school) can be limited to collaboration between teachers and outside practitioners. When the two other methods are used, students participate in this collaboration as well.

A curriculum unit dealing with the purchase tax was taught in the SLK in the 1988–1989 school year. It was organized using the second method identified earlier (students' independent study of objects and activities in society). The students and the teacher first discussed what issues concerning the purchase tax are current, interesting, or problematic to them. They also discussed whether the students knew persons (parents, relatives, friends, former employers) who are working with these problems. Groups of three students were formed, each focusing on a problem area of interest to them. The groups studied the areas by using the law book, court cases, and news articles, as well as by consulting with the Purchase Tax Office. This consultation was required by the teacher. They also consulted with people working on the problem areas they had selected. The groups wrote their reports and presented them in class. The result was that the students wrote their own 43-page "textbook" on the purchase tax. The teacher concluded that the results were better than the average lessons prepared by the student teachers in the SLK.

The social organization of this kind of studying can be characterized by Philip Coombs's (1985) term *network of learning*. One of the teachers defined the problem as follows.

In the college you should teach knowledge and competencies needed in practical life because we are a vocational college. The thing that should be learned is certain basic matters, a certain point of view, way of thinking. The details are forgotten but it is a way of thinking and an attitude that is important. And for that it is necessary for the teacher to follow what is happening in practice. The teacher should also practice what he teaches, not only study the things he teaches. But how? Another job, an additional job to which the school has a positive attitude. It is almost a necessary condition. It is impossible to study these things from books alone. (Teacher 10)

A classic collective in the educational context consists of an educational researcher and teachers planning, performing, and evaluating teaching experiments. Although this kind of group connects theory and practice, the problem is that it is limited to the educational context alone. In light of what was said earlier, it is questionable whether this type of collaboration can overcome the division between school learning and societal practices outside the school (Engeström, Hakkarainen, & Hedegaard, 1984).

Projects completed in SLK provide examples of another type of collaborative network. Here the connection is basically between school and work practices. The limitation is that the production of new knowledge (research) in content areas and instructional solutions is not included in the network. As a result, there is the risk that learning is limited to repetitive acquisition of practical procedures prevalent in the work activities.

A third type of collaborative network includes researchers of certain content areas, teachers, parents, and students. The "Water and Vantaa River" project is an example of this kind of collaboration. In this project, students and parents participated in research activities during the summer without the teachers. Within such a network, learning processes can take place independently of the teachers in the classroom context.

A fourth type of collaboration is still broader. It includes educational researchers, researchers from relevant subject fields, practitioners, teachers, parents, and students. There are several examples of this kind of collaboration. A project called "Art and Built Environment" was carried out in England from 1976 to 1982. In this project, the network consisted of architects, community planners, teachers, and students. The idea was to study the surroundings of the school and to give the students models and instruments to influence their environment. The motto of the project was "Democracy in planning begins at the schools." The architects participated a few hours a week in the teaching and studying process. The local school administration paid their fees. Again, more than knowledge was transmitted in this process. The fears, aspirations, hopes, and world-view of the researchers and practitioners were conveyed.

An excellent example of a large network was the project "Man in Changing Society (MIS)," carried out in northern Sweden from 1985 to 1987. The premises and experiences of this project have been analyzed by Sutter and Grensjö (1988). They describe how three "ingredients" or societal intentions were united into the idea of the project. The first one was pedagogical and psychological. The intention was to surpass the traditional school learning and to foster explorative learning in school. The second one was to study local history by utilizing historical source materials, especially parish records. The third ingredient was the intention to utilize computers at schools in a productive way. The project involved forming an expanding network of actors with different interests.

MIS started as [a] consequence of societal discovery of the usefulness of the parish records and their "modernization" by microcards and computers. In its turn this is a part of a larger [trend toward] using the archives in general more effectively. . . . MIS is not restricted to the domain of school. . . . From the beginning others interested in knowledge have contributed to the work: employees of museums, archives and libraries, parents, genealogists, local historians, retired people, researchers at the university (outside the project team) and others. . . . From its start MIS has deliberately used what we have named a "cooperative way of working." A network of relations – not only schools but other institutions as well, and also laymen – was established through personal contacts and, as the project grew, more and more with the aid of the project journal. (Sutter & Grensjö, 1988, pp. 43, 50)

It was the object and idea of this project – local history research by means of parish records and computers – that made this kind of a network necessary. The network was the only way to make the necessary knowledge, intellectual resources, and source materials available to teachers and students.

The researchers describe how this kind of expanding teaching-learning process raises new kinds of problems in the planning, organization, and evaluation of the process and its results. The project was criticized for not having systematically evaluated the learning outcomes in students. The researchers agree with this criticism, pointing out that they had to abandon much of the intended evaluation when the project grew in size and acceptance. The expert group assessing the project wrote in its report: "The interest among teachers as well as pupils has been broad and the response of the school community in northern Sweden almost overwhelming." The researchers made their choice. The devoted their efforts to the practical development of the new activity. This exemplifies the methodological dilemma of research driven by the development of truly new and expansive forms of activity (see also Gardner, 1990, p. 104).

The social composition of a network of learning is basically dependent on the object of the learning. The object of learning and the composition of the network are also culturally specific. The examples presented earlier are taken from schools of European cities. Luis Moll and James Greenberg (1990) reported on networks of learning in a Hispanic working-class community in Tucson, Arizona. The aim of their project was to foster educational innovation by studying the possibility of utilizing the "funds of knowledge" embedded in the network of households and activities of the community. The researchers founded an after-school "laboratory" to provide teachers with assistance in developing educational innovations in literacy instruction. The authors describe "modules" of study in which writing was connected to the use of community resources. Members of the community came into the school, and the students went to study and acquire knowledge in the community. Robert Serpell's recent study of schooling in Zambia is another example of cultural variations in the formation of networks of learning (Serpell, 1993).

Conclusion

School learning or school-going activity is a historical result of separating knowledge from its movement, from its societal generation and use. The object of school learning is primarily the school text, now mainly in the form of grade-specific standard textbooks and packaged materials. To expand the limits of school learning, new kinds of objects – societal activities, knowledge in use – and a corresponding collective subject, a network of learning, are needed.

In light of the arguments presented in this chapter, it is evident that responsibility for planning the contents and forms of instruction will rest primarily at the school and community level. The prevalent rationalistic conception of curriculum planning is giving way to a view of curriculum planning as ongoing, multivoiced discourse and experimentation in a network that brings together actors representing various interests, types of expertise, and cultural backgrounds.

References

Apple, M. (1983). Curricular form and the logic of technical control. In M. Apple & L. Weiss (Eds.), *Ideology and practice in schooling.* Philadelphia: Temple University Press.

Apple, M. (1986). *Teachers and texts: A political economy of class and gender relations in education.* New York: Routledge.

Bourdieu, P., & Passeron, J.-C. (1990). *Reproduction in education, society, and culture* (2nd ed.). London: Sage.

Bowles, S., & Gintis, H. (1976). *Schooling in capitalist America: Educational reform and the contradictions of economic life.* New York: Basic Books.

Coombs, P. H. (1985). *The world crisis of education.* New York: Oxford University Press.

Cuban, L. (1982). Persistent instruction: The high school classroom, 1900–1980. *Phi Delta Kappan, 64*(2), 113–118.

Cuban, L. (1984). *How teachers taught: Constancy and change in American classrooms 1890–1980.* New York: Longman.

Davydov, V. V. (1982). The psychological structure and contents of learning activity in school children. In R. Glaser & J. Lompscher (Eds.), *Cognitive and motivational aspects of instruction.* Berlin: Deutcher Verlag der Wissenschaften.

Davydov, V. V. (1988). Learning activity: The main problems needing further research. *Multidisciplinary Newsletter for Activity Theory, 1*(1–2), 29–36.

Denscombe, M. (1982). The "hidden pedagogy" and its implications for teacher training. *British Journal of Sociology of Education, 3,* 239–265.

Dewey, J. (1898). The primary education fetish. *Forum, XXV*(3), 316–328.

Dewey, J. (1906). *The school and the child. Being selections from the educational essays of John Dewey* (J. J. Findlay, Ed.). London: Blackie and Son.

Dewey, J. (1938). The determination of ultimate values or aims through antecedent or a priori speculation or through pragmatic or empirical inquiry. In G. Whipple (Ed.), *The twenty-seventh yearbook of the National Society for the Study of Education.* Bloomington: Public School Publishing.

Dewey, J. (1961). *Democracy and education.* New York: Macmillan.

Dewey, J., & Childs, J. (1933). The socio-economic situation and education. In W. Kilpatrick (Ed.), *The educational frontier.* New York: Appleton-Century.

Driver, R. (1983). *The pupil as scientist?* Milton Keynes: Open University Press.

Elliot, D. L., & Woodward, A. (Eds.). (1990). *Textbooks and schooling in the United States. 89th yearbook of the National Society for the Study of Education. Part 1.* Chicago: NSSE.

Engeström, Y. (1987). *Learning by expanding. An activity-theoretical approach to developmental research.* Helsinki: Orienta-Konsultit.

Engeström, Y., Hakkarainen, P., & Hedegaard, M. (1984). On the methodological basis of research in teaching and learning. In M. Hedegaard, P. Hakkarainen, & Y. Engeström (Eds.), *Learning and teaching on a scientific basis.* Aarhus: Aarhus Universitet, Psykologisk Institut.

Fichtner, B. (1984). Learning and learning activity – two different types of learning in school and the historical-societal contexts of their development. in E. Bol, J. P. P. Haenen, & M. A. Wolters (Eds.), *Education for cognitive development.* Den Haag: SVO.

Gardner, H. (1990). The difficulties of school: Probable causes, possible cures. *Daedelus, 119*(2), 85–113.

Goodlad, J. L., & Klein, M. F. (1970). *Behind the classroom door.* Worthington: Charles A. Jones.

Haber, S. (1964). *Efficiency and uplift: Scientific management in the progressive era, 1890–1920.* Chicago: University of Chicago Press.

Hoetker, J., & Ahlbrand, W. (1969). The persistence of recitation. *American Educational Research Journal, 2,* 145–167.

Kliebard, H. (1971). Bureaucracy and curriculum theory. In V. Haubrich (Ed.), *Freedom, bureaucracy and schooling.* Washington, DC: National Education Association.

Kliebard, H. (1986). *The struggle for the American curriculum 1893–1958.* Thetford: Routledge.

Leiwo, M., Kuusinen, J., Nykänen, P., & Pöyhönen, M.-R. (1987). *Kielellinen vuorovaikutus opetuksessa ja oppimisessa II (Verbal interaction in teaching and learning II).* Jyväskylä: Jyväskylän yliopisto. Kasvatustieteen tutkimuslaitoksen julkaisusarja A. Tutkimuksia 3.

Leon'tev, A. N. (1978). *Activity, consciousness, and personality.* Englewood Cliffs: Prentice-Hall.

Lundgren, U. (1979). *Att organisera omvärlden. Introduktion till läroplansteori.* Stockholm: Liber.

Moll, L. C., & Greenberg, J. B. (1990). Creating zones of possibilities: Combining social context for instruction. In L. C. Moll (Ed.), *Vygotsky and education: Instructional implications and applications of sociohistorical psychology.* Cambridge: Cambridge University Press.

Normann, R. (1983). *Luova yritysjohto (Creative business managment).* Espoo: Weilin & Göös.

Olson, D. R. (1980). On the language and authority of textbooks. *Journal of Communication, 30*(1), 186–196.

Popkewitz, T. S., Tabachnick, R., & Wehlage, G. (1982). *The myth of educational reform: A study of school responses to a program of change.* Madison: University of Wisconsin Press.

Resnick, L. B. (1987). Learning in school and out. *Educational Researcher, 16*(9), 13–19.

Serpell, R. (1993). *The significance of schooling: Life-journeys in an African society.* Cambridge: Cambridge University Press.

Sutter, B., & Grensjö, B. (1988). Explorative learning in the school? Experiences of local historical research by pupils. *The Quarterly Newsletter of the Laboratory of Comparative Human Cognition, 10*(2), 39–54.

Thorndike, E. L. (1962). *Psychology and the science of education. Selected writings of Edward L. Thorndike.* New York: Teachers College Press.

Tyson-Berstein, H. (1988). *America's textbook fiasco: A conspiracy of good intentions.* Washington, DC: Council for Basic Education.

Tyson, H., & Woodward, A. (1989). Why students aren't learning very much from textbooks. *Educational Leadership, 47*(3), 14–17.

Whitehead, A. N. (1929). *The aims of education.* London: Williams & Norgate.

Wise, A. (1977). Why educational policies often fail: The hyperrationalization hypothesis. *Curriculum Studies, 9,* 43–57.

Wolcott, H. F. (1977). *Teachers versus technocrats: An educational innovation in anthropological perspective.* Eugene: Center for Educational Policy and Management.

Zumwalt, K. (1988). Are we improving or undermining teaching? In L. Tanner (Ed.), *Critical issues in curriculum. Eighty-seventh yearbook of the National Society for the Study of Education.* Chicago: University of Chicago Press.

Part IV

Technology and work

21   The theory of activity changed by information technology

Oleg K. Tikhomirov

Introduction

Progress in informatics and information technology has greatly influenced theoretical psychology. On the other hand, psychological knowledge is increasingly used to support the processes of applying and developing information technology.

In this chapter, I discuss these mutually dependent tendencies from the viewpoint of the psychological theory of activity. I focus on problems and prospects of creativity and creative activity in conditions of rapid development and pervasive implementation of information technology in various spheres of human activity.

The delegation of certain human functions to computers presents the theory of activity with new problems. What is the nature of the activity performed by humans in the context of advanced computerization? How does human activity change when humans use computers?

Computer science constantly uses the notions of *routine* and *creative*. Focusing on creativity reveals a large gap between psychological studies of activity and psychological studies of creativity. Theories of activity and theories of creativity have developed as separate domains of inquiry.

We witness both the tendency of negation of the theory of activity by the theory of creativity and the tendency of negation of the theory of creativity by the theory of activity. It has been claimed that among the most important trends in the development of the psychology of creativity in Russia are the "gradual substitution of the principle of activity by the principle of interaction and . . . substitution of the activity concept by the systems concept" (Lomov & Anzyferova, 1989, p. 28).

Are these counterpositions well grounded? In my opinion, they are not. To make the *general* scientific notion of system absolute for theoretical psychology usually means to ignore the study of *specific* and concrete systemic characteristics of human psychological functioning. L. S. Vygotsky

347

long ago introduced the notion of *psychological system* (Tikhomirov, 1989). He argued for the necessity of distinguishing between qualitatively different systems.

To speak today of the systems concept without differentiating systems according to their types means to go backward from the ideas of Vygotsky. Unfortunately, we sometimes see this happen in today's psychology, including the psychology of creativity. The concept of activity in psychology is a systemic concept, for activity is considered as a system (Leont'ev, 1975). We can compare (or even counterpose) different types of systemic concepts in psychology. But to present the systems concept and the concept of activity as opposites is unjustified. This also applies to the counterposition of the categories *activity* and *interaction* and *activity* and *communication*. Through activity, humans interact with the surrounding world. Communication is an integral aspect of joint activity. Under certain conditions, communication becomes activity in and for itself (need for communication, communicative goals, etc.).

The categories of *activeness* and *process* are also used as substitutes for the category of activity. However, it is not difficult to see that activity is a specifically human type of activeness and that activity has the character of a process. This means that the concept of process is an aspect of the analysis of activity rather than an alternative to activity.

Now let us view the opposite tendency – that of negating by the theory of activity the problems of studying creativity. Here we must consider the contents of the notion *theory of activity*. This notion includes ideas about the structure of activity, its types, its dynamics and development, its functions, and its mechanisms of realization. The theory of activity contains claims about the relation between activity and its subject and between activity and consciousness. It also includes notions about the functions of the theory of activity, the ways it has developed, and its relation to other psychological theories. General notions about activity have been specified in psychology by differentiating its types: practical and theoretical, external and internal, orienting and performing, individual and collective. Creative activity as an independent activity type is not usually discussed.

In discussions of the general structure of activity, the components of this structure are usually treated as established, not as generated. According to Leont'ev, activity is "a unit of life processed by psychic reflexion, the real function of which is to orientate the subject in the world of objects" (Leont'ev, 1975, p. 82). However, both reflexion and orientation can exist without distinct phenomena of creativity.

Inconsistency in the development of the concept of activity, demonstrated by a reduction of activity to actions and by neglect of the complexity of motivational-emotional regulation of activity, of the regulation of meanings and goals, also contributes to the negation of the problems of creativity. This situation not only limits the sphere of applicability of activity theory in psychology but also hinders the solution of new problems – problems that have appeared in the theory and practice of information technology use.

Theory of creative activity

I see the resolution of the problem in a differentiation between creative and routine activities as relatively independent types of activity. Both practical and theoretical activities can be routine or creative. In the context of broad use of information technology, intellectual activity, activity with knowledge, is of primary importance.

The theory of the orientating function of the psyche, the understanding of the psyche as orientating and researching activity, offers a step forward. There are actions with complete and incomplete orientation bases. However, the overrating of complete orientation hinders the understanding of the original character of creative activity. Theoretical and experimental studies show that in solving sufficiently complex problems, complete orientation is impossible. The only possible way to solve these problems is to act on an incomplete orientation basis. Psychological study of orientation should include not only the question of its completeness, but also the stereotypical or nonstereotypical character of orientation (see, e.g., Kaloshina, 1985).

It is necessary to differentiate between types of psychic reflexion, between processes connected to the existing and those connected to the possible. It is the latter that are specific to creative acts. According to Leont'ev, object-orientedness is the constituting characteristic of activity. The object of activity appears primarily in its independent existence, as subjugating and transforming the subject's activity, and secondarily as the object's image or a product of the psychic reflection of the object's properties, which can only be realized as a result of the subject's activity. In creative activity, the object appears in two other forms: as a new product of activity, a product that didn't exist before, and as an image of a yet to be created object. Whereas in noncreative activity the functions of comparison, reproduction, assimilation, and copying are of primary importance, in creative activity the functions of construction, generation, and creation of the new are most important. Subjectivity is transformed into objectness. It is necessary to differentiate between two types of activity's productivity – the repetitive creation of stereotyped products and the creation of new, original ones.

Creative activity is characterized not only by motives, goals, and operations (which exist also in routine activity), but also by acts generating new motives, goals, and operations. This activity undergoes functional development in the course of its realization. Creative activity can be defined as a unit of life that includes the generation of new psychic formations, the real function of which is giving humans the opportunity to generate a new world of objects. New psychic formations in activity precede and prepare the production of new, tangible results (products) of activity.

New needs and new motives are important sources of creative activity. Initial motivation can change in the course of activity. Hierarchical relations between motives can also change. Motives are not just conditions for developing actual intellectual activity, but also factors influencing its productivity and structure. Motivation is characterized not only by the content, but also by the dynamics and level of development.

The functional development of cognitive needs (study by E. E. Vasiukova, unpublished data) is characterized by changes in the objective content (type of knowledge), in the dynamic properties (stability), in relations with other needs, and in the level of realization. In this development we can isolate different specific levels of micro- and macrogenesis. The generation and characteristics of cognitive need, which appears in a concrete situation, depend not only on the exposition of the subject to the noncorrespondence of his or her known methods of action to the requirements of the problem, but also on the general level of the development of the subject's stable cognitive need. The general level of the development of a stable cognitive need defines the correlation between reproductive and creative components of intellectual activity – the level of its "creativity" rises with the rise of this level.

Studies of creative activity demand an analysis of the relations between activity and personality in a specific creative act. I. L. Zinovieva (unpublished data) studied these relations, specifically the dependence of intellectual activity's organization on the level of the subject's confidence. It appeared that the confident subjects had a higher goal orientation, which leads to the "cutting off" – by way of categorical evaluations – of the hypotheses of all information that does not lead to the goal, as well as higher trust in existing conclusions and higher integration between generalizations. The nonconfident subjects demonstrated chaotic and disintegrated organization of the search, the result of approximate evaluations of the value of the components in the field of meanings, which generates numerous directions of the search having equal attractiveness – and this hinders effective completion of the goal.

A study by I. A. Vassiliev and N. N. Khussainova (unpublished data) showed that personality determines the level of the organization of creative activity and activity's field of meaning (objective content of the problem, subjective-objective content of the problem, broader life context). The psychological mechanisms of "escapes" from creative activity devoted to the solution of a specific problem include broadening the activity's field of meaning beyond the objective content of the problem, that is, the inclusion of the "I," the experimenter and broader life context in the activity as meaningful reference points. A typology of escapes from creative intellectual activity was established by the direction of the escape into one of the fields of meaning.

Goal formation (generation of new goals in the subject's activity) is one of the central acts in the structure of creative activity. The term *goal* defines the image of the future desirable results indirectly connected with the motive. The achieved result of the action always contains something new in relation to the goal: by-products of a goal-oriented action, results of involuntary activeness of the subject. Besides needs and motives, the prerequisites of the generation of new goals in individual creative activity include (1) the assimilation of new knowledge about possible goals (results); (2) the reception of new demands for action; (3) the appearance of new results of individual actions; (4) the nonachievement of the anticipated results; and (5) the appearance of new, unrealized anticipations of the future results of the action. Transformation of demands into individual goals is one of the common variants of goal formation. In independent goal formation (i.e., when a directly formulated demand is lacking), the process can develop voluntarily or involuntarily (Tikhomirov, 1988, pp. 111–152).

Among the psychological mechanisms of goal formation are (1) transformation of motives into motive-goals with their realization; (2) transformation of by-products of action into goals by connecting them with the motive and realization of the result; (3) transformation of unrealized results into realized results; (4) isolation of intermediary goals as a function of an obstacle; (5) joint practical activity; (6) correlation of the object with several needs; and (7) partial satisfaction of the need by the object of this need (Tikhomirov, 1988, pp. 111–152).

In 1975 Leont'ev wrote that goal formation is "a process almost not studied at all" (p. 106). Today the situation is different. Among the objects of research are the role of motives and emotions in the acts of goal formation, the role of evaluations of the available possibilities of the object situation and of the perspectives of its transformation, the role of the evaluations of the attainability of the anticipated result, the role of memory, and the dependence of goal formation on meaning formation (Tikhomirov, 1988).

Studies of the operational content of activity include analysis of the generation of nonverbalized research operations, factors of their organization, and interrelations with verbalized operations. Differentiation between creative and routine activity demands not only a new approach to the traditional units of activity analysis from the viewpoint of their generation in the course of activity's self-development, but also the isolation of new components. Let me mention just two examples.

Studies of creative intellectual activity have shown that this activity includes both processes subjected to a conscious goal and nonverbalized anticipations of future results. The latter processes can be more intense than the goal-oriented actions themselves. Experimental studies of the generation of intermediary goals have demonstrated that nonverbalized anticipations may precede the formation of a new conscious goal, coexist with this goal and even behind it. Studies of goal formation have also shown that in the formation and functioning of the conscious goal, evaluations of the attainability of the result, unrealized by the subject, join in.

An important place in the analysis of creative activity belongs to studies of its emotional regulation. The following parameters are central in these analyses: (1) emotional saturation of the activity, (2) objective content (direction) of emotions, (3) characteristics of emotional fixation, (4) emotional targeting and correction, and (5) emotions' modality. Creative activity is characterized by the generation and complex dynamics of emotional evaluations, which appear as a new formation, no less meaningful than motives and goals (Tikhomirov, 1988, pp. 91–110).

Concrete human activity includes an "amalgamation" of creative and noncreative components. Depending on their domination, one can speak of a predominantly creative or noncreative activity. Attempts to proclaim every activity creative contradict the realities of division of labor in the society.

Psychological effects of the computerization of activity

Creative activity, while remaining the prerogative of humans, is considerably changed in the context of computer use. In conditions of computerization, a real development of creative activity can be witnessed.

New forms of creative work, education, and play appear, forms that are simply impossible without computers. At the same time, new types of stereotyped, routine activity appear.

Computerization typically entails sharp increases in external prestige motivation, as well as intensive development of personality's cognitive needs. We witness both fear of using computers and the unbridled optimism connected with their use. A transformation takes place in the whole system of motives, stable meanings of personality, and personality's goals in participating in the regulation of creative activity. One can also note a double tendency toward broadening the possibilities of creating and attaining goals, on the one hand, and toward narrowing these processes, on the other hand.

The contradictory character of the psychological effects of computerization makes it necessary to analyze these effects in a concrete fashion, to work purposefully toward positive results, and to correct possible negative consequences. All this demands a differentiated analysis with regard to different professional, ethnic, and age groups, as well as to computers of different types and generations, different languages and principles of programming. The computer is not only a universal data-processing device, it is also a universal means of influencing human activity and, consequently, the human psyche. This influence can be both purposeful and spontaneous. The specific character of such influence is defined, first of all, not by a computer, but by the organizational and social conditions of its use and by the characteristics of the activity.

Experimental psychological studies of goal formation as a manifestation of creativity in the dialogue with computers have shown the potential of broadening human creative activity. This potential is expressed in an increase in the number of formulated goals and in the heightening of their originality. It has been also demonstrated that the use of computers leads to a qualitative transformation of goal formation processes, manifested in new properties of the object situation that are unapproachable without computers. This change is also manifested in the broadening of the zone of independent selective search. At the same time, studies have shown that the development of creative activity in the computerized context can be considerably enhanced with the help of psychological maintenance of computerization. In the opposite case, there is a likelihood of the formation of a stereotyped, clichéd thinking supported by the computer's "authority" (Tikhomirov, 1988, pp. 180–190).

In performing any of the social roles when participating in a joint activity, one can isolate both routine and creative components. The transfer of routine components to the computer means its inclusion in the performance of a social role – and, consequently, the transformation of the content of the social roles. New roles appear.

Tikhomirov and Gurieva (1989) studied the psychological effects of computerization of the activity of psychodiagnosticians. The study included an analysis of the transformation of the motives of computerized activity, the changes in the processes of goal formation in this activity, and the changes in its operational content. The study used three evaluation scales: "positive vs. negative" effects, "real vs. potential" effects, and "governed vs. ungoverned" effects.

Real positive changes in the motivation of the psychodiagnosticians were expressed in the formation of "known" motives connected to the advantages of computer use. This manifested itself in the admission of the computer as a means and in the trust in its data.

Real negative changes in motivation were generated by the realization of computers' limited abilities in solving problems and by the discovery of technical defects in computers. The phenomena of "psychological barrier" and "hypertrust" were observed.

Potential positive changes in motivation consisted in the affirmation of the professional value of the psychodiagnosticians and in an emphasis on their responsibility for the results of computerized psychodiagnostics. Potential negative changes in motivation are based on faulty assessments of the importance of computer use in psychodiagnostic studies, which can lead to a broad dissemination of incorrect psychodiagnostic decisions.

Real positive changes in goal formation were connected to the reduction of certain stereotyped goals in the interpretation of test results and to the development of such goals as nonformalized analysis of test data, more qualitative interviews with the examined person, and a greater number of interviews in a specific period of time. More attention was paid to the concretization and specification of the goals initially formulated in a general form. The level of prognostic goal formation was rising.

Among real negative changes in goal formation were the setting of goals connected to the preparation, regulation, and control of the computer's results in the process of solving a psychodiagnostic problem (these computer-specific goals, though necessary to attain a productive result, have a less meaningful and auxiliary character; they make the achievement of a productive result more complex). Computerized testing of the examined persons without preliminary preparation makes them constrained and produces in them a fear of the computer as a technical device. This leads to unauthentic data or to a refusal to work with the computer. At this stage, a combination of manual and computerized types of activity makes it possible to optimize the process, but it simultaneously leads to lower productivity.

Potential positive changes in goal formation may consist in an optimal prevalence of creative components of computerized psychodiagnostic activity over the stereotyped components. Potential negative changes in goal formation are connected to setting inadequate or unrealistic goals – for example, the goal of full substitution of the psychodiagnostician by a computer.

Real positive changes in the activity's operational content consist in the reduction of the operational load and in the possibility of using the results of more perfect operations carried out by the computer. Real negative changes in the activity's operational content include new types of operations constituting auxiliary work with comparatively low social value and inefficiently performed sensomotoric operations, produced by inconvenient data presentation on the display, irrational organization of the computer keyboard, and deficient instructions and manuals. The tempo of operations dictated by the computer can also be negative.

Potential positive changes in the activity's operational content are noted in the course of learning, rationalization of the display, and the user's work routines. Potential negative changes in the operational content can consist in an inadequate evaluation of the importance of operations for efficient psychodiagnostic activity, which may lead to a lack of convergence between real and expected results and to the formation of hypertrust in computer data.

Activity theory and theory of artificial intelligence

Recent decades have seen an intensive interaction between psychology and the theory of artificial intelligence. Both psychologists and cognitive scientists have made many attempts to use the apparatus of artificial intelligence and the operational principles of artificial systems in the study of cognition, creativity, and behavior.

One manifestation of the influence of the theory of artificial intelligence is broad dissemination of ideas about creativity and activity as processes of algorithm realization. An *algorithm* is an instruction, the fulfillment of which guarantees the solution of a certain class of problems. This fulfilling of an instruction is sometimes declared to be an act of creativity and a model of human activity.

Our concept of creative activity can be interpreted as a nonalgorithmic model of creativity (Ponomarev & Saarinen, 1986, pp. 1–8). Creative activity is in a sense contrary to an algorithm, an "antialgorithm." The nonalgorithmic nature of motivational-emotional regulation is expressed in the fact that the need proper (as an unspecified state of want) lacks the "rules" of need's transfer into motive, which appears only as a result of a meeting between a need and the object of its satisfaction. The widening of the so-called insatiable needs – which include cognitive needs – is also not preprogrammed into the properties of needs. Relations between motives are also not fixed. They are established and changed in the course of activity's realization and can be especially complex in the situation of conflicting motives. Generation and transformation of emotional evaluations in activity are also not algorithmic. Relations between motives and goals can also be nonalgorithmic. The relation between goals and motives is especially ambiguous in situations of goal formation. The process of need satisfaction does not necessarily include the isolation of conscious goals. The transition from motive to goal and the goal formation process proper do not have an algorithmic character.

The theory of heuristic programming as part of the theory of artificial intelligence has attracted attention to the heuristic organization of the human search for solutions. Usually no consideration is given to the difference between formal and nonformal heuristic principles, selective mechanisms that can work on both verbalized and nonverbalized levels. The change in these mechanisms, the transition from one search zone to another, is an important trait of creative activity.

Let us now consider certain new aspects of the analysis of traditional structural components of activity. These new aspects become manifest as a result of interaction between activity theory and the theory of artificial intelligence.

Operations in the functioning of an artificial intelligence system differ from operations in the structure of human activity. Not all of the latter can be transferred to artificial systems. Human operations are not only performed, but also generated and transformed.

The term *goal*, which denotes the differentiating characteristic of action in the theory of activity, is also used in the theory of artificial intelligence. However, there it has a different meaning: a finite situation, set by a formal description (e.g., in the form of a list of indications), and achieved during the functioning of a certain system. In this context the goal loses its connection to the motive, which is crucial in the theory of activity.

Comparison of the motivational-emotional regulation of creative activity with the evaluating functions of artificial intelligence systems shows that humans use not only constant but also situationally occurring and dynamically changing evaluations. There is a considerable difference between verbal-logical and emotional evaluations. As to needs and motives, they are absent in artificial systems – which constitutes the main difference between the work of a human and that of a machine, a difference central to the theory of activity.

Taking into consideration the active development of expert systems, it is necessary to discuss the correlation between the categories "knowledge" and "activity." Knowledge can be a specific product initially generated by human thinking activity and a means of performing this activity. Knowledge can be reproduced – as in reproduction proper or in recalling. Along with formalized, easily described knowledge, there exists nonformalized (or ill-formalized) knowledge. It includes mundane notions, empirical generalizations, and complexes, which should not be regarded as second-rate.

From the viewpoint of the theory of creative activity, even such complex information technologies as expert systems do not reproduce human activity, though they transform it. Needs, goal formation, and the generation of emotional evaluations remain specifically human characteristics. However, activity theory and the theory of artificial intelligence are united by the necessity to develop a theory of activities that use artificial intelligence systems.

The dialogue between human and computer is characterized by the emerging personification of the computer, that is, its perception as an entity with certain personal traits and conscious properties and its corresponding treatment. Interaction between the human operator and the computer takes on more and more traits of joint activity (cooperation or rivalry). The need for communication with the computer is actualized. A motive of competition with the computer appears, manifested in the formation of goals such as "to win over the machine," "to take revenge on the machine," and so on.

The notion of *artificial* is connected with more than the discussion of computers' possibilities. Generally, this term denotes everything created by humans (Simon, 1969). Correlation of the artificial and nonartificial in human intellectual activity constitutes an important scientific problem, which can be reformulated as the problem of correlation between routine and creative processes. The former can be artificial, as they are produced by other people and adopted by the individual. The nonartificial in intellectual activity is not limited, in our opinion, to the natural prerequisites of this activity (Simon, 1969); it also relates to the new formations appearing in the course of activity. To ignore this type of the nonartificial is to ignore the creative nature of human intellectual activity.

In this context, it is necessary to specify the role of instruction in intellectual development, the thesis about the mind's social and historical development, with which the theory of activity is traditionally associated. The content of individual human experience includes not only mastered social experience, but also personal experience, the experience of an activity's realization, which determines the readiness and selectiveness of acquisition.

Social experience is transferred not only to other people, but also to information technology – for instance, in the form of computer programs. In this connection, we must differentiate between the processes of "appropriation" of social experience by a human being and by a computer. Such differentiation is decisive for the evaluation of the concept of psychology as a "science of the artificial"; it leads to broader notions about the functions of human activity.

In successfully acquiring and mastering specific social experience, a human being also accumulates certain personal experience – for example, in the form of traces of emotional experiences generated by the first acquaintance with the material, by deeper acquaintance with the material, and so on. One of the regularities of individual psychological development is that in appropriating sociohistorical experience, one also acquires individual experience. This annuls both counterposition and identification of social and individual experience, as well as differentiating between the processes of appropriation of social experience by humans and by computers.

Conscious intellectual activity of human beings is governed by objective circumstances, that is, those not dependent on the will of persons living in society, setting certain goals and attaining these goals, never able to foresee all the consequences of their actions. This thesis remains valid in regard to instructional and educational activity, and does not allow us to adopt the opinion that a single person's activity and psyche are nothing more than the product of surrounding people, that they are artificial. From the viewpoint of the theory of creative activity, psychology cannot be regarded as a science of the artificial.

Conclusion

The development of informatics and information technology not only produces considerable changes in human activity, it requires development of the theory of activity. This theory has a new function: to interpret the psychological nature of human activity in the information society and the challenges it presents to the development of psychological science.

References

Kaloshina, I. P. (1985). *Normative analysis of creative activity.* Moscow: MGU (in Russian).

Leont'ev, A. N. (1975). *Activity, consciousness, and personality.* Moscow: Misl (in Russian).

Lomov, B. F., & Anzyferova, L. (Eds.). (1989). *Tendencies in the development of psychological science.* Moscow: Nauka (in Russian).

Ponomarev, J. A., & Saarinen, L. (Eds.). (1986). *Proceedings of the first Finnish–Soviet symposium on creativity.* Helsinki: Suomen ja Neuvostoliiton välinen tieteellis-tekninen yhteistoimintakomitea.

Simon, H. A. (1969). *The sciences of the artificial.* Cambridge, MA: MIT Press.

Tikhomirov, O. K. (1988). *Psychology of thinking.* Moscow: Progress.

Tikhomirov, O. K. (1989). *Vygotsky's theory as methodological basis for crosscultural study of the impact of information technology in education on child psychological development.* Paper presented at the Third International Conference, "Children in the Information Age," Sofia, May 19–23.

Tikhomirov, O. K., & Gurieva, L. P. (1989). The experience of analyzing the psychological effects of computerization of psychodiagnostic activity. *Psychologicheskii zhurnal, 2,* 33–45 (in Russian).

22 Activity theory, transformation of work, and information systems design

Kari Kuutti

Introduction

We are living in a period of transition – a search for a new paradigm for information systems (IS) is going on. New research approaches, based on different assumptions, are emerging, and the discussion is being broadened and intensified. At the core of the debate lies the question of how to handle contextuality in IS design and therefore in IS research. It now seems to be generally accepted that designing the technical "core system" alone is insufficient, and that in order to design and implement a successful IS some kind of "context" has to be taken into account – a context that includes people and their relations. Thus, the question is how to obtain reliable, useful results when the object of study belongs – at least partially – to the realm of the social sciences.

Earlier there was also much discussion about the technical or social nature of IS and the practical consequences of this distinction – how social systems can be studied and developed. During the 1970s, the original, strictly technologically oriented view was challenged by the "sociotechnical" school of design, which gained a firm footing especially in the United Kingdom and Scandinavia. During the 1980s, however, the differentiation of research approaches gained new momentum and considerable visibility, with the emergence of a new wave of approaches. These sought their conceptual foundation in the realms of the various social sciences and proceeded much further than the sociotechnical school has done. The Manchester colloquium of 1984 (Mumford, Hirschheim, Fitzgerald, & Wood-Harper, 1985) was an open manifestation of this diversity, and the search for a new conceptual base for IS research and design was one of the main themes of the ISRA-90 conference (Nissen, Klein, & Hirschheim, 1991).

The purpose of this chapter is to inquire why this discussion has developed just now. It is suggested that the main reason may be the ongoing transformation in the organization of work. The relationship between work and information technology is nowadays very close – in fact, the implementation of IS may be the most common means of changing the way work is done in organizations. Thus, changes in work will commonly occur through IS development projects. The newly organized work will need a new kind of support from information technology. These needs cannot be studied using the old concepts, hence the search for new frameworks and background theories.

In the following section, I give an overview of the IS research discussion, based on some earlier attempts to classify this discussion. I then analyze the ongoing transformation of work organization and compare the needs of this changing work with the goals of the new IS research and design approaches. They are found to be quite similar. After that, I discuss some major problems in recent IS research and compare them with the properties of activity theory. The latter is found to be a promising alternative as a new background theory for IS research and design.

The debate surrounding information systems research

The ongoing debate regarding paradigmatic questions within IS research has been characterized by Klein and Hirschheim in the following way:

It is possible, therefore, to speak of an IS orthodoxy, one where fundamental tenets are shared and form a general conception of how information systems can and should be developed. Recently, however, it is possible to note the emergence of some radically different approaches to ISD [information systems design], ones which do not share the same paradigm, which possess an underlying philosophy that is quite different from the orthodoxy, and which challenge the basic assumptions, values and beliefs of the past. (Klein & Hirschheim, 1987, pp. 275–276)

A review of this long debate in depth is beyond the scope of this chapter. Only a short overview will be given. This can be done conveniently and, for our purposes, accurately enough by using some recent attempts to classify the discussion, namely, those presented by Bansler (1989), Hirschheim and Klein (1989), Iivari (1991), and Nurminen (1988).

Bansler and Nurminen

Because the classifications proposed by Nurminen and Bansler overlap significantly, they are here considered together. Bansler restricts his analysis by considering only Scandinavian research traditions, whereas Nurminen attempts to be more general.

	Systems theoretical tradition	Sociotechnical tradition	Critical tradition
Knowledge interest	profit maximizing	job satisfaction participation	industrial democracy
Notion of the organization	cybernetic system	sociotechnical system	framework for conflicts
Notion of the labor force	objects (systems components)	actors (individuals)	actors (groups)
Notion of capital/ labor relations	common interests	common interests	opposing interests

Figure 22.1.   Classification of IS research traditions proposed by Bansler (1988).

Both Bansler and Nurminen have found three major directions of research. Nurminen calls them *systems theoretical, sociotechnical,* and *humanistic.* Bansler also has a systems theoretical and a sociotechnical faction, but he names the third one *critical.* He condenses the classification as shown in Figure 22.1.

The classification proposed by Nurminen can be condensed as in Figure 22.2. According to Nurminen, the main emphasis in the emerging new approach is on recognizing active, individual subjects. For Bansler, the main factor separating the new from the old is the recognition and acceptance of conflicts. Both have a similar view of the systems theoretical and sociotechnical schools. Both connect the systems theoretical tradition with Tayloristic work organization.

The basic ideas of the theory of information systems are in many respects identical with the ideas expressed by Taylor in his "Principles of Scientific Management" from the beginning of this century. Taylor and the system theoretical school share the same mechanistic view of organizations, and they have the same goals – control and regularity. (Bansler, 1989, s. 9)

Hirschheim and Klein

The classification of Hirschheim and Klein is based on the influential work of Burrell and Morgan (1979), who derived their classification from an analysis of general social theories applied to organizational theories. Hirschheim and Klein go one step further and apply the classification to the IS domain: "We see the framework proposed by Burrell and Morgan – with some modification – as best depicting the different classes

	Systems theoretical	Socio-technical	Humanistic
Ideal type	integrated total system	no clear type	personal systems
Notion of knowledge	objectivistic	objectivistic, some instrumental	subjectivistic
Notion of human being	rational system element	Theory Y	individualistic
Notion of actions	according to rules	humans as actors, IS also actor	humans only actors, IS tool
Notion of communication	IS equal comm. partner	IS equal comm. partner + unofficial comm.	all communication between humans
Notion of organization	Tayloristic, bureaucratic	two parallel systems, bureaucratic	handicraft-like
Notion of IS development	by experts; use and development separated	users notified, design of social system	by users, incremental

Figure 22.2. Classification of IS research traditions proposed by Nurminen (1988).

of systems development approaches, relatively speaking" (Hirschheim & Klein, 1989, s. 23).

The authors recognize four classes, which they term *functionalism, social relativism, radical structuralism,* and *neohumanism.* Their characterizations are extended in Figure 22.3 to the corresponding system developers, and some references are made to projects in which such approaches have been implemented.

Iivari

Iivari's analysis (Iivari, 1991) adopts a different viewpoint, studying only those approaches that are documented in textbooks. This method has the drawback, or benefit, that only stabilized, influential approaches are considered. Iivari recognizes the existence of seven well-established schools:

1. Software engineering
2. Database management
3. Management information systems

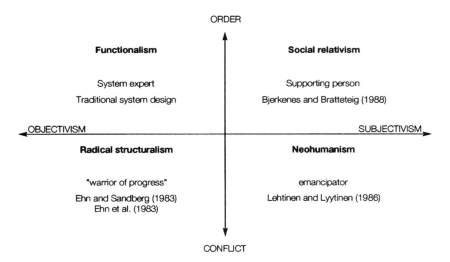

Figure 22.3. Classification of IS research traditions proposed by Hirschheim and Klein (1989).

4. Decision support systems
5. Implementation research
6. Sociotechnical approach
7. Infological approach

Iivari's goal is not to construct a clear-cut typology. His framework has several dimensions with more accurate classes that are not mutually exclusive. There are similarities to the framework of Burrell and Morgan, but Iivari has taken into account criticisms leveled against these authors.

Iivari's results are remarkably similar over the various approaches. Their ontological assumptions are basically the same, the main distinguishing feature being the range of social aspects considered relevant. Their epistemological assumptions are unanimously positivistic, although there is more variance in the methodologies than one would expect. Their ethical values are means–end oriented and depend mainly on the economic goals of the organizations, although there are also some other criteria.

Comparison

Although differences exist between the classifications, there are also considerable similarities, and some conclusions can be drawn. For the first, the results of Iivari seem to prove that there really exists an

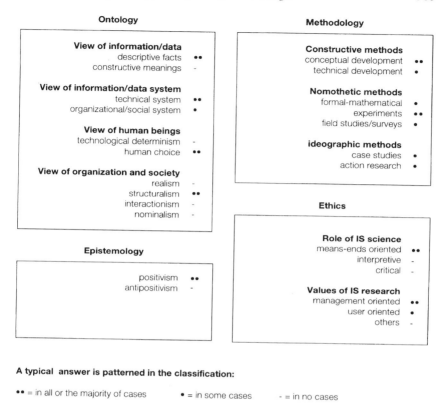

A typical answer is patterned in the classification:

•• = in all or the majority of cases   • = in some cases   - = in no cases

Figure 22.4. Iivari's (1994) classification of IS research approaches.

"orthodoxy," a group of schools that to a great extent share basic assumptions. Simplifying slightly, we can state that the whole group belongs to the functionalist class in Hirschheim and Klein's classification. Iivari's results nevertheless show that it is also incorrect to consider the group as a whole except in the roughest of analyses.

Second, both Bansler and Nurminen consider the sociotechnical school as an entirely separate class, but Iivari sees only minor differences and Hirschheim and Klein do not identify it at all. We could perhaps interpret this as suggesting that for Bansler and Nurminen the sociotechnical school is "more close to the origo" than the others in the functionalist class.

Third, although Bansler and Nurminen have partially the same classes, there is some "orthogonality" in their classifications. Both seem to use only one axis of the Hirschheim and Klein classification — and not the same one. Bansler makes his distinctions only in the order–conflict classification, whereas Nurminen is interested only in features found in the subjectivistic–objectivistic classification.

To summarize, there seems to be a consensus regarding an orthodoxy, from which the sociotechnical approach can be distinguished more or less accurately. In addition, a variety of clearly distinguishable emerging new approaches are identified as the opposition.

Reasons for the emergence of the new approaches

How is the emergence of alternative approaches explained by the authors? Iivari does not consider the reasons for this development, because he concentrates only on orthodoxy. But Bansler sees his three phases in a temporal succession:

1. Systems theoretical tradition: Close connection to Tayloristic work organization – and with its problems.
2. Sociotechnical tradition: Criticism of Taylorism and a search for consensus by developing work satisfaction. Originates in opposition to strictly technological systems and in the spread of sociotechnical ideas in working life.
3. Critical tradition: Criticism of consensus and support for workers in alliance with trade unions. Originates in the change in trade union attitudes: growing attention paid to detrimental influences on labor.

Nurminen sees relationships between the systems theoretical and sociotechnical views in a quite similar way to Bansler. He does not see the emergence of the humanistic view as resulting from opposition to consensus, explaining it more by the need for a new, decentralized type of system.

Hirschheim and Klein explain this development by suggesting that functionalistic orthodoxy has encountered problems of systems legislation and implementation caused by insufficient understanding of the basic social nature of IS. The new approaches are attempts to overcome these problems by starting with different basic assumptions and values. Hirschheim and Klein recognize that the origin of change lies in the new values and attitudes accepted by individual designers. In an earlier paper, the authors summarized their explanation as follows.

We postulate that the divergence of perspectives and methods in recent information systems development research can be explained by the following fundamental conjecture: there exists a link between new research directions in information systems development and social change in society, such that all of the alternatives to the currently accepted ISD orthodoxy are inspired by the same kind of forces or influences that in general drive social change in industrial societies. Social change thus affects which approaches to ISD are socially acceptable and appropriate. The question of how social change actually affects the emergence of new directions in IS and ISD research has not received much attention by the IS community.

The basic contention, and the line of reasoning to argue its case, is that research interests in general are inextricably bound up with societal norms, values and beliefs. If society changes, so too will its values and beliefs. As such changes are likely to cause dissatisfaction with old beliefs and norms which govern existing practices of ISD, the latter is eventually forced to change in a way which is consistent with societal change, or to justify its current approaches and results in a different way. (Klein & Hirschheim, 1987, p. 276)

I agree with the first part of the argument – that the emergence of new perspectives is caused by a change in society. But the second part – that the change is channeled into ISD research through changing values and attitudes – is more problematic. Although values are certainly changing, one could perhaps establish more direct and objective links between societal change and new perspectives. In the following section, I consider the ongoing change in work organization in order to gain a better insight into this question.

Discussion on new forms of work organization

In order to distinguish the new from the old, some kind of historical perspective is necessary. Here I use the following simple model of ideal types to describe the historical development of work organization (Figure 22.5).

The term *handicraft* refers to a type of work in which the methods and tools develop or have been developed mainly in practical situations. Using the terms of Braverman (1974), conception and execution are still united. The outcome is not strictly defined beforehand but may evolve during the process. The tools used are simple and not based on theoretical mastery of the properties of the object of the work, but have gradually evolved during a long tradition.

The archetypal work organization is the master–apprentice relationship in traditional craft workshops, in which a novice learns the tacit knowledge required to perform his tasks and tacit skills for their execution during his apprenticeship by growing into a particular work culture. The craftsman is the active subject of his work.

The term *Taylorized* refers to the type of work that has evolved since the beginning of the Industrial Revolution, the ideas of which are perhaps

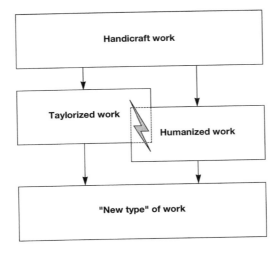

Figure 22.5. Ideal types of work organization.

most clearly stated in the works of F. W. Taylor on *scientific management*. Even though Taylorism is no longer very popular, much shop floor work is still of this type. Tacit knowledge is not sufficient: Knowledge concerning the objects and methods of production must be collected and objectified, often at the level of scientific reasoning. The objectified knowledge is embodied many times over in machines and detailed instructions. The real subject of the work is management, whose motives guide the outcome and process. A well-known problem of such *rationalized* work is alienation – manifested in difficulty in maintaining the motivation of workers who have no control over their work process or its results, which in turn causes problems of quality assurance and other problems. According to Braverman (1974), the crucial idea of scientific management is the strict separation of conception from execution. The archetypal organization of work is the assembly line, where work consists of simple, repetitive operations and its pace is determined by the line.

   The term *humanized* refers to the type of work that has evolved in opposition to the rationalized type and as an answer to the problems created by it. Its origins lie in the sociotechnical school. This approach directs attention to the human resources of an organization and attempts to motivate the workers by giving them more control over their work. There are two major levels in humanized work: (1) arrangements at the individual level, such as job rotation, job enlargement, and job enrichment, and (2) more fundamental work reorganization, typically by forming semiautonomous

QWL in the 1970s	High performance in the 1990s
personnel administration technique	human resource management strategy
aims to reduce costs of absenteeism and labor turnover and increase productivity	aims to improve organizational flexibility and product quality for competitive advantage
based on argument that increased autonomy improves quality of work experience and employee job satisfaction	based on argument that increased autonomy improves skills, decision making, adaptability, and use of new technology
had little impact on the management function beyond firstline supervision	involves change in organizational culture and re-definition of management functions at all levels
quick fix applied to isolated and problematic work groups	takes 2 to 3 years to change attitudes and behavior throughout the organization

Figure 22.6. Major differences between humanized (quality of working life) and new (high-performance) types of work (after Buchanan & McCalman, 1989, p. 63).

work groups in which some parts of the design and planning of the work process are done by the workers themselves. Autonomy is restricted to the work process, however; the workers have no influence on product design and many other matters. A limited amount of conception with regard to the process has been "given back" to the workers in this model.

How can the emerging new type of work be separated from the humanized type? Buchanan and McCalman (1989) maintain that although some ideas developed during the initial period of humanization are still useful, the overall situation has changed so radically that the humanized and new types are incompatible. They condense the differences into the table shown in Figure 22.6.

What are the most obvious distinguishing features of the new work organization, and what kind of new worker is needed? The following quotations each describe some aspect of the emerging new form of organization.

If there is a hidden thread connecting these principles, it is that knowledge workers are the only corporate assets that last. They embrace machines and engender new systems, which they ultimately outgrow. (Clark, 1989, p. 98)

Workers will need a broader range of skills in order to perform a greater variety of tasks as they adopt a systems approach to the new technology. Many technicians already work in common design networks and have to cooperate across job boundaries with theoretical knowledge matched by diagnostic skills. (Gerwin, Sorge, & Warner, 1986)

Such *intelligent* organizations are ephemeral, formed when problems surface, disbanded when they are solved; they often include suppliers and other people from the outside. The structure they assume is based on how the problem is posed. A company's ultimate

Features of the "new work"	Desirable "new" system properties
flexibility	flexibility
integration	communication support
continuously evolving	craft enhancement
cooperation	group work support
own work planning and control	personal tools, human-scale systems
theoretical thinking with models, better understanding of work	understandability, visibility as systems attributes
large, flexible assortment of skills	skill conservation and development
new motivation, responsibility for a larger area than own tasks	emancipation of interests, democratization of working life

Figure 22.7. Comparison between features of the new work organization and the properties needed in new information systems.

success, therefore, depends on how effectively it can shift from measuring and controlling costs to choosing and managing projects that enhance its organizational capabilities. . . . They push at the margins of their expertise, trying on every front to be better than before. They strive to be dynamic, *learning* organizations. . . . Worker skills are critical to a company's success; a layoff could mean permanent loss of that resource. At the same time, companies need to encourage cooperation among workers, to reinforce the value of long-term employment. People work best with people they know. The most important variable costs for an advanced manufacturing company may well be the costs of training and retraining people. (Hayes & Jaikumar, 1988, pp. 84–85)

Workers at all levels add value not solely or even mostly by tending machines and carrying out routines, but by continuously discovering opportunities for improvement in product and process. (Reich, 1987, pp. 80–81)

For workers, this path means accepting flexible job classifications and work rules; agreeing to wage rates linked to profits and productivity improvements; and generally taking greater responsibility for the soundness and efficiency of the enterprise. (Reich, 1987, p. 83)

The *informated* organization does move in another direction. It relies on human capacities for teaching and learning, criticism and insight. It implies an approach to business improvement that rests upon the improvement and innovation made possible by the enhanced comprehensibility of the core processes. It reflects a fertile interdependence between the human mind and some of its most sophisticated productions. (Zuboff, 1988, p. 414)

The characteristic features of the emerging new type of work are compared in Figure 22.7 with the desired properties of IS, as expressed by the opposition in the IS debate. The IS properties are collected from

Alvarez and Klein (1989), Bansler (1989), Hirschheim and Klein (1989), and Nurminen (1988).

The lists in Figure 22.7 show a remarkable similarity. It is evident that the link between the demands for developing work and attempts to generate a new paradigm for IS research is much more direct than has thus far been recognized within the IS debate. The transforming of work needs new kinds of support and poses new problems. Old conceptual tools are inadequate for solving them, and the IS debate is searching for new frameworks for doing precisely that.

Activity theory and problems of IS research

What kinds of problems are faced by the IS community? At the most general level, three areas of difficulty can be defined: IS research should be able to deal with active individuals, societal change, and multi-disciplinarity.

Traditionally, the users of IS have been treated as more or less passive and predetermined parts of organizational information processing machinery. This view has been one of the major objects of criticism in the IS debate. Information systems should be able to support active individuals while still preserving the organizational viewpoint. This has been difficult to achieve within the existing frameworks of IS research and design.

It is interesting to note that besides the debate within IS research, there is another one going on within the human–computer interaction (HCI) research community, especially since it seems to be centered on questions very similar to those affecting the whole IS level (see Bannon, 1990a; Carroll, 1991). One of the major criticisms in that debate concerns the neglect of active individuals, as expressed in the slogan "From human factors to human actors" (Bannon, 1990b).

This discussion is mostly restricted to the individual level. However, there is a third discussion concerning the same themes in which the collective and societal levels are also taken into account. Research on computer-supported cooperative work (CSCW) gained popularity very rapidly during the latter half of the 1980s, and it is apparent that the "co-operative work" referred to by many authors is very close to the "new type of work" described earlier (Bannon & Schmidt, 1991; Lyytinen, 1989; Sørgaard, 1987).

In studying the context of an IS, one becomes aware of topics that definitely belong to some other discipline, such as psychology, social psychology, sociology, or economics. IS research should be able to take these into account and use them as parts of the whole picture. But if research results from several different disciplines should be used, how can they be fitted together? Currently, each researcher tends to use his or her own framework and concepts, which rarely are integrated or even comparable to any marked extent.

As if the problem of contextuality is not difficult enough, the situation is made far worse by the fact that contexts are not static. The larger the context we try to study, the more probable it is that it will be in a state of change, driven by factors that we should be able to recognize and utilize. On the other hand, designing an IS should mean mastering change in its context. Again, the conceptual tools for analysis and design contain the implicit assumption of a static, well-defined environment.

A wide variety of approaches have been suggested to enable IS research to cope with the situation, many of them based on some recognized theoretical framework such as transaction cost theory (Ciborra, 1987), speech act theory (Lyytinen & Lehtinen, 1984), critical social theory (Lyytinen & Klein, 1985; Ngwenyama, 1991), grounded theory (Calloway & Ariav, 1991; Toraskar, 1991), phenomenology (Boland, 1985; Ratswohl, 1991), hermeneutics (Boland, 1991), or semiotics (Andersen, 1991), to name just a few. However, no one approach has yet been able to make a major breakthrough and establish a new standard paradigm. Could activity theory do any better?

Thus far, only a handful of researchers have made the first groping attempts to apply activity theory in the IS research field (for a recent collection, see Nardi, 1996). However, it can already be seen that the theory has interesting features that may be beneficial.

Activity theory may help maintain adequately the relationship between the individual and social levels in the objects to be studied, especially in situations where there is a need to grasp emergent features in individual and social transformation. This notion is supported by the fact that activity theory has already been applied, at different levels, to HCI problems (Bødker, 1989; Bannon & Bødker, 1991), CSCW (Engeström, Engeström, & Saarelma, 1988; Kuutti, 1991b), and information systems (Bødker, 1991; Kuutti, 1991a).

By its very nature, activity theory is multidisciplinary. If we hold to the basic assumption that activities are minimal meaningful objects of study – the *molar units* of Leont'ev (1978) – in which essentially human qualities have to be taken into account, we must then admit that activities as wholes cannot be exhaustively studied by any individual discipline. In fact, one arrives at the conclusion that several disciplines should actually have the same context with respect to the research object, namely, the context formed by activity. Although they are focused on different aspects of activity, all the other context-forming parts must be also taken into account in order to preserve the validity of the research. This common context of the object of study could dramatically enhance the possibilities for different disciplines to discuss with and benefit from each other. This is a research program rather than an actual situation, of course, but steps have already been taken in that direction.

Activity theory has elaborated a conceptual apparatus for studying and mastering developmental processes. It regards contexts as dynamic systems mediated by cultural artifacts. Moreover, activity contexts are seen as internally contradictory formations, which implies transformations and discontinuous development.

Finally, activity theory is interventionist in its methodological approach. Seeing humans as creators of their activity contexts, it aims at reconstructing contexts in practice so that people are not just objects or subordinate parts but regain their role as creators. Accepting this challenge leads to approaches such as *developmental work research,* a relatively recent application of activity theory in work organizations (Engeström, 1991).

Conclusion

This chapter is a broad overview, bringing together three general topics: IS debate, discussion of new forms of organizing work, and activity theory. There is a connection between the ongoing transformation of work and the paradigmatic problems in IS research. New approaches must be established in order to master the change, and since activity theory was developed precisely to study individual and social transformation, it is a strong candidate for forming a background for such new approaches. The potential of activity theory must be demonstrated in practice. This can be done only within concrete IS development projects.

References

Alvarez, R., & Klein, H. K. (1989). Information systems development for human progress? In H. K. Klein & K. Kumar (Eds.), *Systems development for human progress* (pp. 1–20). Amsterdam: North-Holland.

Andersen, P. B. (1991). A semiotic approach to construction and assessment of computer systems. In H.-E. Nissen, H. K. Klein, & R. Hirschheim (Eds.), *Information systems research arena of the 90's* (pp. 465–514). Amsterdam: Elsevier.

Bannon, L. (1990a). From cognitive science to cooperative design. In *Proceedings of a symposium on theories and technologies of the information society* (pp. 33–58). Aarhus: Centre for Cultural Research, Aarhus University.

Bannon, L. (1990b). From human factors to human actors: The role of psychology and human–computer interaction in systems design. In J. Greenbaum & M. Kyng (Eds.), *Design at work* (pp. 25–44). Hillsdale: Lawrence Erlbaum.

Bannon, L., & Bødker, S. (1991). Beyond the interface: Encountering artifacts in use. In J. M. Carroll (Ed.), *Designing interaction: Psychological theory at the human–computer interface* (pp. 227–253). Cambridge: Cambridge University Press.

Bannon, L., & Schmidt, K. (1991). CSCW: Four characters in search of a context? In J. M. Bowers and S. D. Benford (Eds.), *Studies in computer supported cooperative work* (pp. 3–17). Amsterdam: North-Holland.

Bansler, J. (1989). Systems development research in Scandinavia: Three theoretical schools. *Scandinavian Journal in Information Systems, 1*(1), 3–20.

Bødker, S. (1989). A human activity approach to user interfaces. *Human–Computer Interaction, 4*(3), 171–195.

Bødker, S. (1991). Activity theory as a challenge to systems design. In H.-E. Nissen, H. K. Klein, & R. Hirschheim (Eds.), *Information systems research arena of the 90's* (pp. 551–564). Amsterdam: Elsevier.

Boland, R. J. (1985). Phenomenology: A preferred approach to research on information systems. In E. Mumford, R. Hirschheim, G. Fitzgerald, & A. T. Wood-Harper (Eds.), *Research methods in information systems* (pp. 193–201). Amsterdam: North-Holland.

Boland, R. J. (1991). Information systems use as a hermeneutic process. In H.-E. Nissen, H. K. Klein, & R. Hirschheim (Eds.), *Information systems research arena of the 90's* (pp. 439–458). Amsterdam: Elsevier.

Braverman, H. (1974). *Labor and monopoly capital.* New York: Monthly Review Press.

Buchanan, D. A., & McCalman, J. (1989). *High performance work systems: The digital experience.* London: Routledge.

Burrell, G., & Morgan, G. (1979). *Sociological paradigms and organizational analysis.* London: Heinemann.

Calloway, L. J., & Ariav, G. (1991). Developing and using qualitative methodology to study relationships among designers and tools. In H.-E. Nissen, H. K. Klein, & R. Hirschheim (Eds.), *Information systems research arena of the 90's* (pp. 175–194). Amsterdam: Elsevier.

Carroll, J. M. (Ed.). (1991). *Designing interaction: Psychological theory at the human–computer interface.* Cambridge: Cambridge University Press.

Ciborra, C. U. (1987). Research agenda for a transaction cost approach to information systems. In R. Boland & R. Hirschheim (Eds.), *Critical issues in information systems research* (pp. 253–274). Chichester: Wiley.

Clark, K. B. (1989). What strategy can do for technology. *Harvard Business Review, 67*(6), 94–98.

Engeström, Y. (1991). Developmental work research: Reconstructing expertise through expansive learning. In M. I. Nurminen & G. R. S. Weir (Eds.), *Human jobs and computer interfaces.* Amsterdam: Elsevier.

Engeström, Y., Engeström, R., & Saarelma, O. (1988). Computerized medical records, production pressure and compartmentalization in the work activity of health center physicians. In *Proceedings of the 2nd Conference on Computer-Supported Cooperative Work* (pp. 65–84). New York: ACM.

Gerwin, D., Sorge, A., & Warner, M. (1986). The role of human resources in the computerized factory. *Human Systems Management, 6*(3), 193–196.

Hayes, R. H., & Jaikumar, R. (1988). Manufacturing's crisis: New technologies, obsolete organizations. *Harvard Business Review, 66*(5), 77–85.

Hirschheim, R., & Klein, H. (1989). Four paradigms of information systems development. *Communications of the ACM, 32*(10), 1199–1216.

Iivari, J. (1991). A paradigmatic analysis of contemporary schools of IS development. *European Journal on Information Systems, 1*(4), 249–272.

Klein, H., & Hirschheim, R. (1987). Social change and the future of information systems development. In R. Boland & R. Hirschheim (Eds.), *Critical issues in information systems research* (pp. 275–305). Chichester: Wiley.

Kuutti, K. (1991a). Activity theory and its applications to information systems research and design. In H.-E. Nissen, H. K. Klein, & R. Hirschheim (Eds.), *Information systems research arena of the 90's* (pp. 529–550). Amsterdam: Elsevier.

Kuutti, K. (1991b). The concept of activity as a basic unit for CSCW research. In L. J. Bannon, M. Robinson, & K. Schmidt (Eds.), *Proceedings of the 2nd ECSCW* (pp. 249–264). Amsterdam: Kluwer.

Leont'ev, A. N. (1978). *Activity, consciousness, and personality.* Englewood Cliffs: Prentice-Hall.

Lyytinen, K. (1989). *Computer-supported cooperative work – issues and challenges.* Manuscript. University of Jyväskylä, Department of Computer Science.

Lyytinen, K., & Klein, H. K. (1985). The critical theory of Jürgen Habermas and information systems. In E. Mumford, R. Hirschheim, G. Fitzgerald, & A. T. Wood-Harper (Eds.), *Research methods in information systems* (pp. 219–235). Amsterdam: North-Holland.

Lyytinen, K., & Lehtinen, E. (1984). Discourse analysis as information system specification method. In M. Sääksjärvi (Ed.), *Report of the 7th Scandinavian research seminar on systemeering* (pp. 146–198). Helsinki: Helsinki School of Economics.

Mumford, E., Hirschheim, R., Fitzgerald, G., & Wood-Harper, A. T. (Eds.). (1985). *Research methods in information systems.* Amsterdam: North-Holland.

Nardi, B. (Ed.). (1996). *Context and consciousness: Activity theory and human–computer interaction.* Cambridge, MA: MIT Press.

Nissen, H.-E., Klein, H. K., & Hirschheim, R. (Eds.). (1991). *The information systems research arena of the 1990s: Challenges, perceptions and alternative approaches.* Amsterdam: North-Holland.

Ngwenyama, O. K. (1991). The critical social theory approach to information systems: Problems and challenges. In H.-E. Nissen, H. K. Klein, & R. Hirschheim (Eds.), *Information systems research arena of the 90's* (pp. 267–280). Amsterdam: Elsevier.

Nurminen, M. (1988). *People or computers: Three ways of looking at information systems.* Lund: Studentlitteratur.

Ratswohl, E. J. (1991). Applying Don Idhe's phenomenology of instrumentation as a framework for designing research in information science. In H.-E. Nissen, H. K. Klein, & R. Hirschheim (Eds.), *Information systems research arena of the 90's* (pp. 421–438). Amsterdam: Elsevier.

Reich, R. B. (1987). Entrepreneurship reconsidered: The team as hero. *Harvard Business Review, 65*(3), 77–83.

Sørgaard, P. (1987). A cooperative work perspective on use and development of computer artifacts. In P. Järvinen (Ed.), *Report of the 10th IRIS seminar.* Acta Universitatis Tamperensis B 27 (pp. 719–734). Tampere: University of Tampere.

Toraskar, K. (1991). How managerial users evaluate their decision support. A grounded theory approach. In H.-E. Nissen, H. K. Klein, & R. Hirschheim (Eds.), *Information systems research arena of the 90's* (pp. 195–226). Amsterdam: Elsevier.

Zuboff, S. (1988). *In the age of the smart machine: The future of work and power.* New York: Basic Books.

23 Innovative learning in work teams: Analyzing cycles of knowledge creation in practice

Yrjö Engeström

Introduction

Innovative organizational learning is collaborative learning in work organizations that produces new solutions, procedures, or systemic transformations in organizational practices (Engeström, 1995). Studies of innovative organizational learning have thus far produced relatively general conceptual tools (e.g., Argyris & Schön, 1978; Senge, 1990). Although it is commonly acknowledged that innovative learning at work has a complex cyclic character (e.g., Dixon, 1994), there have been few detailed attempts to theorize about such cycles and to model their steps as they occur in learning processes in work teams.

One of the most interesting attempts is the recent book by Nonaka and Takeuchi (1995). These authors focus exclusively on innovative learning, which they prefer to call *knowledge creation* in organizations. Nonaka and Takeuchi propose a theory of knowledge on which they build a model of cycles of knowledge production. Their examples are drawn primarily from practices and cases of new product development in Japanese companies.

In my research projects on work teams in American and Finnish organizations, we have identified and analyzed a number of innovative learning processes within and between teams (for recent examples, see Engeström, 1994a, 1995; Engeström, Engeström, & Kärkkäinen, 1995). We typically videotape series of team meetings and interactions at work and analyze transcripts of these interactions as our prime data. This approach enables us to conduct very detailed data-driven analyses of the discursive processes, practical actions, and mediating artifacts that are employed in the step-by-step production of an innovative solution or idea.

On the other hand, my analyses employ theoretical tools from cultural-historical activity theory and developmental work research (see Engeström, 1987, 1991a, 1993a). Three characteristics make this theoretical

377

framework particularly well suited for analyses of innovative learning at work. First, activity theory is deeply contextual and oriented at understanding historically specific local practices, their objects, mediating artifacts, and social organization (Cole & Engeström, 1993). Second, activity theory is based on a dialectical theory of knowledge and thinking, focused on the creative potential in human cognition (Il'enkov, 1977; Davydov, 1990). Third, activity theory is a developmental theory that seeks to explain and influence qualitative changes in human practices over time.

In this chapter, I discuss the applicability of the theoretical framework of Nonaka and Takeuchi (1995) in analyses of learning and problem solving in teams. This discussion makes evident certain advantages but also certain shortcomings of the framework, calling for alternative and complementary approaches. I present a conceptual framework based on activity theory and on the theory of expansive learning (Engeström, 1987). As concrete examples, I analyze an innovative learning process that took place in two successive meetings of a shop floor work team located in a large machining plant in southern California. I conclude with a discussion of the uses of the two theoretical frameworks as toolkits for understanding innovative learning in work teams.

Nonaka and Takeuchi's cycle as a framework of explanation

Nonaka and Takeuchi's (1995) theory of knowledge creation is based on a matrix of conversions between tacit and explicit knowledge. The matrix leads to a cyclic model of phases (Figure 23.1). The process of knowledge creation begins with socialization, or sharing of tacit, sympathized knowledge. The next phase is construction of explicit conceptual knowledge, also called *creating concepts*. After that, there is the phase of combining and constructing systemic knowledge, also called *justifying concepts*. Finally, the product is converted into operational and internalized knowledge. The authors divide this phase into two: *building an archetype* and *cross-leveling knowledge*. In a complex process of new product development, for example, this cycle is repeated over and over again.

Nonaka and Takeuchi present their theory in universal terms. Yet their concrete cases are taken from large-scale processes of new product development over extended periods of time. Curiously, they all but neglect the small cycles of team-based continuous improvement, or *kaizen*, commonly seen as the foundation of creative renewal in Japanese companies.

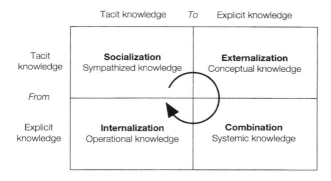

Figure 23.1. The cycle of four modes of knowledge conversion (adapted from Nonaka and Takeuchi, 1995, pp. 62, 71, 72).

The model presents a rather deterministic order of events in the creation of knowledge. However, such a model may always also be interpreted as a flexible heuristic rather than as a strict algorithmic rule. What is more problematic is the theoretical basis on which the phases of the cycle are built. Nonaka and Takeuchi construct their dynamic cycle out of a static matrix of four fields. These four fields are based on the distinction between tacit and explicit knowledge. Thus, the four fields, which are turned into four phases of a cycle, are essentially different modes of representing knowledge: tacit-sympathized, explicit-conceptual, explicit-systemic, and tacit-operational. The crucial question is: Are such representational modes of knowledge an appropriate basis for discerning phases and recurrent sequential patterns in processes of knowledge creation? In other words, is Nonaka and Takeuchi's leap from a matrix to a cycle justified?

I strongly doubt that a theoretically and empirically viable cyclic model can be built on the foundation of modes of knowledge representation. Modes of knowledge representation are instrumentalities, implementations of different toolkits of cognitive and discursive work. There is little evidence of any inherent order in the employment of such toolkits. Rather, they seem to be used in accordance with situationally constructed needs and opportunities, often in a probing manner and in opportunistic combinations. The few serious attempts to construct developmental models on the basis of successive representational modes, notably Bruner's (1966) *enactive, iconic,* and *symbolic,* have not gained much general currency. Although Nonaka and Takeuchi construct their cycle in a logical fashion, they offer little in terms of empirical evidence or compelling theoretical support for it. Their cases seem to be partly hand-picked and stream-lined to fit the theory; in part, they are so ambiguous that they could be made to fit many competing and contradictory theories.

Nonaka and Takeuchi's categories may themselves be used productively to analyze different types of knowledge representation that are employed in the course of collaborative knowledge creation. Such an analysis would be useful as a way of identifying and rectifying possible biases in a team's style of learning and problem solving. For example, an exclusive emphasis on explicit conceptualization may be unproductive if the exchange of sympathized knowledge is neglected.

Nonaka and Takeuchi's framework does not seem to account effectively for sequences of formulating and debating a problem, in which knowledge is represented as an open, multifaceted *problematic*. Nor does the framework make explicit provision for sequences of analyzing and debating a problem systematically, in which knowledge is represented as a problematic field to be circumscribed and dimensionalized. Nonaka and Takeuchi's model has no place for debate and analysis, although their descriptive case materials do indicate that such processes take place, particularly in the early phases of the cycle (Nonaka & Takeuchi, 1995, pp. 106–107).

Nonaka and Takeuchi's theory takes the initial existence of a fairly clear problem, task, or assignment as a given. Their cycle begins with the sharing of tacit knowledge *about a relatively clearly defined task,* captured by the authors in their notion of *organizational intention* that is formulated by the management. Thus, the framework excludes the phases of goal and problem formation, delegating them to the management as an unexamined black box.

Activity theory and expansive learning as a framework of explanation

The cultural-historical theory of activity (activity theory, for short) approaches human cognition and behavior as embedded in collectively organized, artifact-mediated activity systems (Leont'ev, 1978; Engeström, 1987; Cole & Engeström, 1993). Activities are social practices oriented at objects. An entity becomes an object of activity when it meets a human need. The subject constructs the object, "singles out those properties that prove to be essential for developing social practice," using mediating artifacts that function as "forms of expression of cognitive norms, standards, and object-hypotheses existing outside the given individual"

(Lektorsky, 1984, p. 137). In this constructed, need-related capacity, the object gains motivating force that gives shape and direction to activity. The object determines the horizon of possible actions (Engeström, 1995).

Objects are not to be confused with goals. Goals are attached to specific actions. Actions have clear points of beginning and termination and relatively short half-lives. Activity systems evolve through long historical cycles in which clear beginnings and ends are difficult to determine. Goals do not explain the emergence of actions; goals and plans are formulated and revised concurrently as one acts, and they are commonly explicated clearly only retrospectively (Weick, 1995). An activity system constantly generates actions through which the object of the activity is enacted and reconstructed in specific forms and contents – but being a horizon, the object is never fully reached or conquered. The creative potential of activity is closely related to the *search actions* of object construction and redefinition.

This situation-specific reconstruction and instantiation of the object of an activity system often takes the form of problem finding and problem definition. Simon's (1973) dictum that there are initially only ill-structured problems and that problem solving consists essentially of structuring and constraining the problem is quite appropriate against this background. What this dictum overlooks is that "one can never get it right, and that innovation may best be seen as a continuous process, with particular product embodiments simply being arbitrary points along the way" (von Hippel & Tyre, 1995, p. 12).

The mediating artifacts include tools and signs, both external implements and internal representations such as mental models. It is not particularly useful to categorize mediating artifacts into external or practical ones, on the one hand, and internal or cognitive ones, on the other hand. These functions and uses are in constant flux and transformation as the activity unfolds. An internal representation becomes externalized through speech, gesture, writing, manipulation of the material environment – and vice versa, external processes become internalized. Freezing or splitting these processes is a poor basis for understanding different artifacts. Instead, we need to differentiate between the processes themselves, between different ways of using artifacts.

For this purpose, I have suggested four types of artifacts (Engeström, 1990). The first type is *what* artifacts, used to identify and describe objects. The second type is *how* artifacts, used to guide and direct processes and procedures on, within, or between objects. The third type is *why* artifacts, used to diagnose and explain the properties and behavior of objects.

Finally, the fourth type is *where to* artifacts, used to envision the future state or potential development of objects, including institutions and social systems.

Although certain artifacts are typically used in certain ways, there is nothing inherently fixed in an artifact that would determine that it can only be, for instance, a why artifact. A conceptual model may typically function as a dynamic diagnostic tool, but it may also become a frozen definition used only as a what artifact to identify and classify phenomena. A hammer may typically be used as a what artifact for identifying objects that may be hammered (such as nails). But it may also become a where to artifact used as a symbol for workers' power.

The artifact-mediated construction of objects does not happen in a solitary manner or in harmonious unison. It is a collaborative and dialogical process in which different perspectives (Holland & Reeves, 1996) and voices (R. Engeström, 1995) meet, collide, and merge. The different perspectives are rooted in different communities and practices that continue to coexist within one and the same collective activity system.

"Perspective" is a further elaboration of concepts that link activity systems to one another and to structures and dynamics of power and privilege. It allows one to speak more directly to agency in Marx's work, to the capacity of humans to apprehend the conditions of their activity and through their practice change those very conditions. (Holland & Reeves, 1996, p. 272)

As Holland and Reeves (p. 274) point out, *perspective* is a hedge against simplified views of context that ignore the unsettled and conflicted relations between different positions and actors. The concept of perspective opens up intriguing questions: Can and should perspectives merge? Is it possible or desirable to have a completely shared object in an activity?

The theory of expansive learning (Engeström, 1987) is based on the dialectics of ascending from the abstract to the concrete. This is a method of grasping the essence of an object by tracing and reproducing theoretically the logic of its development, of its historical formation through the emergence and resolution of its inner contradictions. A new theoretical idea or concept is initially produced in the form of an abstract, simple explanatory relationship, a *germ cell*. This initial abstraction is enriched step by step and transformed into a concrete system of multiple, constantly developing manifestations. In an expansive learning cycle, the initial simple idea is transformed into a complex object, a new form of practice. At the same time, the cycle produces new theoretical concepts – theoretically grasped practice – concrete in systemic richness and multiplicity of manifestations.

In this framework, *abstract* refers to partial, separated from the concrete whole. In empirical thinking based on comparisons and classifications, abstractions capture arbitrary, only formally interconnected properties. In dialectical-theoretical thinking, based on ascending from the abstract to the concrete, an abstraction captures the smallest and simplest, genetically primary unit of the whole functionally interconnected system (see Il'enkov, 1977; Davydov, 1990; also Bakhurst, 1991; Falmagne, 1995).

The expansive cycle begins with individual subjects questioning the accepted practice, and it gradually expands into a collective movement or institution. The theory of expansive learning is related to Latour's actor-network theory in that both regard innovations as stepwise construction of new forms of collaborative practice, or technoeconomic networks (Latour, 1987, 1988; see also Engeström & Escalante, 1996).

Ascending from the abstract to the concrete is achieved through specific epistemic or learning actions. Together these actions form an expansive cycle or spiral. An ideal-typical sequence of epistemic actions in an expansive cycle may be described as follows (see also Engeström, 1994b).

- The first action is that of questioning, criticizing, or rejecting some aspects of the accepted practice and existing wisdom. For the sake of simplicity, I call this action *questioning*.
- The second action is that of *analyzing* the situation. Analysis involves mental, discursive, or practical transformation of the situation in order to find out causes or explanatory mechanisms. Analysis evokes "why?" questions and explanatory principles. One type of analysis is *historical-genetic;* it seeks to explain the situation by tracing its origination and evolution. Another type of analysis is *actual-empirical;* it seeks to explain the situation by constructing a picture of its inner systemic relations.
- The third action is that of *modeling* the newly found explanatory relationship in some publicly observable and transmittable medium. This means constructing an explicit, simplified model of the new idea that explains and offers a solution to the problematic situation.
- The fourth action is that of *examining the model,* running, operating, and experimenting on it in order to fully grasp its dynamics, potentials, and limitations.
- The fifth action is that of *implementing the model,* concretizing it by means of practical applications, enrichments, and conceptual extensions.

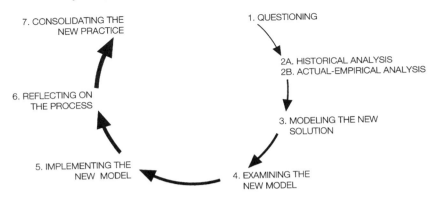

Figure 23.2. Sequence of epistemic actions in an expansive learning cycle.

- The sixth and seventh actions are those of *reflecting* on and evaluating the process and *consolidating* its outcomes into a new, stable form of practice.

These actions bear a close resemblance to the six learning actions put forward by Davydov (1988) as constituents of learning activity that follows the logic of ascending from the abstract to the concrete. Davydov's theory is, however, oriented to learning processes within the confines of a classroom where the curricular contents are determined ahead of time by more knowledgeable adults (Engeström, 1991b). This probably explains why it does not contain the first action of critical questioning and rejection, and why the fifth and seventh actions, implementing and consolidating, are replaced by *constructing a system of particular tasks* and *evaluating* – actions that do not imply the construction of actual, culturally novel practices.

The process of expansive learning should be understood as construction and resolution of successively evolving tensions or contradictions in a complex system that includes the *object* or *objects*, the mediating *artifacts*, and the *perspectives* of the participants. The entire ideal-typical expansive cycle may be diagrammatically depicted with the help of Figure 23.2.

The theory of expansive learning has thus far been applied mainly to large-scale transformations in activity systems, often spanning a period of 2 or 3 years (Engeström, 1991a, 1993b). On such a scale, the action phases of the expansive learning cycle are interpreted as lengthy periods of collaborative work dominated by a given action type (e.g., historical analysis, modeling). This corresponds roughly to the scale of events analyzed by Nonaka and Takeuchi.

In this study, the scale is radically changed. Instead of entire corporations, the focus is on teams. I am looking at phases and cycles that take minutes, perhaps an hour, instead of months and years. Can such miniature cycles be considered expansive?

The answer is yes and no. Miniature cycles of innovative learning should be regarded as *potentially* expansive. A large-scale, expansive cycle of organizational transformation always consists of small cycles of innovative learning. However, the appearance of small-scale cycles of innovative learning does not in itself guarantee that an expansive cycle is going on. Small cycles may remain isolated events, and the overall cycle of organizational development may become stagnant, regressive, or even fall apart. The occurrence of a full-fledged expansive cycle is not common, and it typically requires concentrated effort and deliberate interventions. With these reservations in mind, the expansive learning cycle and its embedded actions may be used as a framework for analyzing small-scale, innovative learning processes.

Both Nonaka and Takeuchi's theory and the theory of expansive learning focus on the creation and practical application of powerful new concepts. Both theories regard knowledge creation as an escalating process.

Thus, organizational knowledge creation is a spiral process, starting at the individual level and moving up through expanding communities of interaction, that crosses sectional, departmental, divisional, and organizational boundaries. (Nonaka & Takeuchi, 1995, p. 72)

However, although for Nonaka and Takeuchi (p. 72) "tacit knowledge of individuals is the basis of organizational knowledge creation," the theory of expansive learning sees different modes of knowledge representation (including the whole issue of tacit vs. explicit knowledge) as instrumentalities or toolkits that may be used in many different orders and combinations. The theory of expansive learning puts a lot of weight on the local discursive construction of a shared object and intention in knowledge creation – something Nonaka and Takeuchi seem to take for granted, tacitly delegating it to management. It also emphasizes the central role of contradictions and debate in knowledge creation. The whole process is seen as energized and often radically refocused by negation: questioning, criticizing, even rejecting the accepted wisdom.

The two cases

The company in which the data were collected is a leading manufacturer of mid-range industrial gas turbines and turbomachinery systems. It has approximately 4,400 employees at its headquarters and manufacturing facilities. In recent years, the company has invested heavily in teaming in all departments and at all levels of the organization. The teaming philosophy is based on the concept of self-directed work teams, systematically presented in Orsburn, Moran, Musselwhite, and Zenger (1990). Management has created a rather impressive system of training and internal support to teams.

Our field research has been conducted in the Cold CAM section of the manufacturing plant (CAM = certified assembly manufacturing), where we have observed, videotaped, and interviewed three adjacent production teams since May 1995. According to its mission statement, the Cold CAM section produces "components that are large and structural in nature, with surface precision and accuracies critical to engine alignment and clearances."

The data used in this chapter are from the biggest of the three teams, established in 1994. In the spring of 1995, this team had 15 members, of whom 10 were machinists, 3 assemblers, and 2 welders. For purposes of production efficiency, the team was divided into two zones, A and B. Zone A had six workers (including two welders and an assembler); Zone B had nine workers. The team's elected coordinator was a machinist from Zone B. Zone A had its own zone leader (also a machinist). The team as a whole was responsible for late parts. In the weekly team meetings, three experts with at least partially supervisory roles participated regularly: the area coordinator, the resource planner, and the quality control expert (precision inspector).

The data used in this chapter are taken from two successive meetings of the team, held on May 30 and June 6, 1995. We videotaped both meetings, collected the written documents used in or produced to record the meetings, and conducted interviews with several participants. The analyses reported in this chapter are based on the transcripts of the videotaped conversations.

In the first meeting, the key issue discussed was whether or not the team should purchase new backup tooling. The new tooling was proposed by the area coordinator. The suggested new tooling holds inserts that make the machines work. It is supposed to be more precise, more durable, and more expensive than other forms of tooling used thus far and has been experimental at the company. In the second meeting, the key issue was how to deal with scrap parts produced in the team. The company holds ISO 9001/9002 quality system certifications, and the official policy requires that scrap parts must be reported in written form with the help of a Withholding Notice (WN). The official procedure for handling WNs is called *corrective action*. It requires that the operator responsible for the discrepant part attend a meeting outside the work team, where the issue is discussed and rectified.

The two cases used in this chapter represent innovative organizational learning at different levels. In the first case, the team produced a novel solution to a contested issue: whether or not to purchase new backup tools of a certain type and make. Team members initially disagreed on the issue, and it seemed to become a deadlock. The solution was based on a proposal to first test just one new tool in use and to decide on the purchase on the basis of the experiences gained. I previously called this type of outcome a *solution innovation* (Engeström, 1995). In the second case, the team produced a novel procedure for reporting and discussing causes of scrap parts. The team designed a procedure that deviated from the existing standard procedure in the plant. I have called this type of outcome a *trajectory innovation* (Engeström, 1995). A solution innovation typically applies only to the specific case for which it was invented, whereas a trajectory innovation is aimed at becoming a more or less permanent, repeatedly used procedure. Of course, it is possible that a solution innovation is subsequently repeated consciously in similar new situations, thus becoming a trajectory innovation. Conversely, a trajectory innovation may fail to generalize beyond the first application, thus effectively becoming a one-time solution innovation.

Analysis of the cases

I analyzed the transcripts of the two meetings in great detail with the help of Nonaka and Takeuchi's categories. I found instances of all the four basic phases depicted in Figure 23.1. In particular, creating concepts, justifying concepts, and constructing operational knowledge were relatively easy to identify. Sharing sympathized knowledge was much more difficult to find, although I finally identified two brief sequences that could be classified as representing that category.

Nonaka and Takeuchi develop and demonstrate the uses of their categories in cases of new product development that are much more global and long-term than the discursive processes analyzed in this chapter. The fact that it was possible to use their categories with these data indicates that the categories do have some analytical power and validity even when applied to processes of innovative learning in singular team meetings.

Table 23.1. *Phases of knowledge creation in the two team meetings*[a]

Meeting 1		Meeting 2	
Turns	Phase	Turns	Phase
01–08	*Formulating/debating a problem*	01–12	*Formulating/debating a problem*
09–92	*Analyzing/debating a problem systematically*	13	Creating concepts
		14–19	Justifying concepts
93–99	Sharing sympathized knowledge	20–46	Constructing operational knowledge
100–132	*Analyzing/debating a problem systematically*	[47–63]	[Different topic discussed]
		64–175	*Formulating/debating a problem*
133–153	Constructing operational knowledge	176–178	Creating concepts
		179–181	Sharing sympathized knowledge
154–189	*Analyzing/debating a problem systematically*	182–224	Justifying concepts
190–200	Creating concepts	225	Creating concepts
201–207	Constructing operational knowledge	226–239	Constructing operational knowledge

[a] The phases follow the framework of Nonaka and Takeuchi (1995). Phases not recognizable within this framework are indicated by italics.

Table 23.1 shows the two discussions broken into phases that follow Nonaka and Takeuchi's model as far as possible. "Turns" refers to numbered turns of talk in the discussion. The phases that could not be identified using Nonaka and Takeuchi's categories were scrutinized separately and given provisional names that try to describe their character without any particular theoretical assumptions. These "unrecognizable" phases are indicated by italics in the table.

Table 23.1 reveals that two types of sequences in the team discussions were impossible to categorize with the conceptual framework of Nonaka and Takeuchi. I descriptively call these sequences of *formulating/debating a problem* and sequences of *analyzing/debating a problem systematically*. Interestingly enough, clearly the largest single chunks of discussion (measured by the number of turns of talk), namely, those consisting of turns 09–92 in meeting 1 and turns 64–175 in meeting 2, belonged to the two types that did not fit the framework.

Formulating/debating a problem covers sequences of discussion in which the participants present or argue about an issue or question to be discussed and resolved. In other words, there was a debate about whether an issue was a problem or not. In these sequences, knowledge was represented as fuzzy, multifaceted *problematic,* to be somehow clarified and constrained. There was tension and pressure, but there was no clear assignment to work out or design an innovative solution.

In the team we observed, the sequences of *formulating/debating a problem* were examples of *problem finding* rather than problem solving. The team may have seemed to begin with a clear task, but soon enough the task itself became problematized and problem construction took over. In other words, the processes of innovative knowledge creation in the team we observed were much heavier on the initial problem definition and problem construction than Nonaka and Takeuchi's model would allow.

In Nonaka and Takeuchi's model, a group of employees begins the cycle, with a clear organizational assignment in mind, by socialization, sharing their experiences in brainstorming camps, focused apprenticeships, and similar fields for creating *sympathized knowledge.*

At Matsushita, team members apprenticed themselves to the head baker at the Osaka International Hotel to capture the essence of kneading skill through bodily experience. At Honda, team members shared their mental models and technical skills in discussing what an ideal car should evolve into, often over *sake* and away from the office. These examples show that the first phase of the organizational knowledge-creation process corresponds to socialization. (Nonaka & Takeuchi, 1995, p. 85)

The sequences of *formulating/debating a problem* were not at all like the socialization described by Nonaka and Takeuchi. The *sharing of sympathized knowledge* played a rather marginal part, appearing twice in the two meetings, certainly not the foundational role of starting the cycle, as the theory would predict. The first of these two situations occurred in the middle of an intense debate. The second situation occurred at the end of a debate, immediately after one of the participants had proposed an innovative solution to the issue at hand. Both were brief exchanges of sympathy, not the kind of extensive socializing described by Nonaka and Takeuchi.

Analyzing/debating a problem systematically is the second category missing in the framework of Nonaka and Takeuchi. This type of discourse played a central role in the first team meeting. The problem of whether or not to buy new backup tools for the team was tackled by means of a systematic force field analysis, listing the pros and cons of each alternative solution. In the framework of Nonaka and Takeuchi, there seems to be no place for this type of discourse. This was certainly not mere socialization and sharing of tacit knowledge – the procedure was very explicit. But this was also not yet creation of new concepts or innovative ideas. The focus was on laying out and assessing what the team members already knew.

Table 23.2. *Phases of knowledge creation in the two team meetings*[a]

Meeting 1		Meeting 2	
Turns	Phase	Turns	Phase
01–08	*Formulating/debating a problem*	01–12	*Formulating/debating a problem*
09–61	Actual-empirical analysis	13	Modeling a new solution
62–73	Questioning	14–19	Historical analysis
74–189	Actual-empirical analysis	20–46	*Reinforcing the existing practice*
190–192	Modeling a new solution	[47–63]	[Different topic discussed]
193–203	Examining the new model	64–88	Questioning
204–207	Implementing the model	89–175	Actual-empirical analysis
		176–178	Modeling a new solution
		179–236	Examining the new model
		237–239	Implementing the model

[a] The phases follow the framework of Engeström (1987). Phases not recognizable within this framework are indicated by italics.

Both meetings we analyzed started with *formulating/debating a problem*, and both ended with *constructing operational knowledge*. Beyond this rather minimal similarity, the different phases observed in the two meetings did not follow any fixed order or identifiable sequential pattern. To the contrary, it seems that the different forms of knowledge suggested by Nonaka and Takeuchi may appear in many different orders and combinations in the course of a process of innovative knowledge creation.

In Table 23.2, the framework of expansive learning is applied to the transcripts of the two team meetings. As the table shows, the framework of expansive learning leaves three phases in the two processes unidentified. The framework of Nonaka and Takeuchi (Table 23.1) left six phases unidentified.

Interestingly enough, the first phase in both meetings (*formulating/debating a problem*) does not fall into the categories of *questioning* or *analysis*, whereas turns 64–175 in Meeting 2 do fall into these two categories. In both meetings, the first phase consisted of a presentation and discussion of the issue prepared *for* the team, not initiated and constructed *by* the team. In Meeting 2, for example, the team coordinator and the resource planner introduced the issue of how to deal with scrap parts. Although the coordinator did open his turn with a question, this was immediately qualified with an authoritative statement, followed by the resource planner's even more authoritative presentation of the economic costs involved. The resource planner was not questioning – he was telling the others what to do.

The other unidentifiable sequence was named *reinforcing the existing practice.* In the framework of Nonaka and Takeuchi, turns 20–46 of Meeting 2 fell into the category of *constructing operational knowledge.* This would seem to correspond to *implementation* in the framework of expansive learning. But in this framework, the *object* is of decisive importance: implementation of *what*? The sequence covering turns 20–46 contains no new object. It contains an attempt to eliminate deviations from the accepted correct practice. It is not about operationalizing an innovation; it is about operationalizing an already existing rule, represented by the managerial expertise of the resource planner. We might say that this phase, as well as the initial phases of *formulating/debating a problem* in both meetings, are unidentifiable within the theory of expansive learning because *they are in fact nonexpansive.* In other words, processes of innovative knowledge creation are not pure. They contain both expansive and nonexpansive phases, both steps forward and digressions.

In spite of the differences, there seems to be a fair amount of similarity between Tables 23.1 and 23.2. Are the differences between the two frameworks perhaps only terminological? What added explanatory power does Table 23.2 offer?

The potential value of this framework lies in the opportunity it offers for examining closely the constitutive actions of expansive learning. Now that we have previously identified those actions in the discourse data, we can look in detail at their dynamics.

Questioning in expansive learning

The action of *questioning* is interesting in that it is all but missing in Nonaka and Takeuchi's framework. In the first team meeting, in the middle of systematic analysis of pros and cons, questioning erupted as a challenge, initiated by a machinist. Instead of engaging in a verbal fight or struggle over authority, the area coordinator used the force field on the whiteboard as a mediating artifact, transferring the machinist's argument into an externalized, jointly observable form on the whiteboard. Externally, the analysis of pros and cons continued. However, after the challenge, the dynamic of the discussion was changed. There was tension that demanded a resolution. The exact contents of the tension were not clear at the outset. Much of the subsequent cognitive and discursive work in the meeting was devoted to turning the fuzzy tension into an analytically manageable problem.

In both meetings, the action of *questioning* was initiated by one participant but accomplished through collaborative argumentation. Basically these were actions of *collective refocusing,* though the new object was captured only in a fuzzy and ambiguous form. In Meeting 1, the focus was shifted from mere technical comparison of features to an underlying opposition of alternative policies, although the shape of these alternative policies remained unclear. In Meeting 2, the focus shifted from an operational maintenance issue that had nothing to do with scrap parts (turns 49–63) to reopening the issue of scrap parts and corrective action. Most participants thought this discussion was already closed and left behind as an issue of simply reinforcing the existing policy.

Analysis in expansive learning

The actions of *analysis* are also missing in Nonaka and Takeuchi's framework. In our data, *historical analysis* appeared only in Meeting 2. History was used to clarify the origination of the present policy. Interestingly enough, the very dilemma and tension of the meeting, which would come to the table only later when the machinist initiated the action of questioning, was implied in the way the area coordinator hesitated in his historical account: "*But then again,* uh, we have said officially and unofficially that if, uh, the cost of parts is less than the cost of WN [withdrawal notice] that we would go the variance route rather than writing it up. *But, then again . . .*"

Actual-empirical analysis was used extensively in both meetings. In Meeting 1, it was structured with the help of a mediating artifact, the force field analysis, which took the physical shape of a matrix of pros and cons. During the analysis, the object of analysis itself was renegotiated and revised. Also, the mediating artifact itself, the force field analysis matrix, was revised in the middle of the analysis.

Although the force field matrix gave structure to the analysis, it had its own problems. It did not differentiate between specific descriptive features and general principles as possible pros and cons. It seemed almost too easy to throw in some feature as a pro or a con, without explaining why it should be interpreted as such. This led to ambiguous interpretations that required repair. Correspondingly, the outcomes of the force field analysis were far from conclusive. The analysis resulted in evolving lists of pros and cons from which the team could not derive a clear-cut solution.

The inconclusive, almost endless nature of the force field analysis led the area coordinator to press repeatedly for some sort of closure to the discussion, if only in the form of a postponement of a decision. Two members of the team responded by rejecting the postponement, thus increasing pressure to find a solution immediately. Though seemingly constraining, this kind of pressure toward a decision may in practice facilitate innovation rather than compromise (Perrow, 1984).

In Meeting 2, actual-empirical analysis took a different shape. It became a struggle between *principles*, much more explicitly so than in Meeting 1. To a large extent, this difference was probably a consequence of the different nature of the issues discussed. On the other hand, the use of the force field matrix as a mediating artifact in Meeting 1 may also have played a role, as indicated previously.

The analytical debate spanning turns 89–175 was basically a confrontation between two major principles of work organization: *individual responsibility/accountability* and *equal responsibility/fairness.* After the questioning sequence, the area coordinator began to justify the practice of the individual corrective action procedure that requires reporting scrap parts outside the team. He invoked the principle of individual responsibility/accountability – only to receive an immediate rebuttal from the machinist, who invoked the principle of equal responsibility/fairness.

The machinist received support from some of the team members, most notably from another machinist who repeatedly paraphrased and clarified his point of view, acting as a scaffold to support the formation of an emerging idea. This represents an interesting variation of the mechanism of the zone of proximal development, first discovered by Vygotsky (1978).

In themselves, the competing principles of individual responsibility and equal responsibility were logically fully compatible: Individual responsibility can apply to everyone equally. In this case, their incompatibility was caused by a subprinciple attached to individual responsibility, namely, the subprinciple of *cost efficiency.* This subprinciple was enforced as a reservation: If individual responsibility becomes too costly, that is, if the external corrective action procedure costs more than an average scrap part, then full individual responsibility is not applied. The team was divided into Zone A and Zone B. Parts handled in Zone A were cheaper. Thus the principle of individual responsibility was fully applied only to workers in Zone B – which, in turn, violated the principle of equal responsibility.

This analysis undertaken in Meeting 2 was not mediated by graphic artifacts such as the force field matrix used in Meeting 1. Words and gestures were the primary mediating artifacts in this debate. Beyond that, verbally formulated principles were employed as decisive "why" artifacts. The whole debate was an example of *analysis* in the important sense that general principles were analytically separated from various descriptive details and explicated in such a way that the central disagreement became evident.

Modeling a new solution in expansive learning

In both meetings, the new solution was formulated in a brief sequence, almost as a sudden flash of insight. In Meeting 1, the solution – testing just one new machine in practice before deciding on the purchase – was suggested by a machinist and supported by another machinist sitting next to him.

This sequence was remarkable in that the first machinist made his suggestion in spite of first having been fairly forcefully overridden by the resource planner. The first machinist basically recaptured the initiative by force, with significant vocal and mimetic encouragement from the second machinist. The second machinist's support had a dual function: It encouraged the first machinist, and it gave immediate weight to his suggestion in the eyes of the other participants. The new solution was a joint achievement. Again, this may be seen as an example of Vygotsky's (1978) zone of proximal development unfolding in innovative team learning.

A careful analysis of previous events reveals that the new solution was not, after all, a sudden flash of insight. Before being formulated, the first machinist's idea was silenced at least once before in the course of the meeting. At that point, the second machinist began to introduce the first one's novel idea. But the initiative was taken by others, who started joking about purchasing the backup tools with the area coordinator's Visa card. Instead of remediating the discourse toward a solution, joking here diverted it from the emerging new idea.

In Meeting 2, the new solution was modeled equally briefly, this time by the resource planner. He introduced the principle of *teaming* as a way out of the deadlock between the principles of individual responsibility and equal responsibility. His suggestion was powerfully mediated by the rhetorical device of reported speech (see Goodwin, 1990; Lucy, 1993). This device was used to make vividly concrete both the negative and positive alternatives.

Again, careful examination reveals that the solution had antecedents in the discussion. At the very beginning of the meeting, the team coordinator suggested the notion of *internal corrective action*, although at that point conservatively, limited to Zone A, where even management did not demand external corrective action due to its costs. He used the protective argument that "nobody needs to know" rather than pushing offensively for the team principle. He did not even mention the word *team* at this point. This anticipatory but premature attempt to model the new solution was left without a collaborative response and elaboration. However, the term *internal corrective action* was picked up later and played a decisive role in the conceptualization of the solution – though invested with conceptual content different from that initially suggested by the team coordinator.

Examining the new model in expansive learning

In both meetings, the new solution model was collectively *examined* immediately after its formulation. In Meeting 1, this involved only one reservation from the area coordinator. The second machinist immediately began to concretize the model – again using reported speech. After that, the conclusion was evident and the area coordinator, too, expressed his approval.

In Meeting 2, the examination was more critical and comprehensive. First, the resource planner's model of corrective action within the team received warm support from three outspoken machinists. But the discussion soon took the shape of a debate between the resource planner and the area coordinator. Both used reported speech. Soon the resource planner also employed the mediating device of analogy, comparing the work team to a baseball team.

The decisive artifact turned out to be the principle of teaming – a powerful "why" artifact. A third machinist added the important aspect or variable of *expertise* to the examination. He argued that in external corrective action, reports are made to people who do not know the local process; thus, why not keep the reporting inside the team, where the expertise exists? He made the distinction between "inside" and "outside" the team the crux of the matter by means of corresponding significant hand gestures ("outside" being signaled by pointing up with a hand, "inside" by pounding on the table).

The examination came to a close when the team's quality control expert forcefully reformulated the resource planner's model of internal corrective action and the team principle behind it. The crucial distinction between outside and inside was again expressed with the mediating hand gestures used earlier by the third machinist. After this authoritative input, participants expressed general agreement and a decision was reached quickly.

Implementing the new model in expansive learning

In both meetings, *implementation* of the new model was a rather technical and brief ending sequence of the discussion. In Meeting 1, the only substantive step toward implementation was a summary of the decision formulated by the team coordinator. In Meeting 2, the team's quality control expert was appointed, together with the team coordinator, to take the team's proposal of internal corrective action to management.

The quality control expert accepted the task, simultaneously stating his doubts: "I know we have team power, but how much team power do we have?" The question was prophetic. After an initially positive response, management eventually turned down the team's proposal for full-scale internal corrective action.

Innovative learning as an uncommon event

In both of the team meetings analyzed, the team constructed a problem and an innovative solution to it. In what sense was there learning and knowledge creation?

The first solution was to test a single tool in practice before deciding to purchase a whole set of similar tools. This does not seem to be a particularly original idea. Yet, there was disagreement on the benefits and drawbacks of the new tools, and no consensus was in sight. The only reasonable decision seemed to be postponement of the decision – in itself no guarantee of anything better. The testing solution was clearly novel for the team. It may have remained a singular innovation. On the other hand, it may provide a model and resource for proceeding in other similar situations.

Whether sustained learning in the classical sense (similar stimulus situation – novel behavior) actually occurred is an open issue until a similar situation is observed in the team. This occurrence is not at all unlikely: Technological investments are often debated in such a rapidly developing field. It is more than likely that in such an event the team will work with more options than *yes, no,* and *delay* – the three alternatives it started out with in the first meeting analyzed. As to knowledge creation, the actual material implementation of the innovation, that is, the practical testing of the single new tool, was itself the embodiment of new knowledge in this case. It was very much "knowledge in the world" (Norman, 1988) or "between people" (Engeström et al., 1995), not necessarily conceptualized or internalized "knowledge in the head."

The second solution was to adopt a new procedure of internal corrective action for the entire team in dealing with scrap parts – a trajectory innovation meant for permanent use. This was a deliberate deviation from the accepted company policy. Had this innovation been accepted by management, the reporting (corrective action) behavior of the team would certainly have become qualitatively different from what it had been and from what it was expected to be in the surrounding organization. Since the proposal was rejected, the innovation remains a potential innovation only. However, it was given a name (*internal corrective action*) and conceptualized to such a degree that it has taken a life of its own in the discourse, thinking, and practice of the team: It has become a new mediating knowledge artifact in the local activity. When an innovation is rejected but has conceptual coherence and need-based anchoring in the daily realities of a collective activity system, it is not likely to disappear. Reappearances in modified forms are much more likely.

The importance of object formation

Both meetings testify to the importance of critical questioning and rejection of the accepted wisdom as a triggering action in innovative learning. Tjosvold and Tjosvold (1994) emphasize the importance of *constructive controversy* in teamwork. Bartunek and Reid (1992) discuss the positive potential of conflicts in organizational change. Although a related phenomenon, questioning is a more specific action than the global notions of controversy or conflict. It is an action of challenging and negating the prevalent authoritative view or policy, much in line with what Litowitz (1990) aptly characterized as "just say no."

Both meetings also demonstrate the crucial role of object/problem construction in innovative learning. The initial existence of a shared problem or task can rarely if ever be taken for granted in work teams. In fact, actions directed toward constructing a shared understanding of the problem took the lion's share of both discussions. The innovative solution itself seemed to emerge as a final burst after the painstaking period of object construction.

The formation of a shared object is a major collaborative achievement. It is above all an analytical achievement, involving the formation and use of historical explanations, systematic comparisons, and explanatory principles. Here the theory of expansive learning differs very clearly from Nonaka and Takeuchi's theory of knowledge creation. The latter emphasizes socialization and sharing of sympathized, tacit knowledge as the step leading to an innovative solution. In the theory of expansive learning and in the data analyzed earlier, such a phase has no prominent role. There are at least two possible explanations that may mediate this difference. First, analysis is never purely conceptual and explicit; it always includes more tacit and experiential aspects, too. Second, Nonaka and Takeuchi may refer to groups that have little shared experiential background to begin with, being selected from various departments of a company. In such a case, the socialization phase may indeed be necessary. This, however, in no way diminishes the importance of subsequent or parallel analytic actions.

The role of artifacts

In the two meetings, an array of mediating artifacts were used. The primary *what* artifacts included, above all, talk and gestures used to construct the object/problem and its solution. Reported speech and analogy were among the rhetorically powerful *what* artifacts used in the meetings. Joking about purchasing the new tools was used in Meeting 1 in a way that diverted the discourse from the emerging innovative solution – an instance that may be seen as an antidote to optimistic assumptions about the innovation-facilitating potential of humor (Hatch & Ehrlich, 1993). In Meeting 2, the significant hand gestures indicating "outside" and "inside" were used by two participants in the decisive phase of examining the new solution model.

A number of seemingly fixed and finished theoretical concepts, obviously obtained from above through training and instruction, were also used as *what* artifacts in the meetings. These included concepts used to convey authority, such as *ISO* ("That's a hit against ISO"), but also concepts used as tools appropriated for practical use, such as *inventory* and *WN*. Some concepts like *continuous improvement* might be in the middle, in the process of becoming increasingly common for the participants. The seemingly fixed and finished character of these concepts should not be taken for granted either. *Corrective action* was obviously a theoretical concept given from above. But the team transformed it into the idea of *internal* corrective action, which gave it an entirely different meaning. This corresponds to Vygotsky's (1986) idea of the bidirectional and negotiated character of the formation of theoretical concepts. Such concepts "grow" from both above and below, and the creative moment is in the meeting of these two directions.

The *how* artifacts included numerous forms of metatalk that were used to guide and constrain the discussion. They might be labeled as "One person at a time"; "Don't argue about who's right and who's wrong"; "Let's not get personal"; "Interpreting what someone else said is not the same as defending that opinion." These are actually procedural rules with various degrees of generality. "One person at a time" is a very general rule in institutional conversations, whereas "Don't argue about who's right and who's wrong" applies specifically to a type of discussion in which the group tries to produce ideas rather than decide on their validity. One could say that procedural rules such as these remain rules as long as they are implicitly constraining the discussion. They become active tools as soon as they are deliberately used by participants in order to maintain or redirect the course of the discussion.

The *why* artifacts included the force field analysis in Meeting 1 and the principles and subprinciples in Meeting 2. The force field analysis is aimed at elucidating justifications for a choice between two alternatives. In other words, it should yield *why* artifacts that can be used to reach a decision. In Meeting 1, the force field analysis seemed to yield mainly descriptive *what* artifacts that were difficult to interpret in any convincing or conclusive manner. Thus, a tool such as this does not inherently determine how it is used – descriptively or analytically. In Meeting 2, the general principles were explicated largely as a response to the persistent and aggressive questioning initiated by the first machinist. He first demanded that a force field analysis be conducted on this issue, too. He then provocatively and repeatedly used the *why* question to challenge the managerial wisdom.

Interestingly enough, in both meetings the solution models were jointly fixed only in spoken discourse. The later written minutes were constructed by the minutes keeper only. The available graphic tools (whiteboard, overheads) were not used to explicate and examine collectively the solutions. Thus, the crucial, newly produced *where to* artifacts remained fairly vague and ambiguous.

Innovative learning as meeting of perspectives

Even though research on work teams has increased greatly in recent years (see Beyerlein & Johnson, 1994; Beyerlein, Johnson, & Beyerlein, 1995), very few studies have focused on detailed analyses of discourse in the team. This is probably due partly to the difficulty of analyzing relatively long multiparty conversations that are embedded in practical activity. The previous analyses indicate that innovative learning processes in teams may not be harmonious brainstorming sessions or situations where "members think alike" (Rentsch & Hall, 1994). To the contrary, in the two meetings, persons presenting different perspectives disagreed and entered into debates. In Meeting 1, the perspective proposing the purchase of new tools and the perspective questioning the purchase collided. In Meeting 2, the perspective advocating individual responsibility/accountability and the perspective advocating equal responsibility/fairness collided.

These perspectives were not merely individual-psychological properties. In both cases, one of them was more anchored in the community of management and supervision, and the other was more anchored among the shop floor workers. However, this distinction alone would be greatly oversimplified. In Meeting 1, the purchase of new tools was both supported and criticized by the workers. In Meeting 2, the perspective of individual responsibility was initially strongly supported by the workers of Zone A but criticized by the resource planner, a representative of the community of management and supervision at the meeting. The demarcation lines were broken from the beginning and remained so. In both cases, the solution went beyond the initial perspectives – a new team perspective emerged. Yet it would be exaggerated to claim that the new perspective was unanimously shared. Reservations were also expressed and played with.

Interestingly enough, the perspectives were not fixed in the sense of stable alliances between individuals. The relationship between the first and second machinists is a case in point. In Meeting 1 these two were the closest of allies, especially toward the end of the discussion, when they pushed together for the innovative solution. In Meeting 2 they were in opposite camps from the beginning, to the point of personal attacks. Toward the end of that meeting, the second machinist changed his mind and suggested a compromise solution. The perspectives as collective formations were robust enough to allow individual movement between them.

Innovation as collaborative achievement

What gave the team's quality control expert the authority to bring the discussion to a unanimous close in Meeting 2? It would be easy to speculate about his position and special expertise. However, there may be another explanation. The new, innovative model of internal corrective action was in fact constructed through several steps of conceptual evolution and enlistment of social support. This stepwise progression could be expressed as a chain of key actors and actions:

> Team coordinator [modeling] →
> Machinist 1 [questioning] →
> Machinist 4 [actual-empirical analysis] →
> Resource planner [modeling] →
> Machinist 3 [examining] →
> Quality control expert [examining] →
> Team coordinator [implementing]

This representation makes evident the collaborative and constructive nature of innovative learning and knowledge creation. The quality control expert could bring the discussion to a close not just by virtue of his personal authority but because sufficient collective weight had been gathered, step by step, behind the innovation, and simultaneously the innovation itself had shaped to an acceptable degree of coherence.

This is in line with both Nonaka and Takeuchi's theory and the theory of expansive learning. The two theories do not have to be seen as mutually exclusive or hostile. Nonaka and Takeuchi's emphases on the alternative *modes of representing* knowledge and the transitions between them offers important insights that may often be overlooked within the theory of expansive learning. On the other hand, the theory of expansive learning, based on the dialectics of ascending from the abstract to the concrete, offers a new framework for analyzing the interplay of the *object* under construction, the mediating *artifacts,* and the different *perspectives* of the participants in a progression of collectively achieved actions. Perhaps the theory of expansive learning can be regarded as a basis for defining the phases of a cycle, whereas Nonaka and Takeuchi's categories are useful in defining the alternative modes of representation available to the participants as complementary instrumentalities in each phase of the cycle.

Deriving the phases of the cycle of knowledge creation from modes of knowledge representation has led Nonaka and Takeuchi to exclude questioning and analysis from their cycle. These actions are tacitly delegated to management. Had the authors analyzed small cycles of innovative learning in work teams, they would have realized that such a split between problem construction and problem solving, or intention and realization, is unrealistic. No matter how clear the intention and assignment may be for management, the object will be creatively reconstructed by those who are supposed to solve the problem. This creative reconstruction often involves questioning, confrontation, and debate. If this is overlooked, the important dimension of power will be artificially separated from object-oriented collaborative work and innovative learning in work organizations and teams.

References

Argyris, C., & Schön, D. A. (1978). *Organizational learning: A theory of action perspective.* Reading: Addison-Wesley.

Bakhurst, D. (1991). *Consciousness and revolution in Soviet philosophy: From the Bolsheviks to Evald Ilyenkov.* Cambridge: Cambridge University Press.

Bartunek, J. M., & Reid, R. D. (1992). The role of conflict in a second order change attempt. In D. M. Kolb & J. M. Bartunek (Eds.), *Hidden conflict in organizations: Uncovering behind-the-scenes disputes.* Newbury Park: Sage.

Beyerlein, M. M., & Johnson, D. A. (Eds.). (1994). *Advances in interdisciplinary studies of work teams: Vol. 1. Theories of self-managing teams.* Greenwich: JAI Press.

Beyerlein, M. M., Johnson, D. A., & Beyerlein, S. T. (Eds.). (1995). *Advances in interdisciplinary studies of work teams: Vol. 2. Knowledge work in teams.* Greenwich: JAI Press.

Bruner, J. S. (1966). *Toward a theory of instruction.* Cambridge, MA: Harvard University Press.

Cole, M., & Engeström, Y. (1993). A cultural-historical interpretation of distributed cognition. In G. Salomon (Ed.), *Distribute cognition: Psychological and educational considerations.* Cambridge: Cambridge University Press.

Davydov, V. V. (1988). Problems of developmental teaching. *Soviet Education, XXX*(8–10) (whole issue).

Davydov, V. V. (1990). *Types of generalization in instruction: Logical and psychological problems in the structuring of school curricula.* Reston: National Council of Teachers of Mathematics.

Dixon, N. M. (1994). *The organizational learning cycle: How we can learn collectively.* London: McGraw-Hill.

Engeström, R. (1995). Voice as communicative action. *Mind, Culture, and Activity, 2,* 192–214.

Engeström, Y. (1987). *Learning by expanding: An activity-theoretical approach to developmental research.* Helsinki: Orienta-Konsultit.

Engeström, Y. (1990). *Learning, working and imagining: Twelve studies in activity theory.* Helsinki: Orienta-Konsultit.

Engeström, Y. (1991a). Developmental work research: Reconstructing expertise through expansive learning. In M. I. Nurminen & G. R. S. Weir (Eds.), *Human jobs and computer interfaces.* Amsterdam: Elsevier.

Engeström, Y. (1991b). Non scolae sed vitae discimus: Toward overcoming the encapsulation of school learning. *Learning and Instruction, 1,* 243–259.

Engeström, Y. (1993a). Developmental studies of work as a testbench of activity theory: The case of primary care medical practice. In S. Chaiklin & J. Lave (Eds.), *Understanding practice: Perspectives on activity and context.* Cambridge: Cambridge University Press.

Engeström, Y. (1993b). The working health center project: Materializing zones of proximal development in a network of organizational innovation. In T. Kauppinen & M. Lahtonen (Eds.), *Action research in Finland*. Helsinki: Ministry of Labour.

Engeström, Y. (1994a). Teachers as collaborative thinkers: Activity-theoretical study of an innovative teacher team. In G. Handal & S. Vaage (Eds.), *Teachers' minds and actions: Research on teachers' thinking and practice*. London: Falmer Press.

Engeström, Y. (1994b). *Training for change: New approach to instruction and learning in working life*. Geneva: International Labor Organization.

Engeström, Y. (1995). Innovative organizational learning in medical and legal settings. In L. M. W. Martin, K. Nelson, & E. Tobach (Eds.), *Sociocultural psychology: Theory and practice of doing and knowing*. Cambridge: Cambridge University Press.

Engeström, Y., Engeström, R., & Kärkkäinen, M. (1995). Polycontextuality and boundary crossing in expert cognition: Learning and problem solving in complex work activities. *Learning and Instruction, 5,* 319–336.

Engeström, Y., & Escalante, V. (1996). Mundane tool or object of affection? The rise and fall of the Postal Buddy. In B. A. Nardi (Ed.), *Context and consciousness: Activity theory and human–computer interaction*. Cambridge, MA: MIT Press.

Falmagne, R. J. (1995). The abstract and the concrete. In L. M. W. Martin, K. Nelson, & E. Tobach (Eds.), *Sociocultural psychology: Theory and practice of doing and knowing*. Cambridge: Cambridge University Press.

Goodwin, M. H. (1990). *He-said–she-said: Talk as organization among black children*. Bloomington: Indiana University Press.

Hatch, M. J., & Ehrlich, S. B. (1993). Spontaneous humor as an indicator of paradox and ambiguity in organizations. *Organization Studies, 14,* 505–526.

Holland, D., & Reeves, J. R. (1996). Activity theory and the view from somewhere: Team perspectives on the intellectual work of programming. In B. A. Nardi (Ed.), *Context and consciousness: Activity theory and human–computer interaction*. Cambridge: MIT Press.

Il'enkov, E. V. (1977). *Dialectical logic: Essays in its history and theory*. Moscow: Progress.

Latour, B. (1987). *Science in action: How to follow scientists and engineers through society*. Cambridge, MA: Harvard University Press.

Latour, B. (1988). *The Pasteurization of France*. Cambridge, MA: Harvard University Press.

Lektorsky, V. A. (1984). *Subject, object, cognition*. Moscow: Progress.

Leont'ev, A. N. (1978). *Activity, consciousness, and personality*. Englewood Cliffs: Prentice-Hall.

Litowitz, B. E. (1990). Just say no: Responsibility and resistance. *The Quarterly Newsletter of the Laboratory of Comparative Human Cognition, 12,* 135–141.

Lucy, J. A. (Ed.). (1993). *Reflexive language: Reported speech and metapragmatics*. Cambridge: Cambridge University Press.

Nonaka, I., & Takeuchi, H. (1995). *The knowledge-creating company: How Japanese companies create the dynamics of innovation*. New York: Oxford University Press.

Norman, D. A. (1988). *The psychology of everyday things*. New York: Basic Books.

Orsburn, J. D., Moran, L., Musselwhite, E., & Zenger, J. H. (1990). *Self-directed work teams: The new American challenge*. Homewood: Irwin.

Perrow, C. (1984). *Normal accidents: Living with high-risk technologies*. New York: Basic Books.

Rentsch, J. R., & Hall, R. J. (1994). Members of great teams think alike: A model of team effectiveness and schema similarity among team members. In M. M. Beyerlein & D. A. Johnson (Eds.), *Advances in interdisciplinary studies of work teams: Vol. 1. Theories of self-managing teams.* Greenwich: JAI Press.

Senge, P. M. (1990). *The fifth discipline: The art and practice of the learning organization.* New York: Doubleday.

Simon, H. A. (1973). The structure of ill-structured problems. *Artificial Intelligence, 4,* 181–201.

Tjosvold, D., & Tjosvold, M. M. (1994). Cooperation, competition, and constructive controversy: Knowledge to empower self-managing work teams. In M. M. Beyerlein & D. A. Johnson (Eds.), *Advances in interdisciplinary studies of work teams: Vol. 1. Theories of self-managing teams.* Greenwich: JAI Press.

von Hippel, E., & Tyre, M. J. (1995). How learning by doing is done: Problem identification in novel process equipment. *Research Policy, 24,* 1–12.

Vygotsky, L. S. (1978). *Mind in society: The development of higher psychological processes.* Cambridge, MA: Harvard University Press.

Vygotsky, L. S. (1986). *Thought and language.* Cambridge, MA: MIT Press.

Weick, K. E. (1995). *Sense-making in organizations.* Thousand Oaks: Sage.

Part V

Therapy and addiction

24 Object relations theory and activity theory: A proposed link by way of the procedural sequence model

Anthony Ryle

Introduction

The aim of this chapter is to consider the relationship between two theories of very different origins, namely, object relations theory and activity theory. The idea of linking the two theories was derived from my development of the procedural sequence model, which evolved in parallel with the development of an integrated approach to psychotherapy – cognitive analytic therapy (Ryle, 1982, 1990). The procedural sequence originated as a restatement, in cognitive terms, of ideas from both cognitive-behavioral and psychoanalytic therapies; the resemblance of this model to aspects of activity theory was pointed out by my colleague Mikael Leiman, and the present exploration was initiated by discussions with him.

In this chapter I (1) present the basic features of the procedural sequence model; (2) outline the way in which ideas from object relations theory were incorporated in it; (3) describe briefly the ideas of Vygotsky and activity theory; and (4) consider the compatibility and complementarity between activity theory and the procedural sequence and object relations models.

Development of the procedural sequence model

A full account of the development of cognitive analytic therapy and of the procedural sequence model will be found in Ryle (1990). This time-limited therapeutic approach has, as its central feature, the joint elaboration by the patient and therapist of a written reformulation of the patient's problems. This takes the form of a letter describing the patient's past history and the strategies developed to cope with it, as well as a description of the patient's current maladaptive "procedures." These

407

procedures are seen as being formed and enacted in the course of the individual's ongoing activity and can be understood only in relation to his or her history and current context.

A full account of a procedural sequence includes the following: a description of the individual's active involvement with his or her surroundings; his or her appraisal of this involvement; the formation and pursuit of goals in this context; the individual's anticipation of the personal capacity to attain these goals and of the consequences of so doing; his or her consideration of the means available and selection and enactment of one of these; the individual's evaluation of the efficacy and consequences of his or her action; and the individual's confirmation, revision, or abandonment of his or her aims and/or means. Such sequences are seen to underlie the organization of aim-directed action.

The model is derived from the ideas of Kelly (1955), Miller, Galanter, and Pribram (1960), and the general field of cognitive-behavioral and social learning theory (Ryle, 1982). Such sequences are normally revised in the light of experience, but neurotic procedures are characteristically both ineffective and resistant to such revision.

Three patterns of neurotic procedures are recognized: (1) traps, which involve negative beliefs and appraisals and forms of action leading to consequences seemingly confirming these negative beliefs and appraisals; (2) dilemmas, which represent false dichotomization of the options for roles or actions; and (3) snags, which are false predictions leading to the abandonment or undoing of appropriate aims. Psychoanalytic concepts can be restated, with some modification, in terms of this model.

Object relations theory and the procedural sequence model

The reconstruction of early development offered in object relations theory (Fairbairn, 1952; Segal, 1964; Guntrip, 1961, 1968; Winnicott, 1965, 1971; Ogden, 1983) has considerable explanatory value where adult personality and relationship patterns are concerned. In varying degrees, however, object relations theorists have used the unsatisfactory "metapsychology" of psychoanalysis, with its neglect of cognition, its pseudobiology, its reifications, and so on. The linking of these key ideas with the procedural sequence model involved restatements in a different language (see Ryle, 1988, 1990) in which the main biological influence is understood in terms of inborn attachment behaviors (Bowlby, 1969) and in which the infant–mother interaction is described in terms of role procedures. The procedural sequence-object relations model account of early development can be summarized as follows.

1. The newborn infant, on the basis of inborn attachment behaviors, using sensorimotor intelligence, is involved from birth in elaborating "role procedures" for relating to her mother (mother is taken to include other caretakers in this discussion).

2. Early role procedures are concerned with only parts or aspects of the mother, and their development precedes the infant's ability to discriminate self from other.

3. A role procedure (unlike a procedure for manipulating a physical object) requires one to predict (as the consequence of one's action) the responses of the other. Hence in each interaction the child learns two role procedures (see Ogden, 1983), one self- and one other-derived. The term *reciprocal role procedure* is used to underline this point.

4. In time, the infant not only predicts and elicits the mother's role, she begins to enact it – for example, feeding the mother or mothering a doll or teddy bear.

5. At a later date, evident from early speech, the child enacts the maternal role toward herself. This internalization of the mother's role is the basis of a capacity for self-care, self-management, and self-consciousness, as well as a liability to internal conflict.

6. The dependent infant can control the environment only by way of communication with the mother, and this communication will have a large affective component. Hence one's sense of the world, oneself, and others, as well as one's capacity to express and control feelings and to act on the world, are all first acquired within the mutual relationship(s) of infancy, experienced through primitive conceptual processes.

7. Early reciprocal role and self-management procedures have a common origin in early reciprocal roles with aspects of the mother; a major task of early childhood is the integration of these part procedures into complex, whole-person procedures.

8. This integration will depend on the capacity of the mother to provide a safely predictable environment appropriate to the child's temperament and developmental level. Separations, deprivations, and more severe disturbances of parenting will interfere with this process, and the capacity to unite contrasting, polarized part procedures, carrying opposing emotional implications,

may be damaged. This, rather than defensive splitting and projection, is seen as the origin of poorly integrated adult personality
disorders.

9. The persistence of nonintegrated part procedures will be man-
    ifest in splitting (persistent, polarized judgments) and in pro-
    jective identification, in which one pole of a poorly integrated
    reciprocal role procedure is elicited from another person.

This developmental account provides an understanding of the origins
of personality structure and of the formation and structure of the appraisal functions that form part of the procedural sequence. Subjectively, it is common to recognize an internal dialogue in which one voice
is commonly identified as a more parental "I" and the other as a more
childlike "me." Individuals may be primarily identified with either the
parental or the child "voice" or with the derivatives of them such as an
ideal self. Awareness of the dialogue between opposing or interrelated
voices may be present, or one or the other voice may be repressed.

In modeling the processes generated by complex personality structures, the work of Horowitz (1979) was of great value. His concept of
states of mind (perhaps better called *states of being*) allows *subpersonalities*
to be identified, each with a characteristic pattern of reciprocal role and
self-management procedures and of emotion. His technique of configu-
rational analysis demonstrates links and shifts between these states.

Horowitz constructed his accounts from taped therapy sessions; in cognitive analytic therapy, sequential diagrams are constructed with the patients in the early reformulation process and become an active tool of the
therapy (Ryle, 1990; Beard, Marlow, & Ryle, 1990).

Sequential processes and structures can both be portrayed more clearly
by visual means than by words. In practice, various forms of diagrams
were used in the early clinical application of this technique, but in time,
a more standard and more theory-based model evolved. In this model,
a schematic representation of the internal structure, described in terms
of dominant *internal parent–internal child* interactions, forms the core of
the diagram from which procedural loops emanate. The focus is on negative internal states and negative, self-perpetuating procedures; hence
procedural loops will feed back, serving to maintain in some way the core
inner state.

Such loops may represent the pursuit of ordinary life aims such as
seeking intimacy or striving for success; may express one or another of
the roles schematically portrayed in the internal parent–internal child

relationship (i.e., projective identification); or may represent attempts to avoid or transform unmanageable repressed core emotions, for example, through symptoms or through avoidance behaviors.

Sequential diagrams made up in this way represent a formal device illustrating, in terms of the procedural sequence object relations model, the relation between historically derived internal structures and current life procedures. Dissociated core states (splitting) can be illustrated in such diagrams. In terms of theory, sequential diagrams extend the original procedural sequence model by incorporating a representation of historically derived structures and by demonstrating the relation between different procedures while retaining the emphasis on repetitive, self-maintaining sequences as explaining neurotic and personality disorders.

By incorporating psychoanalytic ideas in this way, the model is distinguished from those currently put forward within cognitive psychotherapy (e.g., Guidano, 1987; Young, 1990), although the work of Liotti (1987) is close in many ways. Although the procedural sequence model was elaborated by using cognitive concepts to construct a model capable of accommodating psychoanalytic ideas, the broader context offered by activity theory is, I believe, more compatible and adequate.

Vygotsky and activity theory

The main sources of this attempted summary are Vygotsky (1962, 1978) and the valuable critical review of both Vygotsky and later work in activity theory by Wertsch (1985). The feature of this tradition that makes it particularly interesting in this context is the emphasis on internalization. Activity theory, in fact, is a thoroughgoing object relations theory, for Vygotsky saw, in the transformation of interpersonal experience into intrapersonal thought processes, the root of all that is specifically human in human psychology.

Vygotsky (1896–1934) came from a cultured Russian Jewish family and studied law, philosophy, linguistics, aesthetics, and psychology at Moscow University and, simultaneously, at an alternative unofficial university staffed by teachers who had lost their jobs on political grounds. Psychology was his central interest for the last 10 years of his life, during which he was ill several times with the tuberculosis of which he eventually died.

His approach to psychology represented a decisive and deliberate shift of attention from the concerns of the Pavlovian tradition to the study of higher mental functions, often assumed, then as now, to be inaccessible to scientific study. His interest was fueled by his identification with the idealism and intellectual ferment of postrevolutionary Russia and by his nondogmatic Marxism. Marx saw humans' ideas as being the product of their historical activity; in transforming nature, social humans had evolved tools, language, and concepts that served in turn to transform humanity. A recent commentator (Wartofsky, 1979) summarized the implications of this view by saying that "the artifact is to the cultural evolution what the gene is to biological evolution."

Vygotsky's aim was to develop a Marxist psychology, seeking to trace the historical and cultural origins of individual psychology. Although some cross-cultural studies were undertaken (Luria, 1976), the main thrust of Vygotsky's work was at the level of individual development. In an oft-quoted remark, he said, "What the child does with an adult today, she will do on her own tomorrow," and his main research was directed to understanding how this was so, that is, to determine how interpersonal activity, involving tools and/or language, became transformed into intrapersonal, mediated thought. Whereas Piaget, more or less simultaneously, was concerned with the internalization of physical manipulations, Vygotsky's interest was in tool- or sign-mediated activity and especially in the role of language.

The role of speech was considered central and, in an important debate with Piaget, Vygotsky insisted that egocentric speech, rather than being the first form, as Piaget suggested, was in fact a derivation of primitive social speech. Egocentric speech was seen to "go underground" during childhood, to become inner speech, the main medium of "decontextualized" thought. Thinking was described as "quasi-social" dialogue. This dialogic nature of thought is the basis of our capacity to make ourselves and our thoughts the objects of our thinking.

One important idea that emerged from studies of development and learning (including much work with psychologically damaged children) was the concept of the *zone of proximal development,* defined as the gap between a child's actual performance and the level achievable with the help of an adult or a competent peer. Apart from demonstrating how misleading attainment tests can be, the concept pointed to the idea that the task of an educator must be to go ahead of development, leading the child into his or her zone of proximal development and providing the necessary conditions for internalization.

Wertsch (1985) has reviewed later work in activity theory, including his own, which has served to clarify the conditions necessary for internalization; these include the child's active participation in specific tasks with the help of an adult who provides accurate verbal commentary and who transfers responsibility to the child at an appropriate rate (see also Bruner's [1966] concept of the *scaffolding* role of the teacher).

The concept of *activity* is poorly rendered by the English word; in activity theory the implication is of high-level, motivated thinking, doing, and being of an individual in a given social context. This is the chosen focus of the theory, within which, and only within which, the traditional categories of psychological investigation (perception, cognition, memory, feeling, etc.) may be studied and understood (Davydov, Chapter 2, this volume). Two lower levels within activity are identified, namely, action, concerned with the pursuit of specific goals, and operations, whereby goals are pursued in specific contexts (Leont'ev, 1981). This seems a fruitful distinction that might clarify issues in comparative research in psychotherapy.

There are a number of authors in the West whose ideas are closer to those put forward in activity theory, including, for example, Mead (1964) on the self and Berger and Luckmann (1967) on the social construction of reality, and both Vygotsky and Luria were acknowledged influences on Bruner's work in developmental psychology (e.g., Bruner, 1966). In general, however, until the recent growth of interest in activity theory in some European countries in the past few years, the work has been remarkably neglected. In the Soviet Union, the theory was seen to extend into philosophy and sociology as well as psychology, and this broad basis may have saved psychology there from fragmentation.

However, in the two decades following Vygotsky's death there was extensive censorship of his work, and although this was lifted in the 1950s a certain dogmatism persisted and was only recently explicitly discarded (Zinchenko, 1989). One manifestation of recent change has been a switch in attention from the historical-cultural formation of mind to the generation of new thought (creativity) (Engeström, Chapter 1, this volume).

Despite the strong emphasis on interpersonal transactions, the chief emphasis in activity theoretical psychology has been on intellectual development. I am not aware of any work centrally concerned with emotions and personality development. However, the following quotation (Radzikhovskii, 1984, p. 42) suggests a natural convergence with object relations theory:

The thought naturally arises whether the basic structure of human activity is formed in early ontogeny or the basis of internalisation of the structure of joint activity into which the child is drawn from his very birth.

The relation of activity theory to the procedural sequence model of object relations theory

The main differences between activity theory and the procedural sequence object relations model as developmental theories can be summarized as follows: Activity theory is concerned with the normal development of children, especially their intellectual development, through the process of internalization. There is a central emphasis on language. The main applications have been in the field of pedagogy. The "activity theory adult" is an agent of the culture, his or her relationship with the child being by way of shared activity involving tools and language use.

The procedural sequence object relations model, on the other hand, is centrally concerned with abnormal emotional and personality development, and of how these may be traced back to the earliest stages of life. The main observational base and applications are in psychotherapy. The "procedural sequence object relations model adult" is enacting a direct relationship molded by continual affect-laden communication, centered on the needs of the dependent child, the mutually developed and meshing reciprocal roles being concerned with the caring-dependent relationship, although increasingly joint environmental manipulation also occurs. Crucial stages in the relationship antedate the development of mediated thought.

A detailed study of the relationship between Winnicott's ideas and those of the Vygotskian school considered in terms of the procedural sequence object relations model has been developed by Leiman (personal communications). Winnicott's (1971) understanding of the early unity and slow separation of infant and mother, and his description of the *transitional object* and its relation to cultural transmission, places him closer to activity theory than any other psychoanalyst.

In many ways, the procedural sequence object relations model could be regarded as an extension of the developmental theory of activity theory to earlier ages (with a bias toward abnormality). One aspect of its contribution could be epitomized by rephrasing Vygotsky's statement as follows: "What the adult cannot let the child do or know today, the child cannot let herself do or know tomorrow." It would seem to be important for educators as well as therapists to recognize the potential effects of damaging early internalizations, and of how they may inhibit late entry into the (intellectual and emotional) zone of proximal development; the issue seems to have received little attention in activity theory.

At a more general theoretical level, as Radzikhovskii suggests, internalization, in the form of the elaborations of primitive reciprocal role procedures, starts at birth, not only long before speech but before even self–other discrimination is clear or the unity and constancy of the other is established. These early procedures are the bricks from which later whole-person role procedures and self-management procedures are elaborated, and they may be flawed. Moreover, during the phase of the integration of partial procedures (procedures often carrying major and contrasting affective implications), it seems probable that the presence of an integrating parent, providing a reasonably consistent acceptance of the full range of procedures and affects, is essential (Winnicott, 1965).

This stage extends into the time when language acquires a dominant role, and part of the integrating function of the parent may include providing an accurate account of what is enacted between parent and child. The inconsistent or damaging parent may also provide a distorted account, leaving the child with a mistrust of self and others and an untrustworthy inner commentary.

The implications of this account of early development are that primitive, unrecognized role procedures may continue to influence and limit the later learning of children and adults. This recognition is the basis for the emphasis, in psychoanalysis, on understanding transference and countertransference in order to avoid being drawn into forms of reenactment of those early and damaging reciprocal role procedures. However, the way in which psychoanalysts set out to modify the procedures, by offering a nonreciprocating relationship and through interpretation (i.e., by challenging the meaning of the patient's utterances), is, from the viewpoint of activity theory, a peculiar one. The aim of inducing regression and so making primitive procedures manifest is, in most instances, redundant, for it is essentially those that are manifest in the patient's life that are of therapeutic concern, and the idea that regression must precede reconstruction is not firmly established, except in tradition.

Activity theory would suggest that, if we may assume that learning in therapy is at least partly analogous to childhood learning, the best approach is to get the teacher (therapist) to get the pupil (patient) actively involved in tasks for which appropriate concepts are provided and for which responsibility is increasingly handed over. In this respect, the practice evolved in cognitive analytic therapy of jointly elaborating descriptions and diagrams of damaging procedures, which become the jointly used tools of therapy, turns out to be a Vygotskian one.

Sequential diagrams go beyond activity theory in offering an understanding of how different actions are pursued and linked together by structures that serve to limit or distort the individual's activity. Clinically it is a striking fact that patients are often able to learn to recognize the manifestation of hitherto unrecognized damaging procedures, both in their daily lives and in their therapeutic relationship, using these tools. In a minority of patients, the repeatedly enacted and experienced ability of the therapist not to collude with such procedures may need to precede the patient's capacity to use these tools for self-reflection, although even in such cases the descriptive tools are of value to the therapist. The power of verbal and diagrammatic reformulations seems most evident in those cases of poorly integrated personality who usually respond badly to conventional psychodynamic therapy or psychoanalysis, which suggests that in these patients it is not so much the intensity of their conflicts or the failure of their defenses as the absence of an accurate integrating commentary that generates or maintains their difficulties. This view receives some support from within psychoanalysis (Robbins, 1989).

Discussion

In developing the procedural sequence object relations model, the first aim was to find a way of integrating the ideas and practices of different approaches to psychotherapy and the second was to place psychotherapy in a broader theoretical setting. Neither cognitive-behavioral nor psychoanalytic theories are free from serious reductionism in the accounts of human experience, whereas activity theory, however patchily developed at present, proposes a view of individual development that places humans in their full human and historical context. For this reason, its development might offer the best framework within which to place the study of psychotherapy.

At present, there is a remarkable general ignorance of Vygotsky's work, an ignorance that reflects and serves to maintain the fragmentation of psychology. As an example, Posener (1989) described Piaget as offering the only elaborated theory of cognitive development. Moreover, seeing Piaget (a little unfairly) as being concerned only with the child's relation to "affectively neutral objects," this author claimed as the preserve of psychoanalysis the study of the "the patient's highly charged experience of intimate relations with the central figures in his life" and hence the area of drive development, object relations, and incipient structure formation.

Having divided the field in this way, Posener proceeds to note interesting "correlations" between psychoanalytic and Piagetian ideas of the second and third years of life. But these, I would argue, are correlations between inseparable phenomena that develop from the same experiences. Vygotsky was concerned (in a way that Piaget was not) with the "highly charged experiences of intimate relations" of the child because of the emphasis he placed on the adult's role in the process of intellectual growth internalization, and he was interested (in a way that psychoanalysts are not) in the absolute importance of object relations (i.e., sign-mediated joint activity) for culturally shaped cognitive development.

In this chapter, the understandings of activity theory and the procedural sequence object relations model are presented as complementary. Their combination offers a preliminary comprehensive framework for understanding human psychology that, among other things, can illuminate and help integrate psychotherapy.

References

Beard, H., Marlow, M., & Ryle, A. (1990). The management and treatment of personality disordered patients: The use of sequential diagrammatic reformulation. *British Journal of Psychiatry, 156,* 541–545.

Berger, P. L., & Luckmann, T. (1967). *The social construction of reality.* London: Penguin Press.

Bowlby, J. (1969). *Attachment and loss.* London: Hogarth Press.

Bruner, J. (1966). *Toward a theory of instruction.* Cambridge, MA: Harvard University Press.

Fairbairn, W. R. D. (1952). *Psychoanalytic studies of the personality.* London: Tavistock.

Guidano, V. F. (1987). *Complexity of the self: A developmental approach to psychopathology and therapy.* London: Guilford Press.

Guntrip, H. (1961). *Personality structure and human interaction.* London: Hogarth Press.

Guntrip, H. (1968). *Schizoid phenomena: Object relations and the self.* London: Hogarth Press.

Horowitz, M. J. (1979). *States of the mind: Analysis of change in psychotherapy.* New York: Plenum Press.

Kelly, G. A. (1955). *The psychology of personal constructs.* New York: Norton.

Leont'ev, A. N. (1981). The problem of activity in psychology. In J. V. Wertsch (Ed.), *The concept of activity in Soviet psychology.* Armonk: Sharpe.

Liotti, G. (1987). The resistence to change of cognitive structures: A counterproposal to psychoanalytic metapsychology. *Journal of Cognitive Psychotherapy, 1,* 87–104.

Luria, A. R. (1976). *Cognitive development: Its cultural and social foundations.* Cambridge, MA: Harvard University Press.

Mead, G. H. (1964). *On social psychology.* Chicago: University of Chicago Press.

Miller, G. A., Galanter, E., & Pribram, F. H. (1960). *Plans and the structure of behavior.* New York: Holt.

Ogden, T. H. (1983). The concept of internal object relations. *International Journal of Psychoanalysis, 64,* 227–241.

Posener, J. A. (1989). A cognitive perspective on object relations, drive development and ego structure in the second and third years of life. *International Journal of Psychoanalysis, 70,* 627–643.

Radzikhovskii, L. A. (1984). Activity: Structure and units of analysis. *Soviet Psychology, 22*(2), 35–53.

Robbins, M. D. (1989). Primitive personality organisation as an interpersonally adaptive modification of cognition and affect. *International Journal of Psychoanalysis, 70,* 443–459.

Ryle, A. (1982). *Psychotherapy: A cognitive integration of theory and practice.* London: Academic Press.

Ryle, A. (1988). Cognitive theory, object relations and the self. *British Journal of Medical Psychology, 58,* 1–7.

Ryle, A. (1990). *Cognitive analytic therapy: Active participation in change. A new integration in brief psychotherapy.* Chichester: Wiley.

Segal, H. (1964). *Introduction to the work of Melanie Klein.* London: Hogarth Press.

Vygotsky, L. S. (1962). *Thought and language.* Cambridge, MA: MIT Press.

Vygotsky, L. S. (1978). *Mind in society: The development of higher psychological processes.* Cambridge, MA: Harvard University Press.

Wartofsky, M. (1979). *Models: Representation and scientific understanding.* Dordrecht: Reidel.

Wertsch, J. V. (1985). *Vygotsky and the social formation of mind.* Cambridge, MA: Harvard University Press.

Winnicott, D. W. (1965). *The maturational processes and the facilitating environment: Studies in the theory of emotional development.* Madison: International Universities Press.

Winnicott, D. W. (1971). *Playing with reality.* London: Tavistock.

Young, J. E. (1990). *Cognitive therapy for personality disorder: A schema-focused approach.* Sarasota: Professional Resource Exchange.

Zinchenko, V. P. (1989). Is science an integral part of culture? *Impact of Science on Society, 39,* 253–265.

25   The concept of sign in the work of Vygotsky, Winnicott, and Bakhtin: Further integration of object relations theory and activity theory

Mikael Leiman

Introduction

In his recent work, Ryle (Chapter 24, this volume) has introduced the idea of integrating object relations theory and activity theory. A specific aspect of this integrative perspective will be examined, implied in Ryle's work but not elaborated by him. It is the issue of sign mediation, Vygotsky's primary contribution to the methodological problems of modern psychology.

My aim is to show that object relations theory, especially the work of Winnicott, may bring fresh understanding to Vygotsky's early notions. I further claim that, by introducing the contribution of Mikhail Bakhtin and his circle to the notion of sign mediation, the profundity in Winnicott's understanding of the transitional object and of the potential space may be more fully appreciated. At the same time, Winnicott's and Bakhtin's ideas will jointly clarify limitations in Vygotsky's sign conception.

Ryle (Chapter 24, this volume) addresses the possibility of integrating object relations theory with activity theory by using the procedural sequence object relations model, developed by him in the context of an integrated approach to brief dynamic psychotherapy, the cognitive–analytic therapy (Ryle, 1982, 1990).

Ryle's attempt to transcend, by introducing activity theory, some of the limitations in a cognitivist understanding of mental functioning seems to open promising perspectives for examining the classical issue of the relations between psychoanalysis, psychology, and linguistics, addressed by Soviet psychologists in the 1920s (Voloshinov, 1976; Vygotsky, 1979). This early integration failed due to a number of limitations within both classical psychoanalysis and linguistics. A new, and perhaps more fruitful, conception may be built by bringing object relations theory into a

419

dialogue with a modified understanding of signs, freed from their traditional linguistic understanding.

In what follows, the concept of sign is examined by bringing together
the work of three creative scholars – Vygotsky, Winnicott, and Bakhtin.
The contribution of these three authors will be presented in order to elucidate the concept of sign and to examine its relations to the concepts of
intersubjective space, joint activity, and dialogue. This integrative effort
will, hopefully, serve as a next step in the effort to relate object relations
theory with activity theory.

Vygotsky's views of sign mediation

It seems that Vygotsky did not work with a unitary and completed
definition of the sign concept. Like all creative scientists, he allowed it to
develop and obtain somewhat different shades of meaning, depending on
the context in which he used it. Thus the whole issue of sign-mediated
activity in Vygotsky's work covers a broad spectrum from tool-mediated,
practical activity to the process of acquiring scientific concepts.

A separate task of critical analysis, not attempted here, would be to
trace Vygotsky's different views of the sign, a task laudably approached
by Lee (1985) and Wertsch (1985). I exploit some of their insights, combining them with my selective reading of Vygotsky's own writing.

The first thing to note about Vygotsky's understanding of the sign is
his manner of approaching it from a developmental perspective. For him
this perspective did not, however, mean a task of writing a history of the
concept itself. He enriched his definitions of the sign by studying the
genesis and developmental paths of various sign-mediated activities in
children.

Such a contextual definition of the sign in the process of empirical research of children's sign use permitted a truly flexible way of examining
the concrete transformations of sign-mediated activity and its relations
with practical activities. Unfortunately, it also led Vygotsky to adopt,
without critical reflection, an understanding of the sign as it was presented in the prevailing linguistic research, with all its ambiguities and
limitations. Although Vygotsky managed to transcend the unmediated
stimulus–response models of behaviorism, as well as the subjective idealism embedded in introspectionist psychology, he seems to have accepted,
without critical appraisal, the linguistic notions of Sapir (Lee, 1985) and
Yakubinskii (Wertsch, 1985).

Vygotsky correctly postulated that the sign adopts a mediating position in human activity, changing its structure and developmental course. At the same time, he adopted the prevailing epistemological distinction, long nurtured in Western philosophy and psychology, between the object and its representation. This caused a conceptual impoverishment in his conception of the sign and also created and maintained a gap between the two primary mediators of human activity, the tool and the sign.[1]

This problem becomes evident in Vygotsky's definition of the sign, in which he first postulates an analogy between it and the tool but then goes on to emphasize their fundamental difference.

The sign acts as an instrument of psychological activity in a manner analogous to the role of a tool in labor. "The invention and use of signs as auxiliary means of solving a given psychological problem (to remember, compare something, report, choose, and so on) is analogous to the invention and use of tools" (Vygotsky, 1978, p. 52).

There is, however, an important feature that separates the sign from the tool. Tools mediate object-oriented activity, whereas signs, in the form of language, mediate social intercourse. Tools are externally oriented and are used in the modification of objects, whereas signs change nothing in the psychological operation. Signs are multifunctional tools of communication and representation.

For Vygotsky, signs in general and language in particular, as the prime system of signs, are reversible (Lee, 1985). By this he understands that (verbal) signs fall back on their users, that they can serve both as a stimulus and as a response. This property allows their users to employ signs in controlling their own behavior.

Such a view of the sign seems to have been developed by qualifying the tool analogy. What is brought forward from the analogy is the mediating role of signs in psychological processes. But the sign itself remains a rather undeveloped concept. Yet the sign becomes, somewhat indirectly, characterized in Vygotsky's research on internal speech, on the development of word meaning and scientific concepts.

Reviewing this work, Lee (1985) has described two characteristics of the sign that reflect the influence of contemporary linguistics and logic on Vygotsky's thought. First, in his genetic analysis of speech, Vygotsky distinguished between communicative and representative functions of language. Second, when examining the development of word meaning, he singled out meaning and reference as the two structural aspects of linguistic signs. Vygotsky illustrated this with two phrases that refer to

Napoleon. Whether we say "the victor at Jena" or "the loser at Waterloo," we refer to the same person, yet the meaning of the two phrases differs.

Vygotsky made use of this distinction when he began to examine the development of word meanings in ontogenesis. It also played a part in his understanding of everyday versus scientific concepts. In this analysis, his dependence on linguistics became even more pronounced. He asserted that syntactic relations, codified in grammar, played an important role in relating one concept with another. Interconceptual relations were the defining feature of scientific concepts.

Vygotsky's understanding of syntax, and of grammatical relations in general, is fully in line with a Saussurean conception that approaches grammar as a generalized and normative structure of language. As Lee (1985) has emphasized, grammar acts for Vygotsky as the mediating device between the "upward growth" of spontaneous concepts and the "downward growth" of scientific concepts.

Thus, it seems reasonable to conclude that Vygotsky adopted the prevailing linguistic views of words and grammar. His truly creative and fruitful insight, based on the tool analogy, was to understand the mediating role of signs in the construction of mental activity. But he failed to develop the sign concept further on the basis of a genetic analysis of the sign itself. Such an analysis would have shown its material nature, as well as its various developmental changes in object-oriented and communicative activities.[2]

Vygotsky's unduly linguistic conception of the sign can probably explain some of the difficulties in his analyses of speech development and word meaning. It certainly exposes the contradiction we encounter within the three pages of *Mind in Society* (Vygotsky, 1978) where he discusses the tool–sign analogy. Having made a sharp division between material tools and immaterial signs, Vygotsky addresses the problem of internalization. And when describing it, he presents an example, a vignette, that I find to be most important in the attempt to understand the genesis of signifying acts and the material origin of signs.

A good example of this process may be found in the development of pointing. Initially, this gesture is nothing more than an unsuccessful attempt to grasp something, a movement aimed at a certain object placed beyond [the child's] reach; his hands, stretched toward that object, remain poised in the air. His fingers make grasping movements. At this initial stage pointing is represented by the child's movement, which seems to be pointing to an object – that and nothing more.

When the mother comes to the child's aid and realizes his movement indicates something, the situation changes fundamentally. Pointing becomes a gesture for others. The child's unsuccessful attempt engenders a reaction not from the object he seeks but from another person. Consequently, the primary meaning of that unsuccessful grasping movement is established by others. Only later, when the child can link his unsuccessful grasping movement to the objective situation as a whole, does he begin to understand this movement as pointing. At this juncture there occurs a change in that movement's function: from an object-oriented movement it becomes a movement aimed at another person, a means of establishing relations. The grasping movement changes to the act of pointing. As a result of this change, the movement itself is then physically simplified, and what results is the form of pointing that we may call a true gesture. It becomes a true gesture only after it objectively manifests all the functions of pointing for others and is understood by others as such a gesture. Its meaning and functions are created at first by an objective situation and then by people who surround the child. (Vygotsky, 1978, p. 56)

This important account of the genesis of signifying acts is by no means limited to the sphere of gestures. Linguistic signs acquire their proper meaning as well as their individual coloring for the child by similar contextual dynamics. We might continue Vygotsky's description by extending the example. It does not take long for the infant to realize that the gesture of pointing may be expressed by another form of signification, by the request – first in the form of a cry, later by using an articulated word, and still later by using a question. The true magic of words is hidden in the fact that they seem to affect the mother's reciprocating acts as effectively as did the previous physical gesture. The child would never find a motive for speaking unless words did not have this strange aspect of power in themselves.

Vygotsky's example of the development of mediated acts and their transformation represents the first step toward a truly genetic and unified notion of signs that he himself was unable to develop.

Winnicott's concepts of transitional object and potential space

We must now turn to Winnicott in order to elaborate Vygotsky's account of the path from action to gesture as the generative process of meaningful signs.[3]

What was expressed as a sweeping generalization by Vygotsky would become a persistent issue for Winnicott and his theory of transitional objects – the "transforming tool" for the psychoanalytic tradition, which, however, has been unable to incorporate its implications into the classical conceptual apparatus of Freudian metapsychology.

Being a pediatrician, Winnicott had a unique opportunity to observe infants in their primary social settings and in the clinical laboratory of the consulting room. He was able to recognize how tool-mediated activity developed in the early interaction between the baby and the mother and, being a psychoanalyst, he was sensitized to the emotional aspects and implications of this interaction.

One of the earliest writings of Winnicott that addresses the complex pattern of tool mediation and early emotional interaction is "The Observation of Infants in a Set Situation" (Winnicott, 1982). I present a lengthy quotation from this work because the behavior of the infant, as described by Winnicott, is quite important for the understanding of very early forms of tool mediation. The quotation also helps to introduce Winnicott's views of transitional objects.

. . . I ask the mother to sit opposite me with the angle of the table coming between me and her. She sits down with the baby on her knee. As a routine, I place a right-angled shining tongue-depressor at the edge of the table and I invite the mother to place the child in such a way that, if the child should wish to handle the spatula, it is possible. Ordinarily, a mother will understand what I am about, and it is easy for me gradually to describe to her that there is to be a period of time in which she and I will contribute as little as possible to the situation, so that what happens can fairly be put down to the child's account. You can imagine that mothers show by their ability or relative inability to follow this suggestion something of what they are like at home; if they are anxious about infection, or have strong moral feelings against putting things to the mouth, if they are hasty or move impulsively, these characteristics will be shown up. . . .

The infant's behaviour

The baby is inevitably attracted by the shining, perhaps rocking, metal object . . . and I will now describe what, in my opinion, is a normal sequence of events. . . .

Stage 1. The baby puts his hand to the spatula, but at this moment discovers unexpectedly that the situation must be given a thought. He is in a fix. Either with his hand resting on the spatula and his body quite still he looks at me and his mother with big eyes, and watches and waits, or in certain cases, he withdraws interest completely and buries his face in the front of his mother's blouse. It is usually possible to manage the situation so that active reassurance is not given, and it is very interesting to watch the gradual and spontaneous return of the child's interest in the spatula.

Stage 2. All the time, in "the period of hesitation" (as I call it), the baby holds his body still (but not rigid). Gradually he becomes brave enough to let his feelings develop, and then the picture changes quite quickly. The moment at which this first phase changes into the second is evident, for the child's acceptance of the reality of desire for the spatula is heralded by a change in the inside of the mouth, which becomes flabby, while the tongue looks thick and soft, and saliva flows copiously. Before long he puts the spatula into his mouth and is chewing on it with his gums, or seems to be copying father smoking a pipe. This change in the baby's behaviour is a striking feature. Instead of expectancy and stillness there now develops self-confidence, and there is free bodily movement, the latter related to manipulation of the spatula. . . .

The baby now seems to feel that the spatula is in his possession, perhaps in his power, certainly available for the purposes of self-expression. He bangs with it on the table or on a metal bowl which is nearby on the table, making as much noise as he can; or else he holds it to my mouth and to his mother's mouth, very pleased if we pretend to be fed by it. He definitely wishes us to play at as to take the thing into our mouths and spoil the game as a game. (Winnicott, 1982, pp. 52–54)

In this passage, all the important constituents of intersubjective space, all the basic relations between the infant, the physical object, and the adults may be seen in their embryonic forms. Much of Winnicott's later work on transitional objects, as well as his ideas of the potential space,[4] are elaborations of this description, itself backed up by 20 years of clinical experience with infants and their mothers.

In this example we may see how the baby, attracted by the object, immediately checks the attitude of the adults in order to determine the basic meaning of the situation. We may see how intimately emotional aspects are interwoven into the path from perceiving the spatula to grasping it. We recognize the appearance of an active relation to the object and its gradual transformation from a tool of manipulative acts into a device of playful unitedness. I now examine Winnicott's theory of the transitional object more closely.

The following case clearly illustrates the dialogical origin of the infant's transitional objects, as well as the path from mediated joint activity to mediated individual activity, proceeding first on an external and later on an internalized plane.

The mother of a 22-week-old baby noticed that he began to caress his bib toward the end of feeding, when he became relaxed and sleepy. The mother interpreted this act as a sign of falling asleep. Because of frequent dribbling, she had him wear the bib almost all the time he was awake. Thus it was indeed a "frequent companion" for the baby. Having interpreted the baby's caressing of the bib as a sign of drowsiness, the mother then began to give him a similar-sized bright terry towel that soon became a "mediating sign" of the joint preparation for a snooze. Being sensitized, by a book on baby care, to the importance of the meaning of the towel, she handed it to the baby only in these situations. She was, however, (fortunately) only partly aware of the fact that all the good, soothing, and comforting qualities of the towel were created by the good, peaceful, and loving communion between herself and the baby. Only in forgetful intimacy, free of the mother's controlling and overconscious aims, may the transitional object become saturated by its magic.

This standard example of the birth of transitional objects illustrates the necessary components involved in the emergence of such objects. It also demonstrates how intimately their developing properties are connected with the complex joint activity, during which the adult provides the basic meaning of the object.[5]

The infant's own activity is, however, very important in making the object subjectively meaningful and, in the long run, an object enriched by more and more complex experiences, following from both joint and individual activities.

The simple illustration, just quoted, of the mediated character of transitional objects only partly explicates the subtle interplay between the subjective and objective aspects of the intersubjective space. For Winnicott, the meeting point between the internal and the external, between what is subjectively created and objectively existing, is indeed a delicate issue.

A transitional phenomenon or object is a symbol of the union of the baby and the mother (or part of the mother). This symbol can be located. It is at the place in space and time where and when the mother is in transition from being (in the baby's mind) merged in with the infant and alternatively being experienced as an object to be perceived rather than conceived of. The use of an object symbolizes the union of two now separate things, baby and mother, at the point in time and space of the initiation of their state of separateness. (Winnicott, 1974, p. 114)

For me the most important aspect of Winnicott's understanding of the "third area of living," which he approaches by using the concepts of *transitional phenomena* and *potential space,* is the emergence of a symbol at the meeting point of union and separateness.[6]

Compared with Vygotsky's unproblematic view of objectivity as something given and internalized by the child while interacting with the adult, Winnicott has a more interesting view of reality as an interplay between what is given (objectively) and what is created — jointly — in the intersubjective space. Human beings bring their subjectivity into the external world of which they are an inseparable part. In such a view of reality the ancient Cartesian dualism has been radically transcended.

Winnicott's view of *mediation,* although he did not use that term, emphasizes its developmental nature. Transitional objects obtain their specific meaning in the gradual process of experiential separation during which the infant becomes capable of distinguishing between "the object objectively existing" and "the object conceived of."

The end product of such development is the complete separation of the sign from its referent. Yet throughout our lives we retain the intermediate phases of experiencing where the object and its perception merge. Play, art, and religion are those areas of human experience that continue to make full use of the third area of experience.

Trying to relate Vygotsky's views of internalization to Winnicott's understanding of transitional phenomena gives us a rich basis for conceiving the formation of meaning in joint activity. One has to combine both of the previously mentioned aspects. First, the sign (or the tool) acquires meaning only as a sign of union in the process of separation. Second, it has at the same time an objective existence in the shared reality. Whether as physical objects or symbolic artifacts, all that exists will become sub-jectively meaningful – and usable – only when mediating the eternal in-terplay of union and separateness.

This is Winnicott's lesson for Vygotskian scholars. The concept of mediation is enriched by emotional aspects and by the idea of the third area, where reality is found creatively. Perhaps the most important as-pect in this understanding of mediation is its developmental nature. Be-ing initially an unrecognized aspect of reality, combining creation and finding (Winnicott's paradox), mediational patterns change as the infant grows toward a conscious and creative use of objects. Mediation itself changes, as it mediates the developing distinction between the internal and external.

The following theoretical formulation may be summarized from Win-nicott's work on transitional objects: Every act of signification will always involve a three-term relation between (at least) two persons and the "ob-ject." Quotation marks are used here because the object may be anything from parts of the body, from gestures and other actions, to physical things, whether artificial or not, and to signs.

The person–object interchanges constitute indeed an indivisible to-tality, made up of its indissoluble constituents, becoming consumed by each other yet becoming enriched by this ever-evolving mutual consum-mation. It is this mediated coactivity that makes up the intersubjective space within which life is possible.

All meaning is generated within this developing, intercommunicational space, which unites what is seen with what is not yet seen, which trans-forms practical, material transactions into signs, and which materializes symbolic and invisible forms of activity into practical acts and tangible objects. Everything that exists in the human mind – indeed in the world, "humanized" by practical, object-oriented activities – is created within this living, concrete, and material space. It is this radical materialism that places Winnicott's work so close to Vygotsky and especially Bakhtin, as will be shown.

Vygotsky's important discoveries of tool-mediated activity were ham-pered by his linguistic conception of signs that prevented him from seeing clearly the early development of signs and their true materiality as medi-ators. Winnicott was, in his turn, restrained by psychoanalytic views that did not contain any understanding of mediation.

Brought into the methodological context of mediated activity, Winni-cott's views of the creative nature of subjectivity, of the origins of object use in the intersubjective space, and of the quality of transitional objects and their gradual transformation may be regarded as very important contributions to the theory of tool-mediated activity and the origin of signs.

Indeed, in this new context, Winnicott's writings gain simplicity and clarity that do not at all justify claims about the inaccessibility of his thought. It is through Winnicott's work that object relations theory may be integrated with Vygotskian conceptions of sign mediation while at the same time freeing the latter from its linguistic constraints.

The Bakhtinian understanding of signs

To continue my conceptual journey, I explore the work of Mikhail Bakhtin[7] and his collaborators because in the Bakhtinian conception of signs we are going to encounter a synthetic view, not fully covered by either Vygotsky or Winnicott. Yet it has to be added that without the profound insights of these two creative theorists, it would not be possible to disclose the rich implications of Bakhtin's ideas.

The basic Bakhtinian definition of the sign is presented by Voloshinov (1973) in his philosophical study of language:[8]

Any ideological product is not only itself a part of a reality (natural or social), just as is any physical body, any instrument of production, or any product for consumption, it also, in contradistinction to these other phenomena, reflects and refracts another reality outside itself. Everything ideological possesses meaning: it represents, depicts, or stands for something lying outside itself. In other words, it is a sign. (Voloshinov, 1973, p. 9)

The basic thing to note in this quotation is Voloshinov's use of the term *ideological*. Accustomed to its close connections with political jargon, we often invest it with negative connotations. For Voloshinov, ideological does not have these implications. It embraces a far wider domain, in fact everything in human life that may assume the function of a sign.

There are two important aspects in Voloshinov's opening remarks about the sign. First, the sign is part of reality, and in this sense it is as material as any other natural or artificial object. Second, its distinctive and basic property is the ability to mediate between two realities: The sign brings the reality it stands for into the situation where it is used.

To emphasize the materiality of signs, Voloshinov declares later in the text that every ideological sign is not only a reflection, a shadow, of reality, but is also itself a material segment of that very reality. In Voloshinov's definition, there is no place for a dualism of the (material) thing and its (ideal) representation that has characterized the epistemological distinctions made in the Western traditions of philosophy and psychology.

This is, of course, an extremely bold statement. The sign is not merely a mirror, it is the true carrier of the reality it signifies. This peculiarity is pointed out by Holquist (1990), but he does not examine its possible origin. In a more recent paper, Lock (1991) put forward the thesis that this conception of a sign is a direct expression of Bakhtin's religious interests. As a Russian Orthodox, he was well aware of the philosophical writings of the 4th-century Greek Fathers, whose work played an important part in the spiritual revival of prerevolutionary Russia.

In the writings of Gregory of Nyssa, Athanasius the Great, Maximus the Confessor, and others, neo-Platonist dualism was transcended by the biblical understanding of the Incarnation as "the Word that became flesh." The early Fathers developed such a radically materialistic conception of the sign to account for the spiritual experience, shared by the Christians, of the presence of Christ in the sacramental life of the early Church.[9]

In the political climate of the Soviet Union in the early 1920s, such views could not, of course, be espoused openly. It seems, however, that Voloshinov's special emphasis on the sign as a mediator, not as a representation, can best be understood in the light of Patristic writings.

We may now move on to Voloshinov's next thesis of the genesis of signs. He writes:

Signs can arise only on interindividual territory. It is the territory that cannot be called "natural" in the direct sense of the word: signs do not arise between any two members of the species Homo sapiens. It is essential that the two individuals be *organized socially*, that they compose a group (a social unit); only then can the medium of signs take shape between them. (Voloshinov, 1973, p. 12)

Signs as "psychological tools" incorporate the material properties of their origin, their "action energy," so to speak, and the relations into which they originally entered, or by which they were created, as mediators. This is the dynamic aspect of signs. In this passage Voloshinov also introduces the idea of the societal factors that affect the persons and their dialogic relationship, mediated by signs. In a truly dialectical fashion, signs and socially organized persons define each other. Neither may be understood properly without the other.

Having provided the basic constitutive properties of the sign, Voloshinov addresses the problem of language. He delineates four aspects that characterize the word as "the sign par excellence" of all human communication.

First, "the entire reality of the word is wholly absorbed in its function of being a sign." In this sense, a word is the purest mediator of social interchange. It is created in communication, its meaning develops within communication, and the meaning – the word's ability to present another reality in the context of its use – is its constitutive property, its reason for coming into being.

Second, the word is "not only the purest, most indicatory sign but it is, in addition, a neutral sign." Voloshinov clarifies this aspect of the word by contrasting it with other kinds of "semiotic material" that are created and used within a particular field of socially significant activity. Whereas these signs, or symbols, remain inseparable from the domain of their usage, words can "carry out ideological functions of any kind – scientific, aesthetic, ethical, religious."

Third, because of its universality and its intrinsic capacity to mediate, the word is the prime tool of human interchange; it is "preeminently the material of behavioural communication."[10] These implications are also reinforced by the fourth aspect of the word: its specifically human mode of existence:

Although the reality of the word, as is true of any sign, resides between individuals, a word, at the same time, is produced by the individual organism's own means without recourse to any equipment or any other kind of extracorporeal material. This has determined the role of word as the semiotic material of inner life – of consciousness. (Voloshinov, 1973, p. 14)

This aspect of the word comes very close to Winnicott's views. Voloshinov's thesis of the reality of the word, as residing between individuals, may be understood fully in line with Winnicott's understanding of how transitional objects assume their qualities in the potential space. Keeping in mind that signs are true mediators of two interpenetrating realities, the notion of words as transitional objects becomes quite conspicuous.

There is one more aspect of Voloshinov's writings that has important methodological implications for psychology. It is the radical redefinition of consciousness based on his notion of the sign.

Consciousness cannot be derived directly from nature. . . . It takes shape and being in the material of signs created by an organized group in the process of its social intercourse. The individual consciousness is nurtured on signs; it derives its growth from them; it reflects their logic and laws. (Voloshinov, 1973, p. 13)

Voloshinov elaborates this thesis when criticizing the traditions of contemporary psychology. In one passage he comes astonishingly close to Winnicott's definition of the third area of experience: the intersubjective space where human mental life takes shape.

By its very existential nature, the subjective psyche is to be localized somewhere between the organism and the outside world, on the borderline separating these two spheres of reality. It is here that an encounter between the organism and the outside world takes place, but the encounter is not a physical one: the organism and the outside world meet here in the sign. (Voloshinov, 1973, p. 26)

These words speak for themselves, and by relating transitional phenomena with Voloshinov's views, we may see the extremely important and radical implications of Winnicott's thinking. Moreover, his work provides concrete, developmentally relevant substance for Voloshinov's abstract views.

Much of Bakhtin's later work on words and language was done in the context of his unique theory of utterance. This theory, which he kept on revising and extending throughout his life, is far too complex to be presented here. It permitted Bakhtin to explore the word as a living sign that traverses through time and absorbs into itself a treasure of voices, or previous dialogues.

In the context of an utterance, the word always wants to be heard, always seeks responsive understanding. For the word (and, consequently, for the human being), there is nothing more terrible than a lack of response (Bakhtin, 1984).

Words do have strange powers, provided that we can free ourselves from our extremely reduced view of them – generated both by our epistemology and by our lexical-semantic approach. By speaking of the word's wish to be heard, Bakhtin reiterates his early understanding of signs as mediators, as "messengers" from the context in which they were created in the new context of their use.

Conclusion

Given the concept of sign elaborated earlier, it would be tempting to make a critical examination of current, and still popular, cognitive theories about mental representation and concept formation. Another area of investigation would be the increasingly popular constructivist views espoused, for instance, by some social psychologists and within family therapy. Such tasks have to be left to the future. The question posed at the beginning of this chapter concerned the possible relating of activity theory to psychoanalytic object relations theory.

In Chapter 24 of this volume, Ryle expresses his hope of marrying Melanie Klein and Lev Vygotsky. In light of this theoretical investigation, such a marriage does indeed seem possible. However, it will require Winnicott to act as a mediator, and it seems that, in order to bear fruit, such a marriage will require an additional boost provided by Bakhtin. Then the marriage may indeed become a transformative experience for all the participants.

Notes

I want to thank Dr. Anthony Ryle for our discussions and for his helpful comments on the drafts of the chapter. The theoretical research on which this chapter is based was funded by the Academy of Finland and the National Insurance Institution.

1. It might be argued that the later accusations, made by Soviet psychologists, of Vygotsky's intellectualism reflect his dualism concerning the tool as a material object and the sign as an ideal phenomenon. However, the efforts to resolve this dualism by adopting the conception of object-oriented activity led to another dead end. It caused an impoverishment in the psychological understanding of symbolic processes and blocked empirical research on the manifold patterns and transformations of tool and sign mediation.

2. The materiality of signs is much better understood by Winnicott and especially well by Bakhtin. Such a conception of signs as something just as material as everything else in the world may be incomprehensible to us, who have been brought up in the Western tradition of thinking, which distinguishes sharply between object and representation, between "the world out there" and our knowledge of it. The materiality of signs includes their physical characteristics, i.e., the specific sign material, of their external forms. In addition, the materiality of a sign is defined by the intercommunicational activity into which it enters as a mediator. This form of materiality is retained by the sign even in its internalized forms – as a mediator of mental activity. This aspect of the sign will be clarified later when I introduce Bakhtin's conceptions.

3. The quoted passage is so compact that much understanding brought from other sources must be used in order to comprehend its brilliance and depth. By relating Vygotsky's insight with Winnicott's views, I hope to be able to show how much it contains.

4. The concept of intersubjective space, which I will be using, must be separated from Winnicott's concept of the potential space. The former is a general concept, intended to convey the idea that any kind of psychological phenomenon is necessarily embedded in the matrix of mediated intercommunication. Winnicott's potential space is one concrete instance of this, aimed specifically at setting the stage for transitional phenomena and the developmental path by which, in the end, we fully employ the distinctions between the subjective and the objective, between the object and its representation.

5. It is important to note that transitional objects are not only created for soothing purposes. As Eigen (1981) points out, the core of transitional experiencing has to do with an inherent fit between the infant's creativeness and the world, i.e., the mother's sensitivity to the embryonic actions of the baby and her ability to amplify these actions.

6. As will be shown, the Bakhtinian concept of the sign, as a mediator between two interpenetrating realities, and Winnicott's understanding of the symbol come very close to each other.

7. Bakhtin (1895–1975) was an original scholar whose work, together with that of his close associates, embraces a broad field of interests. He is probably best known from his theory of the novel, based on the studies of Rabelais and Dostoevsky, but his work on signs, discourse, and language has begun to attract increasing interest within Western semiotics, linguistics, and psychology (Morson & Emerson, 1990). Recently, his relevance to the Vygotskian tradition has been noted both in the Soviet Union (Zinchenko, 1985) and in the West (Emerson, 1986; Wertsch, 1985).

8. Within the recent tradition of Bakhtinian exegesis, a controversy about authorship has attracted a lot of scholarly interest (Morson & Emerson, 1989, 1990). Although authorship is an important aspect of Bakhtin's own theory of utterance, he himself had quite liberal views about it and regarded creative work as collective productivity. It has been commonly assumed that two books (Voloshinov, 1973, 1976) published in V. N. Voloshinov's name are in fact written by Bakhtin. Voloshinov's authorship of *Marxism and the Philosophy of Language* may be questioned, and some writers try to account for this problem by referring to "Bakhtin/Voloshinov." As this would result in a clumsy presentation, I shall refer to Voloshinov as the author. No substantial damage will ensue, as the concept of sign discussed here will be found throughout the writing of Bakhtin himself.

9. When discussing the concept of symbol and its development in the Orthodox tradition, Schmeman (1990) refers to Maximus the Confessor, a 6th-century Father, who claimed that "The symbol – and this is very important – is thus the very reality of that which it symbolizes. By representing, or signifying, that reality it makes it present, truly represents it" (p. 123). Schmeman gives an example, encountered in the Orthodox liturgy, of such a materialistic view of symbols: "Nowhere is this symbolic realism more evident than in the application by Maximus of the term 'symbol' to the Body and Blood of Christ offered in the Eucharist, an application which, in the context of today's opposition between the symbolic and the real, would be plain heresy." In his last work, Bakhtin (1986), echoing this sacramental understanding of the symbol, writes, "The symbol has a 'warmth of fused mystery'." It may be of interest to note that Winnicott (1974) also points out this peculiarity of Christian sacramentalism in his discussion on transitional objects.

10. For Voloshinov the birthplace of language is the dialogue, the concrete, living speech activity between socially organized persons. During our cultural development we have learned to reproduce verbal signs through extracorporeal material, in writing. This has greatly enhanced the possibilities of indirect communication. It has also seduced philologists throughout centuries, as well as linguists and psychologists of our time, to approach the word from a lexical-semantic point of view, mercilessly criticized by Voloshinov later in his book. The semiotic "materialization" of the word may indeed adopt many forms. It should, however, not make us lose sight of its supreme position in the living communication.

References

Bakhtin, M. (1984). *Problems of Dostoevsky's poetics.* Manchester: Manchester University Press.

Bakhtin, M. (1986). *Speech genres and other late essays.* Austin: University of Texas Press.

Eigen, M. (1981). The area of faith in Winnicott, Lacan, and Bion. *International Journal of Psycho-Analysis, 62,* 413–433.

Emerson, C. (1986). The outer world and inner speech: Bakhtin, Vygotsky, and the internalization of language. In G. S. Morson (Ed.), *Bakhtin: Essays and dialogues on his work.* Chicago: University of Chicago Press.

Holquist, M. (1990). *Dialogism: Bakhtin and his world.* London: Routledge.

Lee, B. (1985). Intellectual origins of Vygotsky's semiotic analysis. In J. V. Wertsch (Ed.), *Culture, communication, and cognition: Vygotskian perspectives.* Cambridge: Cambridge University Press.

Lock, C. (1991). Carnival and incarnation: Bakhtin and Orthodox theology. *Journal of Literature and Theology, 5*, 68–82.

Morson, G. S., & Emerson, C. (1989). *Rethinking Bakhtin: Extensions and challenges.* Evanston: Northwestern University Press.

Morson, G. S., & Emerson, C. (1990). *Mikhail Bakhtin: Creation of a prosaics.* Stanford: Stanford University Press.

Ryle, A. (1982). *Psychotherapy: A cognitive integration of theory and practice.* London: Academic Press.

Ryle, A. (1990). *Cognitive-analytic therapy: Active participation in change. A new integration in brief psychotherapy.* Chichester: Wiley.

Schmeman, A. (1990). *Liturgy and tradition: Theological reflections of Alexander Schmeman* (T. Fisch, Ed.). New York: St. Vladimir's Seminary Press.

Voloshinov, V. N. (1973). *Marxism and the philosophy of language.* Cambridge, MA: Harvard University Press.

Voloshinov, V. N. (1976). *Freudianism: A Marxist critique.* New York: Academic Press.

Vygotsky, L. S. (1978). *Mind in society: The development of higher psychological processes.* Cambridge, MA: Harvard University Press.

Vygotsky, L. S. (1979). Consciousness as a problem in the psychology of behavior. *Soviet Psychology, 27*, 3–35.

Wertsch, J. V. (1985). *Vygotsky and the social formation of mind.* Cambridge, MA: Harvard University Press.

Winnicott, D. W. (1974). *Playing and reality.* Harmondsworth: Penguin Books.

Winnicott, D. W. (1982). The observation of infants in a set situation. In D. W. Winnicott, *Through paediatrics to psycho-analysis.* London: Hogarth Press. (Originally published 1941)

Zinchenko, V. P. (1985). Vygotsky's ideas about units for the analysis of mind. In J. V. Wertsch (Ed.), *Culture, communication, and cognition: Vygotskian perspectives.* Cambridge: Cambridge University Press.

26   From addiction to self-governance

Anja Koski-Jännes

Introduction

It is well known that human beings may become addicted to just about anything, ranging from chemical substances such as caffeine, nicotine, alcohol, and other drugs to commodities such as clothes, shoes, and fancy cars, as well as to various behaviors such as gambling, jogging, working, and even criminal activities. The consequences of these "fatal involvements" are, however, different. Some may lead to fame and riches, others to illness, despair, or even suicide – depending on the society's but also on the individual's biopsychosocial responses to the behavior in question.

Originally, the Latin verb *addico*, from which *addiction* is derived, referred to devoting or giving oneself up to someone or something – either good or bad. The meaning of the word was value free. From the 19th century on, with the rise of the temperance and antiopium movements, it became used in place of *intemperance* and *inebriety*, thereby gaining a mainly negative connotation. It referred to the heavy consumption of intoxicating substances and, in the narrow sense, to drug abuse alone (Alexander & Schweighofer, 1988).

Today, however, the scope of the term *addiction* has widened again. It now refers to all kinds of more or less harmful dependencies. It is my aim here to look at this issue from this wider perspective, even though the focus of this chapter is mainly on the addiction to alcohol.

Addictive behavior as a form of activity

How should we characterize these harmful dependencies? Typical features of addictive behaviors are a strong desire or sense of compulsion, impaired capacity to control the behavior, discomfort and distress when the behavior is prevented or stops, and the tendency to persist with the behavior despite clear evidence that it is leading to problems (Gossop, 1989, pp. 1–2). Addictive behaviors can thus be characterized as fixed, compulsive, and highly repetitive action patterns that limit the perception of and involvement in alternative behaviors. Generally they bring immediate gratification but long-term harm to the individual – and often to surrounding others as well.

As specific kinds of action patterns, addictions could be approached from the activity-theoretical frame of reference (Leont'ev, 1978). This was done, for instance, by Bratus (1974), who described excessive drinking as a form of activity that tends to suppress all the other motives and respective forms of activity of the person in question.

How does this tendency develop? Bratus (1980, pp. 140–142) describes the initial attraction of alcohol as follows. In most cultures alcohol is a common accompaniment of various festivities. These social events awaken, even by themselves, happy expectations. This mental preparation usually goes unnoticed. Hence the resulting euphoria is attributed to the beverage consumed. The link between the drink and the unconsciously prepared frame of mind is the seed from which the special attraction of alcohol is to grow.

That people also drink for other purposes – to relax, to forget, to medicate themselves, to get courage and inspiration – further illustrates that the psychophysiological effects of alcohol are relatively diffuse. Through the projection of drinking-related expectancies, alcohol may, however, turn into a "magic elixir," a universal means for reaching desired states of mind (Marlatt, 1985).

In addition to various social and psychological factors that push an individual toward a drinking career, the development of excessive drinking is therefore, according to Bratus (1980, pp. 144–146), a consequence of growing reliance on alcohol as a means of need satisfaction and conflict resolution.

The chances of satisfying one's needs and solving one's problems are generally improved through social object-related activity. While drunk, these ends are, however, reached on an illusory level – and with much less effort – or they are pushed away from consciousness. The motivation for excessive use thus stems from the conflict between what is and what is wanted, between the instrumental and motivational aspects of personality, and from the illusory-compensatory solution of this contradiction (Bratus, 1980, pp. 146–147).

Other addictions could be described in a similar fashion. A point to note is, however, that the psychological *object* of addiction in all these cases is not a substance, a commodity, or an activity. The object of addiction is an experience, a particular state of body and mind (Peele, 1985, p. 225). An addiction could therefore be regarded as an attempt to manipulate the internal state with the help of chemicals, commodities, or activities. And the faster the effect occurs, the better it serves its purpose. In the short run, this kind of activity may provide remarkable relief, but when driven to excess, the detrimental effects usually override. From the point of view of personality development, drug and alcohol addictions are particularly harmful because they interfere with the person's cognitive functioning and do not allow the individual to develop his or her capacity to meet the shifting demands of everyday life. On the contrary, they tend to narrow this capacity and to destroy the ability to reach one's goals in life.

Why is it so difficult to break the habit?

Addictive behaviors are known to be resistant to change; relapses are common. The concept of *trap* suggested by Anthony Ryle (1982) provides a way to understand this difficulty and thereby to extend the theoretical frame presented so far.

A trap is defined as a circular kind of self-perpetuating disturbance in goal-directed activity. Its typical sequence consists of an inappropriate belief, which "leads to a form of action intended to correct it, but in fact serving to maintain or reinforce it" (ibid., p. 25). Traps are typical in neurotic behavior, but they are also common in the area of character pathology. Usually the person perceives the situation in a distorted way and/or chooses a wrong means to the goal he or she is striving for.

An alcoholic trap could be described as follows (see Figure 26.1). A negative emotion due to, for instance, unsolved life problems leads one first to look for a way out. Low frustration tolerance directs the person to look for a fast solution. Alcohol is a substance that is believed to provide fast relief from emotional pain. This expectancy leads one to think about taking a drink. Rationalizations and the denial of possible negative consequences are drawn in to justify the indulgence. The combination of positive outcome expectancies and these cognitive manipulations then leads to drinking (Marlatt, 1985), which is followed by short-term relief and a long-term increase in negative emotion (McNamee, Mello, & Mendelson, 1968; Tamerin & Mendelson, 1969). After piling up for a while, negative emotions trigger the alcoholic trap again.

A further example is provided by an attempt to cure sleep disturbances by drinking. Alcohol may, in fact, help a person to fall asleep, but the

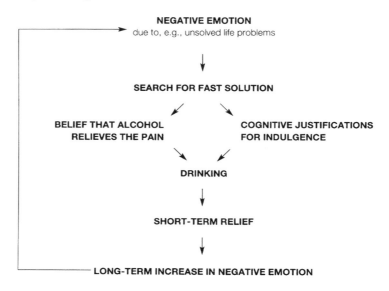

Figure 26.1. An alcoholic trap.

quality of the sleep is inferior and too early awakening is common due to the metabolism of alcohol in the body. In this way, sleep disturbances continue and increase instead of disappearing, but getting out of the trap is improbable as long as the person adheres to faulty beliefs about the beneficial effects of alcohol.

Similar positive feedback loops that increase the initial disturbance instead of diminishing it often appear in other spheres of life, too. Divorce, loss of a job, or loss of a place to live are processes that more often increase the initial disturbance than help the person out of the trouble.

The self-perpetuating nature of traps makes them difficult to change. In the treatment of addictions, it is therefore essential to identify these self-serving patterns of thinking and acting and then to push a wedge into the vicious circle so that the person gets a chance to stop for a while and start to reconstruct his or her thoughts and behavior in regard to the necessity of indulgence in addictive practices. With the term *wedge* I refer to the use of signs as psychological tools of change in the Vygotskian sense (Vygotsky, 1978). Therapeutic change and healing could thus be approached in the same way as any other developmental transformation of human behavior. The tools of change in this area may, however, have some peculiarities that are less pronounced in other areas of personality development.

The role of signs in the process of recovery

All human behavior is regulated by signs. According to Peirce (1985), the founder of semiotics, signs come in the form of icons, indices, and symbols. *Icons* represent their objects by resemblance. Pictures, images, maps, and models are examples of icons. *Indices* are used to point to or identify specific objects. *Symbols* are arbitrary signs used to generalize over a class of objects.

Alcohol research provides ample evidence that the urge to drink is triggered by all these different types of signs. For example, heavy drinking models (iconic sign) increase the level of consumption in their peers, particularly if the model is liked (Collins, Parks, & Marlatt, 1985). The smell of alcohol (indexical sign) increases salivation and craving in alcoholic subjects compared to nonalcoholics (Pomerleau, Fertig, Baker, & Cooney, 1983). Celebrations symbolize the time to drink for most of us.

In contemporary alcohol research, these different antecedents of drinking are usually called just *cues.* They may be perceptual cues, contextual cues, internal cues, and so on. There are, however, some advantages in looking at them from the previously described semiotic perspective (see Koski-Jännes, 1989). Here I elaborate on just one point.

To overcome the addiction to alcohol, a person has to learn to control the urge to drink connected to the signs that usually trigger the drinking response. This is possible with the help of other, more powerful signs that are used to master the temptation and to direct one's attention to alternative behaviors. But what makes some signs "more powerful" than others? To clarify the issue, let us look at some examples of signs used in the process of recovery.

First, it should be pointed out that there are several paths to recovery. For some people, it is enough just to write down what they drink. For others, the route to recovery may be paved by a new challenge, which is incompatible with excessive drinking. Yet, in the case of many heavy drinkers, the change seems to require decisive experiences that function as turning points in their lives.

For instance, Alcoholics Anonymous (AA) literature abounds in stories of drunkards who, after a devastating drinking bout, finally end up in an AA meeting. There they suddenly feel that they have finally come home (Räsänen, 1989). This experience is often so strong that the ties to the group are established on the first encounter.

Similarly, stories of spontaneous recovery (Ludwig, 1988) often credit special life events, such as getting sick, getting divorced, or being fired as the reason for change. These events possess no intrinsic or fixed meaning. They may even appear trivial to others, but they gain their crucial significance from the perceptions and interpretations of the individual in question.

A case description by Ludwig (1988) may be used here as an illustration. An engineer had drinking-related problems with his family and difficulties at work. Because of his diabetes and kidney trouble, he was warned by his physician that he would die if he continued to drink. "Ignoring this threat he got out of his bed in the middle of one night to get some liquor when he saw his wife crying. He felt so guilty and awful over what he was doing to her that he decided to quit drinking" (pp. 70–71).

Yet, events like this had probably occurred several times before. Why did this specific incident suddenly have such a profound effect on this man? Ludwig (1988, p. 73) speaks about subconscious ripening of motives. A semiotic perspective on this event, however, provides another hint to what could have been going on in this situation. According to Peirce (1931–1932, I, 448), the most powerful or "perfect signs are those in which the iconic, indicative and symbolic characters are blended equally." It may be assumed, therefore, that similar events that before had only iconic and indicative functions for this person now somehow also conveyed a more generalized symbolic meaning for him. He was forced to ask himself what he was doing to his wife in a more global sense than just with regard to this specific situation. A whole new life perspective may have been opened up for him through this decisive insight into his wife's suffering.

The story shows the role of strategic, emotionally laden images in the change process. A similar experience is involved in the feeling of "coming home" described earlier. This experience is a particularly powerful iconic, indicative, and symbolic sign for a person who has been adrift for a long time.

Therapeutic case stories provide further illustration of this point. The next one is taken from my own experience. A couple of years ago, I had a young client with features of borderline character pathology in an inpatient clinic where I worked. He was an impulsive, difficult, but also amiable person who, despite his youth, had already completely messed up his life with drinking and drug taking. He stayed in the clinic twice for several weeks, but both treatments ended prematurely due to his return to drinking and drug use.

Because he lived in another city, I could not maintain regular contact with him after his discharge. He nevertheless phoned me every now and then, and we met four times during the following 2 years. And eventually, something began to happen. First, he dropped the drugs. He still drank, but much less than before. Consequently, he did not need to be hospitalized because of pancreatitis, whereas before this had occurred several times a year. After some trials, he met an understanding woman whom he married. He even began to keep some jobs for more than a couple of weeks at a time.

Some time ago, we discussed this change. To him the crucial message was mediated on a single occasion after the treatment when he suddenly realized that "if Anja can really care about me, perhaps I am not such a total failure; perhaps there is also somebody else who can care about me." Shortly after that, he met the woman he married. In his opinion, he would not have been able to maintain the relationship without this basic change in his self-image and his perception of self-worth.

This is, of course, only one aspect of the whole story. But it says something interesting about psychological healing. This process often involves certain momentary revelations that are believed to push the person onto another track. In AA literature these experiences are described as hitting a personal low or "bottom," but the lever of change may just as well be an uplifting experience. Religious conversions are described in the latter way.

The core of these significant events seems to be basically identical. The old, highly overlearned self-schemata are somehow challenged by a deeply personal new perspective, idea, or image, which simultaneously bears a generalized meaning for the person in question. These powerful events often serve as incentives for change, but they may also be used to maintain the change. In the latter case, they serve as an intrinsic contract with oneself taking the form: "Because I had this important experience, I'll stick to this choice rather than do something else."

In his early work *The Psychology of Art*, Vygotsky (1981) pointed out that some signs wake up emotions, and by analyzing them we can approach the emotional regulation of behavior. It is obvious that in the recovery stories described earlier this is just what is going on – people learn to regulate their behavior with the memories of these crucial events.

From addiction to self-governance

Summing up, addictive behavior represents a trapped form of goal-directed activity. To break the vicious circle, one has to push a lever or wedge into this pattern of self-serving consummatory behavior. Many things can be used as tools of change, but a decisive incentive for change is often provided by some emotionally significant event. The memory of this event may later be used as means of maintaining the change. It serves as a special kind of mediating sign, as an inner conract with oneself concerning the decision once made.

It is important to note, however, that these changes seldom happen in a vacuum. The person's immediate social network also plays a role. In a sample of Finnish inpatient alcoholics (Koski-Jännes, 1992), it appeared that subjects who had children at home, who identified with AA, and who had spouses who seldom or never drank with them had a much better prognosis than subjects without these supporting and obliging social relationships. Group therapy also significantly improved the outcome. In other words, people need other people to internalize the necessity to cut down their drinking. This is why the term *self-governance* was chosen here as the opposite to *addiction,* instead of more commonly used terms such as *self-control* or *life control.*

The problem with *self-control* is that it is usually conceived as solitary behavior. It is equal to saying "no" to one's desires, which in itself does not provide a worthwhile goal to strive for. *Life control,* preferred by some researchers, sounds somewhat unrealistic, implying control over one's entire life. In contrast to these concepts, the term *self-governance,* introduced by Mack (1981), acknowledges the essential interdependence of the self and others. Mack uses it in the context of AA, arguing for the role of surrounding social structures in aiding a person to govern the impulse to drink. *Self-governance* as a psychosocial term thereby refers to the sense of being and the power to be in charge of oneself together and with the help of others (Mack, 1981, p. 133). In this sense, it comes closest to the Vygotskian idea of internalizing socially created external means of governing one's thought and behavior with regard to the object of addiction.

References

Alexander, B. K., & Schweighofer, A. R. F. (1988). Defining "addiction." *Canadian Psychology, 29*(2), 151–162.

Bratus, V. S. (1974). *Psihologicheskij analiz izmenenij lichnosti pri alcogolizme.* Moscow: Izdatel'stvo Moskovskogo universiteta.

Bratus, V. S. (1980). O dvizyshih protivoretsiyah razvitiya lichnosti. In B. V. Zeigarnik & V. S. Bratus, *Ocherki po psihologij anomalnogo razvitija lichnosti.* Moscow: Izdatel'stvo Moskovskogo universiteta.

Collins, R. L., Parks, G. A., & Marlatt, G. A. (1985). Social determinants of alcohol consumption: The effects of social interaction and model status on the self-administration of alcohol. *Journal of Consulting and Clinical Psychology, 53,* 189–200.

Gossop, M. (Ed.). (1989). *Relapse and addictive behavior.* London: Tavistock/Routledge.

Koski-Jännes, A. (1989). Learning to control one's drinking – semiotic analysis. In F. Duckert, A. Koski-Jännes, & R. Rönnenberg (Eds.), *Perspectives on controlled drinking.* Helsinki: Nordic Council for Alcohol and Drug Research.

Koski-Jännes, A. (1992). Alcohol addiction and self-regulation. A controlled trial of a relapse prevention program for Finnish inpatient alcoholics. Helsinki: Alko-holitutkimussäätiö.

Leont'ev, A. N. (1978). *Activity, consciousness, and personality.* Englewood Cliffs: Prentice-Hall.

Ludwig, A. M. (1988). *Understanding the alcoholic's mind: The nature of craving and how to control it.* New York: Oxford University Press.

Mack, J. E. (1981). Alcoholism, A.A., and the governance of the self. In M. H. Bean, E. J. Khantzian, J. E. Mack, G. Vaillant, & N. E. Zinberg (Eds.), *Dynamic approaches to the understanding and treatment of alcoholism.* New York: Free Press.

Marlatt, G. A. (1985). Relapse prevention: Theoretical rationale and overview of the model. In G. A. Marlatt & J. R. Gordon (Eds.), *Relapse prevention.* New York: Guilford Press.

McNamee, H. B., Mello, N. K., & Mendelson, J. H. (1968). Experimental analysis of drinking patterns of alcoholics: Concurrent psychiatric observations. *American Journal of Psychiatry, 124,* 1063–1069.

Peele, S. (1985). *The meaning of addiction: Compulsive experience and its interpretation.* Lexington: Lexington Books.

Peirce, C. S. (1931–1932). *Collected papers of Charles Sanders Peirce* (Vols. I and II). Cambridge, MA: Harvard University Press.

Peirce, C. S. (1985). Logic as semiotic: The theory of signs. In E. Innis (Ed.), *Semiotics: An introductory anthology.* Bloomington: Indiana University Press.

Pomerleau, O. F., Fertig, J., Baker, L., & Cooney, N. (1983). Reactivity to alcohol cues in alcoholics and non-alcoholics: Implications for a stimulus control analysis of drinking. *Addictive Behaviors, 8,* 1–10.

Räsänen, S. (1989). *Toipuminen. Suomalaiset alkoholistit puhuvat* (*Recovery: Finnish alcoholics speak*). Helsinki: WSOY.

Ryle, A. (1982). *Psychotherapy: A cognitive integration of theory and practice.* London: Academic Press.

Tamerin, J. S., & Mendelson, J. H. (1969). The psychodynamics of chronic inebriation: Observations of alcoholics during the process of drinking in an experimental group setting. *American Journal of Psychiatry, 125,* 886–889.

Vygotsky, L. S. (1978). *Mind in society: The development of higher psychological processes.* Cambridge, MA: Harvard University Press.

Vygotsky, L. S. (1981). *The psychology of art.* Cambridge, MA: MIT Press.

Author index

445

Subject index

452

The Learning in Doing series was founded in 1987 by Roy Pea and John Seely Brown